Southern Biography Series
William J. Cooper, Jr., Editor

In Pursuit of Reason

NOBLE E. CUNNINGHAM, JR.

In Pursuit of Reason

The Life of
THOMAS JEFFERSON

Louisiana State University Press
Baton Rouge and London

Designer: Laura Roubique
Typeface: Baskerville
Typesetter: G&S Typesetters, Inc.

Library of Congress Cataloging-in-Publication Data
Cunningham, Noble E., 1926–
    In pursuit of reason.

(Southern biography series)
    Bibliography: p.
    Includes index.
    1. Jefferson, Thomas, 1743–1826.   2. Presidents—
United States—Biography.   3. United States—Politics
and government—Revolution, 1775–1783.   4. United
States—Politics and government—Constitutional
period, 1789–1809.   I. Title.   II. Series.
E332.C95   1987   973.4'6'0924 [B]   86-27626
ISBN 0-8071-1375-1

It rests now with ourselves alone to enjoy in peace and concord the blessings of self-government, so long denied to mankind: to show by example the sufficiency of human reason for the care of human affairs and that the will of the majority, the Natural law of every society, is the only sure guardian of the rights of man.

—Thomas Jefferson
February 12, 1790

Contents

Illustrations

Preface and Acknowledgments

On April 13, 1943, during the dark days of World War II, President Franklin D. Roosevelt stood before the gleaming marble of the recently completed Jefferson Memorial in Washington and declared: "Today, in the midst of a great war for freedom, we dedicate a shrine to freedom. To Thomas Jefferson, Apostle of Freedom, we are paying a debt long overdue." It was the two-hundredth anniversary of Jefferson's birth, and the words and deeds of the Revolutionary patriot and third president seemed particularly appropriate to a nation engaged in a struggle for survival. The thirty-second president, drawing numerous parallels between the challenges America faced in Jefferson's day and in his own day, declared: "Thomas Jefferson believed, as we believe, in Man. He believed, as we believe, that men are capable of their own government, and that no king, no tyrant, no dictator can govern for them as well as they can govern for themselves." He concluded his address by proclaiming Jefferson's ringing words chiseled into the marble of the memorial: "I have sworn upon the altar of God, eternal hostility against every form of tyranny over the mind of man."[1]

Roosevelt, who had been the moving force behind the building of the monument, had played a major role in bringing Jefferson back into the consciousness of Americans. Jefferson's profile and the image of his home at Monticello replaced the Indian and the buffalo on the nickel coin, and his portrait appeared on the three-cent stamp, then the common stamp for first-class mail. Roosevelt proudly claimed Jefferson as the founder of the Democratic party; yet the revival of interest in Jefferson resisted the boundaries of partisanship. With the new awareness came a growing appreciation of Jefferson that went beyond his role as a political figure and recognized the broadness of his intellect, interests, and accomplishments. Less than two decades after Roosevelt extolled Jefferson as the champion of liberty, another president, John F. Kennedy, speaking at a White House dinner honoring Nobel Prize winners from throughout the Western Hemisphere, addressed his guests as "the most extraordinary collection of talent, of human knowledge, that has ever been gathered together at the White House, with the possible exception of when Thomas Jefferson dined alone."[2]

The breadth of Jefferson's intellectual world was strikingly displayed during the bicentennial of the American Revolution in 1976 in the exhibition presented by the National Gallery of Art under a banner that read THE EYE OF THOMAS JEFFERSON.[3] As this extraordinary exhibition showed, public interest in Jefferson as a political figure had been joined by an appreciation of his intellectual versatility and accomplishments. Behind the new perception of Thomas Jefferson in the second half of the twentieth century lay a renaissance of historical scholarship that brought the launching of the definitive edition of the rich and voluminous collection of Jefferson's papers under the editorship of Julian P. Boyd and the monumental biography of Jefferson by Dumas Malone appearing in six volumes between 1948 and 1981. Simultaneously, a wealth of specialized scholarly studies enriched our understanding of Jefferson and his age. Indeed, the body of scholarly literature relating to Jefferson has become so extensive that few besides specialists in the history of the early nation can attempt to master it.

The present volume is designed to bridge the gap between public interest in Jefferson and the world of scholarship that has widened our knowledge of the man and his times. In offering a one-volume biography that may interest the informed reader, the scholar, and the student alike, I have been fully aware of the difficulties of the task. Recognizing that in any single volume of reasonable length it is impossible to provide a complete account of Jefferson's long life, complex thought, and many interests, I have been selective. But I hope that I have been fair and representative and that a complete portrait of the man emerges. By the subjects that I have chosen to treat in some detail and the words of Jefferson that I have selected to quote, I have imposed an interpretative framework that every historian imposes on the records of the past, but I believe that the material presented and the analysis provided offer an interpretative biographical portrait that the historical record supports.

Despite Jefferson's diverse interests and accomplishments, certain basic tenets motivated his life and shaped his actions in whatever challenge he faced. Of these, none was stronger than his belief in "the sufficiency of reason for the care of human affairs." As a man of the Enlightenment who believed in the application of reason to society as well as to nature, Jefferson throughout his life pursued the use of reason as the means by which mankind could obtain a more perfect society. This fundamental conviction can be sensed in the quotation from Jefferson that I have employed as epigraph for this book. That passage succinctly expresses Jefferson's commitment to reason and to natural law, from which flowed his devotion to the rights of man and his faith in majority rule. His belief that "knowledge is power, that knowledge is safety, that knowledge is happiness" flowed from that same source and inspired him to rise to the challenge of establishing a state university long after he had closed his political career.[4] Thus, the title *In Pursuit of Reason* indicates what in my judgment best defines the influential and productive life of Thomas Jefferson. It was a faith that nourished his belief in progress, undergirded his political principles, explained his devotion to learning and to educational opportunity for every person, and produced the optimistic outlook that failed him only as he approached the end of a very long life.

Because Jefferson achieved his place in history as a public figure, not as a political philosopher, I have incorporated my account of his political thought into the narrative of his public career, rather than separating his philosophy from the context of the times in which he acted. Throughout his adult life, Jefferson saw himself as pursuing reason, and I have allowed him to present his own ideas in his own terms and, as much as possible, in his own words.

I am indebted to William J. Cooper, Jr., of Louisiana State University for encouraging me to undertake the task of putting into a single volume the portrait of Jefferson that has developed in my own mind during a number of years of study of the man and his era. Like everyone who spends time studying the records left by Jefferson, I have continued to learn from him and to discover avenues that still demand further study. My colleague Gerard H. Clarfield kindly read long sections of the manuscript, and I have profited from discussing the complications of early American diplomacy with him. By mastering word processing, Patty Eggleston, of the staff of the Department of History, University of Missouri, Columbia, has speeded my work, already indebted to her efficient typing and that of Ida Mae Wolff, a member of the same staff. Beverly Jarrett of the Louisiana State University Press has been unfailingly helpful throughout the course of my work on this book, and I am appreciative of her continuing support. For the careful editing of the manuscript for publication, I am greatly indebted to the splendid editorial talents of John Easterly of the Louisiana State University Press. To my wife, Dana, I am particularly grateful for help in the indexing of this book. Finally, I gratefully acknowledge my debt to the University of Missouri, Columbia, for providing me with a research leave to complete the writing of the book and to the university's Research Council for its support of my research.

In Pursuit of Reason

I

The Formative Years

Shadwell, a modest frame house built in a red-clay clearing, stood on the western fringes of settlement in the colony of Virginia. From its well-chosen site below the gap in the Southwest Mountains, the Blue Ridge could be seen in the distance. Closer by, heavily forested slopes proclaimed an unspoiled land and marked the seasons with splendorous displays. In 1735 Peter Jefferson patented one thousand acres along the Rivanna River in the newly opening area that would become Albemarle County. He soon added another four hundred acres and moved his wife and two young daughters to Shadwell not long before his first son, Thomas, was born there on April 13, 1743.

Thomas Jefferson would always feel a closeness to nature and identify with the simpler society of the Virginia upcountry, but his birth on the edge of the wilderness was of less immediate influence on his future than his birth into the ranks of the Virginia gentry—a circumstance that promised the young Jefferson economic security, educational opportunity, and privileged status. His father was a rising young planter and slaveholder, though he was never among the very large landowners of the region. A justice of the peace— one of those influential gentlemen who composed the powerful county courts in eighteenth-century Virginia—he was ultimately elected to the House of Burgesses. Jefferson later recalled, "My father's education had been quite neglected; but being of a strong mind, sound judgment and eager after information, he read much and improved himself."[1] One result had been to establish himself as a successful surveyor and map maker. His son noted with pride his father's association with Joshua Fry, former professor of mathematics at the College of William and Mary, in continuing the boundary line between Virginia and North Carolina and in making the first real map of Virginia. Jefferson owed his lifelong interest in exploration to his father, and he was the beneficiary of his father's determination that his education should not be neglected.

Shadwell was named for the London parish in England where Jefferson's mother had been born into one of the Virginia colony's wealthiest, most influential, and well-established families—the Randolphs. She was christened Jane. Her father, Isham Randolph, as a young ship captain had married in England but returned to Virginia to settle down as the master of Dungeness in Goochland County. Jane was his oldest daughter and nineteen in 1739 when she married the thirty-two-year-old Peter Jefferson, whose forebears had been early settlers, though they were far less prominent than the Randolphs. Late in life Thomas Jefferson would look back on his origins and comment lightly that the Randolphs "trace their pedigree far back in England and Scotland, to which let every one ascribe the faith and merit he chooses."[2] Jefferson always stressed environment over ancestry, but he could not have failed to appreciate the influence his family connections played in his own life.

Jefferson's earliest memories were not of Shadwell and its wilderness setting, but of Tuckahoe, the plantation of William Randolph on the James River in a more thickly settled area to which Peter Jefferson moved his family when Thomas was two or three years old. By the time he was nine, the family, which now included five children, had returned to Shadwell, but Thomas was away at school much of the time after that and mainly spent his vacations at home. Yet the young Jefferson put deep roots into the soil of Albemarle, and one day he would inherit Shadwell and build his own home, Monticello, on a hilltop that was part of the tract first patented by his father. Though he had no recollection of the sparsely populated wild that his father had known and though he never experienced the wilderness as his father had, he felt a closeness to the land that was an important part of his being. He would never cease to think of himself as a man of the soil.

The records relating to Jefferson's adult years are voluminous, but little material relating to his childhood has survived. The earliest letter of Jefferson's known today was written when he was sixteen; it concerned his plans to go to college.[3] Any earlier papers or family letters that may have once existed were probably destroyed by a disastrous fire at Shadwell in 1770. No correspondence between Jefferson and either his father or his mother has survived, and Jefferson said little about his childhood in his brief and never-completed autobiography. The most traumatic event of his early years was the death of his father, whom he remembered as a strong and vigorous man but who died at age forty-nine when Thomas was fourteen. Jefferson later recalled that "at 14 years of age, the whole care and direction of my self was thrown on my self entirely, without a relation or friend qualified to advise or guide me."[4] This was an exaggeration, for his father had left his affairs in good order, and his executors were men that Jefferson could and did consult. But the recollection vividly reflects his sense of loss and suggests the strong influence his father had exerted in directing his early education and molding the habits that would shape his life. The remark also indicates that the young Jefferson did not see his mother as having provided major direction in the past and that he did not turn to her for advice upon the death of his father.

Despite the prominence of her family, Jefferson's mother is a little-known figure. She bore Peter Jefferson ten children. Two of them died in infancy, but the other eight lived to maturity.[5] The youngest—twins—were not yet two years old when her husband died, and though she survived him by nineteen years, her whole life was devoted to rearing a large family. She continued to live at Shadwell until her death in March, 1776, but the only references to her in Jefferson's papers are in his account books. In later years he made only rare mention of her in the surviving record. The evidence is too thin to speculate upon his relationship with his mother, but there is nothing to suggest that it was a warm one, and it may have been strained.[6]

Jefferson's schooling began while the family was at Tuckahoe. The move there after William Randolph's death had been made in accordance with Randolph's will, which named his "dear and loving friend" Peter Jefferson one of his executors. Randolph's wish was that Peter Jefferson (whose wife was William's first cousin) move his family to Tuckahoe to look after his lands and his three young, motherless children until his only son, Thomas Mann Randolph, came of age. The boy was only four when his father died, and Peter and Jane Jefferson did not remain at Tuckahoe until the child reached his majority, but they did stay for some six years. During this time Peter Jefferson directed the education of both the Randolph children and his own, employing a tutor to conduct classes in a small building in the yard at Tuckahoe. Jefferson later referred to this as the "English school," and it was there that he began his education at the age of five.[7]

When the Jefferson family returned to Shadwell, Thomas was either left behind to continue his schooling or sent back soon thereafter. At this time, at the age of nine, he was placed by his father in

the Latin school of the Reverend William Douglas, a Scottish clergyman who was minister of St. James Parish in Goochland County.
He boarded at the clergyman's house during school terms and continued under his instruction for five years, learning from Douglas,
according to his pupil's later account, the rudiments of the Latin
and Greek languages, along with French. Jefferson placed the emphasis on rudiments, for he remembered Douglas as "but a super-
ficial Latinist, less instructed in Greek."[8] These were probably the
unhappiest years of Jefferson's childhood, distant from home for
long periods of time and without the stimulus of an inspiring
teacher. In contrast, the next period of his schooling was among
the happiest times of his youth.

At fourteen, after the death of his father, Jefferson enrolled in
the school conducted in Albemarle County by the Reverend James
Maury, rector of the Fredericksville Parish, who had a log school-
house on his farm twelve miles from Shadwell. Too far for daily
commuting, it was close enough to go home on the weekends. More
important than the location of the school was the character of the
schoolmaster, one of the colony's best-educated men, whom Jefferson admiringly described as "a correct classical scholar."[9] Jefferson
got none of his ideas about religious toleration from this rigid
churchman, but after two years in his school he could read Greek
and Roman authors in the original, a proficiency that he never lost.
He also got some exposure to English literature and other areas of
learning, and because he boarded with the Maury family during
the week, he had access to Maury's extensive library of over four
hundred volumes. It was the beginning of Jefferson's lifelong love
of books.

During the period that Jefferson attended Maury's school, one of
his father's executors recorded payment to a dancing teacher for
six months' instruction to five of the Jefferson children. We may assume that Thomas was among them, for accomplishment in dancing was expected of every young Virginia gentleman. By this time
also, Thomas had learned to play the violin. He would later describe music as "the favorite passion of my soul."[10] Much earlier he
had learned the skills of the outdoors—to ride and to hunt—also
demanded of every eighteenth-century Virginia gentleman.

After two years of scholarly application under Maury's able direction and with his seventeenth birthday approaching, Jefferson was
ready for college. He wrote to one of his guardians that "by going
to the College I shall get a more universal Acquaintance, which may
hereafter be serviceable to me; and I suppose I can pursue my

Studies in the Greek and Latin as well there as here, and likewise learn something of the Mathematics." Jefferson said also that he was losing about one-fourth of his time because of the interruptions caused by company at Shadwell. His habits of industry and application had already become well fixed, as indeed they must have been before his father's death. "It is while we are young that the habit of industry is formed," he later reflected. "If not then, it never is afterwards." He would also later tell his own daughter: "Determine never to be idle. No person will have occasion to complain of the want of time, who never loses any. It is wonderful how much may be done, if we are always doing." [11]

In the spring of 1760 Jefferson, not quite seventeen, entered the College of William and Mary in Williamsburg, and he would ever regard this as one of the major transforming experiences of his life. "It was my great good fortune, and what probably fixed the destinies of my life," he later wrote, "that Dr. William Small of Scotland was then professor of Mathematics, a man profound in most of the useful branches of science, with a happy talent of communication, correct and gentlemanly manners, and an enlarged and liberal mind. He, most happily for me, became soon attached to me and made me his daily companion when not engaged in the school; and from his conversation I got my first views of the expansion of science and of the system of things in which we are placed." [12] Unfortunately, no letters written during the first two years of his studies in Williamsburg survive to trace his intellectual growth, but it was surely immense, for what Dr. Small introduced to his bright and inquiring pupil was the world of the Enlightenment. Jefferson ever after would be one of the most devoted disciples of that Age of Reason.

The academic community in Williamsburg was small and not very distinguished when Jefferson went there. The entire faculty of the college, including the president, consisted of seven men—all of them, except Small, Anglican clergymen. The student body, divided among the grammar school, the Indian school, the philosophy school (in which Jefferson was enrolled), and the divinity school, numbered less than a hundred. As a result of circumstances that proved fortuitous for him, Jefferson had most of his work under Small. During his first year the chair of moral philosophy became vacant, and Small was appointed to fill it on an interim basis in addition to his chair of natural philosophy. Small, it appears, taught almost everything. Jefferson recorded that he was the first person to give regular lectures in ethics, rhetoric, and belles lettres. "It is a highly significant fact," the eminent biographer Dumas Malone wrote of Jefferson's college years, "that the early teacher who did most to fix the destinies of his life was the only layman in the faculty of the College." It was also Small who introduced Jefferson to George Wythe, with whom Jefferson would read law, and to Governor Francis Fauquier, whom Jefferson regarded as the ablest man who had ever filled that office and whose father had worked for Sir Isaac Newton. It was probably after Jefferson completed his college study in two years and began to read law with Wythe that he was admitted as the fourth member of a frequent dinner group of Small, Wythe, and Fauquier at the governor's table, where, said Jefferson, he "heard more good sense, more rational and philosophical conversations, than in all my life besides."[13]

Jefferson's Williamsburg years were not quite those of a disciplined, cloistered scholar that his later reflections and advice to his own children suggested. He admitted that he had been one of six members of the college's secret Flat Hat Club, which he confessed "had no useful object."[14] During his Christmas vacation in 1762 he wrote to his college chum John Page more about girls than about studies, saying of his first love, Rebecca Burwell, sister of a college friend, that "there is so lively an image of her imprinted in my mind that I shall think of her too often I fear for my peace of mind, and too often I am sure to get through Old Cooke [Coke] this winter: for God knows I have not seen him since I packed him up in my trunk in Williamsburgh."[15] As this and several other letters that he wrote to Page during the following months suggest, the young law student, despite contrived efforts to make light of it, was deeply enamored of the sixteen-year-old Rebecca, whom he also called Belinda. At nineteen, Jefferson may have been intellectually mature enough to have shared the company of Small, Wythe, and Fauquier, but emotionally he was still an adolescent. Because John Page preserved these private letters in which Jefferson revealed his feelings, we are able to sense his anxiety, timidity, and ultimate disappointment.

Jefferson apparently planned to spend the winter months of 1763 at Shadwell studying the writings of Sir Edward Coke, which every aspiring student of law was expected to master. Instead, he got an eye infection that kept him from reading, missed his friends in Williamsburg, pined for Rebecca, and was generally miserable. "All things here appear to me to trudge on in one and the same round," he wrote to Page; "we rise in the morning that we may eat breakfast, dinner and supper and go to bed again that we may get up the next morning and do the same." From one who would later glory in the rural tranquillity of Albemarle County, this is strong evidence of his youthful restlessness. But above all, he was undecided about the course he should follow in regard to Rebecca Burwell. "Had I better stay here and do nothing, or go down and do less?" he asked his friend Page. "Inclination tells me to go, receive my sentence, and be no longer in suspence: but, reason says if you do and your attempt proves unsuccessful you will be ten times more wretched than ever." [16] Throughout his letters there was an underlying fear of being rejected, and he talked of traveling to Europe to be cured of love.

Page warned his anguished friend that there was a rival for Rebecca's affection and that Jefferson ought to return to Williamsburg and "go immediately and lay siege in form." [17] Nevertheless, Jefferson did not return to Williamsburg until October, 1763, and by then he had persuaded himself that he should go to England before he took a wife. His long stay at home has led one biographer to suspect that his mother may have been discouraging the courtship, but there is no proof of this. It is known that in February he changed his talked-of plans to return to Williamsburg in May because there was smallpox in Williamsburg. [18]

In any event, by the time he finally danced with Rebecca in the Apollo Room of the Raleigh Tavern in Williamsburg on the night of October 6, he had apparently decided to ask her to wait for him while he went to England. This proved an unattractive prospect to Rebecca, and the next morning he was miserable. "Last night, as merry as agreeable company and dancing with Belinda in the Apollo could make me, I never could have thought the succeeding sun would have seen me so wretched as I now am!" he confessed to Page. He had polished in his mind the words he would say, but when the time came, "a few broken sentences, uttered in great disorder, and interrupted with pauses of uncommon length, were the too visible marks of my strange confusion!" he lamented. He later was able to speak his piece, but with no better results. Resigned to being rebuffed, apparently not ready for marriage at twenty, he dropped his pursuit of Rebecca (who soon married another man), stopped his talk of going to England, and plunged into the study of law. He had said that "if Belinda will not accept of my service it shall never be offered to another," and for a time it appeared that he meant it. [19]

Jefferson devoted five years to reading law with George Wythe. During that period he spent many months away from Williamsburg

and seems not to have spent much time serving in an appren-
ticeship role to Wythe. The latter type of training was the most
common method of learning law in a time when there were no law
schools and training in law in America was not well structured as in
England, but Jefferson was more inclined to learning law from
books than from practice. Shortly after he was admitted to the bar,
he gave his opinion that "the placing of a youth to study with an
attorney was rather a prejudice than a help. We are all too apt by
shifting on them our business, to incroach on that time which
should be devoted to their studies. The only help a youth wants is
to be directed what books to read, and in what order to read them."[20]

What Jefferson valued most was the direction that Wythe gave to
his reading. Wythe started him on *Coke upon Littleton*—the first part
of the *Institutes of the Laws of England*—which is where he would
probably have started had he gone to England to study at one of
the Inns of Court. Sir William Blackstone's famous *Commentaries on
the Laws of England* was not completed until 1769, two years after
Jefferson was admitted to the bar. Thus, his initial exposure was
not to that orderly and lucid work that was soon to become the
most influential teacher of lawyers in both England and America,
but to the dense prose of that seventeenth-century legalist Sir
Edward Coke. "Well, Page," he told his friend when he was just beginning his reading, "I do wish the Devil had old Cooke, for I am
sure I never was so tired of an old dull scoundrel in my life." But
Jefferson went on to conquer Coke and in time came to admire his
"uncouth but cunning learning." Coke had been a leader of the
popular party in opposition to James I and Charles I and prominent in the drafting of the Petition of Right (1628), and his role as
the champion of English rights and liberties would place him in
good standing with Americans in their struggle with George III.
Years after the Revolution, Jefferson would say of Coke that "a
sounder whig never wrote, nor of profounder learning in the or-
thodox doctrines of the British constitution, or in what were called
English liberties."[21]

From Coke's *Institutes* Jefferson went on to study the various reports of cases before the King's Bench compiled by William Salkeld,
Robert Raymond, George Andrews, and others. His reading also
included Lord Kames's *Historical Law Tracts*, Sir John Dalrymple's
history of feudal property in Great Britain, and Bernard Hale's
History of the Common Law. It is possible to be this precise about what
Jefferson read, because he made notes on his reading in a com-

monplace book, as he had earlier done while reading in literature and history.[22] "When I was a student of the law," Jefferson recalled years later, "after getting through Coke Littleton, whose matter cannot be abridged, I was in the habit of abridging and common-placing what I read meriting it, and of sometimes mixing my own reflections on the subject."[23] Jefferson's commonplace books, which survived the 1770 fire at Shadwell, leave abundant proof of his dili-gence and system as a serious student of law, and his abstracts of cases show the importance that he gave to the case method of studying law.

While Jefferson was reading law under Wythe, he reached his majority and received the inheritance provided by his father's will. The long periods that he spent at Shadwell may in part be ex-plained by the new responsibilities that he then assumed. He would not come into possession of Shadwell until after the death of his mother, who had a life interest in the house and 400 surrounding acres, but he took possession of the major portion of the lands that his father had acquired on the Rivanna, which totaled 2,650 acres (including the 400 acres in the Shadwell tract). Jefferson had the choice of the Rivanna lands or another tract of about equal size on the Fluvanna River, which after he chose the Rivanna tract would ultimately go to his only brother, Randolph. As the residu-ary legatee, Jefferson also received various other tracts of land that his father had acquired and that brought his patrimony altogether to around 5,000 acres. By his father's will, Jefferson also inherited twenty-two slaves.[24]

Until he was twenty-one, Jefferson had no part in the supervision of his father's estate, but after he received his inheritance he as-sumed the active management of his property. In addition, he rented from his mother the 400 acres at Shadwell, which were farmed together with his larger Monticello tract and other lands on the Rivanna, and he hired slaves from her to work the lands. He also inherited the gristmill that his father had built on the Rivanna River and operated it until it was swept away by a flood in 1771. In the year that he turned twenty-one, Jefferson sold 700 acres of land in Amherst County, presumably because he needed the cash. As time passed, he both bought and sold other tracts, mostly at a distance. But he held on to his major holdings in Albemarle, and over the years he would consolidate and add to them.[25] In view of the sizable inheritance that came into his possession when he was twenty-one, Jefferson's persistence in his study of law shows that he had ambitions beyond being a planter. His experiences in Williamsburg had exposed him to a world beyond the hills of Albemarle, and however much he loved that land, he was also attracted to the broader world.

Jefferson's years in Williamsburg were more than a time for college studies and reading law and more than a time to enjoy the company of college friends and his mentors Small and Wythe. These were also the years when Jefferson first came into contact with the men who directed the affairs of the colony and managed its government. As the capital of Virginia, Williamsburg was the seat of power in England's largest colony. Its major buildings, observed the Oxford-trained Reverend Hugh Jones in 1724, "are justly reputed the best in all the English America, and are exceeded by a few of their kind in England." In words that would equally apply to Williamsburg in Jefferson's day, Jones noticed that "at the Capitol, at publick times, may be seen a great number of handsom, well-dressed, compleat gentlemen. And at the Governor's House upon birth-nights, and at balls and assemblies, I have seen as fine an appearance, as good diversion, and as splendid entertainment . . . as I have seen any where else." [26]

During the "publick times" in the spring and fall when the General Court and the House of Burgesses were in session, the leading men from throughout the province crowded into Williamsburg and nearby plantations, nearly doubling the town's normal population of about 1,500. From the college, at one end of the Duke of Gloucester Street, Jefferson could easily walk the broad, straight, mile-long thoroughfare to the Capitol. At George Wythe's stately house on the palace green, he was only a few hundred feet from the Governor's Palace. After he became acquainted with Governor Fauquier, he also came to know some of the influential men who composed the Governor's Council. Well connected by birth, Jefferson was no doubt curious to see his mother's cousin Peyton Randolph, the king's attorney, in action, and his acquaintance with Edmund Pendleton and Patrick Henry heightened his interest in hearing them speak in the oldest legislature in America. Thus, Jefferson was often in the Capitol to listen to the debates and also, as a student of law, to observe the proceedings of the General Court.

In view of the lively issues that came before the House of Burgesses in the 1760s, it may be suspected that Jefferson was more often attracted to the proceedings of the legislature than the court. It is certain that he was there often enough to gain an invaluable political education. He was standing at the lobby door of the House on May 30, 1765, when Patrick Henry spoke in support of the Stamp Act Resolutions and connected the name of George III with Julius Caesar and Charles I. The exact words that Henry used are in dispute, but the governor reported that "very indecent language" was employed, and Jefferson later recalled vividly shouts of treason and Henry's "presence of mind with which he closed his sentence and baffled the charge vociferated."[27] Whether Jefferson's memory, at the distance of half a century, was wholly accurate is of less importance than the fact that he was an eyewitness to so important a scene. Never to become a great orator himself, Jefferson was an early admirer of Henry's oratorical skills, and none of his speeches left a more indelible impression on the young political observer than this dramatic moment in the House of Burgesses.

In May, 1766, not long after his twenty-third birthday, Jefferson made a trip of some two months to Annapolis, Philadelphia, and New York—his first trip outside of Virginia; returning to Virginia by sea, he experienced his first ocean voyage. That he made Annapolis, a neighboring provincial capital, his first major stop and went to watch the Maryland legislature in session was indicative of his interests. In the only letter that has survived from this journey, he devoted more time to reporting on the Maryland Assembly— where he was surprised by the lack of decorum—than to any other subject. He also commented on the houses, gardens, and public buildings of Annapolis, showing an observant eye for architecture.[28] Unfortunately, no letters are extant to record Jefferson's first impressions of Philadelphia and New York, but it is known that his main reason for going to Philadelphia was to be inoculated against smallpox. The fact that he carried out that purpose made him one of the pioneers of that then risky experiment and placed him firmly on the side of advancing science. Jefferson was nearing the end of his formal education when he made this journey and would begin to practice law in the following year. In a sense the trip marked his transition from a student to a man of an ever-widening world.

In the spring of 1766, before his trip to Maryland, Pennsylvania, and New York, Jefferson began what would become his Garden Book, recording the first entry at Shadwell on March 30: "Purple hyacinth begins to bloom." Before he left for Maryland, he noted that the wild honeysuckle in the woods had opened and that the blue flowers in the low lands had vanished. Thus began the close and systematic observations of plant life that interested Jefferson throughout his days, for he would make the last entry in his Garden Book in the autumn of 1824, only two years before his death.

Soon after starting the book, he recorded the preparations for the gardens of flowers, fruits, vegetables, and other plants that he would make flourish in the red soil of Monticello. It was another year before he would have the mountaintop cleared to begin his house there, but he was already developing stock for his gardens.[29]

The beginnings of his gardens and of his nearly lifelong building project at Monticello coincided with another major step in his life: setting up an active practice of law in Albemarle and neighboring counties. Jefferson's close identification with the land and Monticello and the prominence of his later political career have tended to obscure the fact that he began his working years as a practicing lawyer. Though he may have enjoyed the study of law more than the practice of it, he threw himself into his new vocation with considerable application. In his autobiography Jefferson recorded that George Wythe presented him before the General Court in Williamsburg in 1767, and his casebook shows that he got his first client in February, 1767.[30] His legal practice was soon carrying him from Albemarle to Staunton, Winchester, and neighboring county seats, to Richmond, and to the General Court in Williamsburg. During his first year as a lawyer, he listed in his casebook a total of 68 cases. During the second year he recorded 115, and by 1769 he was employed in 198 cases. But these did not include all of his legal business; his pocket memoranda and account books show numerous additional clients. When he received £370 in fees in his third year of practice, it was clear that he had achieved success as a lawyer.[31]

Matters dealing with landownership, as was common in that era, predominated in his practice, but his casebook shows a wide variety of litigation. He numbered among his clients both the humble and the great. During his second year of practice, he recorded that "the Honble Wm. Byrd (Charles city) retains me generally," and his casebook lists other prominent Virginia names. It also lists many obscure persons and shows that he declined fees in some circumstances, including all actions to establish the liberty of persons claimed as slaves. He represented plaintiffs and defendants with about equal frequency.[32]

As a young lawyer, Jefferson was better known for thorough preparation than for courtroom oratory, in which he never rivaled Patrick Henry. As Edmund Randolph observed, "Mr. Jefferson drew copiously from the depths of the law, Mr. Henry from the recesses of the human heart." But Randolph also said that "without being an overwhelming orator," Jefferson was an "impressive speaker, who fixed the attention."[33] Jefferson drew not only from the depths of English law but also on occasion called up the law of nature. In a case in 1770 he argued that "under the law of nature, all men are born free, every one comes into the world with a right to his own person, which includes the liberty of moving and using it at his own will."[34]

The case involved a man whose grandmother was a mulatto, born to a white woman and a black man. According to a law of 1705 the grandmother had been subject to servitude until age thirty-one. Before reaching that age, she had given birth to a child, who according to a law of 1723 also was subject to service until age thirty-one. In turn, that daughter, before attaining her freedom, had given birth to a son, and he, like his mother and grandmother before him, was being held to service until age thirty-one. He sought release from servitude before that age, and Jefferson, without fee, pleaded his case. After a detailed exposition, the young, slaveholding lawyer concluded that the act of 1705 "subjected to servitude the first mulatto only. That this did not, under the law of nature, affect the liberty of the children. Because, under that law we are all born free." It took the act of 1723 to subject such children to servitude, he pointed out and, with no hiding of his own convictions, concluded that "it remains for some future legislature, if any shall be found wicked enough, to extend it to the grandchildren and other issue more remote." What Jefferson adroitly ignored was that the act of 1723 applied to the children born to any female mulatto held to servitude until age thirty-one and that the statute thus operated with equal effect on the plaintiff's mother as it did upon his grandmother.[35] After listening to Jefferson's arguments, the court ruled against his client before the other side even presented its position. If Jefferson's reference to the law of nature was startling to the judges, such concepts were already well fixed in his own mind. He was finding practical application for them well before he would marshal them in a wider cause.

In his carefully kept casebook he entered his last case—number 939—on November 9, 1774, and soon turned over his pending business to Edmund Randolph. Although during a brief period in 1782 Jefferson prepared some six legal opinions for clients, he never fully returned to the practice of law after the Revolution.[36] Before that epochal event he had already turned his legal skills in new directions and entered another career—one that he repeatedly professed to hate but never abandoned—politics.

II
Public Life and Private World

In December, 1768, Jefferson stood for election as a delegate from Albemarle County to the Virginia House of Burgesses. The poll taken at that election has not survived, and only the names of the persons elected were reported in the press. But enough is known about the conduct of elections in Jefferson's Virginia to reconstruct the scene that brought his Albemarle neighbors to the courthouse in Charlottesville on election day. There the freeholders (white adult men who owned twenty-five acres with a house, or one hundred acres of unoccupied land, or a house and lot in town) gave their votes orally before the sheriff and within the hearing of numerous onlookers who crowded into the courthouse. Seated in the center of a long table, the sheriff, who conducted the election, was flanked by several justices of the peace, by the clerks who recorded the votes, and by the candidates themselves. The candidates were expected not only to be present on the grounds on election day but also to provide refreshments (rum punch and cookies were common) for the voters, who were free to accept the hospitality of all candidates regardless of their political preferences. That Jefferson provided such treats at his first election is known because he recorded the expenses in his account book.[1] To fill the two seats to which each county was entitled in the House of Burgesses, each freeholder voted for two persons and on this occasion chose from among three candidates. Two of them, Dr. Thomas Walker and Edward Carter, had been members of the previous Assembly, but during the last session Carter had failed to attend. This circumstance no doubt played a part in Jefferson's becoming a candidate. When the poll closed, Walker had been reelected, and Carter, a large Albemarle landowner, had lost to the young, well-educated lawyer whose father had been one of the earliest settlers in the county.

On May 8, 1769, Jefferson—just turned twenty-six—took the

oath of office and was seated in the House of Burgesses. It was fortunate that the new member arrived promptly in Williamsburg to
be present when the session opened, for the burgesses were to sit
for only ten days before the governor dissolved them. Yet during
that short period Jefferson drafted his first state paper—resolutions in answer to the governor's speech—a purely ceremonial exercise but one that showed that his talents as a writer were already
known to some of the members. His draft of the address, however,
was objected to by some members of the committee and recast—a
reminder that he was still a new member.[2] The young burgess from
Albemarle County was also named to two important committees:
Privileges and Elections, and Propositions and Grievances, indicating that Jefferson entered the House with influential connections,
including his mother's cousin Peyton Randolph, who was elected
Speaker.[3]

Tensions with Great Britain had mounted since Jefferson had listened to Patrick Henry denounce the Stamp Act four years before.
Now the Townshend duties, voted by Parliament two years earlier,
were the focus of colonial protests. On the ninth day of the session,
the burgesses by a unanimous vote passed resolutions declaring
that they had the sole right to levy taxes on the colony, affirming
the right of petition, and protesting the removal of accused persons
to England for trial. On the next day Governor Botetourt dissolved
the House of Burgesses. Later that day "the late Representatives of
the People" gathered in the Apollo Room of the Raleigh Tavern.
"Judging it necessary that some Measures should be taken in their
distressed Situation, for preserving the true and essential Interests
of the Colony," they reassembled on the following day (May 18,
1769) and passed a series of nonimportation resolutions and formed
an association to implement them.[4] Some members had come to
Williamsburg prepared to act, and the resolutions appear to have
been based on a paper that George Washington brought with him
from Mount Vernon. Although the authorship of the resolutions
has never been fully established, the new member from Albemarle
was not among the drafters.[5] He was, however, one of the signers,
and he fully supported the actions. It was a dramatic moment to
begin his political career, and the unity of the burgesses in asserting
the rights of the colony could only have confirmed the views that
already were becoming fixed in Jefferson's own mind.

In August, 1769, Governor Botetourt issued a writ for a new
election, which was held in September. Jefferson was again elected,
as were most of the other members of the dissolved Assembly. He

observed that the only burgesses not reelected were the few who declined to support the proceedings at the Raleigh Tavern. The new Assembly convened on November 7 and lasted six weeks. Jefferson was named to the same standing committees as in the previous session and during the session served on several select committees, reporting two committee bills to the house. Though he must have found this session less exciting than the previous one, he got his first real taste of the business of legislating. Toward the end of the session when he was named to the committee to examine enrolled bills, it was evident that he had become one of those members who gave close attention to his duties and to the work of the House. When he returned to Williamsburg in the spring of 1770 for the next session, Jefferson's contributions were similar.[6] His legislative service had become important to him, and he devoted himself to it with characteristic application.

In the same year that he entered the House of Burgesses, Jefferson ordered a small shipment of books from London. Their titles are significant not only in relation to his own legislative career but also in view of the growing constitutional struggle with Great Britain and the onrush of events in which he would participate. Among the books he received were John Locke's *Two Treatises on Government*, Montesquieu's complete works, Jean Jacques Burlamaqui's *Principes du Droit Naturel*, Anthony Ellys' *Tracts on the Liberty, Spiritual and Temporal, of Protestants in England*, and Adam Ferguson's *An Essay on the History of Civil Society*.[7] One writer who has questioned Jefferson's direct contact with Locke's work at this important period in his life has asserted that the Locke volume perished almost immediately after Jefferson received it in the fire that ravaged his mother's house at Shadwell on February 1, 1770. But Jefferson had access to Locke's *Two Treatises on Government* in 1772, for he cited it several times in legal notes on divorce.[8] Although Locke's *Two Treatises* was not among Jefferson's books received by the Library of Congress in 1815, it was listed in his manuscript catalogue of his library.[9] Furthermore, of the thirteen works purchased in 1769, seven from Jefferson's library are in the Library of Congress today.[10] The books are all in editions described in the 1769 invoice that listed the titles that were being shipped, and all have publication dates prior to 1769.

The existence of these volumes suggests that this key shipment of books was not lost at Shadwell. Indeed, the books may not have reached there before the fire. Jefferson was informed by letter from London, dated October 2, 1769, and an accompanying invoice that his order of books was being shipped to Virginia on board the *Industry* captained by James Lowes.[11] On December 7, 1769, Purdie and Dixon's *Virginia Gazette*, published in Williamsburg, announced that the *Industry* under the command of Captain Lowes had arrived in the James River from London after seven weeks' passage. It is certain that this was the ship that carried Jefferson's box of books. How soon thereafter or where Jefferson uncrated the books is not known, but he was in Williamsburg attending the meeting of the House of Burgesses when the *Industry* arrived in the James River, and it may be that the letter and the two invoices came on the same ship. It is of interest that these papers were not destroyed by the fire at Shadwell and are the earliest extant papers addressed to Jefferson. It is also known that Jefferson kept some books in Williamsburg, for in 1773, when he made a count of the books at Monticello, he specifically noted that the count did not include his books in Williamsburg.[12] Books on political subjects, such as those received in the 1769 shipment, seem the type of volumes that he might have kept in the provincial capital for reference during legislative sessions.

The destruction at Shadwell was extensive. Jefferson said that he lost "every paper I had in the world, and almost every book," and calculated the loss of books at £200. "To make the loss more sensible it fell principally on my books of common law," he wrote, "of which I have but one left, at that time lent out."[13] Jefferson did not mention his new shipment of books in reporting the details of the fire to his friend John Page, but the weight of evidence suggests that those books, rather than being destroyed, provided a new beginning for Jefferson's library. That circumstance may have meant that the books were the more closely read for being all he had.

While dividing his time between his law practice and his legislative duties, Jefferson also began to give increasing attention to another interest that more and more would absorb his attention: building a house on the mountaintop that would become the seat of his lands in Albemarle and the center of his dreams. "I have lately removed to the mountain from whence this is dated," Jefferson wrote February 20, 1771, in one of the earliest known letters from Monticello. "I have here but one room, which, like the cobler's serves me for parlour for kitchen and hall. I may add, for bed chamber and study too. My friends sometimes take a temperate dinner with me and then retire to look for beds elsewhere. I have hopes however of getting more elbow room this summer." This letter was written from the earlier of the two small pavilions that today flank the main house—then far from finished in its first state and not to be completed in its final form for four decades. Jefferson had had the mountaintop cleared and leveled in 1768; the following year the cellar of the first pavilion was excavated, a well dug, bricks made, and other work on the site begun. By November, 1770, the first building was sufficiently completed to enable Jefferson to move there, an event no doubt speeded by the fire at Shadwell the previous February. After that disaster, he was away much of the time on law business, at a session of the legislature, and on various visits before establishing himself at Monticello.[14]

Jefferson was both the builder and the architect of Monticello, and it became for him nearly a lifetime avocation. His home was the first of a series of architectural achievements, many of them late in life, that support a leading architectural historian's assessment of Jefferson as America's "first great native-born architect." The first American to make working drawings as well as architectural designs, Jefferson produced more than five hundred such drawings—the earliest ones in planning the building of Monticello. Twenty-one architectural drawings date between 1767, when he first started planning his home on the little mountain, and the end of 1770, when he moved there; another six drawings were probably completed by early 1771. He would ultimately produce over two hundred drawings, sketches, and surveys that scholars have identified as connected with his building, rebuilding, and remodeling of Monticello.[15]

Jefferson learned architecture from observation and from books. Although no record of his first impressions of the architecture of Williamsburg survives, Jefferson's later comments were harsh. He was restrained in his critique of the Capitol and the Governor's Palace, but he called the college and the hospital buildings "rude, misshapen piles, which, but that they have roofs, would be taken for brick-kilns." When he first saw Annapolis, he judged the houses there better than in Williamsburg. Most of the houses in Virginia were built of wood, and he thought it "impossible to devise things more ugly, uncomfortable, and happily more perishable. . . . The genius of architecture seems to have shed its maledictions over this land," he wrote. "Buildings are often erected, by individuals, of considerable expence. To give these symmetry and taste would not increase their cost. . . . But the first principles of the art are unknown, and there exists scarcely a model among us sufficiently chaste to give an idea of them." This seems a severe assessment in view of the existence of such James River mansions as Carter's Grove,

Westover, and Berkeley. But, as Edmund Randolph would observe, Jefferson "panted after the fine arts, and discovered a taste in them not easily satisfied with such scanty means, as existed in a colony." Randolph also said that "it constituted a part of Mr. Jefferson's pride to run before the times in which he lived." [16]

If Jefferson found no models about him to imitate, he discovered them in books, and it was to those sources that he owed his earliest architectural accomplishments. He is said to have purchased his first book on architecture while a student at William and Mary, and by the time he started drawing his plans for Monticello, he had the beginnings of an architectural library. In his early drawings for Monticello he used James Gibbs's *Book of Architecture* and his *Rules for Drawing* along with Robert Morris' *Select Architecture*. [17] Gibbs's books, popular in America for a generation, probably introduced Jefferson to the ideas of the Italian master Andrea Palladio, whose *Four Books of Architecture* he would ultimately acquire in no less than five editions and whose ideas would be dominant in Jefferson's architectural thinking before he went to France in 1784. The first state of Monticello clearly reflected the Palladian influence. Robert Morris, who designed buildings in spheres and perfect cubes, also appealed to Jefferson's mathematical mind. He liked the simplicity of Morris' designs and their adaptability to small scale. Jefferson's first idea for a house seems to have come from Morris' *Select Architecture*, for one of his earliest drawings is a tracing from a plate in that work. Another of Jefferson's early studies for Monticello was taken directly from one of the plates in Gibbs's *Book of Architecture*, which in turn was similar to a plate in Palladio's second volume. Both Gibbs and Morris used the octagonal shape, which Jefferson found attractive for both houses and gardens, first employing the design at Monticello. [18]

By 1770 Jefferson had decided on a center block with flanking wings for the main house. His drawings show it dominated by a two-story portico of two orders with stronger Doric capitals supporting Ionic columns, as Palladio recommended. Once the foundation walls were up, he decided to add octagonal bays to the parlor and the ends of the house. There is some question as to whether the upper portion of the portico was ever built before later remodeling began. The Marquis de Chastellux, visiting Monticello in 1782, reported entering the house "through two porticoes ornamented with columns," but whether he meant a two-story portico is unclear. [19]

One of the most distinctive features of Jefferson's plan was to group under one roof the scattered outbuildings—kitchen, laundry room, woodhouse, storage rooms, and the like—that filled the grounds around most Virginia plantations and connect these supporting buildings with the main house. He acquired the basic idea from Palladio and adapted it to his mountain site by devising a plan by which the dependencies were built on the basement level, opening on one side to ground level, and covered with terraces. When the Marquis de Chastellux visited Monticello, he was impressed with the main house, which he described as "in an Italian style" and "quite tasteful," and he was struck with the arrangement of the dependencies. Altogether he found the place "resembles none of the others seen in this country; so that it may be said that Mr. Jefferson is the first American who has consulted the Fine Arts to know how he should shelter himself from the weather."[20]

When Chastellux made these observations, Jefferson had been building at Monticello for a dozen years and had not yet completed his original plans, but it was evident by then that Jefferson conceived of his home as an extension of himself, his interests, and his ideas. Building Monticello was a means of creative expression, an absorbing hobby, and an exciting adventure. Nowhere else did he find so wondrous a setting. "Where has nature spread so rich a mantle under the eye?" he asked. "How sublime to look down into the workhouse of nature, to see her clouds, hail, snow, rain, thunder, all fabricated at our feet! And the glorious Sun, when rising as if out of a distant water, just gilding the tops of the mountains, and giving life to all nature!" Thoughts of Monticello summoned his deepest feelings, and he once wrote, "All my wishes end, where I hope my days will end, at Monticello."[21]

At the time he started building his home, Jefferson did not know who would share it with him, but he soon was interrupting his work to visit Martha Wayles Skelton at the Forest, her father's house in Charles City County, near Williamsburg. These visits began in October, 1770, and increased in frequency during 1771. In June of that year Jefferson sent to England for a pianoforte "worthy the acceptance of a lady for whom I intend it," and in August he confided that "in every scheme of happiness she is placed in the fore-ground of the picture, as the principal figure. Take that away, and it is no picture for me."[22] This was Jefferson's first serious romantic attachment since his adolescent love affair with Rebecca Burwell. In the intervening years nothing in the record indicates his being attracted to any women except for an imprudent advance to Betsy Walker, wife of his friend John Walker. Years later he admitted that "when young and single I offered love to a handsome lady," and he acknowledged "its incorrectness."[23] This appears to have been an exceptional circumstance, and until he met Martha Skelton, he seems to have been less interested in women than in establishing himself in law and in politics. During these years he had taken seriously his responsibilities to his mother and to his younger sisters and brother. He had been much shaken in 1765 by the death of his oldest sister, Jane, who was twenty-five and had been particularly close to him. Thus, a number of circumstances may have contributed to what appeared to be a lack of interest in finding a wife. All of this changed when he fell in love with Martha.

Five and a half years younger than Jefferson, Martha Wayles Skelton was the young widow of Bathurst Skelton, whom Jefferson had known while Skelton was a student at William and Mary. The daughter of John Wayles, a prosperous lawyer with a large landed estate, Martha had married Bathurst Skelton when she was eighteen, borne a son at nineteen, and become a widow before she was twenty. It was about two years after this that Jefferson met her, probably in Williamsburg in the autumn of 1770, and soon thereafter began to pay her increasing attention. Indeed, he apparently courted her with all the formality that the word suggests. Within a year she had agreed to marry him, and on the first day of January, 1772, they were married at the Forest. Martha was twenty-three and Jefferson twenty-eight—somewhat older than most Virginia men married in his day. In the summer before their marriage, her son, John Skelton, not yet four, died, and Jefferson never gained the stepson for whom he had already begun to make plans.[24]

No portrait of Martha Wayles Jefferson survives, and the rare contemporary descriptions of her offer few details. Family tradition describes her as beautiful and musically talented. Her brother-in-law Robert Skipwith told Jefferson not long before their marriage that she was a woman "with the greatest fund of good nature" and "all that sprightliness and sensibility which promises to ensure you the greatest happiness mortals are capable of enjoying."[25] No description of Martha in Jefferson's own hand survives, nor any letter between them, for he apparently destroyed such private papers as might have revealed his deepest personal feelings. But there is every reason to believe that he found Skipwith's prediction to be true and that their marriage was a happy one.

There are no portraits of Jefferson at the time of his marriage, and none would be painted until he went to Europe after the Revolution. Nor are there any written descriptions dating from that time. But we know from later descriptions that he was over six feet tall and somewhat lanky; his eyes were hazel, his hair reddish, and he tended to freckle in the sun. Unlike other times of his life, at this period he appears to have been careful about his dress. While courting Martha, he even ordered from London "a large Umbrella with brass ribs covered with green silk, and neatly finished."[26] He had already shown a shyness that he would only gradually overcome and a sensitivity that he would never lose. He was never referred to as handsome, but the impression that he made on others was generally pleasing. As he made his mark in the world, others would more often record these impressions. When he took Martha to Monticello as his wife, neither of them could have anticipated the events that would make him known beyond the Virginia society into which they both had been born and in which they expected to live out their lives.

Their first-born daughter, Martha, would one day relate that she had heard from her father the story of the newlyweds' arrival at Monticello late at night in the midst of a snowstorm, finding all the fires out and the servants in bed. The next day Jefferson recorded in his garden book that the snow in Albemarle was about three feet deep, "the deepest snow we have ever seen." This entry was made on January 26; he would make no other entry until March 30.[27]

Just how much of Monticello had been completed when the newly married couple arrived there is uncertain. That the main house was not finished is clear, but more may have been finished than the small pavilion that had been Jefferson's bachelor's quarters. It may be that one wing of the main house was sufficiently completed to be occupied, but the tradition is that the small outbuilding was their first home.[28] Regardless of when they moved into the main house, construction would continue throughout their marriage. It was not finished before the Revolution. Building continued throughout the war years, and work remained to be done when the Chevalier de Chastellux visited there in 1782.

Jefferson did not attend the session of the House of Burgesses that met in early February, 1772, soon after his marriage, and he was at Monticello in late September when their first child, Martha, was born.[29] But in the years ahead he would be drawn away from home more than he wished by events as unforeseen as they would be epoch-making. Though he had not realized it at the time, he had already witnessed and participated in the first steps on the road to revolution.

III
The Road to Revolution

Virginia was quiet at the beginning of the 1770s. A new ministry headed by Lord North took office in London, and in April, 1770, Parliament repealed the Townshend duties except for the levy on tea. Though Parliament still asserted its right to tax and to pass other laws binding on the colonies, "nothing of particular excitement occurring for a considerable time," Jefferson observed, "our countrymen seemed to fall into a state of insensibility to our situation."[1] He would later recall this lull in public concern as dangerous to the American cause, but as a young husband and a new father, he may not have been unduly concerned by the fact that Virginia's Governor Dunmore kept the House of Burgesses prorogued for another year following the 1772 session that he had missed. When Dunmore did summon the Assembly to meet in March, 1773, Jefferson was there to participate, and by then his concern about colonial rights was rising sharply.

The burning of the revenue schooner *Gaspee* by Rhode Islanders in 1772 brought the creation of a royal commission of inquiry with powers to send offenders to England for trial. Seeing the revival of that crucial issue as demanding attention, Jefferson joined a group of young burgesses who believed that many older and leading members lacked the "forwardness and zeal which the times required." This younger group, which included Patrick Henry, Richard Henry Lee, Francis Lightfoot Lee, and Dabney Carr, began meeting privately in the evenings at the Raleigh Tavern. "We were all sensible," Jefferson said, "that the most urgent of all measures was that of coming to an understanding with all the other colonies to consider the British claims as a common cause to all, and to produce an unity of action."[2] The plan they proposed was an intercolonial system of committees of correspondence.

The group prepared a series of resolutions introduced in the

House of Burgesses by Dabney Carr and passed on March 12, 1773, without a dissenting vote. Peyton Randolph, the Speaker, was chosen to chair the committee of correspondence called for by the resolutions. Jefferson and all those whom he identified as being members of the Raleigh Tavern group were also named to the committee, which was instructed to open communications with the other colonies. Meeting the next day, the committee composed a circular letter sent to all colonies along with a copy of the resolutions. The creation of committees of correspondence by the various colonies provided the structure for a revolutionary political union. Acknowledging the earlier establishment of committees of correspondence within Massachusetts, Jefferson nonetheless claimed for Virginia the leadership in the creation of the intercolonial network.[3] Governor Dunmore either did not recognize or preferred to ignore the significance of the Virginia action, reporting to London "some resolves which show a little ill humour in the house of Burgesses, but . . . so insignificant that I took no matter of notice of them."[4] He thus did not dissolve the Assembly but prorogued it after a session of only eleven days. By repeatedly proroguing it, he kept it from meeting until May, 1774.

Jefferson was not among the three members named as a standing committee by the committee of correspondence at its first meeting, and he left Williamsburg after the proroguing of the Assembly. In the year between the sessions of 1773 and 1774, Jefferson's personal life was greatly affected by the death of his best friend and brother-in-law, Dabney Carr, and the death of his father-in-law, John Wayles. Carr had been his boyhood chum at Maury's school, had married his sister Martha in 1765, and had recently entered the House of Burgesses. Jefferson felt his death keenly, and when he wrote the epitaph for his tombstone, he signed it, "Thomas Jefferson, who of all men loved him most." Carr was the first person to be buried at Monticello. Later, probably in 1781, Martha Carr and her children would come to live at Monticello. Shortly after Dabney Carr's death John Wayles died, and Mrs. Jefferson inherited a sizable estate of over 11,000 acres and 135 slaves. Approximately half of the land had to be sold to pay her share of her father's heavy debt, but the inheritance, by Jefferson's calculations, doubled their wealth, while increasing his responsibilities of management.[5] These considerations must have played a part in Jefferson's decision to cease practicing law, for within six months following Wayles's death, he closed his practice. The release from the demands of an active law business provided more time for the management of his own, his mother's, and his wife's property and also left Jefferson freer for public service. The latter would increasingly command his attention.

When the Virginia Assembly convened in May, 1774, relations with Great Britain were in a heightened state of crisis. During the previous year the ailing East India Company had been given special privileges to sell tea in America, and once its marketing operations were set up in the colonies, the cry of monopoly joined the cry against the tax on tea. After protesters boarded three ships in the Boston harbor and dumped chests of tea into the bay, Britain responded with the Boston Port Bill, closing the Boston harbor to all commerce effective June 1, 1774. The news of the British action reached Williamsburg in May in the midst of the legislative session.[6]

Jefferson was among those who took the lead in designing the swift Virginia reaction. He joined with Patrick Henry, Richard Henry Lee, Francis Lightfoot Lee, and several other younger members who believed that Virginia must take an unequivocal stand in the support of Massachusetts. As a means of arousing Virginians from lethargy, this group hit upon the idea of calling for a day of general fasting and prayer. Using the library in the council chamber, they searched through John Rushworth's *Historical Collections* (London, 1659–1701), found a model in a proclamation issued by Charles I in 1642, and prepared a resolution to proclaim June 1, 1774, a day of fasting, humiliation, and prayer "to implore heaven to avert us from the evils of civil war, to inspire us with firmness in support of our rights, and to turn the hearts of the King and parliament to moderation and justice."[7] The details that Jefferson remembered years later about rummaging through Rushworth looking for precedents and modernizing phrases in the model adopted suggest that he had a principal hand in drafting the resolution, but Robert Carter Nicholas, whose religious character was more in unison with the resolution, presented it to the House of Burgesses on May 24. The resolution passed immediately without opposition. It was promptly printed in a broadside that Governor Dunmore held in his hand two days later when he summoned the burgesses to the council room and dissolved them, protesting that the resolution was "conceived in such Terms as reflect highly upon his Majesty and the Parliament of *Great Britain*." It was a sign of the growing distance between the royal government and the colony that the dissolution was unexpected and that more spirited resolutions were being withheld until the business of the Assembly could be completed.[8]

After being dissolved, the burgesses reassembled in the Apollo Room of the Raleigh Tavern. On May 27 along with eighty-eight other members, Jefferson signed an association to refrain from using tea and to boycott most other commodities sold by the East India Company. Even more important, the signers agreed that "an attack, made on one of our sister colonies, to compel submission to arbitrary taxes, is an attack made on all British America," and called upon the committee of correspondence to contact the other colonies regarding a general congress "to deliberate on those general measures which the united interests of America may from time to time require."[9]

The next day Jefferson attended the meeting of the committee of correspondence, which sent letters to all the colonies transmitting the Virginia action and soliciting sentiments on the appointment of delegates to a general congress. Jefferson was also present two days later at a meeting of burgesses still in Williamsburg summoned by Peyton Randolph to respond to newly arrived dispatches in which Bostonians appealed for the adoption of a strict nonimportation and nonexportation agreement. Because that was a measure the association formed at the Raleigh Tavern on May 27 had shunned, the new gathering felt unable to commit Virginia and called another meeting for August 1 in Williamsburg. Jefferson was one of the signers of the printed letter sent to all members of the late House of Burgesses reporting the appeal from Boston, summoning the Williamsburg meeting, and urging all representatives meanwhile to collect the sense of the people in their counties.[10]

Returning to Monticello, Jefferson was soon at his writing table drafting resolutions and putting his thoughts on paper in preparation for the August meeting. The first of his efforts was a series of resolutions adopted by the freeholders of Albemarle County on July 26, 1774, at the time of the election of Jefferson and John Walker to represent the county in the Virginia convention in Williamsburg. The resolutions asserted that "the several states of British America" were subject only to the laws adopted by their own legislatures. Proclaiming that "no other legislature whatever may rightfully exercise authority over them," they protested that "their natural and legal rights have in frequent instances been invaded by the parliament of Great Britain." The resolutions supported nonimportation and nonexportation measures until the port of Boston was reopened, taxes were repealed, and restrictions on American trade and manufacturing lifted.[11] Jefferson also prepared a similar series of resolutions for submission to the Virginia convention and drafted a set of proposed instructions to the Virginia delegates to the Continental Congress scheduled to convene in Philadelphia in September. He intended to propose these instructions at the convention, but he became ill en route and returned home.

He did, however, send two copies of his paper to Williamsburg. One was addressed to Patrick Henry, who never communicated it to anyone. Jefferson later wondered if he had taken time to read it. The other copy went to the chairman of the convention, Peyton Randolph, who laid it on the table as coming from an absent delegate. Although the proposals in Jefferson's draft were not taken up by any member nor offered to the convention, some members arranged to have the paper printed. It appeared in Williamsburg under the title *A Summary View of the Rights of British America* and was soon reprinted in Philadelphia and London. The author was listed on the title page of the twenty-three-page pamphlet only as "A Native, and Member of the House of Burgesses," but Jefferson's authorship was generally known. He later thought that his propositions were considered too bold for the times and that "tamer sentiments were preferred." In time he came to believe that a moderate course had been wise and that he had proposed a leap too long for most of his fellow citizens. He also admitted that his paper was based on an interpretation of the relationship of the colonies to Great Britain that, except for George Wythe, he had never been able to convince others to accept.[12]

A Summary View of the Rights of British America was indeed a bold statement. Although too extreme for 1774, it would not long be so regarded. Its circulation propelled Jefferson into the front ranks of the champions of American rights and established those credentials that two years later placed him on the committee to draft the Declaration of Independence. In addition to a broad statement of principles, Jefferson presented a detailed enumeration of American grievances against both Parliament and the crown, formulating the list of charges that he would add to and incorporate into the Declaration of Independence.

Jefferson based *A Summary View* on the contention that the only connection between the settlements in America and Great Britain was through the crown. He began his argument by going back to the migrations of the Saxons. "Our emigration from England to this country gave her no more rights over us, than the emigrations of the Danes and Saxons gave to the present authorities of the mother country over England," he said in summarizing his pamphlet.[13] The pamphlet itself explained:

Our ancestors, before their emigration to America, were the free inhabitants of the British dominions in Europe, and possessed a right, which nature has given to all men, of departing from the country in which chance, not choice has placed them, of going in quest of new habitations, and of there establishing new societies, under such laws and regulations as to them shall seem most likely to promote public happiness. . . . Settlements having been thus effected in the wilds of America, the emigrants thought proper to adopt that system of laws under which they hitherto lived in the mother country, and to continue their union with her by submitting themselves to the same common sovereign, who was thereby made the central link connecting the several parts of the empire thus newly multiplied.[14]

As he had proclaimed in the Albemarle resolutions, Jefferson insisted that "the British parliament has no right to exercise authority over us." This was not a widely shared view. More prevalent was the position that Parliament had a right to regulate commerce and to lay duties on it for the purposes of regulation but not of raising revenue.[15]

Having denied the authority of Parliament, Jefferson appealed to the king to recommend to Parliament the total revocation of those acts causing discontent. But in repudiating Parliament, Jefferson had no intention of strengthening the power of the king, and he cautioned George III that the king was "no more than the chief officer of the people, appointed by the laws, and circumscribed with definite powers, to use, and consequently subject to their superintendance." Detailing the acts of Parliament and the policies of monarchs and ministers that proved "a deliberate, systematical plan of reducing us to slavery," Jefferson laid these grievances before the king "with that freedom of language and sentiment which becomes a free people, claiming their rights as derived from the laws of nature, and not as the gift of their chief magistrate. Let those flatter, who fear: it is not an American art." He urged George III to "no longer persevere in sacrificing the rights of one part of the empire to the inordinate desires of another." Though affirming no wish to separate from Great Britain, the mere mention of the possibility showed how far Jefferson was prepared to go. In conclusion he affirmed that "the god who gave us life, gave us liberty at the same time: the hand of force may destroy, but cannot disjoin them."[16]

Most Americans in 1774 were not ready to go so far as the thirty-one-year-old Albemarle delegate. That was evident in the resolutions adopted by the Virginia convention, which were primarily concerned with creating a vigorous nonimportation association and halting all exports of tobacco and other products to Great Britain after August 10, 1775, if American grievances were not redressed by then.[17] Some Virginians in fact used Jefferson's paper to emphasize the moderation of the convention's approach. In a preface added upon publication, the editors applauded the "faithful accuracy" with which the sources of the differences with Great Britain were examined and the "manly firmness" with which "the opinions entertained by every free American" were expressed. Then they added, "It will evince to the world the moderation of our late convention, who have only touched with tenderness many of the claims insisted on in this pamphlet, though every heart acknowledged their justice."[18]

Like most of Jefferson's political writings, *A Summary View* was written for a specific political purpose, not as an abstract political treatise. Nevertheless, since it was Jefferson's first published writing and a precursor to the Declaration of Independence, the sources of his ideas at this stage of his thinking are of particular interest. Because Jefferson did not record all of his reading in his commonplace book and did not date any of the entries, it is impossible to be precise about what Jefferson was reading at any specific time, but there is evidence to indicate some of the leading works that he had in his possession or was familiar with prior to writing *A Summary View*.[19] We know the titles of the volumes in the important shipment of books he received from London in December, 1769. Among his major purchases then were Montesquieu's complete works, Locke's *Two Treatises on Government*, and Burlamaqui's *Principes du Droit Naturel*.[20] Although his acquisition of these works in 1769 suggests Jefferson's familiarity with them before he wrote his pamphlet in 1774, he would also have been familiar with the concept of natural rights from reading other works whose authors were influenced by Locke. Entries in his commonplace book show, for example, that Jefferson read extensively in the works of Lord Kames, who was much influenced by Locke. After a study of Jefferson's commonplace book, Gilbert Chinard concluded that Jefferson found in this Scottish lord a complete exposition of the theory of natural rights.[21] That Jefferson copied little from Locke in his commonplace book may suggest familiarity with ideas well known in Virginia rather than neglect of so important a political thinker.[22]

What Jefferson regarded as key works on political thought at the time he wrote *A Summary View* can be glimpsed in the selected reading list that he prepared three years earlier for Robert Skipwith.

Under the heading "Politicks, Trade," he listed eight titles, headed
by Montesquieu's *Spirit of Laws*, Locke's *Treatises on Government*,
and Algernon Sidney's *Discourses Concerning Government*. Jefferson
later called Sidney's work "a rich treasure of republican principles,
supported by copious and cogent arguments, and adorned with the
finest flowers of science. It is probably the best elementary book
of the principles of government, as founded in natural right,
which has ever been published in any language." On his 1771 list
Jefferson also recommended Lord Bolingbroke's political works in
five volumes, to which he himself had been particularly attracted as
a student and from which he had copied extensively in his literary
commonplace book. In addition he included Montesquieu's "Rise
and Fall of the Roman Government" and Sir James Stewart's *Political Economy*—another of the works that he had purchased in 1769.
These were only a few of the best books on politics and trade,
Jefferson wrote Skipwith, while listing additional volumes on history, law, and other subjects that included works by Kames, Locke,
and other political writers.[23]

In addition to ideas absorbed from Europe's major political philosophers, Jefferson also was familiar with the writings of pamphleteers, both British and American. There are reflections in *A
Summary View* of Letter 25 (1769) of "Junius," a pamphleteer of the
"country party" in England, and also of Richard Bland's *An Inquiry
into the Rights of the British Colonies* (1766), a pamphlet written in response to the Stamp Act.[24] Of Bland, a fellow burgess whose library
Jefferson would purchase upon his death in 1776, Jefferson said
that he "wrote the first pamphlet on the nature of the connection
with Great Britain which had any pretension to accuracy" but did
not carry his arguments to their logical conclusion.[25]

A Summary View was in part a legal brief in which Jefferson summarized acts of Parliament affecting the colonies and cited references to the statutes in marginal notes. Elsewhere, he did not cite
his sources, but his study of history was in evidence throughout.
His commonplace book shows that he had given particular attention in his reading to the early populations of Europe and their migrations, and he found evidence that convinced him of the existence of early popular sovereignty and historical confirmation of
the doctrine of natural rights. He was gratified to read in Stanyan's
history of Greece that "the first kings of Greece were elected by the
free consent of the people." He also found examples in ancient history of colonies that governed themselves independently.[26] Such
historical precedents formed the basis of much of Jefferson's rea-

soning in *A Summary View*. He was a lawyer calling up precedents rather than a philosopher constructing abstract theories. At the same time, the reasoning that Jefferson employed in parts of his *Summary View* defied history and prompted John Quincy Adams years later to protest: "The argument of Mr. Jefferson, that the emigration of the first colonists from Great Britain which came to America was an expatriation, dissolving sovereignties, was doubtful in theory and unfounded in fact. The original colonists came out with charters from the King, with the rights and duties of British subjects. They were entitled to the protection of the British King, and owed him allegiance."[27]

Jefferson's contemporaries were more charitable than John Quincy Adams at a distance of half a century. John Adams said of the Jefferson he met in 1775 at the second Continental Congress: "Mr. Jefferson had the Reputation of a masterly Pen. He had been chosen a Delegate in Virginia, in consequence of a very handsome public Paper which he had written for the House of Burgesses, which had given him the Character of a fine Writer."[28] The importance of *A Summary View* rests more upon its political effects in 1775 and 1776 than on its merits as a work of history or political theory. If Jefferson's history was not always sound, the direction of his own thinking toward a separate America was clear.

The Williamsburg convention did not instruct its delegation to the Congress in Philadelphia to present Jefferson's *Summary View* and did not name him among its seven delegates. However, he did tie for eighth place in the voting for delegates.[29] His absence from the Williamsburg convention may have been a factor in his not getting more votes, but this is not at all clear, for Jefferson was still a junior colleague to the leading men chosen to speak for Virginia. Although Jefferson did not participate in the first meeting of the Continental Congress in September, 1774, his *Summary View* circulated among the delegates along with James Wilson's recently published *Considerations on the Nature and Extent of the Legislative Authority of the British Parliament*, which also denied the power of Parliament over the colonies but argued for loyalty to the king.[30]

Sitting from September 5 to October 26, 1774, the first Continental Congress adopted a declaration of rights and grievances, asserting among others the right to "life, liberty and property" and the power of provincial assemblies over taxation and internal polity, subject only to the veto of the crown. It also listed and called for the repeal of all the various acts since 1763 that the colonists found unacceptable.[31] The delegates agreed upon a strict nonimportation, nonconsumption, and nonexportation association modeled on the Virginia association of August, 1774, binding the colonies to halt all importations of British goods after December 1, 1774, and to cease exports after September 10, 1775. To enforce the association, committees were to be created in every county, city, and town, and the names of violators were to be published as enemies of American liberty. Any colony failing to subscribe to the association, or violating it, was to be deemed "unworthy of the rights of freemen, and . . . inimical to the liberties of their country." Jefferson approved the proceedings of the Continental Congress, and when the Albemarle committee was elected to enforce the association, his name headed the list of the fifteen men chosen. He was soon circulating association papers to local captains throughout the county.[32]

The Virginia convention that met in Williamsburg in August, 1774, authorized its chairman, Peyton Randolph, to convene another meeting of the delegates at any time that he deemed proper, thus assuring the continuance of the convention mechanism even if the governor continued to keep the House of Burgesses prorogued. Under this authority Randolph summoned a second convention to meet in Richmond in March, 1775. Jefferson and Thomas Walker were again elected to represent Albemarle County at the convention, and Jefferson was present when the convention opened on March 20.[33]

Jefferson's autobiography is nearly silent on the Richmond convention, which has figured so prominently in the history of the American Revolution as the meeting where Patrick Henry boldly proclaimed, "Give me liberty, or give me death." Of that dramatic occasion Jefferson said little more than that the Richmond convention approved the proceedings of the first Continental Congress and reelected the same delegates to attend the second meeting to be held in May. Perhaps he did not have more to say about the convention because it was Henry who dominated the proceedings, but he might have noted that he was among those who supported Henry's vigorous resolutions to take steps to arm and train a militia for the defense of Virginia. Edmund Randolph recalled that "Jefferson was not silent" and that he "argued closely, profoundly, and warmly" on the same side as Henry. Jefferson also was a member of the twelve-man committee charged with preparing a plan for a militia to put the colony into a posture of defense. Henry was named first to the committee, while Jefferson's name was next to the last. But a draft of the committee's report in Jefferson's hand indicates that he was the principal draftsman of the plan recommended by the committee and adopted by the convention.[34] Jefferson did not stir the passions that Henry evoked, but unlike some members of the Richmond convention, he did not draw back from Henry's advanced position. He was ready for bold action.

The most important thing that the convention did as far as Jefferson personally was concerned was to name him as the deputy to succeed Peyton Randolph in the Continental Congress should Randolph be unable to serve. As the Speaker of the House of Burgesses, Randolph would be forced to absent himself from the Congress should the Virginia governor summon the Assembly into session. Governor Dunmore did just that on May 12, calling the burgesses to meet on June 1. Randolph vacated the chair of the Continental Congress on May 24 to return to Williamsburg. As a member of the House of Burgesses, Jefferson was present in Williamsburg for the opening of the Assembly but soon set out for Philadelphia carrying with him the news of Virginia's response to the rapid movement of events.

In March Jefferson had sat in Saint John's Church in Richmond and listened to Patrick Henry proclaim: "Gentlemen may cry peace, peace—but there is no peace. The war is actually begun!" He knew then that Henry's oratory had risen to hyperbole, but by the time the burgesses met in June, all Virginians knew that Henry's rhetoric had become reality. News of the bloodshed at Lexington and Concord on April 19, 1775, reached Virginia before the end of the month. Soon afterward Jefferson wrote to his former mentor William Small that the Massachusetts events had "cut off our last hopes of reconciliation, and a phrenzy of revenge seems to have seized all ranks of people."[35] When the second Continental Congress met on May 10, it moved speedily to put the colonies in a state of defense.

Meanwhile in Virginia tensions had mounted. On March 28, while the Richmond convention was in session, Governor Dunmore issued a proclamation denouncing the Continental Congress and commanding all officers of the colony to use their utmost efforts to prevent the appointment of delegates to the second Congress. On the night of April 20 Dunmore secretly had the store of gunpowder belonging to the colony transferred from the magazine in Williamsburg to a British warship in the York River—an action that aroused Virginians not only in Williamsburg but also throughout the colony. In the aftermath of this unrest, it was an unpropitious time to summon the House of Burgesses into session. But in May

the conciliatory proposal of Lord North reached the colonial governors with instructions for presentation to the various assemblies,
and Dunmore proceeded to summon the Virginia burgesses to
meet on June 1.

Lord North's plan, approved by the House of Commons in late
February, proposed that whenever any colonial assembly agreed to
make a grant for the common defense of the empire and the support of civil government in the colony, the British government
would refrain from imposing on that colony any other tax for these
purposes. Governor Dunmore presented North's proposal in a conciliatory address, but in light of recent events it was coldly received
by the burgesses. While taking North's propositions under consideration, the House of Burgesses approved the proceedings of the
Continental Congress and the Richmond convention and pressed
an inquiry into Dunmore's removal of the gunpowder from the
Williamsburg magazine. As the situation grew tenser, Dunmore on
the night of June 8 slipped out of the Governor's Palace and took
refuge on a British warship in the York River.[36]

Jefferson was on the committee to prepare the response to North's
conciliatory proposal. In his autobiography he said that Peyton
Randolph was anxious that the response of Virginia harmonize
with the sentiments of the Continental Congress and pressed him
to draft the response, fearful that otherwise it would be done by
Robert Carter Nicholas, "whose mind was not yet up to the mark of
the times." Elsewhere, Jefferson wrote that he attended the Virginia Assembly instead of proceeding immediately to Philadelphia
because he knew the importance of the answer to North's conciliatory proposition and because the leading Virginia Whigs were then
in the Continental Congress.[37] Jefferson needed little persuasion to
accept the task of drafting the Virginia response, and it was largely
his draft that the House of Burgesses approved, though with "a
dash of cold water on it here and there," he said, "enfeebling it
somewhat."[38]

The hand of Jefferson can be seen throughout the Virginia
resolutions. They rejected North's proposal "*Because* the British
Parliament has no right to intermeddle with the support of civil
government in the Colonies. . . . *Because* to render perpetual our
exemption from an unjust taxation, we must saddle ourselves with
a perpetual tax adequate to the expectations and subject to the
disposal of Parliament alone." The British proposals were also
unacceptable because all of the objectionable acts of Parliament
remained unrepealed, standing armies were still to be kept in

America, and the colonies were being threatened by invasions from land and sea. In conclusion the resolutions expressed support for the interest of all the other colonies and advanced the hope that "we may again see reunited the blessings of Liberty, Property, and Union with *Great Britain.*"[39] It was a more moderate statement than Jefferson's *Summary View* and showed the marks of maturing statesmanship, but it lacked nothing in firmness and resolute commitment to the American cause.

On June 11, Jefferson set out for Philadelphia with a copy of his resolutions, which had been agreed upon in the committee of the whole and would be presented to Governor Dunmore the next day. The young delegate was leaving Virginia for only the second time in his thirty-two years and entering the broader world of continental affairs for the first time. He must have recalled his first journey to Philadelphia nine years earlier, and he may have reflected on the changes that had since taken place, both in his own life and in America. There was little outward sign of change in the country through which he rode, and he stopped briefly in Annapolis to buy books and to view the state house.[40] But he well knew that much of British America was on the brink of full revolt that would bring war and changes that could not be foreseen but were bound to be immense. There was talk of reconciliation with Great Britain, but a revolution had in fact begun, and Jefferson was heading for the center of the storm. He was ready for that revolution and prepared for the role that he would play in the momentous events that lay immediately ahead.

IV

At Philadelphia

It was June 21, 1775, when Jefferson arrived in Philadelphia after a ten-day journey from Williamsburg. While he was en route, the Continental Congress named George Washington the commander in chief of all continental forces. Two days after Jefferson's arrival the general departed for Boston amid bands playing and an outpouring of public support. "The war is now heartily entered into," Jefferson wrote, "without a prospect of accomodation but thro' the effectual interposition of arms."[1]

The second Continental Congress had been sitting since May 10, and John Hancock was now presiding, having succeeded to the chair when Peyton Randolph returned to Williamsburg. Jefferson was well acquainted with the Virginia delegation, which after Washington's departure included Richard Henry Lee, Patrick Henry, Richard Bland, Benjamin Harrison, and Edmund Pendleton. But among some fifty other delegates there was no one whom he had ever seen before. The reputations of the leading men, though, were known to him, and he must have been as anxious to meet Samuel Adams, Benjamin Franklin, John Adams, and others as they were curious to see the young Virginian whose reputation as a spokesman for colonial rights had preceded him. Jefferson had become known especially through his *Summary View of the Rights of British America*, which had circulated during the previous Congress. Samuel Ward, a delegate from Rhode Island, wrote just after Jefferson's first appearance in Congress: "Yesterday the famous Mr. Jefferson a Delegate from Virginia in the Room of Mr. Randolph arrived. . . . He looks like a very sensible spirited fine Fellow and by the Pamphlet which he wrote last Summer he certainly is one." Jefferson brought to Congress, John Adams said, "a reputation for literature, science, and a happy talent of composition. Writings of his were handed about, remarkable for the peculiar felicity of expression." Adams also said that Jefferson never spoke in the debates and "during the whole Time I satt with him in Congress, I never heard him utter three Sentences together." At the same time, Adams recalled that Jefferson "was so prompt, frank, explicit and decisive upon committees and in conversation . . . that he soon seized upon my heart."[2]

Jefferson's talents as a writer were called upon shortly after he took his seat in Congress. On June 23, two days following his arrival, Congress named a committee to draw up a declaration to be published by General Washington upon taking command of the forces before Boston. When the committee's draft was presented to Congress, it was recommitted and Jefferson and John Dickinson were added to the committee. Jefferson then wrote a new draft drawing heavily on his *Summary View*, though with a far less declamatory tone than employed earlier. The committee was not yet satisfied and gave Jefferson's draft to Dickinson to rework before submitting the declaration to Congress on July 6. Congress spent the day debating it paragraph by paragraph and approved the manifesto with only slight modification. The publication of the various drafts of this "Declaration of the Causes and Necessity of taking up Arms" by editor Julian Boyd in *The Papers of Thomas Jefferson* shows that the statement was a joint effort to which both Jefferson and Dickinson made important contributions and that the differences between them have been frequently overblown. John Adams said of the declaration: "It has Some Mercury in it, and is pretty frank, plain, and clear. If Lord North dont compliment every Mothers Son of us, with a Bill of Attainder, in Exchange for it, I shall think it owing to Fear."[3]

Accounts of the fighting at Bunker Hill had reached Philadelphia by the time Jefferson wrote to Albemarle neighbor George Gilmer on July 5. He praised the valor of New Englanders and reported heavy losses sustained by the British. While not at liberty to reveal all of the proceedings of the Congress, he could let it be known that Congress had directed the raising of twenty thousand troops and that most of them had already been enlisted. The news was encouraging to Gilmer, who was encamped with a company of Albemarle volunteers outside Williamsburg when Jefferson's letter reached him, but he was alarmed by Jefferson's report of a shortage of gunpowder. On the whole, though, Jefferson's letter was an optimistic one that reported that "nobody now entertains a doubt but that we are able to cope with the whole force of Great Britain, if we are but willing to exert ourselves." The war would be expensive, he said, but individuals would have to sacrifice their private interests. "As our enemies have found we can reason like men," he declared, "so now let us show them we can fight like men also." Gilmer was not the only person to read these stirring words, for the main text of Jefferson's letter was published in Williamsburg on July 28 in Purdie's *Virginia Gazette* as an "extract of a letter from one of the Virginia delegates."[4]

At the same time that they approved the forceful "Declaration of the Causes and Necessity of taking up Arms," members of Congress endorsed a second petition to King George III, and forty-nine delegates, including Jefferson, signed it on July 8. Jefferson recalled that John Dickinson, who had drafted it, signed with much satisfaction, but that some members—among whom he included himself—did so with less enthusiasm. The Virginia delegation certainly put little faith in its success when they reported it to the Virginia convention, for they followed it with an urgent plea for military preparations.[5]

More significant than the petition to the king was Congress' response to Lord North's conciliatory proposal, which had been referred to the continental body by the assemblies of New Jersey, Pennsylvania, and Virginia. On July 22 Benjamin Franklin, Jefferson, John Adams, and Richard Henry Lee were appointed a committee to report on North's proposition. Because Jefferson had drafted the Virginia response and had brought a copy with him, he was delegated the task of drafting the committee's report. Other committee members contributed suggestions, and Congress made some changes before final adoption, but the main lines of the resolutions approved by Congress on July 31 followed Jefferson's draft. He in turn drew on the paper he had prepared for the Virginia House of Burgesses. The result was a vigorous rejection of North's proposal as unreasonable, insidious, and altogether unsatisfactory.[6]

During his first six weeks in Congress, Jefferson thus had a leading role in drafting two major state papers adopted by Congress. Both the "Declaration of the Causes and Necessity of taking up Arms" and the response to Lord North's conciliatory plan would be widely published in newspapers throughout the colonies. Jefferson's name was not publicly associated with either of these declarations, which came from Congress, but to members of that body the papers were early demonstrations of Jefferson's literary and polemical abilities and of his commitment to the American cause. Six weeks after leaving Virginia, he was among the leading men in Congress and in the front ranks of the revolutionists.

After adopting the resolutions in reply to Lord North's proposal, Congress recessed until early September, and Jefferson returned to Virginia. A convention—which by then was the principal govern- ing body of Virginia—was sitting in Richmond; as a delegate from Albemarle, Jefferson stopped there before going on to Monticello. He spent only a week in Richmond but was present long enough to witness his election again to the Continental Congress. No longer last on the list of delegates, he came in third in the voting. With eighty-five votes he was not far behind Peyton Randolph with eighty-nine and Richard Henry Lee with eighty-eight votes; he was chosen ahead of Benjamin Harrison, Thomas Nelson, Richard Bland, and George Wythe.[7] Patrick Henry, having been named commander in chief of Virginia's military force, was considered in- eligible for election. Jefferson could only have interpreted the con- vention's action as a vote of confidence in his service in Congress, but before the month was up he would be wishing for a time when "consistently with duty, I may withdraw myself totally from the public stage and pass the rest of my days in domestic ease and tranquillity."[8] This was the first of many similar declarations that Jefferson would make throughout his public career, but he repeat- edly put public service first, and he did so at this time.

Back home at Monticello, Jefferson wrote a long letter to John Randolph, who was leaving for England, and made arrangements to obtain Randolph's violin, which had earlier been the object of an unusual arrangement between them. In 1771 they had executed an agreement that should Jefferson die first, Randolph could select books valued at £100 from his library; if Jefferson survived Ran- dolph, he was to receive the violin.[9] However much Jefferson cov- eted the violin, Randolph's decision not to support the colonial cause saddened him, and he hoped that their personal friendship might be preserved. He also used the letter as an opportunity to restate the case for the colonies, urging Randolph to promote rec- onciliation by enlightening the British ministry about the true state of the colonies. The ministry had been deceived, Jefferson argued, by their officers in America, who "have constantly represented the American opposition as that of a small faction. . . . They have taken it into their heads too that we are cowards and shall sur- render at discretion to an armed force. . . . Even those in parlia- ment who are called friends to America seem to know nothing of our real determinations. . . . I wish no false sense of honor, no ig- norance of our real intentions, no vain hope that partial conces- sions of right will be accepted may induce the ministry to trifle with accomodation till it shall be put even out of our own power ever to accomodate." He concluded by saying that he would rather be dependent on Great Britain, properly limited, than on any nation on earth. "But I am one of those too who rather than submit to the right to legislating for us assumed by the British parliament, and which late experience has shown they will so cruelly exercise, would lend my hand to sink the whole island in the ocean."[10] The fact that Jefferson's letter today is in the papers of the Earl of Dartmouth, who was then secretary of state for the colonies, indicates that Randolph brought it to the attention of the British authorities. But the course of events suggests that they were little influenced by it.

Jefferson's brief respite at Monticello was darkened by the death of his second daughter, Jane Randolph, born in April, 1774, and he was late in getting back to Philadelphia. When he arrived there on October 1, Congress had been in session since September 13, and he found the delegates struggling with the task of raising, organizing, and maintaining an army. Reports of the dispatch of additional British troops to America were reaching Philadelphia amid fading prospects of any conciliatory response from Great Britain. By November Congress knew that the king had refused to receive its petition and had declared the colonies in a state of rebellion. Among the gloomy reports in his letters to Virginia, Jefferson included the melancholy news of the death of "our good old Speaker," Peyton Randolph.[11]

When Jefferson wrote to John Randolph to inform him of the death of his brother Peyton, he devoted only two sentences to reporting that event, while seizing the opportunity to lay before Randolph the critical state of the times. Previously Jefferson had placed most of the blame for American unrest on Parliament, but in this letter he revealed an important shift in his thinking. He now blamed King George III. "It is an immense misfortune to the whole empire to have a king of such a disposition at such a time," he wrote. "We are told and every thing proves it true that he is the bitterest enemy we have." In his attack on the king, Jefferson also raised the subject of independence. "To undo his empire he has but one truth more to learn, that after colonies have drawn the sword there is but one step more they can take," he declared.

> That step is now pressed upon us by the measures adopted as if they were afraid we would not take it. Believe me Dear Sir there is not in the British empire a man who more cordially loves a Union with Great Britain than I do. But by the god that made me I will cease to exist before I yield to a connection on such terms as the British parliament

propose and in this I think I speak the sentiments of America. We want neither inducement nor power to declare and assert a separation. It is will alone which is wanting and that is growing apace under the fostering hand of our king. One bloody campaign will probably decide everlastingly our future course; I am sorry to find a bloody campaign is decided on.[12]

Randolph was in England, and Jefferson was trying to send a message to the British, but the letter leaves little doubt that Jefferson's own position was shifting toward independence and that he was beginning to see separation from Britain as inevitable.

In the three months before Jefferson took leave of Congress on December 28, he served on numerous committees, proving again that he was a hardworking member more active in committees than in debates. Yet none of his work in these months was as important as during his first service in June and July. Meanwhile he grew desperate for news from home. "I have never received the scrip of a pen from any mortal in Virginia since I left it," he wrote to Francis Eppes after six weeks in Philadelphia. Nor had he been able by inquiries to hear any news of his family. "The suspense under which I am is too terrible to be endured," he told Eppes, whose wife was Mrs. Jefferson's sister, with whom she was staying. "If any thing has happened, for god's sake let me know it."[13]

Congress anticipated a winter recess in December, 1775. Jefferson himself drafted a committee report on the unfinished business before the body and another on the powers of a committee to sit during recess.[14] But Congress continued to sit, and Jefferson's anxiety mounted. In view of the fact that each delegation had one vote and because the Virginia delegation was large, his absence would not present problems; other members also came and went during the session. Since he had left home in September, the war had come to Virginia. Norfolk and other coastal areas had been attacked. The slowness and sparsity of news from Virginia heightened his concerns, and he was worried about his family. After three months away from home and with no immediately compelling matter before Congress, he set out from Philadelphia for Monticello at the end of December and did not return for four months.

Part of his stay at Monticello was a regenerating one, but on March 31 his mother died unexpectedly at the age of fifty-seven, and Jefferson was soon seized by one of his periodic headaches that immobilized him for a month. Jefferson later described one such attack as "a paroxysm of the most excruciating pain" that "came on everyday at sunrise, and never left me till sunset." The spells usually lasted two or three weeks and occurred about every six to eight years until after he left the presidency. They came on when he was suffering from extreme tension, and this was one of his most difficult attacks.[15] One can only speculate on the source of the tension, but it was a period of unusual stress that may have extended beyond the loss of his mother to the uncertainty of the expanding war. He had already committed himself to the revolution and had much—indeed everything—to lose if it failed. We do not know how his wife stood in regard to what he was doing, because he destroyed all of the letters that passed between them. We do know that she did not accompany him to Philadelphia, as some wives did their husbands, but we also know that it was an arduous journey and she was not physically strong. Whatever the stresses, Jefferson surmounted them, and after he returned to Philadelphia, he entered one of the most productive periods of his life.

It was May 14 when Jefferson resumed his seat in Congress. In the interval of his absence news reached Philadelphia of George III's speech at the opening of Parliament in October declaring that "the rebellious war now levied . . . is manifestly carried on for the purpose of establishing an independent empire." Despite heated arguments from the opposition, Parliament by large majorities backed the king and approved waging war to return the American colonies to their allegiance. Meanwhile the king and his ministers contracted for German mercenaries to fight in America. These steps forced many Americans who had previously sought only to secure what they regarded as their rights within the empire to consider the alternative of independence. The decision of the British government to wage war, said John Adams, "makes us independent in Spight of all our supplications and Entreaties." Amid the bleak news from Britain, Thomas Paine's *Common Sense*, appealing to Americans to proclaim their independence immediately, appeared anonymously in Philadelphia in January, 1776. Paine's passionate pamphlet was soon being read by thousands of Americans—among them Thomas Jefferson, to whom Thomas Nelson sent a copy from Philadelphia early in February.[16]

We have no contemporary record of Jefferson's response to the news from Britain or to Paine's pamphlet, and he skipped over these months in his autobiography. In April his old friend John Page, assuming that Jefferson was in Philadelphia, wrote him, "For God's sake declare the Colonies independent at once, and save us from ruin." Another Virginian wrote him about the same time that the notion of independence was spreading rapidly in Virginia and would no doubt be adopted at the next convention. Jefferson would find these letters waiting for him in Philadelphia, but while in Virginia he had already taken pains to collect the opinions of the people and had concluded that in Albemarle and neighboring counties nine out of ten were for independence.[17]

He had been back in Philadelphia less than two weeks when the Virginia delegates received the resolutions adopted by the Virginia convention on May 15 instructing them to propose, and give Virginia's assent to, independence.[18] Read to the Congress on May 27, the resolutions were followed on June 7 by Richard Henry Lee's motion, on behalf of the Virginia delegation, for independence. Jefferson was soon to be involved in the event that would bring him his most lasting fame. But before he stood with other delegates in that July of 1776 to approve the declaration that he had largely drafted, he would spend more time at his writing desk drafting a proposed constitution for Virginia than in composing the Declaration of Independence.

The same resolutions adopted by the Virginia convention on May 15 calling for independence also provided for the appointment of a committee to prepare a plan of government for Virginia. Even before the delegates in Congress received these resolutions, the Congress had adopted recommendations to the colonies to form new governments, and immediately upon arriving back in Philadelphia, Jefferson turned his attention to the plan of government for Virginia. "It is the whole object of the present controversy," he wrote, "for should a bad government be instituted for us in future it had been as well to have accepted at first the bad one offered to us from beyond the water without the risk and expence of contest." So keenly did he want to participate in designing the new government for Virginia that he suggested that the Virginia convention might want to recall its delegates from Congress for a short time to join in the constitution-making process. His letter hardly had time to reach Virginia before he learned that the drafting of a constitution was already under way, with George Mason taking the lead in preparing the plan.[19]

Mason rather than Jefferson thus had the major hand in drafting the Virginia constitution, though Jefferson's papers show that his contribution to it was greater than has sometimes been recognized.[20] The detailed plan that Jefferson prepared with great care and put through three drafts reached the Virginia convention too late to be considered except as a basis for making additions to, or changes in, a draft that was already far advanced. When George

Wythe arrived in Williamsburg on June 23 with Jefferson's draft, he
found the plan of the drafting committee before the whole house.
Wythe reported to Jefferson that two or three parts of his plan
were inserted with little alteration, "but such was the impatience of
sitting long enough to discuss several important points in which
they differ . . . that I was persuaded the revision of a subject the
members seemed tired of would at that time have been unsuccess-
fully proposed."[21] The most important change incorporated from
Jefferson's draft was the addition of a preamble containing a bill of
charges against George III justifying the change in government. If
this list sounded much like the later one in the Declaration of Independence, it was because Jefferson used the same composition draft
of these charges in writing the preamble for his draft of the Virginia
constitution and in drafting the Declaration of Independence.[22]

As a record of Jefferson's views on government at the time of the
Revolution, Jefferson's draft of a constitution for Virginia is of considerable interest.[23] In general it was more democratic than that
adopted by the convention, proposing a broader suffrage and
more equal representation in the legislature. Jefferson would have
broadened the suffrage to include adult male taxpayers as well as
property holders, and he would have liberalized landholding by
providing that every adult not owning fifty acres would be entitled
to a grant of fifty acres or whatever land needed to raise his holdings to fifty acres. Jefferson also would have reduced the heavier
representation of the eastern part of the state in the Assembly by
substituting representation proportional to population for equal
representation from each county. The new constitution, however,
retained the existing property qualifications for voting without
providing for land grants and kept the colonial system of two delegates from each county in the House of Delegates.

Both Jefferson's plan and the constitution as adopted specified an
assembly of two houses but differed in the method of electing the
senate. Jefferson proposed that the senate be chosen by the lower
house, whereas the constitution provided for popular election by
districts. Though in most instances the Virginia convention tended
to continue colonial practices rather than follow Jefferson's more
forward-looking ideas, in this instance the convention, rather than
Jefferson, seemed to be on the side of greater democracy. The argument that he made to Edmund Pendleton on the subject appears
discordant with his many statements in subsequent years affirming
faith in the people. "I have ever observed that a choice by the
people themselves is not generally distinguished for it's wisdom,"

Jefferson wrote. "The first secretion from them is generally crude and heterogeneous. But give to those so chosen by the people a second choice themselves, and they generally will chuse wise men." His aim was, he said, "to get the wisest men chosen, and to make them perfectly independent when chosen." [24]

Jefferson later admitted that his vision of republicanism at the time of the Revolution was limited. "In truth, the abuses of monarchy had so much filled all the space of political contemplation, that we imagined everything republican which was not monarchy," he recalled. "We had not yet penetrated to the mother principle, that 'governments are republican only in proportion as they embody the will of their people, and execute it.'" [25] Following the conventional political science of mixed government, Jefferson did not think in terms of a senate representing the people. In truth, few contemporaries understood the implications of the changing role of American senates embodied in the Virginia constitution of 1776. The idea that the people might have two legislative branches speaking for them at the same time was a revolutionary change in political concepts that not even Jefferson appreciated. [26] He did not propose a democratically elected senate, because he looked upon it as a chamber of independent wise men, not as spokesmen for the people. Both the Virginia Constitution of 1776 and Jefferson's draft provided for the annual election of the governor by the legislature and placed the supreme power of the state in the General Assembly. The executive was to be subordinate to the legislature. Jefferson, in fact, proposed to call the governor "the administrator," though his plan would have left the executive with more authority than the constitution was to permit.

Like Jefferson's draft, the Virginia Declaration of Rights, written by George Mason and approved by the Virginia convention prior to adopting the constitution, provided for religious freedom, but Jefferson went further to strike at the established Anglican church by proposing that no person "be compelled to frequent or maintain any religious institution." [27] Jefferson also drafted a provision to prohibit the importation of slaves into Virginia—a proposal that the convention did not accept, though Jefferson's condemnation of George III for allowing the slave trade to continue was retained in the preamble.

Altogether Jefferson did not regard the Virginia constitution as going far enough in initiating the changes that he thought the Revolution should effect. George Wythe anticipated Jefferson's disappointment, confiding to him that the new system required reformation. Meanwhile, Edmund Pendleton counseled Jefferson to use his talents "to nuture the new constitution, while pruning it of its defects."[28] Such comments strengthened Jefferson's own desire to return to Virginia. There can be no doubt that his dissatisfaction with the first Virginia constitution explains much of his later effort to achieve by legislation reforms that he had originally hoped to see written into the fundamental law of the state. Before he would turn his attention to those concerns, however, he had to complete the task of justifying to mankind the natural right of Americans to determine their own destiny.

On June 7, 1776, Richard Henry Lee introduced in Congress the resolution "That these United Colonies are, and of right ought to be, free and independent States, that they are absolved from all allegiance to the British Crown, and that all political connection between them and the State of Great Britain is, and ought to be, totally dissolved."[29] Congress considered this resolution on June 8 and again on June 10, when action on it was postponed until July 1. In the course of these debates it appeared that some colonies "were not yet matured for falling from the parent stem," Jefferson noted, "but that they were fast advancing to that state," and "it was thought most prudent to wait a while for them."[30] It was not a question of whether the resolution would pass or fail, for its adoption was not in doubt. What was sought was unanimity.

Meanwhile, a committee was appointed on June 11 to draft a declaration to announce and justify the anticipated act. The committee, composed of Thomas Jefferson, John Adams, Benjamin Franklin, Roger Sherman, and Robert R. Livingston, delegated to Jefferson the task of preparing a draft. He did so, working alone in his lodgings, using a portable lap desk recently made to his specifications by a Philadelphia cabinetmaker.[31] Why was Jefferson chosen to do the drafting? In old age Adams said that he and Jefferson had been named a subcommittee to prepare a draft and each had pressed the other to do so. Adams even reconstructed the conversation that followed when Jefferson proposed that Adams prepare the draft.

> Adams: "I will not."
> Jefferson: "You should do it."
> Adams: "Oh! no."
> Jefferson: "Why will you not? You ought to do it."
> Adams: "I will not."
> Jefferson: "Why?"

Adams: "Reasons enough."

Jefferson: "What can be your reasons?"

Adams: "Reason first—You are a Virginian, and a Virginian ought to appear at the head of this business. Reason second—I am obnoxious, suspected, and unpopular. You are very much otherwise. Reason third—You can write ten times better than I can."

Jefferson: "Well, if you are decided, I will do as well as I can."

Adams: "Very well. When you have drawn it up, we will have a meeting."[32]

When Jefferson learned of Adams's recollections, he said Adams was mistaken. There had never been any subcommittee, and it was the entire committee that "unanimously pressed on myself alone to undertake the draught." Jefferson said that at age eighty he would not claim any advantage of memory over Adams at eighty-eight, but he insisted that his notes made at the time did not support Adams' version.[33] Though Adams may have recorded an imaginary conversation, the reasons that he gave for Jefferson being chosen to draft the Declaration ring true. He probably remembered a subcommittee because, after preparing his draft, Jefferson submitted it separately to Adams and to Franklin for their suggestions and corrections before presenting it to the full committee. Both men made alterations in their own handwriting on Jefferson's draft, producing a unique and historic document that still survives today. Jefferson then made a fair copy for the committee, which made a few changes and reported it to Congress on June 28.[34]

Before considering Jefferson's Declaration, Congress had to act on Lee's resolution for independence and resumed debate on it on July 1. The following day it was adopted with the affirmative votes of all delegations except New York, whose delegates were bound by instructions that obligated them to abstain. By July 15 they would receive new instructions and make approval of independence unanimous. Debate on the Declaration of Independence began on July 2 and continued through three days. In the course of the debates, Congress considerably altered Jefferson's draft as approved by the committee, cutting about a quarter of the text, polishing the wording, and in some instances making substantive changes. The most significant alteration came when Congress struck from Jefferson's text his condemnation of George III for allowing the slave trade to continue—a strongly worded passage in which Jefferson had denounced the slave trade as a "cruel war against human nature itself." Jefferson said the change was made in compliance with the wishes of South Carolina and Georgia but added that "our Northern brethren also I believe felt a little tender under those censures; for tho' their people have very few slaves themselves yet they had been pretty considerable carriers of them to others."[35] Most of the changes that Congress made in shortening and revising the wording of the document improved it, though the sensitive author believed that his draft was the stronger statement. When he sent copies of the Declaration as approved by Congress to a few of his friends, he sent a paper showing the original draft and the alterations so they could judge whether it was made better or worse by his critics.[36] After the various revisions were made, Congress adopted the Declaration on July 4. Although Jefferson stated that it was signed on the same day, there is no evidence to corroborate this. If any signing took place on July 4, it was not the official signing, for not until July 19 did Congress order the Declaration to be engrossed and signed. The signing of the engrossed parchment took place on August 2.[37]

Despite the changes made by the committee and by Congress in his draft, Jefferson could still rightly claim authorship of the Declaration of Independence, and he would subsequently come to regard it as one of the three most important accomplishments of his life. The sources of the ideas that Jefferson drew on in writing the Declaration would later become a source of interest to his contemporaries and of continuing fascination to historians. Richard Henry Lee thought Jefferson had copied from John Locke's treatise on government. John Adams in old age charged that the essence of Jefferson's ideas could be found in fellow New Englander James Otis's pamphlet *The Rights of the British Colonies Asserted and Proved* (Boston, 1764). When Jefferson heard this, he said flatly that he had never seen Otis's pamphlet. He did not deny that he had read Locke, but he insisted that he had "turned to neither book nor pamphlet while writing it." At the same time, Jefferson claimed no originality for the Declaration of Independence. "I did not consider it as any part of my charge to invent new ideas altogether, and to offer no sentiment which had ever been expressed before," he said.[38] His aim was "to place before mankind the common sense of the subject, in terms so plain and firm as to command their assent," and to justify independence. "Neither aiming at originality of principle or sentiment, nor yet copied from any particular and previous writing," he wrote, "it was intended to be an expression of the American mind."[39]

Before writing the Declaration of Independence, Jefferson must have read the draft of the Virginia Declaration of Rights largely composed by George Mason and printed in the form that came from the drafting committee of the Virginia convention on May 27. That draft was published in Philadelphia in the *Pennsylvania Evening Post* on June 6 and reprinted two days later in the *Pennsylvania Ledger*, and it appeared again in the *Pennsylvania Gazette* on June 12. Jefferson could hardly have missed seeing it. There were certainly similarities between the draft of the Virginia declaration and Jefferson's draft of the Declaration of Independence. Mason began by affirming, "That all men are born equally free and independent, and have certain inherent natural rights, of which they cannot, by any compact, deprive or divest their posterity; among which are, the enjoyment of life and liberty, with the means of acquiring and possessing property, and pursuing and obtaining happiness and safety." Jefferson wrote in the second paragraph of his "original Rough draught" of the Declaration of Independence: "We hold these truths to be sacred and undeniable; that all men are created equal and independent, that from that equal creation they derive rights inherent and inalienable, among which are the preservation of life, and liberty, and the pursuit of happiness."[40] Jefferson need not have had Mason's words before him when he wrote, because they were part of the shared philosophy that Jefferson was seeking to communicate—"an expression of the American mind."

Nor did Jefferson have to turn to books or pamphlets when he took up his pen, for he had earlier read deeply in history and political philosophy and had already absorbed the basic ideas of natural rights and made them a part of his own political philosophy. He was familiar with Locke, Kames, and Burlamaqui; he had probably received a strong dose of Francis Hutcheson when he studied under William Small at William and Mary.[41] He did not need any of their works before him to state the political principles that sanctioned the action he sought to justify to the world. It was only "common sense" to begin by referring to "the laws of nature and of nature's god." He did not originally use the word *self-evident* when he began to list the natural rights of man, writing initially, "we hold these truths to be sacred and undeniable." But he soon changed that to "self-evident" (whether on his own or another's initiative is not clear),[42] for self-evident truths were precisely what he was seeking to enumerate. The first of these was that "all men were created equal and independent" and from this condition derived certain rights. Jefferson significantly did not start with Locke's rights of life, liberty, and property (which the Continental Congress had asserted in its Declaration of Rights and Grievances in October, 1774), but

in the earliest surviving draft he defined the "inherent and inalienable" rights of man more broadly as "the preservation of life,
and liberty, and the pursuit of happiness."[43] He also affirmed at the
outset that governments were established to protect these rights
and derived their just powers from the consent of the governed.
Whenever any government became destructive of these ends, "it is
the right of the people to alter or abolish it and to institute new government." These assertions were retained largely unchanged in the
final Declaration.

How could a slaveholder write that "all men are created equal"?
As he had demonstrated six years earlier in a case before the General Court in Williamsburg, Jefferson accepted the Enlightenment
view that all men were born free and that slavery was contrary to
the law of nature.[44] Unenlightened monarchs or wicked legislatures
might allow slavery to exist or in other ways restrict personal liberty
by decree or statutory law. Such acts could be revoked or repealed,
as he fully expected the laws regarding slavery would be in the
course of time. When not contravened by statutory law, the law of
nature applied to all men. Once kings or legislatures abolished slavery, slaves would regain their natural status as free men.

In the scope of history the opening passages of the Declaration
of Independence containing the affirmation of natural rights, government by the consent of the governed, and the natural right of
revolution gave to that document its lasting influence. But the longest part of the Declaration was devoted to specifying the causes that
had led the American colonies to renounce the government of
Great Britain. In the weeks just before he wrote his draft of the
Declaration of Independence, Jefferson had been occupied in writing his proposed constitution for Virginia. He had begun that work
with a bill of charges against King George III, and he had that composition draft before him when he drew up a similar list of charges
for inclusion in the Declaration of Independence. Thus, the two
papers shared a common origin and had many similarities, though
after he and Congress finished their editing, the Declaration of Independence was distinctive. While the charges against the king
were designed to arouse support for the American cause at home
and abroad, and many of the grievances might have more logically
been charged to Parliament rather than to the king, none of the
charges was without a historical basis. Jefferson put an American
gloss on history, but he did not invent the grievances. His contemporaries recognized clearly enough what he was talking about. The
Declaration of Independence was a brief for the American posi-

tion, not an impartial summary of recent events. Jefferson was America's advocate.

In its revisions Congress incorporated Lee's resolution for independence into the final paragraph of the Declaration but retained Jefferson's stirring concluding words: "We mutually pledge to each other our Lives, our Fortunes and our sacred Honor." On July 1 New Hampshire's Josiah Bartlett wrote: "The Declaration before Congress is, I think, a pretty good one. I hope it will not be spoiled by canvassing in Congress."[45] As it turned out, Bartlett was unnecessarily concerned. In its final form, the Declaration of Independence was a succinct and moving statement that Americans would take to their hearts, as they would one day take its principal author.

Congress on July 4 ordered the Declaration of Independence to be printed in handbills and sent to all units of the army and to all cities, towns, and counties for its proclamation throughout the country. "It compleats a Revolution, which will make as good a Figure in the History of Mankind, as any that has preceeded it," John Adams wrote with enthusiasm, convinced that "all America is remarkably united." But Adams also said that he was "well aware of the Toil and Blood and Treasure, that it will cost Us to maintain this Declaration, and support and defend these States. Yet through all the Gloom I can see the Rays of ravishing Light and Glory. I can see that the End is more than worth all the Means."[46]

Jefferson, who was more reserved than Adams in expressing his feelings, left no similar reflections, but there is nothing in the record to suggest that he would not have agreed fully with his Massachusetts colleague. The Declaration of Independence attracted no public attention to Jefferson, for his authorship was not then publicly known, and his own pride of authorship was muted by all of the changes that Congress had made in words that he had chosen so carefully. In time that disappointment would fade, and the Declaration would bring glory to him and to the new nation that proclaimed it. Though neither Jefferson nor his contemporaries could foresee it in 1776, the Declaration of Independence was to become the most cherished document in American history, not solely because of its proclamation of independence but also because of its affirmation of the political principles that would undergird the new American republic.

V

Virginia Reformer

Once independence was proclaimed, Jefferson was anxious to return to Virginia. He had already decided to give up his seat in Congress at the end of the year for which he had been elected and had written to friends that he did not wish to be a candidate for reelection. The Virginia convention knew this before balloting, but Jefferson's letter formally withdrawing as a candidate had not yet been received, and the convention proceeded to reelect him. When he learned of this, Jefferson again asked to be relieved of his duties. "I am sorry the situation of my domestic affairs renders it indispensably necessary that I should sollicit the substitution of some other person here in my room," he wrote. "The delicacy of the house will not require me to enter minutely into the private causes which render this necessary: I trust they will be satisfied I would not have urged it again where it not necessary." [1]

The concern that prompted this letter was his wife's health, which continued to alarm him as he waited in Philadelphia for a replacement. In June, 1776, the Virginia convention had reduced the size of the delegation from seven to five members, leaving less flexibility for members to be absent and still maintain a state quorum. Thus, Jefferson found himself waiting for Richard Henry Lee to return to Philadelphia before he could depart. "For god's sake, for your country's sake, and for my sake, come," he wrote to Lee on July 29. "I receive by every post such accounts of the state of Mrs. Jefferson's health, that it will be impossible for me to disappoint her expectation of seeing me at the time I have promised, which supposed my leaving this place on the 11th of next month." But Lee was unable to promise to get to Philadelphia before August 20. It turned out to be later, and Jefferson did not get away until September 3. Meanwhile, Mrs. Jefferson's health improved. [2]

Although Jefferson's concern for his wife's well-being was genuine, other factors also help to explain his willingness to give up his seat in Congress. Like many Americans, he expected the war to be short. He said in July, 1776, that it was the universal opinion that the next three months would be the severest test of the conflict.[3] He did not foresee at this juncture the critical role that Congress would be called upon to perform before independence was established and peace obtained. Moreover, Jefferson was eager to participate directly in the government of Virginia. He viewed the new states as the real arenas where the government and society of the new nation were being formed and saw what was happening there as more important than what Congress was doing. At the very moment that he was trying desperately to get away from Philadelphia, a plan of confederation was before Congress. That Jefferson was concerned about such a confederation is shown in the detailed notes he kept on the debates, but he did not attach the importance to the instrument of confederation that he did to the constitution of Virginia. He regarded the fundamental powers of government as residing in the states. Confederation was essential, and he strongly supported the union of states, but he did not look upon confederation as a step toward a national government. Thus, his concern for the structure of government and for establishing the rights of the people centered in Virginia.

Jefferson regretted that he had had no larger role in the making of the Virginia constitution, and he wanted to be on the scene when the Assembly began to implement it. He was encouraged in this thinking by Virginia friends, such as Edmund Pendleton, who urged him to return to take a post in the judiciary. "You are also wanting much in the Revision of our Laws and forming a new body, a necessary work for which few of us have adequate abilities and attention." Pendleton was disappointed when Jefferson expressed no interest in a judgeship, but he was quick to acknowledge Jefferson's usefulness in the legislature.[4] Pendleton's reference to the revision of the laws reinforced Jefferson's interest in that subject and quickened his desire to participate in the work. During the years immediately ahead, Jefferson would give no subject greater attention. When he took his seat in the Virginia House of Delegates in October, 1776, he would embark upon what has been called "one of the most far-reaching legislative reforms ever undertaken by a single person."[5]

Reaching Monticello on September 9, 1776, six days after leaving Philadelphia, Jefferson remained there less than three weeks before leaving to attend the opening of the Virginia General Assembly.

Mrs. Jefferson accompanied him to Williamsburg, where George Wythe made his home available to them while he and Mrs. Wythe were in Philadelphia. The Jeffersons had not yet settled into that handsome residence, which Jefferson had visited so often as a student, when a special messenger from Philadelphia caught up with him on October 8 and delivered a confidential dispatch naming him as a commissioner to France. He was to join Benjamin Franklin and Silas Deane in seeking to negotiate a treaty with France. The unexpected appointment had been made by Congress on September 26, and an accompanying letter from John Hancock informed him that as soon as his reply was received, a ship would be dispatched to take him to France. Jefferson kept Hancock's messenger waiting three days while he made up his mind what to do. The mission obviously was an important one, and Hancock's letter was written in language that assumed that Jefferson would accept. But he had been back in Virginia scarcely a month, his wife was not strong, and they had been in Williamsburg for only a week. Could he leave her again so soon for what was certain to be an extended mission? After agonizing over the question, he decided that he could not. "No cares for my own person, nor yet for my private affairs would have induced one moment's hesitation to accept the charge," he wrote to Hancock. "But circumstances very peculiar to the situation of my family, such as neither permit me to leave nor to carry it, compel me to ask leave to decline a service so honorable and at the same time so important to the American cause."[6]

In the House of Delegates Jefferson plunged immediately into the work of legislative reform. He was not always in harmony with a majority of his fellow delegates. Some of his proposals were not enacted for years; others never became law. But no one took a more leading role in the critical legislative proceedings that followed immediately after independence and the adoption of the first Virginia constitution, and in the long run no one had more influence.

Jefferson's papers reflect the matters that most concerned him at this time. He compiled detailed lists of all the acts of Parliament and of the Virginia Assembly relating to religion, and he gave much attention to drafting bills establishing courts of justice. His interest in religious liberty coincided with a rising popular excitement over that issue in the state.[7] The Virginia Declaration of Rights in June, 1776, had affirmed the principle of religious freedom but had stopped short of disestablishing the Anglican Church. The new constitution was silent on the issue. It soon became clear that Virginia's leaders had not gone as far as most of the people wanted. Dissenters—now more numerous than Anglicans in Virginia—soon bombarded the legislature with petitions seeking implementation of the Declaration of Rights. They wanted full equality in the exercise of religious beliefs and the disestablishment of the Church of England.

On October 11 Jefferson was named to a nineteen-member committee on religion to which these petitions were referred. When James Madison was added to the committee shortly thereafter, Jefferson gained an important ally in the twenty-five-year-old delegate from Orange County who had been a leading voice for religious freedom in the Virginia constitutional convention. It was also the beginning of a friendship between the two men that lasted as long as they lived. Jefferson later said that the dissenters' petitions "brought on the severest contests in which I have ever been engaged."[8] It would be ten years before his own ideas would triumph in the Virginia statute for religious freedom, for he favored nothing less than the disestablishment of the Church of England and complete freedom of religion. He drew up resolutions to effect those purposes in 1776, but the outcome of the legislative struggle stopped with the repeal of all acts oppressive to dissenters and the passage of a bill exempting dissenters from contributing to the support of the Church of England. The act specifically left unresolved the question of a general assessment to support the clergy of all denominations. As Jefferson noted, "although the majority of our citizens were dissenters . . . a majority of the legislature were churchmen."[9] In 1779 the law providing salaries for the established clergy was repealed, but the issue of a general assessment to support the ministers of all Christian sects was not resolved. Neither the idea of a general assessment nor Jefferson's bill for complete religious freedom, introduced as part of the revisal of the laws in 1779, could command a majority in the Assembly at this time. Jefferson would be in France when his statute for religious freedom, a bold assertion of the sovereignty of reason, was finally adopted in 1786.[10]

Jefferson was one of those Americans who wanted the Revolution to bring more changes than simply separation from Great Britain. Along with his concerns about the structure of government and the place of the church, he was anxious that access to land be broadened and that the influence of landed aristocrats be diminished. He had proposed to the Virginia constitutional convention that persons not owning fifty acres of land be granted enough land to raise their holdings to that minimum amount. Having failed there, the first bill that he introduced in the new House of Delegates after the adoption of the constitution was one to abolish entails. Many recipients of large land grants in early Virginia had perpetuated their families and estates by conveying their lands to their descendants in fee tail, that is, by limiting the inheritance of property to a specified, unalterable succession of heirs. The entailing of land had been permitted by English law and had been widely practiced in the older eastern areas of Virginia. The only way that an entail could be altered was by an act of the legislature. This practice, known as "docking," had become common by Jefferson's day and was a troublesome practice to many. To Jefferson, who had once presented a petition for docking on behalf of his wife, it was more than a bother. It was a system that perpetuated an artificial aristocracy of wealth.

Primogeniture likewise perpetuated an aristocracy. Only if a person died without a will did the law require that his property descend to his eldest son, and most large landowners wrote wills. But the practice had contributed to the concentration of wealth and to inequalities at all levels of society. Jefferson himself had been neither the victim nor the beneficiary of either primogeniture or entail, for his own father had provided for all of his children by will, and his land was not entailed. But Jefferson considered the abolition of both practices as vital to a republican society. The attack on entails and primogeniture, he later told John Adams, "laid the axe to the root of Pseudo-aristocracy." [11] To end the influence of this aristocracy was "essential to a well ordered republic," he believed; it would make "an opening for the aristocracy of virtue and talent, which nature has wisely provided for the direction of the interests of society, and scattered with equal hand through all it's conditions." [12] Though the ending of primogeniture would have to wait a decade, Jefferson's bill to abolish entails, introduced on October 14, 1776, promptly passed the House of Delegates and was agreed to by the Senate on November 1.

On the same day that the House agreed to receive a bill regarding entails, it also gave permission for the preparation of a bill for the general revisal of the laws. To Jefferson no subject was more important. "When I left Congress, in 76," he later recalled, "it was in the persuasion that our whole code must be reviewed, adapted to our republican form of government, and, now that we had no negatives of Councils, Governors and Kings to restrain us from doing right, that it should be corrected, in all it's parts with a single eye to reason, and the good of those for whose government it was framed." [13] A bill for revisal drafted by Jefferson received final ap-

proval on October 26, and on November 5 he was chosen by balloting in both houses to head the revision committee. With Edmund
Pendleton, George Wythe, George Mason, and Thomas Ludwell
Lee as the other members of the committee, it was a distinguished
one, and Jefferson's choice to head it was evidence of his stature.
His selection was also recognition of his rare ability to combine a
concern for broad principles with an attention to detail. There was
an order and meticulousness to all of Jefferson's papers that his colleagues must have recognized when they charged him with so demanding a task.

The act gave the committee full authority to revise, amend, or
repeal all or any of the laws of Virginia and to introduce new ones,
subject to the approval of the General Assembly.[14] To begin the
large undertaking, the committee met in Fredericksburg on January 13, 1777, to decide on procedures and to distribute the work.
"The first question was whether we should propose to abolish the
whole existing system of laws, and prepare a new and complete Institute, or preserve the general system, and only modify it to the
present state of things," Jefferson said. To his surprise Edmund
Pendleton, "contrary to his usual disposition in favor of antient
things," favored a completely new code. But in the end the committee agreed on a plan of revisal and modification rather than a new
code, deciding not to meddle with the common law of England except for essential alterations and to revise and digest the statutes.
In dividing its work among the five members, the committee took
into account that neither Mason nor Lee was a lawyer, promising
them assistance and assigning less demanding tasks. Soon afterward Mason resigned from the committee because of poor health,
and Lee died the next year without having undertaken his assignment. The committee's work was then divided among Jefferson,
Wythe, and Pendleton, with Jefferson assuming the largest share of
the burden. During the next two and a half years Jefferson devoted
an incredible amount of time to the reformation of the laws, while
pressing before each session of the legislature bills that he thought
should not be delayed until the full revision of the laws was completed. Jefferson has been called "a veritable legislative drafting bu-
reau" during these years; he was responsible for the introduction
and adoption of more bills than any other single member of the
Virginia Assembly from 1776 to 1779.[15]

By February, 1779, the committee members had completed their
individual assignments, and Jefferson and Wythe met in Williamsburg to combine their drafts and review the result. By June their

finished work was ready to go to the General Assembly. The two bundles of papers that comprised the report submitted on June 18, 1779, filled ninety folio pages when printed. Including several bills that had already been presented to the Assembly, the report offered the drafts of 126 bills, ranging from Jefferson's famous plan for a system of public education to a bill for apprehending horse thieves. The report also presented a revised criminal code in which the death penalty would be inflicted only for treason or murder. Jefferson believed that the 126 proposed acts digested as much of the body of the British statutes and the acts of the assembly as necessary to make the laws of Virginia consistent with "republicanism."[16]

Because each bill was considered separately and some of them had already been brought forward, the initial treatment of the report did not lead to the prompt enactment of a revised code that the committee had envisioned, but rather to a prolonged legislative process in which the report as a whole was not brought forward for action until 1785. By that time with the war over, the peace signed, and the general pulse of reformation weaker than in 1776, about half of the bills were enacted, and the revisal was never put into effect as a unit.[17] Jefferson was then in France, and Madison, who had joined in support of Jefferson's reform efforts in the Assembly, was left with the task of rescuing as many of Jefferson's reforms as he could put through the legislature. One of the successful efforts was the enactment of Jefferson's bill for establishing religious freedom, which provided a comprehensive guarantee of religious freedom for all, without any qualifications whatsoever. Jefferson, who received the news in Paris, proudly circulated the text of the act in Europe and would come to regard this as one of the three major contributions of his life.

Another of Jefferson's major reforms adopted at this time was the bill to change the rules of descent and to abolish primogeniture. Jefferson regarded the repeal of the laws of entail, the abolition of primogeniture, and the establishment of religious freedom as three of the four major measures that formed "a system by which every fibre would be eradicated of antient or future aristocracy; and a foundation laid for a government truly republican." The fourth cornerstone of this system was to be found in his proposed bill "for the more general diffusion of knowledge." Introduced in the House of Delegates in December, 1778, and presented again in June, 1780, the measure was not seriously considered until 1786 when Madison brought it up along with other bills of the *Report of the Committee of Revisors*.[18] Jefferson said in 1786 while the bill was pending that he thought it the most important one in the whole report, and in the bill's preamble he extolled the vital importance of education to republican government.[19]

The plan that Jefferson offered called for each county to be divided into "hundreds" and a school built in each hundred so conveniently located that all free boys and girls might attend daily. For three years all children would receive free schooling, and any child might attend longer at private expense. Pupils would be taught reading, writing, and common arithmetic and become acquainted with Greek, Roman, English, and American history through the books used for reading. From each group of about ten elementary schools one boy "of the best and most promising genius and disposition" whose parents were too poor to continue his schooling would be chosen each year to proceed to one of the grammar schools serving several counties. He would be boarded and his tuition paid by the state. Other qualified students whose parents could support their education also would be admitted to the grammar schools, where they would be taught Latin, Greek, English grammar, geography, and advanced arithmetic. After one year, the least promising third of the state-supported scholars would be cut, and after two years only one—"the best in genius and disposition"— would be allowed to continue at public expense for another four years. With twenty grammar schools proposed, Jefferson envisioned "twenty of the best geniuses raked from the rubbish annually." From this select group, each grammar school in alternate years would send the most promising scholar to the College of William and Mary to be educated, boarded, and clothed at state expense for three years. In a system with twenty grammar schools, ten "public foundationers" would thus annually reach the peak of the educational pyramid.[20]

As Jefferson saw his proposal, "The ultimate result of the whole scheme of education would be teaching all children of the state reading, writing, and common arithmetic: turning out ten annually of superior genius, well taught in Greek, Latin, geography, and the higher branches of arithmetic: turning out ten others annually, of still superior parts, who, to those branches of learning, shall have added such of the sciences as their genius shall have led them to." The system would also furnish the wealthier part of the people convenient schools at which their children might be educated at their own expense.[21] As his summation indicates, Jefferson's plan was a combination of public and private education. To twentieth-century Americans three years of free public education may seem less than enlightened, but at the time of Jefferson's proposal there was no public education at all in Virginia.

The heart of Jefferson's plan was not equal universal education but a system by which the most talented children from whatever condition of society could be given an opportunity for education. An "aristocracy of virtue and talent" thus could be recruited from all classes. Jefferson's interest in education rested on his conviction that the only way of preserving republican government and preventing those entrusted with political power from resorting to tyranny was "to illuminate, as far as practicable, the minds of the people at large." Also, in order to have the best laws and well-administered government, it was important that those persons "whom nature hath endowed with genius and virtue" be liberally educated and called to government service "without regard to wealth, birth or other accidental condition or circumstance."[22]

Jefferson's education bill was not enacted by the General Assembly when the report of the revisors of the laws was under consideration, and it was not until 1796 that any plan for establishing public schools passed. That act retained some of Jefferson's phraseology but authorized only the establishment of elementary schools and left it up to each local community to decide on the expediency of doing so.[23] Jefferson's scheme for selecting and educating the most talented was never adopted. Fortunately, this early rejection did not diminish his lifelong interest in education.

As part of his work on the revisal of the laws, Jefferson expended an extraordinary effort in drafting a criminal code—a favorite reform activity of the Enlightenment. His draft of a bill, replete with elaborate marginal notes citing sources and ostentatiously displaying a broad erudition in law and philosophy, showed the attention he had lavished on the project. He had been particularly influenced by Beccaria's *An Essay on Crimes and Punishments*, and in the preamble to his bill Jefferson summarized the reasoning behind his proposals. It was a government's duty to restrain criminal acts by inflicting punishment, he said, but a person "committing an inferior injury, does not wholly forfeit the protection of his fellow citizens." It was thus the duty of the legislature "to arrange in a proper scale the crimes" to be repressed with "a corresponding graduation of punishments." Capital punishment "should be the last melancholy resource" imposed only for treason or murder. Although Jefferson's bill contained some lapses from humane and liberal standards, the main intent of the reform was humanitarian.[24] Had Virginia followed Jefferson's proposal to abolish the death

penalty for all crimes except treason and murder, the common-
wealth would have been in advance of every other state in the
Union, but the legislature by a single vote rejected the new code.
Madison reported to Jefferson after its final defeat that "the rage
against Horse stealers had a great influence on the fate of the Bill."
Horse stealing was a capital crime, and as Madison concluded,
"Our old bloody code is . . . fully restored." [25]

The most important aspect of Virginia society that the reformers
did not significantly alter in the revisal of the laws was slavery. In his
Notes on the State of Virginia, written while legislative action on the
report of the revisors was pending, Jefferson listed as one of the
major proposed alterations a bill to emancipate all slaves born after
the passage of the act. He went on to explain that the measures reported by the revisors did not contain this proposition but that an
amendment had been prepared to be introduced in the legislature.
According to Jefferson, this amendment provided that children
born to slaves should continue with their parents until a certain
age, then be brought up and trained at public expense in farming
or other skills, and at the age of eighteen for females and twenty-
one for males be colonized outside the state as "a free and indepen-
dant people" under the protection of Virginia until strong enough
to prevail on their own. Jefferson expected to be asked why the
blacks should not be retained and incorporated into the state. And
he answered, "Deep rooted prejudices entertained by the whites;
ten thousand recollections, by the blacks, of the injuries they have
sustained; new provocations; the real distinctions which nature has
made; and many other circumstances, will divide us into parties,
and produce convulsions which will probably never end but in the
extermination of the one or the other race." [26]

There is no record that the amendment for emancipation was
ever introduced, and Jefferson in his autobiography said that "it
was found that the public mind would not yet bear the proposition." In an appendix to the *Notes on Virginia*, Jefferson published
his draft of a constitution for Virginia containing a provision that
all persons born after December 31, 1800, would be free. Prepared
in 1783 in expectation of a constitutional convention that was never
called, that proposition also received no serious consideration.
Though these proposals showed Jefferson in advance of the general sentiment in Virginia of his day, the arguments for emancipation and deportation that he outlined in his *Notes on Virginia* rested
on the assumption of innate racial differences. Jefferson believed
at the time of the Revolution, as he did in old age, that "noth-

ing is more certainly written in the book of fate than that these people are to be free," but he also was convinced that it was no less certain that "the two races, equally free, cannot live in the same government."[27]

Ahead of his time in his stand on emancipation, Jefferson was much the product of his age in his views on race. The views that he expressed in his *Notes on Virginia*, written in the early 1780s in the full tide of his revolutionary fervor, stopped short of accepting the equality of blacks, though he recognized the blacks as equal in "moral sense." Ready to make allowances for differences of condition, education, conversation, and the sphere in which slaves moved, Jefferson still subscribed to the theory of black inferiority. He said that he advanced it "as a suspicion only that the blacks . . . are inferior to the whites in the endowments both of body and mind," but most of his arguments tended to support that suspicion. After reading Jefferson's *Notes on Virginia*, David Ramsay, a South Carolina surgeon and historian, wrote to him that he admired his "generous indignation at slavery; but think you have depressed the negroes too low."[28] It may be argued that Jefferson's suspicion of black inferiority was the only means by which he could deal psychologically with his own sense of guilt in owning slaves. As John C. Miller pointed out, Jefferson could never have lived with the thought that white Americans might be denying opportunity to a black Isaac Newton, a black Francis Bacon, or a black John Locke.[29] To the twentieth-century mind Jefferson's views on race stand in contrast to the liberal stance that he took on most of the major issues of his day; yet his repeated condemnation of the institution of slavery and his insistent arguments that steps must be taken to bring it to an end placed him in advance of most—but far from all—eighteenth-century persons.

The *Notes on Virginia* included an impassioned condemnation of slavery, which Jefferson described as a system destroying the morals of society. "The whole commerce between master and slave is a perpetual exercise of the most boisterous passions, the most unremitting despotism on the one part, and degrading submissions on the other," he wrote, seeing slavery as encouraging passion rather than reason. He condemned statesmen for "permitting one half of the citizens thus to trample on the rights of the other." And he asked: "Can the liberties of a nation be thought secure when we have removed their only firm basis, a conviction in the minds of the people that these liberties are of the gift of God? That they are not to be violated but with his wrath? Indeed I tremble for my country when I reflect that God is just: that his justice cannot sleep for ever." At the time he wrote this, Jefferson said he thought "a change already perceptible, since the origin of the present revolution. The spirit of the master is abating, that of the slave rising from the dust, his condition mollifying, the way I hope preparing, under the auspices of heaven, for a total emancipation, and that this is disposed, in the order of events, to be with the consent of the masters, rather than by their extirpation." [30] By the end of his life, hope would be replaced by growing despair, but he never wavered in his conviction that slavery was an evil that must be extinguished.

By emphasizing the leading reform proposals of the report of the revisors, Jefferson obscured the full magnitude of his extraordinary effort. The failure of the Assembly to adopt the report as a revised code also impaired the public perception of the accomplishment. But those close to Jefferson fully understood his contribution. Madison recognized him as the leading figure in the revisal of the laws, and he later said that the effort "exacted perhaps the most severe of his public labours. . . . The work tho' not enacted in the mass as was contemplated has been a mine of Legislative wealth; and a Model also of Statutory Composition." [31]

From 1776 to 1779 Jefferson devoted most of his public effort to drafting bills and reforming the laws. American spirits rose and fell as the fortunes of the war shifted, but Jefferson pressed on with his work, always thinking in terms of a new society that would follow the war, never proceeding on any premise other than ultimate American success. While the war raged, he was contemplating the establishment of a state-supported library in Richmond to promote "the researches of the learned and curious." When he drafted a bill to that effect, he added a provision that "if during the time of war the importation of books and maps shall be hazardous" or the cost too high, the directors of the library could accumulate the annual appropriation "until fit occasions shall occur of employing them." [32] Most of Jefferson's contemporaries were more concerned with the immediate problems at hand, and his bill for a library never was enacted, but it showed that Jefferson had a vision for the future that not even the darkest days of the war could dispel.

VI
Wartime Governor of Virginia

On June 1, 1779, by joint ballot of both houses of the Assembly, Jefferson was elected governor of Virginia to succeed Patrick Henry, who had served three one-year terms and was ineligible to succeed himself. In a close contest no candidate received a majority on the first ballot. Jefferson led with fifty-five votes, followed by John Page (a member of the Governor's Council since 1776) with thirty-eight and Thomas Nelson (commander of the Virginia militia) with thirty-two. The voting on the second ballot between Jefferson and Page gave Jefferson sixty-seven votes and Page sixty-one. Although the election was close, the outcome was not unexpected. Edmund Pendleton had predicted Jefferson's election the day before the balloting.[1] Page promptly assured his old college friend that he would "do every thing in my Power to make your Administration easy and agreeable to you." In response Jefferson wrote Page that he had been distressed that the zeal of their respective friends had placed them as competitors but that "the difference of the numbers which decided between us, was too insignificant to give you a pain or me a pleasure [had] our disposition towards each other been such as to have admitted those sensations."[2]

Considering the critical state of the war and the problems facing Virginia, the burden of the governorship was hardly a cause for congratulations. Indeed, Jefferson told one well-wisher that condolences would be better suited to the occasion. To Richard Henry Lee he wrote that "in a virtuous government, and more especially in times like these, public offices are, what they should be, burthens to those appointed to them which it would be wrong to decline, though foreseen to bring them intense labor and great private loss."[3] Even then, it is unlikely that Jefferson anticipated the difficulties, labor, and strain the governorship would impose. The thirty-six-year-old governor hardly would have expected to ask to be relieved of those burdens before the end of the three consecutive one-year terms permitted to him by the constitution. However, a few months after accepting reelection in 1780, he was contemplating retiring from office and would do so at the end of his second term.[4] That date in June, 1781, came during one of the darkest periods of the war in Virginia, and he would leave office tired, frustrated, and disappointed. Had he endured the strain another five months, he could have experienced as governor the exhilaration of Cornwallis' defeat at Yorktown.

Offering little glory and much labor, especially in wartime, the governorship was a post without real authority or the resources that effective leadership required. Totally dependent upon the legislature, to which the constitution of 1776 assigned supreme power, the governor had no veto and unlike royal governors could not dissolve the Assembly. He exercised the executive authority with the advice of a council of state composed of eight members elected by the Assembly, and he sometimes was prevented from acting because of the absence of the required quorum of four council members. Yet the governor was responsibile for administering the laws, and to do so on a daily basis required the working out of certain relationships with the council that permitted him to use some discretion. Jefferson was particularly adept at this, and within six months after taking office the council had given him authority to act in certain cases when the council was not sitting and its concurrence could be expected. Jefferson recalled that it was also understood that where the council was divided in opinion or could not be assembled, the governor was free to act on his own opinion and responsibility and that he did so during the invasions of the state by the British. Minutes of the council confirm Jefferson's recollection.[5] Periods of almost daily contact between the governor and the council of state brought a close working relationship with James Madison, who was a member of the council when Jefferson took office, further strengthening their growing friendship.

The war necessitated more administrative machinery than the Virginia constitution envisioned. In May, 1779, the Assembly passed bills, drafted by Jefferson, to establish a Board of War and a Board of Trade. These measures were implemented early in his governorship. The boards, however, proved too cumbersome for effective administration. By the end of his first year as governor the boards were replaced by a commercial agent, a commissioner of the navy, and a commissioner of the war office—all appointed by the governor with the advice of the council and under the direction of both.[6] These changes show Jefferson's efforts to improve the administrative structure of the executive and indicate his early attention to administrative mechanisms, so characteristic of his style in executive posts in later years.

Although the governor of the commonwealth lacked the power that colonial governors had exercised, he was still addressed as His Excellency. Jefferson, like Patrick Henry before him, moved into the palace that royal governors had once occupied. He was to live in that elegant house—whose architectural style he never admired—for less than a year, however. Soon after he was elected governor, the Assembly passed an act to move the capital from Williamsburg to Richmond. The new capital was only a hamlet, but it was more centrally located to a population that was constantly moving westward. Jefferson favored the move. In fact, he had drafted a bill in 1776 to move the capital westward (without specifying Richmond), because the equal rights of all inhabitants required that the seat of government be as nearly central to all as possible. The exposure of Williamsburg to an invading enemy was also a consideration behind Jefferson's proposal. That danger was even greater in May of 1779, when the Assembly resurrected Jefferson's bill and, after minor changes, enacted it into law.[7]

Richmond was unprepared to receive the state government. Buildings for offices had to be hastily acquired, and the governor had to find his own dwelling. His wife and two daughters having joined him in the palace at Williamsburg, he was anxious to keep his family with him. Happily he accomplished this when he rented one of Richmond's few brick houses from Colonel Thomas Turpin and shipped forty-eight crates of furniture and furnishings from the palace in Williamsburg. While this permitted him to live with as much style and elegance as the circumstances permitted—a habit of living that he always followed—his greatest interest was in planning the future capital. When the legislature named him to head the nine-man committee of directors of the public buildings, he immediately began drawing plans for the city.[8] It would be some years before these plans would mature and Jefferson would send from Paris the model for the Virginia state capitol. Before those accomplishments could be recorded, the independence of Virginia had to be secured. When the capital moved to Richmond in May, 1780, the war was far from won, and the end was not in sight.

The Revolutionary War was a disorganized, joint military effort of the states and the Continental Congress. In the absence of any real national government the role of state governments in prosecuting the war was far greater than in any later American war. To be governor of Virginia from 1779 to 1781 was to be an executive actively involved in administering a state at war, and Virginia was the largest of the American states in population and in territory, stretching westward along the Ohio River to the Mississippi. The Board of War headed its letters "War Office, Williamsburg," and the military situation demanded that the governor be constantly concerned with enlistments, arms, military clothing and supplies, prisoners of war, and, at times, the invasion of the state by the enemy.

It was Jefferson's unhappy fate to be governor of Virginia during one of the darkest times of the war and the period in which Virginia was most directly threatened by British military conquest. In November, 1779, the Board of War predicted that the British army would begin offensive operations in the state during the coming winter and among other measures of preparation recommended the appointment of a general officer to implement the orders of the executive. "Civil Bodies," the board wrote, "tho [they] may dictate to, are Illy calculated to direct military ones." The council responded that the executive had no authority to appoint such an officer until an actual invasion had taken place, thus leaving the responsibility of preparing for an invasion in the governor's hands. Jefferson was not fully convinced that the British were planning to invade the Chesapeake Bay that winter, but on December 11, 1779, General Washington informed him that Sir Henry Clinton was embarking eight thousand troops from New York reportedly headed for the Chesapeake.[9] As it turned out, Clinton's destination was Charleston. Though this removed the immediate threat to Virginia, it bode ill for the future. The British were shifting their major military effort to the South, and the war was soon to enter one of its most critical phases.

By the spring of 1780 the Continental war effort was in desperate straits. No period of the Revolution had been more critical than the present moment, Madison wrote to Jefferson from Congress in March: "Our army threatened with an immediate alternative of disbanding or living on free quarter; the public Treasury empty; public credit exhausted, nay the private credit of purchasing Agents employed, I am told, as far as it will bear, Congress complaining of the extortion of the people; the people of the improvidence of Congress, and the army of both; our affairs requiring the most mature and systematic measures, and the urgency of occasions admitting only of temporizing expedients and those expedi-

ents generating new difficulties." A few weeks later Washington was
pleading with Jefferson to procure clothing for the Virginia line
that he had detached from his own forces and sent to join General
Benjamin Lincoln in South Carolina.[10] These bleak letters were
written at a time when it was hoped that Clinton's operations in the
South might be repulsed, but on May 12 Charleston fell to the British, and with it the Virginia forces sent to South Carolina were surrendered. It was June 5 before certain intelligence of this disaster
reached Jefferson in the new capital at Richmond.[11] Three days before learning the dark news from Charleston, Jefferson had been
reelected to a second term as governor.

Jefferson's final year in office was even more difficult than his
first. The financial situation of the state was desperate, inflation
rampant, and state currency becoming worthless. The military
situation in the South deteriorated rapidly, as British troops moved
northward after the fall of Charleston. Jefferson urgently appealed
to Congress for military stores, stressing that state supplies were inadequate even for arming the militia, while assuring Congress that
as far as they would go, state resources would be "chearfully submitted to the common cause." But state resources were either lack-
ing or not effectively mobilized, and General Horatio Gates was
soon complaining that Virginia militia were being sent to join his
command in North Carolina without arms and ammunition and
even without adequate clothing.[12]

In October, 1780, a British fleet of sixty sail entered the Chesapeake Bay, and light horse units made a landing near Portsmouth.
"We are endeavouring to collect as large a body to oppose them as
we can arm," Jefferson wrote to Washington. "This will be lamen-
tably inadequate if the Enemy be in any force; it is Mortifying to
suppose it possible that a people able and zealous to contend with
their Enemy should be reduced to fold their Arms for want of the
means of defence; yet no resources that we know of, ensure us
against this event." On this occasion Virginia was saved only by the
departure of the British fleet for Charleston on November 22. This
was a reprieve only, for at the end of December Benedict Arnold
arrived at the head of an invading British army intent on carrying
the war into the heart of the Old Dominion. Meanwhile General
Nathanael Greene, who had assumed command from General Gates
in North Carolina, described to Jefferson the wretched state of
Gates's army when he took command, and he lectured the Virginia
governor: "Your troops may literally be said to be naked. . . . It will
answer no good purpose to send men here in such a condition, for

they are nothing but added weight upon the army and altogether incapable of aiding in its operations. . . . No man will think himself bound to fight the battles of a State that leaves him to perish for want of covering." [13]

Jefferson was under pressure from all sides: from the Congress to supply money for the war effort and troops for the continental line; from the imperiled army in the South seeking arms, supplies, and clothing; and from his own citizens, who saw their state left exposed to an invading enemy. Though the situation could hardly be blamed on the governor, Virginia was unprepared for the crisis at hand. The state's contribution to the general cause had been large, and many of its people had sacrificed for the common good, but the state had not been mobilized for a war that was to last so long. The dimensions of that neglect were evident by 1780, and though chargeable more to the General Assembly than to the governor, Jefferson as a member of the Assembly from 1776 until his election as governor in 1779 must share in that failure.

Virginia, like most of the other states, had not developed the supply and distribution system needed to support the war effort. The result was that Jefferson as governor was directly involved in such details as calculating the number of uniforms that could be cut from 1,495 yards of cloth. When he was found to have miscalculated, he was informed that the 1,495 yards that he had counted upon as sufficient to make 400 suits would make no more than 370 coats because it was of a narrow width. "I should have imagined that the width as well as the length of the cloth would have been reported to your Excéllency," the colonel in charge of clothing new recruits wrote, as if the governor had no greater responsibilities than keeping track of the width of cloth for uniforms. [14] This was no exceptional case. Jefferson personally requested cartridge paper and cartouche boxes from Philadelphia, wrote out the orders of the officer of a flag-of-truce vessel to proceed up the James, and secured land for the erection of a magazine near the foundry at Westham. [15] At the same time, he was involved in strategic planning for the war, particularly with regard to the West, where he played a major role in supporting the campaigns of George Rogers Clark to secure the Virginia frontier on the Ohio River all the way to its juncture with the Mississippi. [16] He corresponded regularly with General Washington and with the president of Congress, reporting on the military situation in Virginia and relaying information from farther south.

Jefferson faced the difficulties of the war almost philosophically.

Amid the pressures he remained outwardly calm. Despite the reluctance of many of his countrymen to fight or to sacrifice, he retained his faith in the cause and in the ultimate destiny of the American people to prevail. General Daniel Morgan would explode, "Great god what is the reason we cant Have more men in the field—so many men in the country Nearly idle for want of employment." But the governor would explain to Lafayette, "Mild Laws, a People not used to war and prompt obedience, a want of the Provisions of War and means of procuring them render our orders often ineffectual, oblige us to temporize and when we cannot accomplish an object in one way to attempt it in another."[17] To General Nathanael Greene, Jefferson's temporizing appeared to be indifference to the critical state of the war. "The struggle here is great, the situation of the Army precarious," the general wrote from North Carolina in March, 1781. "The least misfortune will bring the war to your doors. You will feel the necessity, therefore of giving me immediate support." Jefferson replied that reinforcements were on the way, but added: "An Enemy 3000 strong, not a regular within our State, nor Arms to put into the Hands of the Militia are Circumstances which promise Difficulties. Yet I shall think it essential to do every Thing we can for you to prevent the Return of Cornwallis's Army."[18]

The war was in fact already at Jefferson's door. In January, 1781, a British fleet sailed up the James River to Westover and landed Benedict Arnold's invading army for an attack on Richmond. Governor Jefferson called up the militia of adjacent counties, hastily began moving records and military stores out of Richmond, and evacuated his family from the city. With no regular troops in the area and no militia in place to defend the capital, Arnold's army entered the city unopposed and sent a detachment to destroy the foundry at Westham. After twenty-four hours Arnold's forces left the city, but not before setting fire to some public and private buildings and carrying off wagonloads of arms, munitions, and military stores that Virginia could ill afford to lose.[19] Never far away, Jefferson spent several active and anxious nights across the James River near Richmond and returned to the capital within thirty-six hours of the British withdrawal. He was soon recording the loss of 150 muskets from the Capitol loft, 150 wagons on the Brook Road, 5 tons of powder from the magazine, 120 sides of leather from the quartermaster, and other distressing losses.[20]

Arnold's withdrawal to Portsmouth was only temporary. In March he was reinforced by the arrival of General William Phillips and

2,000 men. Superseding Arnold in command, Phillips moved up the James River to Petersburg in mid-April and occupied Manchester, south of Richmond across the James. Only the timely arrival of Lafayette with a detachment of 900 Continental troops, who had made a forced march from Annapolis, dissuaded the British from crossing the river to attack the capital. With Lafayette controlling the north bank of the James, the British dropped down the river. But again it was only a temporary maneuver. Cornwallis was already implementing a plan to march into Virginia and link forces with Phillips. When he arrived in Petersburg on May 20 and assumed command of all British forces in Virginia, the American military situation became critical. Even with 1,200 to 1,500 militia added to his forces, Lafayette was no match for the British force of about 7,200. Governor Jefferson had summoned more militia into service, but he had been unable to assure Lafayette that his requests would produce sufficient reinforcements. "I shall candidly acknowledge," Jefferson wrote to Lafayette on May 14, "that it is not in my power to do any thing more than to represent to the General Assembly that unless they can provide more effectually for the Execution of the Law it will be vain to call on Militia."[21] When Cornwallis crossed the James River on May 24 to attack Richmond, Lafayette had no choice but to withdraw rapidly northward toward Fredericksburg.

Meanwhile the General Assembly, scheduled to convene in Richmond on May 7, had difficulty in making a quorum, and on May 10 the members present adjourned to meet in Charlottesville on May 24. Departing the capital on May 15 to be present for the convening of the Assembly, Jefferson was already at Monticello when Cornwallis arrived outside Richmond. Although Jefferson earlier had announced his intention not to accept a third year as governor when his term ended in June, the moment was an inopportune one to contemplate leaving the governorship. He satisfied himself of its propriety by reasoning that his likely successor would be General Thomas Nelson, who commanded the state militia, and that "the union of the civil and military power in the same hands, at this time would greatly facilitiate military measures," especially because he himself was "unprepared by his line of life and education for the command of armies."[22]

On the last day of May, Cornwallis abandoned his pursuit of Lafayette and dispatched Lieutenant Colonel Banastre Tarleton with 250 cavalry to raid Charlottesville in hope of capturing members of the Virginia Assembly and perhaps even Governor Jefferson. The

plan might well have succeeded had not Tarleton's movement toward Charlottesville been observed about forty miles away by Captain Jack Jouett, a militia captain who rode through the night along
back roads to bring the warning to Jefferson and the legislators.
Even then, the delegates barely had time to flee across the mountain
toward Staunton, and several laggards were, in fact, caught. Jefferson himself escaped on horseback through the woods as British
troops ascended the hill at Monticello.[23] Years later Jefferson wrote:

> Would it be believed, were it not known, that this flight from a troop of
> horse, whose whole legion too was within supporting distance, has
> been the subject, with party writers, of volumes of reproach on me,
> serious or sarcastic? That it has been sung in verse, and said in humble
> prose that, forgetting the noble example of the hero of La Mancha,
> and his windmills, I declined a combat, singly against a troop, in which
> victory would have been so glorious? Forgetting, themselves, at the
> same time, that I was not provided with the enchanted arms of the
> knight, nor even with his helmet of Mambrino. These closet heroes
> forsooth would have disdained the shelter of a wood, even singly and
> unarmed, against a legion of armed enemies.[24]

These comments were written in 1816, seven years after he retired
from the presidency. That Jefferson retained such feeling about
this experience of his governorship thirty-five years distant shows
what a political issue was made of his fleeing from the British and
how deeply hurt he was by the charges.

Jefferson's agony over the final days of his governorship began
almost immediately. When Tarleton swept into Charlottesville on
June 4, Jefferson's term as governor had actually expired two days
earlier on June 2, but the recently assembled legislature had not yet
chosen his successor. In fleeing from Monticello on June 4, Jefferson did not head for Staunton, where the legislature would recon-
vene, but went instead with his family to Poplar Forest, a farm in
Bedford County inherited by his wife, ninety miles southwest of
Monticello. Having declared his intention not to accept another
year as governor and his term of office having expired, he was
not required to attend at Staunton. But until the legislature chose
Thomas Nelson as governor on June 12, the state was without a
chief executive in a desperately critical moment. However clearly
Jefferson had earlier made known his determination to retire, his
disappearance from the scene at this time of crisis was bound to
arouse criticism. He should not have been surprised when such an
attack was not long in coming.

On June 12, 1781, George Nicholas moved in the House of Delegates that at the next session of Assembly an inquiry be made into the conduct of the executive during the last twelve months.[25] The resolution, which had the backing of Patrick Henry—an act never forgotten by Jefferson—passed the same day. John Beckley, the clerk of the House, immediately sent Jefferson a copy, though it did not reach him until August 7. Meanwhile Jefferson learned of it from friends in the Assembly, some of whom supported the inquiry, confident, as one member explained to Jefferson, that it "would do you Honor."[26] Immediately after returning to Monticello from Poplar Forest in late July, Jefferson wrote to Nicholas asking for the specific incidents that were to be investigated. Nicholas responded that "no particular instance of misconduct was specified" but went on to list several matters that he believed wanted explanation. Mentioning first "the total want of opposition to Arnold on his first expedition to Richmond," he enumerated other charges relating to the militia and the loss of arms.[27]

Although the resolution specified an inquiry into the conduct of the executive rather than the governor, thus embracing members of the council, the charges appear to have been directed toward Jefferson; he immediately began to prepare his defense. When one of the members of the House of Delegates from Albemarle County resigned to accept a state appointment, Jefferson sought his seat, was elected, and was present in the Assembly on December 12, 1781, the date set for the inquiry. By then Cornwallis had surrendered at Yorktown, and George Nicholas did not even appear in the House of Delegates to press his charges. When no one else moved to begin the inquiry, Jefferson himself rose from his seat, holding in his hand a paper on which he had listed the expected charges, having obtained a more detailed list than the one that Nicholas had sent him. He then proceeded to read the charges and to answer each in turn.[28]

When he sat down, the House unanimously passed a resolution of commendation and thanks, explaining that "popular rumours, gaining some degree of credence, by more pointed Accusations, rendered it necessary to make an enquirey into his conduct, and delayed that retribution of public gratitude, so eminently merited; but that conduct having become the object of open scrutiny, tenfold value is added to an approbation founded on a cool and deliberate discussion." The final resolution as amended by the Senate was less profuse in apology but none the less clear in its verdict. It read:

"*Resolved*, that the sincere Thanks of the General Assembly be given to our former Governor Thomas Jefferson Esquire for his impartial, upright, and attentive administration whilst in office. The Assembly wish in the strongest manner to declare the high opinion which they entertain of Mr. Jefferson's Ability, Rectitude, and Integrity as chief Magistrate of this Commonwealth, and mean by thus publicly avowing their Opinion, to obviate and to remove all unmerited Censure."[29]

Though publicly vindicated, Jefferson was bitter that charges based on rumors had ever been introduced.[30] But like other witnesses to the controversy, he believed that the matter had been put to rest. It would be as unexpected as it was, in his eyes, despicable that years later, when he was a candidate for president of the United States, attacks would be made upon him relating his conduct as governor of Virginia.[31]

Jefferson's resentment against the unfair charges made against him was understandable. Less easy to comprehend was his decision to withdraw from public life when he left the governorship. At that moment the revolutionary cause to which he had devoted most of his energies since the beginning of the war was still unresolved. If he could not endure another year of strain and frustration as governor of Virginia, there were other places where his services were still needed. The Continental Congress in fact lost no time in calling for them. On June 14 the Congress named him along with Benjamin Franklin, John Jay, and Henry Laurens, to join John Adams in Paris as one of the peace commissioners to negotiate with Great Britain.[32] By the time Jefferson received word of this appointment, he had also been informed of the scheduled inquiry into his conduct as governor, and he declined the appointment on the grounds of "a temporary and indispensable obligation" to remain within the state.[33] When Edmund Randolph suggested that the negotiations would probably be delayed long enough for his temporary disability to be removed, enabling him to proceed on the mission, Jefferson was forced to weigh other considerations. When he did so, he still insisted on declining. "Were it possible for me to determine again to enter into public business there is no appointment whatever which would have been so agreeable to me," he wrote to Randolph. "But I have taken my final leave of every thing of that nature, have retired to my farm, my family and books from which I think nothing will ever more separate me."[34] After accepting election to a seat in the House of Delegates to defend his conduct as governor, he refused reelection to the next Assembly. He also declined election to the Continental Congress. The pull of home, family, and Monticello was always great throughout his life, and he now yielded to the impulse to return to private life. That decision was not understood by many of his friends, most of whom were unaware of the delicate state of his wife's health, which figured prominently in his determination. Even James Madison wrote: "Great as my partiality is to Mr. Jefferson, the mode in which he seems determined to revenge the wrong received from his Country, does not appear to me to be dictated either by philosophy or patriotism. It argues indeed a keen sensibility and a strong consciousness of rectitude." [35] Madison was then a member of the Continental Congress in Philadelphia, and he did not know that, at the very moment he wrote, Mrs. Jefferson lay ill at Monticello with little prospect of recovery.

The two frustrating years as governor were important to Jefferson's political education. While he had shown less leadership skills than the times required, the blame was not wholly his, for the powers of his office were ill suited to the demands of a state at war. At the same time, he demonstrated more administrative ability than is frequently recognized. Although he withdrew from the scene with the intention of retiring from public affairs, future circumstances would alter that decision. He would never forget his difficult days as governor, but those memories would not deter him from later returning to public life.

VII
Withdrawal, Sorrow, and Return

In late November, 1780, just after the British fleet that had been threatening Virginia since October sailed from the Chesapeake, Governor Jefferson wrote that he was busily employed in answering queries about Virginia for François Marbois (later Marquis de Barbé-Marbois), secretary to the French minister at Philadelphia, who had circulated among members of the Continental Congress a list of queries concerning the various states.[1] His questions sought useful information on population, geography, natural resources, governments, laws, religion, education, the military, commerce and manufacturing, navigation and seaports, the native Indians, and various other matters. John Sullivan, the delegate from New Hampshire whom Marbois asked to gather data on that state, described the French inquirer as "one of those useful Geniuss who is Constantly in Search of knowledge."[2] It is not surprising that when Joseph Jones, the Virginia delegate queried by Marbois, forwarded the list of questions to Jefferson, the busy governor searched for time to provide answers. He had long been collecting information on Virginia and recording it on loose memoranda kept in bundles at Monticello. Marbois' queries would enable him to put those to good use. Such was the origin of the only book that Jefferson ever authored, his *Notes on the State of Virginia*, now widely regarded as one of the most important scientific and political works written by an American in the eighteenth century and one of the most famous products of the Enlightenment in America.[3]

Jefferson's last year as governor left little time for the enterprise. A month after he started the project, Benedict Arnold's army invaded Virginia, and he would not have an opportunity to return to the work until after he left the governorship. Even then, he did so with difficulty. Forced to flee Monticello as his term ended in June, 1781, and unable to return until August, he turned to composing his answers for Marbois at a time when the military fortunes of Virginia hung in the balance. Only his unshakable faith in the ultimate triumph of the American cause could have enabled him to direct his powers of concentration to such a project. Jefferson could do most of the writing in the isolation of Monticello, but he was unable to collect all of the data needed until after the fighting ended. "The general confusion of our state put it out of my power to procure the information necessary till lately," he explained to Marbois when he sent him his compilation in December, 1781. Although Jefferson's answers to Marbois' questions were fuller than those of any of the other few respondents who bothered to reply, he regarded them as "very imperfect," and as soon as he finished the manuscript, he began to revise it.[4]

On the same day that he sent the work to Marbois, Jefferson wrote to Charles Thomson, secretary of the Congress and fellow member of the American Philosophical Society, asking his opinion on expanding the work as a contribution to the society. Having been elected a councillor of the society while governor, he said that though he was unsure of his responsibilities, he did not wish to be counted "as a drone in any society." Thomson strongly encouraged Jefferson to pursue the work. The American Philosophical Society, he noted, had for its object "the improvement of useful knowledge more particularly what relates to this new world. It comprehends the whole circle of arts, science and discoveries especially in the natural world and therefore I am persuaded your answer to Mr. Marbois queries will be an acceptable present. This Country opens to the philosophic view an extensive, rich and unexplored field." While expressing his regret at Jefferson's retirement from politics, Thomson congratulated posterity on the advantages that they might derive from Jefferson's "philosophical researches." Jefferson already had become so interested in the project that he undoubtedly did not require Thomson's encouragement, but he welcomed his interest. When he later published the work, he included as an appendix a series of observations that Thomson sent him after reading the manuscript. Jefferson corrected and enlarged the work during the winter of 1782 and continued to make revisions as late as 1784 before having it printed in 1785.[5]

The commentaries in the *Notes on the State of Virginia*, as Jefferson modestly insisted, were incomplete, and some topics were treated far more extensively than others. Although most of the work centered on Virginia, Jefferson ranged far beyond his own state on certain subjects, such as the aborigines and the animals in the New

World. When he cited men of genius that America had produced, he pointed to Washington, Franklin, and Rittenhouse, only one of whom was a Virginian. Much of the work was descriptive, factual data about Virginia. He began by describing its boundaries and rivers, providing an amazing amount of information about the waters that flowed through Virginia or along its borders, including the Mississippi. In treating that channel of the future commerce of the western country, he also included its principal source, the Missouri. Even in largely descriptive passages he added opinion, calling the Ohio "the most beautiful river on earth"—a verdict that he had gleaned from others, for he had never seen it himself.[6]

His chapter "Productions Mineral, Vegetable and Animal," the longest in the book, displayed the Virginian's keen interest in natural history and included detailed lists of trees, plants, animals, and birds. The most extensive part of the chapter was Jefferson's argument refuting the theory of the Comte de Buffon, probably the best known and most widely respected naturalist of his day, that the animals and aborigines of the New World were smaller and generally degenerate in comparison with their European equivalents. To provide data, he had friends everywhere measuring and weighing animals, large and small.[7] Jefferson himself was not innovative as a scientist, always valuing the practical over the theoretical, but his section on natural history attracted considerable notice, and throughout his life he would be unexcelled as a promoter of science.[8]

The second longest section of the book was devoted to the constitution and the laws of Virginia, in which he sharply criticized the Virginia Constitution of 1776. Noting that it "was formed when we were new and unexperienced in the science of government," he was critical of the denial of the franchise to a large number of freemen and also of the unequal representation of the central and western portions of the state in comparison with the old tidewater counties. In addition, he opposed the consolidation of power in the hands of a single branch of government, even the legislature. The concentration of the executive, legislative, and judicial powers of government in the same hands was "precisely the definition of despotic government," he wrote. "It will be no alleviation that these powers will be exercised by a plurality of hands, and not by a single one."[9]

Jefferson devoted a chapter to the American aborigines, and in response to Buffon he argued that "we shall probably find that they are formed in mind as well as in body, on the same module with the

'Homo sapiens Europaeus.'"[10] In a section on laws he discussed slavery and the black race, expressing both his strong condemnation of slavery and his suspicion that blacks were not intellectually equal to whites.[11] He also used most of a brief chapter on manners to describe the effects of slavery on slaveholders. One of the most famous passages of the book was found in a section on manufactures, devoted largely to glorifying agriculture as superior to manufacturing.

> Those who labour in the earth are the chosen people of God, if ever he had a chosen people, whose breasts he has made his peculiar deposit for substantial and genuine virtue. . . . While we have land to labour then, let us never wish to see our citizens occupied at a work-bench, or twirling a distaff. Carpenters, masons, smiths, are wanting in husbandry: but, for the general operations of manufacture, let our workshops remain in Europe. . . . The mobs of great cities add just so much to the support of pure government, as sores do to the strength of the human body. It is the manners and spirit of a people which preserve a republic in vigour.[12]

No brief examination of the work can adequately display the erudition of the author or convey the scope of the analytical and speculative content of the book. Throughout it revealed Jefferson's intense interest in the environment and in natural history, his passionate concern for government and the laws, and his committed involvement in the new society in which he lived. Just before its publication, Charles Thomson urged him to give the book a broader title and pronounced it "a most excellent Natural history not merely of Virginia but of North America and possibly equal if not superior to that of any Country yet published."[13]

When the Chevalier de Chastellux visited Jefferson at Monticello in the spring of 1782, he found Jefferson in his element and was charmed by his experienced and learned host. He described "a man, not yet forty, tall, and with a mild and pleasing countenance, but whose mind and attainments could serve in lieu of all outward graces; an American, who, without ever having quitted his own country, is Musician, Draftsman, Surveyor, Astronomer, Natural Philosopher, Jurist, and Statesman . . . and finally a Philosopher." Chastellux, a major general in Rochambeau's army, man of letters, and member of the French Academy, was captivated by his host's house and its setting and by the breadth of Jefferson's mind and interests. "It seems indeed," he wrote, "as though, ever since his youth, he had placed his mind, like his house, on a lofty height, whence he might contemplate the whole universe." Chastellux also mentioned Jefferson's "gentle and amiable wife" and their "charming children whose education is his special care," as he sought to explain why Jefferson preferred to remain at Monticello rather than accept a commission to Europe. Chastellux's visit to Monticello came at a high moment of domestic felicity in Jefferson's life, surrounded by a family to cherish, "a house to embellish, extensive estates to improve, [and] the arts and sciences to cultivate."[14] But it turned out to be a fleeting moment. Before six months had passed, Jefferson's private life had plummeted from the splendid mountaintop that Chastellux described to the depth of gloom and despair.

Less than a month after Chastellux left Monticello, Jefferson recorded in his memorandum and account book on May 8, "Our daughter Lucy Elizabeth (second of that name) born at one o'clock A.M."[15] The first Lucy Elizabeth had died in infancy little more than a year earlier in April, 1781. That loss had been the third Jefferson child (two daughters and one son) to die in infancy or early childhood, and the parents felt the grief particularly intensely, coming as it did at a time of great public stress when the British were threatening a second attack on Richmond.[16] The joy of the birth of a second Lucy Elizabeth was muted by the weakness of her mother, who in ten years had borne six children and repeatedly had suffered difficult pregnancies and childbirths. On May 20 Jefferson wrote to Monroe that "Mrs. Jefferson had added another daughter to our family. She has been ever since and still continues very dangerously ill."[17]

Martha Jefferson never regained her health, and Jefferson watched helplessly as her life slipped away. Years later his eldest daughter, Martha, who was ten at the time and called Patsy, remembered that her father had constantly attended her mother during this final illness. "For four months that she lingered he was never out of Calling," she recalled. "When not at her bed side he was writing in a small room which opened immediately at the head of her bed."[18] Sometime during her declining months Martha Jefferson copied, with slight modification, from *Tristram Shandy* the poignant lines:

> Time wastes too fast: every letter
> I trace tell me with what rapidity
> life follows my pen. The days and hours
> of it are flying over our heads like
> clouds of windy day never to return—
> more every thing presses on—

This much was in her own hand, but it was left to her devoted husband to complete the passage:

> and every time I kiss thy hand to bid adieu,
> every absence which follows it,
> are preludes to that eternal separation
> which we are shortly to make! [19]

When Martha's faltering life came to an end on September 6, 1782, Jefferson's despondency was so intense as to excite the concern of those about him. Years later Patsy recalled: "A moment before the closing scene, he was led from the room in a state of insensibility by his sister, Mrs. Carr, who, with great difficulty, got him into the library, where he fainted, and remained so long insensible that they feared he never would revive." The ten-year old Patsy was not allowed to witness what followed, but when she sneaked into his room at night, she long remembered her shock at his emotion. Her father stayed in his room three weeks, she recalled. "He walked almost incessantly night and day, only lying down occasionally, when nature was completely exhausted, on a pallet that had been brought in during his long fainting-fit." When at last he left his room, "he was incessantly on horseback, rambling about the mountain, in the least frequented roads, and just as often through the woods." Accompanying him on these "melancholy rambles," the young Patsy found the scenes "beyond the power of time to obliterate." [20]

It was a period of deep depression, and not until mid-October did Jefferson find himself "emerging from that stupor of mind which had rendered me as dead to the world as she was whose loss occasioned it," he admitted in November. [21] By then his friends had rallied to his rescue in an effort to draw him away from the scene of his grief. Prompted by Madison, the delegates to the Continental Congress unanimously voted to renew the appointment earlier offered him as one of the ministers plenipotentiary for negotiating a peace. [22] Jefferson received the news of the appointment on November 25, accepted immediately, and a month later was in Philadelphia waiting for passage to France. "I had folded myself in the arms of retirement, and rested all prospect of future happiness on domestic and literary objects," he wrote to Chastellux on the same day he accepted Congress' commission. "A single event wiped away all my plans and left me a blank which I had not the spirits to fill up." [23] Now Congress had provided him the challenge to fill that void, and he seized it eagerly. The man who had quitted the governor's office in despair eighteen months earlier was back in public service. His life again had meaning.

With the French frigate that was to carry him to France blocked by ice below Baltimore, Jefferson spent his time in Philadelphia studying documents in the Department of Foreign Affairs, attending meetings of the American Philosophical Society, and renewing his friendship with James Madison. After a month he journeyed to Baltimore to await the freeing of the frigate from the ice.[24] Soon more than ice delayed his passage. British cruisers blocked the entrance to the Chesapeake. Meanwhile word reached America that a provisional peace treaty had been signed in November, and Congress decided to delay his mission. Jefferson returned to Philadelphia to await instructions, and on April 1, 1783, he was released from the mission. However much he welcomed the news of peace, he was disappointed in missing a trip to France that he had eagerly anticipated. But he had now made the adjustment back into the world of public affairs. He shortly returned to Virginia and immersed himself in drafting proposals for a new constitution for the commonwealth. His willingness to return to Philadelphia, however, was not overlooked by his friends, and on June 6 the Virginia Assembly elected him a delegate to Congress for a term that was to begin in November.

Jefferson had planned to take his daughter Patsy with him on the canceled voyage to France, and he now made plans for her to accompany him to Philadelphia to continue her schooling there while Congress was in session. His two younger children were left in Virginia in the care of his sister-in-law Elizabeth Wayles Eppes. As he prepared to spend the next winter in Philadelphia, he learned that Congress had decided to meet in Princeton. Nevertheless, he continued with arrangements for Patsy in Philadelphia, and they proceeded there in October before he went on to Princeton. No sooner than he arrived in Princeton, Congress adjourned to meet three weeks later in Annapolis.

This was the first Congress to meet after the peace treaty had been signed, and the site of the meeting of Congress and the location of the capital of the new nation were matters of intense interest and political maneuvering. The move to Annapolis was part of the effort to fix the seat of government south of Philadelphia at a more centrally located site, but this was only the beginning of a lengthy competition that would not be settled until after a new Constitution was adopted and George Washington was inaugurated as president. Jefferson would later play an important role in the final bargaining that placed the capital on the Potomac, but at this moment he would have preferred that Congress meet in Philadelphia—a city whose cultural life he found attractive, where he had friends, and where he could spend time with his daughter.

When Jefferson departed from Philadelphia for Annapolis at the end of November, he left Patsy under the care of Mrs. Thomas Hopkinson, the widowed mother of Francis Hopkinson, a fellow signer of the Declaration of Independence. His children would provide companionship for Patsy, who would also get to know the children of David Rittenhouse, a man whose knowledge of astronomy her father admired so much. Jefferson himself would have preferred to remain in this circle rather than to spend the winter in Annapolis, but he left Philadelphia confident that he had procured for Patsy "the best tutors in French, dancing, music, and drawing," and that she would be "more improved" there than with him in the Maryland capital.[25]

Once in Annapolis, Jefferson continued to worry about Patsy and his responsibilities for her education. "The plan of reading which I have formed for her is considerably different from what I think would be most proper for her sex in any other country than America," he wrote to Marbois. "I am obliged in it to extend my views beyond herself, and consider her as possibly at the head of a little family of her own. The chance that in marriage she will draw a blockhead I calculate at about fourteen to one, and of course that the education of her family will probably rest on her own ideas and direction without assistance. With the best poets and prosewriters I shall therefore combine a certain extent of reading in the graver sciences." Jefferson did not expect Patsy to accomplish all of this in a winter in Philadelphia, where her time would be chiefly occupied in acquiring a taste for such of the fine arts as she could not so easily acquire in Virginia.[26] It was clear that his daughter's future— and even that of anticipated future grandchildren—was much in his mind during a lonely season in Annapolis. His stay there also provided the occasion for the beginning of a remarkable series of letters with his daughter—letters that are immensely revealing of his relationship with her and the heavy burden he placed upon her to meet his expectations.

In his first letter to Patsy from Annapolis he sent her a schedule to follow in filling the hours of her days: from eight to ten in the morning, "practise music"; from ten to one, "dance one day and draw another"; from one to two, "draw on the day you dance, and write a letter the next day"; from three to four, "read French"; from four to five, "exercise yourself in music"; from five until bedtime, "read English, write, etc." He also made clear his fatherly expectations, beginning his letter by writing stiffly that "the acquirements which I hope you will make under the tutors I have provided for you will render you more worthy of my love, and if they cannot increase it they will prevent it's diminution." He closed the letter by declaring: "I have placed my happiness on seeing you good and accomplished, and no distress which this world can now bring on me could equal that of your disappointing my hopes. If you love me then, strive to be good under every situation and to all living creatures, and to acquire those accomplishments which I have put in your power, and which will go far towards ensuring you the warmest love of your affectionate father."[27]

However well-meaning, this was a heavy charge to impose on an eleven-year-old motherless child, and it reveals a theme that ran through Jefferson's subsequent letters to Patsy, as it would be found in letters to his daughter Mary, when she, too, reached the age of letter writing. Repeatedly he reminded his daughters that they should strive to be worthy of his love. That he loved his children cannot be doubted, but he found it difficult to express that love, and as a father he was demanding. In this earliest known letter to Patsy, he told her that he expected her to write him by every post, to tell him what books she had read and what tunes she had learned, and to send him copies of her best drawings. He also urged her to write to her aunts in Virginia and instructed her to watch her spelling. As if this long lecture were not sufficient, he added a postscript: "Keep my letters and read them at times that you may always have present in your mind those things which will endear you to me."[28] That Patsy preserved these letters as her father directed is suggestive of the bond that was early formed between them. Patsy would strive to merit her father's love, and she would do so throughout his long life.

The Congress of the Confederation in which Jefferson sat in Annapolis in 1783 and 1784 was not so distinguished or influential a body as the Continental Congress, of which he had been a member in 1775 and 1776, but Jefferson witnessed in this session some of the final acts of the events that the earlier Congress had set into motion. He participated in the ratification by Congress of the definitive treaty of peace, and he was present on December 23, 1783, when General Washington at a formal audience granted by Congress resigned his commission as commander in chief in a dramatic and symbolic ceremony. It was Jefferson who headed the committee of arrangements and drafted a response to Washington's address. One eyewitness to the moving event reported that there was hardly a member of Congress who did not shed tears as the general bade an affectionate farewell to the Congress under whose orders he had so long acted and took his leave of "all the employments of public life." [29] No one could have anticipated at this moment that thirteen years later Washington would make another, and even more famous, farewell address upon leaving an office that then did not even exist: the presidency of the United States. Jefferson was a younger man than Washington, and he had recently returned to public service, but he, too, must have viewed the events more as the ending of an era than the beginning of a new one. Yet he was ever forward-looking, and this was demonstrated in the major contribution that he made during the remaining months that he sat in the Confederation Congress.

On March 1, 1784, Jefferson presented a committee report of a plan for the government of the western territory already ceded, or to be ceded, by the states to the United States. This report became the basis of the Land Ordinance of 1784, an act that never went into effect before being replaced by the Northwest Ordinance of 1787. It did, however, lay the foundation for that more famous act and established the basic principles of American territorial policy. Although Jefferson has sometimes been given credit for all of the ideas in the report, he drew on considerable previous congressional discussion of the issue. Congress did not adopt all of the proposals in the report, but it confirmed the fundamental principle that the western territories should be formed into distinct republican states and admitted into the Union on the basis of equality with the original thirteen states. This was not an idea that originated with Jefferson, though he was one of its early proponents, having included a similar provision in his draft of a constitution for Virginia in 1776. In 1780 the Continental Congress had given preliminary approval to a Virginia resolution introduced by Joseph Jones and James Madison stating the same principle, but it had not then been finally adopted. [30]

In 1784 Jefferson proposed the creation of fourteen new western states, though the exact number was not specified in the report, which suggested names for ten. [31] His list included Saratoga and Washington, but most of the names were Indian derivatives with classical endings, among them Assenisipia, Cherronesus, and Pelisipia. The measure adopted specified neither the names nor the exact number of states, but it included a modified version of Jefferson's plan for two tiers of new states between the Atlantic coast states and the Mississippi River, each new state covering two degrees of latitude from north to south. Under this projection, the Ohio River would not have formed a state boundary line in the westernmost tier of states, and all the territory both north and south of that river was to be organized under the same provisions. Because the Ordinance of 1784 was thus to apply to all of the western territory, the committee's proposal that after 1800 slavery be prohibited there was of considerable importance. This provision, however, failed to pass Congress. Jefferson and Hugh Williamson of North Carolina were the only southern delegates to support it. Later the principle would be revived in the Ordinance of 1787 and prescribed for the territory north of the Ohio River. The plan of government for the territories agreed to by Congress in 1784 provided for stages of territorial government, beginning with the right of settlers to form a temporary government by adopting the constitution and laws of any of the original states. When a territory acquired twenty thousand free inhabitants, Congress would authorize the calling of a constitutional convention to establish a permanent republican government. Once the free population reached the equivalent of that of the least numerous of the thirteen original states, the state would be admitted into the Union on an equal footing with the original states. Thus the 1784 plan, unlike the later Northwest Ordinance, provided for local self-government at every stage.[32] Even if we cannot credit Jefferson with originating all of the ideas that went into the report that he drafted, his advocacy of it showed his vision of an expanding nation of republican states and his faith in western settlers to govern themselves.

Soon after preparing his report on western lands, Jefferson wrote a report for a committee on the national debt, showing that he was not so unprepared on that subject for his later battles with Alexander Hamilton as he is sometimes seen.[33] At the same time he was also working on proposals to make the dollar the American unit of money and to apply, for the first time in history, the decimal system of reckoning to coinage. The latter proposal was part of a broader design to use the decimal system for weights and measures, but that proposition would not be brought forward until later. Although in his autobiography Jefferson gave first place among his principal legislative concerns in 1784 to the system of coinage, his proposal did not actually come before Congress in that session.[34] A year later, Congress would adopt the principle of decimal coinage, and it is understandable that he would look back upon it as one of his chief legislative achievements, but the proposal had not matured before he left the Congress early in May.

Jefferson's service in the Confederation Congress ended abruptly when Congress on May 7, 1784, appointed him as minister plenipotentiary to join John Adams and Benjamin Franklin in Europe to negotiate treaties of amity and commerce. Four days later he left Annapolis, closing a legislative career that during the preceding fifteen years had provided his most important political education and produced some of his most lasting contributions to Virginia and to the new nation. Though he could not anticipate it at the time, he would not again sit in a legislative body, except to preside over the Senate as vice-president, where he would not otherwise be involved in the legislative process.

Within a week after his appointment, Jefferson was back in Philadelphia to pick up Patsy, who was to go with him to France. He did not plan to return home before sailing and sent to Virginia for his mulatto slave ("servant," he called him) James Hemings to come to Philadelphia to accompany him to Europe. He also wrote to William Short, a young Virginian and protégé, to join him as his private secretary, and he sent a power of attorney to Nicholas Lewis of Albemarle County and Francis Eppes, husband of his late wife's sister Elizabeth, in whose home his two younger daughters had been living since his wife's death.[35] It would be three years before he again saw his daughter Mary, then called Polly; she would join him in Paris. He would never again see his youngest child, Lucy Elizabeth, who succumbed to the whooping cough a few months after he left America.

Jefferson decided to sail to Europe from Boston partly because he wanted to see New England. Never having been north of New York City, he convinced himself that, before negotiating commercial treaties, a tour of the eastern states would better enable him to represent their interests.[36] With John Adams a member of the commission, it was unlikely that New England's interests would be neglected. In fact, Jefferson had been named to the commission to ensure that southern interests had a voice in the negotiations. Yet it is understandable that he would want to see his own country before he saw Europe, and he was assiduous in collecting information in New York and New England. On the way to Boston, he stopped in New Haven and visited with Ezra Stiles, the president of Yale, who recorded in his diary that he found Jefferson "a most ingenuous Naturalist and Philosopher, a truly scientific and learned Man, and every way excellent."[37] His route took him through Hartford, New London, Newport, Providence, and smaller towns before reaching Boston on June 18, and while waiting for passage, he made an additional exploration along the coast and into New Hampshire. Back in Boston on June 26, he sailed on the *Ceres* bound for London early in the morning of July 5. He hoped to be set ashore on the coast of France at Brest.[38]

In addition to the instructions from Congress and the twenty commissions to different countries for Adams, Franklin, and himself that he carried with him, he took the manuscript of his *Notes on Virginia* and a catalog of his library. He also traveled with considerable other baggage, including his phaeton (for which he would hire horses and postilions when he reached France), the skin of a large panther (which he took to convince Buffon that animals in the New World were not smaller than those in the Old World), and the recently painted canvas of a portrait of George Washington by Joseph Wright, completed just before he left Philadelphia.[39]

The Atlantic crossing was exceptionally smooth and swift. Patsy wrote that "we had a lovely passage in a beautiful new ship that had only made one voyage before. There were only six passengers, all of whom papa knew, and a fine sun shine all the way, with the sea . . . as calm as a river. I should have no objection at making another voyage if I could be sure it would be as agreable as the first." Her father, with his passion for meticulous observations, recorded the latitude and longitude at noon each day and calculated the distance covered during the preceding twenty-four hours, along with the direction of the wind and the temperature.[40] Nineteen days after weighing anchor at Boston, the *Ceres* was in fifty fathoms of water off the south coast of England. Jefferson's hope of being put ashore on the French coast was not realized, and he went ashore at West Cowes on July 26. He did not intend to tarry in England, but after Patsy took ill at the end of the voyage, they stopped in Portsmouth for several days. Jefferson summoned a physician and nurses, and Patsy soon recovered her health, while he had his first sights of England. On the evening of July 30 they took a boat across the channel to Le Havre. After a miserable night cramped in a tiny cabin and tossed about in rough seas, they arrived on the coast of France at seven the next morning.[41]

When Jefferson first set foot in France, a stranger in a foreign land, it was the beginning of a new experience that would bring him closer to a culture that he had admired from a distance and also expose him to its defects. He had no idea that it would be five years before he would return to America, for he anticipated a mission of no more than two years; he obviously could not foresee the momentous events that he would witness in France before he departed for Virginia in the fall of 1789. It would be unlike any other period in his life. Although sometimes lonely, he would come to appreciate the experience and cherish the memories. The years in France were broadening and rewarding, but the pull of his own country and his longing for Monticello remained undiminished, and his appreciation of America was even more deeply enhanced.

VIII
The Scene of Europe

Jefferson arrived in Paris on August 6, 1784, six days after landing at Le Havre, where he had endured those difficulties perennially greeting visitors to that shore. Although he knew French, he had difficulty making himself understood, and he was overcharged on handling his baggage. He traveled to Paris in his phaeton with his daughter Patsy and his servant James Hemings, a mulatto slave whom he would emancipate a decade later. The unusual carriage attracted attention everywhere along the route and was frequently surrounded by beggars. Patsy counted nine at one stop to change horses. They stayed two days in Rouen, then followed the road along the Seine to Paris, "thro the most beautiful country I ever saw in my life, it is a perfect garden," Patsy reported. She also commented on the beautiful stained-glass windows in the cathedrals they visited. Jefferson said nothing about the cathedrals, but he, too, was captivated by the farming country along the Seine. "Nothing can be more fertile, better cultivated or more elegantly improved," he wrote. At Marly, near Paris, Jefferson paid to see the celebrated Machine de Marly beside the Seine, where huge wooden wheels raised water from the river and pumping stations carried it to reservoirs on high ground.[1]

In Paris, Jefferson first took lodgings at the Hôtel d'Orléans adjoining the Palais Royal, but after a few days he transferred to another hotel of the same name on the Left Bank. The first thing that this father of a twelve-year-old daughter did upon arriving in Paris was to outfit her in suitable clothes. Two days later he bought himself a pair of lace ruffles, and shortly thereafter he purchased a sword and belt and began fitting himself out in the Paris fashion. He also bought a map of Paris and was soon making his first purchases of books. Jefferson promptly placed Patsy in a convent school (the Abbaye Royale de Panthemont), where no one spoke

English, and she knew hardly a word of French. Though feeling deserted at first, Patsy quickly learned the language and a year later was writing that she was "charmed with my situation." Jefferson said the school was "altogether the best in France, and at which the best masters attend. There are in it as many protestants as Catholics, and not a word is ever spoken to them on the subject of religion." However, Patsy reported that during her first year she saw two nuns take the veil.[2]

In October, 1784, Jefferson leased a house in the Cul-de-sac Taitbout, in the vicinity of the opera. He would remain there for about a year before moving to the Hôtel de Langeac bordering the Champs-Elysées. In that stately and spacious town mansion, he lived in greater style during his last four years in France. His household included David Humphreys, secretary to the American commission, and William Short, his private secretary. After renting a house, Jefferson had to buy furniture and furnishings and to increase his staff. He soon had a sizable establishment, hired a carriage with two horses (which required a coachman), and found that his "first expences or Outfit" exceeded his total initial year's salary.[3]

Jefferson's first winter in Paris was trying. His health was poor, and in January, 1785, Lafayette brought him the sad news from Virginia that his youngest daughter, Lucy Elizabeth, had died. "I have had a very bad winter," Jefferson wrote in March, "having been confined the greatest part of it. A seasoning as they call it is the lot of most strangers: and none I believe have experienced a more severe one than myself."[4] By then the spring sun was improving his health and his spirits. He was walking four or five miles a day and feeling much stronger.

In the summer of 1785, as his first year in France was ending, Jefferson began to reflect on his reactions to Europe. Urging James Monroe, who had read law with him while he was governor of Virginia, to pay him a visit in Paris, he insisted: "The pleasure of the trip will be less than you expect but the utility greater. It will make you adore your own country, it's soil, it's climate, it's equality, liberty, laws, people, and manners. My god! How little do my countrymen know what precious blessings they are in possession of, and which no other people on earth enjoy. I confess I had no idea of it myself."[5]

A few months later Jefferson expanded on his view of French society. "Behold me at length on the vaunted scene of Europe!" he wrote to Carlo Bellini, an Italian friend teaching at the College of William and Mary. "You are perhaps curious to know how this new scene has struck a savage of the mountains of America. Not advantageously I assure you. I find the general fate of humanity here most deplorable. The truth of Voltaire's observation offers itself perpetually, that every man here must be either the hammer or the anvil." The great mass of people were suffering under physical and moral oppression, he felt, while among the privileged class "intrigues of love occupy the younger, and those of ambition the more elderly part of the great." Domestic happiness as experienced in America was unknown in France. In science, the mass of people were two centuries behind Americans, "their literati half a dozen years before us." This latter gap was not so bad, Jefferson reasoned, because it gave time for all the nonsense that was published to be weeded out before it reached America. Although he began with negative comments, he concluded with positive reactions to French society. He wished that Americans could imitate more the manners of polite society. "Here it seems that a man might pass a life without encountering a single rudeness." He commented favorably on French temperance in drinking. "I have never yet seen a man drunk in France, even among the lowest of the people." But he reserved his highest praise for French culture. "Were I to proceed to tell you how much I enjoy their architecture, sculpture, painting, music, I should want words. It is in these arts they shine." Perhaps the thing that he most envied, he said, was the opportunity the French had to enjoy good music.[6]

This observant, appreciative, yet intensely American visitor expressed similar sentiments to others, but he also found the goodness of the French people and the advantages of their country negated by "one single curse, that of a bad form of government." He was convinced that of the twenty million people in France, nineteen million were "more wretched, more accursed in every circumstance of human existence, than the most conspicuously wretched individual of the whole United States."[7]

Such commentaries are among the most interesting passages in Jefferson's letters from France, but Jefferson had gone to France not as a leisured observer of European society but as a working diplomat to negotiate commercial treaties. As his collecting of data before leaving America indicated, he took his charge seriously, and upon arriving in France, he devoted all of the energies he could muster to that task. By the fall of 1784 he had versed himself on existing treaties with France, the Netherlands, and Sweden and drafted a model treaty for use in negotiating with other nations.[8] The details of the various negotiations that Adams, Franklin, and

Jefferson undertook—most of which were futile—are not essential to this account of Jefferson's life, but an analysis of his role in these commercial negotiations yields several findings of broad relevance. The documents show that Jefferson was assiduous and characteristically systematic in preparing himself for the negotiations, that he became highly versed in commercial matters, and that he sought to use the negotiations to accomplish purposes broader than those of commerce.

He saw the signing of commercial treaties as strengthening the new and shaky union of American states. The only power the Confederation Congress could exercise over commerce was through its treaty-making authority. "If therefore it is better for the states that Congress should regulate their commerce, it is proper that they should form treaties with all nations with whom we may possibly trade," he believed. No strict constructionist at this time, he thought it essential for Congress to regulate commerce, confiding to Monroe:

> You see that my primary object in the formation of treaties is to take the commerce of the states out of the hands of the states, and to place it under the superintendance of Congress, so far as the imperfect provisions of our constitution will admit, and until the states shall by a new compact make them more perfect. I would then say to every nation on earth, *by treaty*, your people shall trade freely with us, and ours with you, paying no more than the most favoured nation, in order to put an end to the right of individual states acting by fits and starts to interrupt our commerce or to embroil us with any nation.[9]

Jefferson's position placed him firmly on the side of those who wished to strengthen the union of states and reform the constitutional apparatus that so fragilely held them together. In addition to this national goal, Jefferson also saw the negotiations as an opportunity to advance important international purposes by improving the existing law of nations. He included in his model treaty an article to permit merchant vessels employed solely in carrying commerce between nations to sail unmolested in time of war and to allow merchants of other countries at the outbreak of war to remain in an enemy country for nine months to collect their debts, settle their affairs, and depart freely. The article also would shield from war "all women and children, scholars of every faculty, cultivators of the earth, artizans, manufacturers and fisherman, unarmed, and inhabitating unfortified towns, villages, or places; whose occupations are for the common subsistence and benefit of mankind."

Another article provided for better treatment of prisoners of war. Frederick the Great of Prussia approved of these enlightened terms, but other powers held back. When the treaty with Prussia was the only one completed, Jefferson's early hope of signing treaties with many nations was rudely dispelled. "They seemed in fact to know little of us, but as rebels who had been successful in throwing off the yoke of the mother country," he later recalled. "They were ignorant of our commerce, which had been always monopolized by England, and of the exchange of articles it might offer advantageously to both parties. They were inclined therefore to stand aloof until they could see better what relations might be usefully instituted with us."[10] It soon became evident to him that commercial negotiations would take far longer than he had anticipated.

Jefferson carried the manuscript of his *Notes on the State of Virginia* with him when he went to France. Before leaving the United States, he completed the revision of the work, now "swelled nearly to treble bulk." Originally planning to have a few copies printed in Philadelphia to give to friends, he found printing costs there so expensive that he decided to defer it until he got to France. In Paris he discovered that the cost of printing would be one-fourth that in Philadelphia and ordered two hundred copies printed.[11]

His intention still was to circulate the work privately. When the book came from the printers in the spring of 1785, he began sending copies to friends, along with notes cautioning them not to trust the book to anyone who might make it public.[12] "My reason is," he explained to Monroe, "that I fear the terms in which I speak of slavery and of our constitution may produce an irritation which will revolt the minds of our countrymen against the reformation of these two articles, and thus do more harm than good."[13] He told Chastellux that he had no objection to his making extracts for the *Journal de Physique*, because these would not include his passages on slavery and the constitution of Virginia.

> It is possible that in my own country these strictures might produce an irritation which would indispose the people towards the two great objects I have in view, that is the emancipation of their slaves, and the settlement of their constitution on a firmer and more permanent basis. If I learn from thence, that they will not produce that effect, I have printed and reserved just copies enough to be able to give one to every young man at the College. It is to them I look, to the rising generation, and not to the one now in power for these great reformations.[14]

When Jefferson sought Madison's advice on the idea of distributing copies to the students at William and Mary, Madison conferred with George Wythe and replied that Jefferson's strictures would displease some, but "we think both the facts and remarks which you have assembled too valuable not to be made known, at least to those for whom you destine them." Wythe suggested, however, that Jefferson deposit the books in the library, rather than distribute them among the students, which "might offend some narrow minded parents." Meanwhile, Charles Thomson had written Jefferson of his distress "that there should be such just grounds for your apprehension respecting the irritation that will be produced in the southern states by what you have said of slavery. However I would not have you discouraged. This is a cancer that we must get rid of." [15]

Before Jefferson received either Madison's response or Thomson's letter, he was already doubting that he could limit the circulation of the book. "I have been obliged to give so many of them here that I fear their getting published," he confided. His fears were soon realized after a copy got into the hands of a bookseller upon the death of one recipient. When he tried to recover this copy, he learned that the bookseller had hired a translator and was about to publish "a very abominable translation." Under these circumstances he accepted the offer of Abbé Morellet, a member of the French Academy and an acquaintance to whom Jefferson had presented a copy, to provide the translation. Despite Jefferson's supervision of the text, the result was undistinguished. [16]

Once the book became public in France, an English edition seemed certain to follow. Madison warned Jefferson that unless he released the original text, the French translation would inevitably be translated back into English and be published in both England and America. Finding Morellet's version unsatisfactory and the prospect of an English translation from it even worse, Jefferson authorized the publication of an English edition by John Stockdale, sending him a carefully corrected copy of the 1785 Paris edition and the plate of a map that he had prepared for Morellet's edition. In July, 1787, Stockdale published a superior edition, which would be the basis for all subsequent editions published during Jefferson's lifetime. Stockdale's edition was the first to carry the author's name on the title page. [17]

Jefferson was now publicly the author of an important book attracting favorable attention, though he was still reluctant to acknowledge its value. At the time of its first printing he reported from Paris to Charles Thomson in Philadelphia that there was nothing new in literature, "for I do not consider as having added any thing to that field my own Notes." Corresponding with Stockdale about the English edition, he stressed that he had never intended to make his *Notes* public, "because they are little interesting to the rest of the world. But as a translation of them is coming out, I have concluded to let the original appear also." Jefferson's deprecatory tone was rejected by his contemporaries. In thanking him for his copy, John Adams wrote that "it will do its Author and his Country great Honour. The Passages upon Slavery, are worth Diamonds. They will have more effect than Volumes written by mere Philosophers." Chastellux, who had been so much impressed with Jefferson when he visited him at Monticello, called it "an excellent memoir" and judged the sections on natural history and politics to be especially valuable.[18] The *Monthly Review* of London gave the book a mildly condescending notice, finding "much to applaud, as well as some things to which we cannot afford a ready assent." The *Mercure de France*, the leading periodical in the French capital, was more enthusiastic, and Abbé Morellet wrote Franklin that Jefferson's work had been very well received in Paris.[19] Whatever Jefferson's reservations—which sprang in part from his not having started out to write a book—his *Notes on Virginia* established him as a man of letters, student of natural history, scientist, and political theorist on both sides of the Atlantic.

Early in 1785 Congress accepted the plea of the seventy-nine-year-old Franklin to return home and elected Jefferson to succeed him as minister to France. Jefferson received his commission on May 2, and two weeks later he went to Versailles to be received by Louis XVI in an elaborate ritual that he described simply as "ceremonies usual on such occasions."[20] John Adams, who had been appointed as minister to England, was delighted that Jefferson was to remain in Europe. Terming Jefferson's stationing in Paris as "a very fortunate Circumstance, both for me and the public," he called Jefferson "an excellent Citizen, Philosopher and Statesman."[21] Jefferson would stay at this post for the next four years, a distant spectator of those important developments in America that culminated in the drafting of the new Constitution of 1787 and its closely contested ratification completed in the summer of 1788. Those momentous changes taking place in his absence would be overshadowed by the even more portentous events that shook Europe, for before he departed for home in October, 1789, Jefferson would witness the dramatic opening incidents of the French Revolution.

As absorbed as Jefferson became in those events, America was always his first concern, and throughout his residence in France he attempted to stay abreast of happenings at home. He early discovered how difficult it was to obtain news from America, and he was solicitous of his friends, especially Madison and Monroe, to keep him informed. "Nothing can equal the dearth of American intelligence in which we live here," he wrote after his first six months in France. "I had formed no conception of it. We might as well be in the moon."[22] To counter this, he made arrangements to have American newspapers from different states sent to him by the French packet that sailed from New York on the fifteenth of every month, and he was careful to keep up his letter-writing contacts in the United States.

Jefferson's initial concerns as minister to France were the same as those that had occupied his attention as a commissioner charged with negotiating treaties of amity and commerce: to promote the independence and economic well-being of the United States. In his autobiography Jefferson remarked that "my duties at Paris were confined to a few objects; the receipt of our whale-oils, salted fish, and salted meats on favorable terms, the admission of our rice on equal terms with that of Piedmont, Egypt and the Levant, a mitigation of the monopolies of our tobacco by the Farmers-general, and a free admission of our productions into their islands." While this list modestly underestimated the importance of these issues and his duties, Jefferson's recollection was accurate in emphasizing the primacy of commercial concerns.[23]

One of the major problems that required Jefferson's attention and attracted his interest while in France was that of the Barbary pirates. The documents that he carried with him from America authorized the opening of negotiations with Morocco, Algiers, and Tripoli, but early initiatives met with little success. A treaty with Morocco at the relative low cost of thirty thousand dollars negotiated by Thomas Barclay in 1787 was the only achievement.[24] The basic problem remained unresolved. The states along the north coast of Africa were accustomed to exacting tributes from most of the nations whose ships sailed the Mediterranean. They enforced their demands by capturing ships and cargoes and holding their crews for ransom. Americans found European governments secretive about the amounts of tributes they were paying, but they surmised that it was considerable and that the demands upon the United States would be substantial—more money, Jefferson thought, than the American people would be willing to pay. Besides, the very idea of paying tribute rankled him. "When this idea comes across my mind, my faculties are absolutely suspended between indignation and impotence," he remarked. He early favored the use of military force over the paying of tribute to protect American commerce. This later opponent of navies suggested in 1784 that "we ought to begin a naval power, if we mean to carry on our own commerce. Can we begin it on a more honourable occasion or with a weaker foe? I am of opinion Paul Jones with a half dozen frigates would totally destroy their commerce . . . by constant cruising and cutting them to pieces by piecemeal." It was his view that "if we wish our commerce to be free and uninsulted, we must let these nations see that we have an energy which at present they disbelieve."[25]

Jefferson quickly recognized the advantages of joining some of the Mediterranean states already at war with the Barbary states. This led him to the idea of some sort of international force to patrol the Mediterranean. In 1786 he brought forward a proposal for a confederation to be managed by a council of the diplomatic representatives of the cooperating powers.[26] Jefferson enlisted Lafayette in support of the plan, and the latter became so committed to the idea that he proposed himself as "a Chief to the Antipiratical Confederacy."[27] Because of differences between Jefferson and Adams regarding dealing with the Barbary issue, Jefferson relied on Lafayette to present the plan to John Jay and other Americans and did not himself directly submit the proposal to Congress or its secretary of foreign affairs. Jefferson later blamed Congress for not providing the naval force necessary to participate in such a confederacy, but French Foreign Minister Vergennes told Lafayette privately that the scheme was foredoomed to failure because of the opposition of France and England.[28] The realities of eighteenth-century political and commercial rivalries precluded the success of the foresighted proposal, but Jefferson revived the idea when he became secretary of state, though with no more success than he had met with earlier. Later as president he would return to his original position that the United States should employ a naval force against the Barbary states, and as commander in chief he would successfully order such an expedition.

Negotiations initiated by Adams in London with Tripoli and Portugal prompted Jefferson to accede to Adams' request that he come to London in the spring of 1786. He also undertook the trip with the dim hope of joining Adams in negotiating a commercial treaty with Great Britain before the expiration of their two-year commission. Nothing came of the negotiations with Tripoli. A treaty was signed with the Portuguese ambassador but rejected by his government, and the British never even agreed to begin talking—altogether a fruitless diplomatic mission. The six-week stay in England was Jefferson's longest sojourn in the land of his ancestors and fixed in his mind impressions that would last throughout his life. These impressions were not favorable. When presented to the king and queen, he sensed that "it was impossible for anything to be more ungracious than their notice of Mr. Adams and myself." At the first conference with the minister of foreign affairs, he found that "the vagueness and evasions of his answers to us, confirmed me in the belief of their aversion to have anything to do with us." [29]

The evasions and excuses of the British about beginning talks left Jefferson with considerable free time. He had leisure to sit for a portrait—the first ever to be taken of him—by Mather Brown, who had recently painted John Adams. With time to travel he made a trip to see Windsor Castle. Later he and Adams made an extended tour of the gardens of England, stopping along the way to see the colleges at Oxford and to visit Shakespeare's birthplace at Stratford-on-Avon. [30] The gardens were the sights that Jefferson most enjoyed in England, and he walked through them carrying a copy of Thomas Whately's *Observations on Modern Gardening* (1770) and jotting down in a notebook his own impressions and critiques. [31] The inquiries that he made about the expenses of maintaining such gardens and other practical considerations showed that he was thinking about how he might apply what he saw to Monticello. Some of his comments were critical. He found the gardens at Hampton Court "old fashioned"; at Chiswick "the garden shows still too much of art; an obelisk of very ill effect"; at Stowe "the Corinthian arch has a very useless appearance." But he found the clumps of trees at Esher-Place "a most lovely mixture of concave and convex," a beautiful Doric temple at Paynshill, and elsewhere he mixed approving comments with criticisms. His overall verdict was that gardening in England "surpasses all the earth. . . . This indeed went far beyond my ideas." [32]

On the other hand, while finding the city of London handsomer than Paris, he thought it not so handsome as Philadelphia. "Their architecture is in the most wretched stile I ever saw, not meaning to except America where it is bad, nor even Virginia where it is worse than in any other part of America, which I have seen." In comparing England and France, he judged the soil better in France, the laboring people better off in England. He admired the British for their "wonderful perfection" in the mechanical arts. Although he found some good things to say about their country, he left England convinced that "that nation hates us, their ministers hate us, and their king more than all other men."[33]

Jefferson was more restrained in his official report to Jay, but the verdict was the same. "The nation is against any change of measures; the ministers are against it, some from principle, others from subserviency; and the king more than all men is against it." Because George III might be expected to have a long reign, Jefferson saw little hope for any improvement in the near future. "Even the opposition dares not open their lips in favor of a connection with us, so unpopular would be the topic. It is not that they think our commerce unimportant to them. I find that the merchants here set sufficient value on it. But they are sure of keeping it on their own terms." The British believed their commerce indispensable to America, he wrote to several correspondents. "They think we cannot unite to retaliate upon them. I hope we can, and that we shall exclude them from carrying our produce, if not suppress their commerce altogether."[34] Jefferson thus returned to Paris more convinced than ever of the necessity of expanding and improving commercial relations with France and more keenly conscious of the importance of the task still before him in the French capital.

IX
Romantic Interlude
and New Adventures

In London Jefferson met John Trumbull, a thirty-year-old aspiring American artist who had studied with Benjamin West. The son of former governor Jonathan Trumbull of Connecticut, he had served on Washington's staff early in the Revolutionary War and was now planning a series of historical paintings of the Revolution—a project that Jefferson encouraged him to pursue. Jefferson's enthusiasm for the fine arts and his characteristic hospitality prompted him to invite Trumbull to visit him in Paris and to make his home with him while in France.[1]

The American minister was already directly involved in employing the fine arts to perpetuate the achievements of the Revolution, having recently carried out a request of the Virginia legislature to commission a statue of General Washington. He had done this in a way that demonstrated his knowledge of the arts and his desire to advance their appreciation in America. The Virginia Assembly would have been satisfied with a statue taken from a painting of Washington, but Jefferson sought out an artist whose reputation was unrivaled in Europe, and engaged Jean-Antoine Houdon to journey to America to make a plaster model of Washington's bust from life and take the necessary measurements to complete the marble statue in Paris. In justification of the expense of Houdon's trip to America, Jefferson told the governor of Virginia that no statue of Washington providing "true evidence of his figure to posterity" could be made from a picture. In seeking the cooperation of Washington for the sittings, he said that Houdon enjoyed "the reputation of being the first statuary in the world."[2] Washington obligingly sat for Houdon at Mount Vernon in October, 1785, and when Houdon returned to Paris with the plaster bust, Jefferson expressed great pleasure with the result.[3] He himself would sit for Houdon in 1789 before leaving France.

Jefferson's encouragement of Trumbull was a different sort of relationship than his commissioning of Houdon, who already was in demand in the courts of Europe, but in each case Jefferson played a role in a major artistic achievement commemorating the American Revolution. Houdon's marble statue of Washington stands today in the Virginia Capitol, and the life-size version of Trumbull's painting of the signing of the Declaration of Independence, completed in 1818, hangs in the rotunda of the United States Capitol.

It was at the Hôtel de Langeac, where the young Trumbull took up temporary residence as part of the American minister's household in late summer of 1786, that Trumbull drew the first sketches for *The Declaration of Independence*. Jefferson himself sketched a rough floor plan of the room in Independence Hall and assisted the artist in forming the composition of the painting depicting the drafting committee and the other signers. Trumbull made his first sketch of the famous painting on the same sheet of paper that Jefferson used to sketch the plan of the room.[4] Trumbull's ambition to draw all of the portraits of the surviving signers from life meant that it would be years before the painting was completed, but one of the first figures to be painted on the canvas was Jefferson, whom Trumbull painted from life in late 1787 or early 1788.[5]

The portrait of the tall, vigorous Virginian with unpowdered hair in the prime of life, the central figure in Trumbull's painting, would provide posterity with an indelible image. But Jefferson would best remember Trumbull, not as the painter of historical scenes, but as the friend who introduced him to Maria Cosway—a young Englishwoman who would upset and enliven his ordered life as no one had done in the four years since the death of his wife. Maria Cosway was young, cultivated, and charming, but also married. Trumbull introduced them in August of 1786 and provided the link to join Jefferson with Trumbull's circle of artists and friends of the arts that Jefferson later would refer to as "our charming coterie in Paris." The group included Jacques-Louis David—whose painting Jefferson admired greatly—Houdon and his young wife, several talented amateurs, and Mr. and Mrs. Richard Cosway of London, like Trumbull visitors to the city.[6]

A successful painter of widely popular miniatures, Richard Cosway was about Jefferson's age, well established but, from all reports, far from handsome—small, foppish, and somewhat eccentric. His wife, Maria, then twenty-seven, had been born in Florence of English parents. Educated in Italy and early exposed to music and art, she was talented in both. Having learned Italian as her native tongue, she spoke English with an appealing accent but was never comfortable writing in English. After the death of her father, her mother had returned with her family to London, where the beautiful and talented Maria two years later, at age twenty-two, married the rich and successful Richard Cosway.[7] Their home became a popular salon, but the marriage was not a happy one.[8] When the Duc d'Orleans invited Cosway to Paris to paint the duchesse and her children in the summer of 1786, the Cosways became close friends of Trumbull's, and their paths soon crossed with that of the American minister.[9]

Jefferson would vividly remember the day that he met Maria Cosway. He had gone to see the Halle aux Bleds, a large municipal grain market covered by a huge dome—a structure that attracted his interest because he was considering plans for a public market in Richmond. He was overjoyed with "this wonderful piece of architecture," but his interest soon shifted to the party to whom Trumbull introduced him. His eyes fixed upon Maria Cosway, and the noble dome and superb arches of the Halle aux Bleds shrank into insignificance. The forty-three-year-old widower was swept off his well-planted feet by the beautiful and charming young Maria. He saw in her all the ideals that he associated with feminity—"music, modesty, beauty, and that softness of disposition which is the ornament of her sex and charm of ours." He contrived to join the party for dinner, sending off a messenger to the Duchesse d'Enville saying that dispatches had arrived requiring his immediate attention and forcing him to break his dinner engagement. After dining together, the new group rode to Saint-Cloud, made other stops, and Jefferson later confessed to contriving to extend the day as long as possible. The adventures of the day were never to be forgotten. "How well I remember them all," he told Maria, "and that when I came home at night and looked back to the morning, it seemed to have been a month agone."[10]

This was only the beginning of a month of nearly constant going. Trumbull recalled that Jefferson joined the party of friends almost daily, exploring the artistic treasures of Paris and nearby points of interest. Richard Cosway, busy with his painting, was apparently absent from many of the excursions, and with Maria at his side Jefferson found every scene enchanting. He recalled the day they went to Saint-Germain. "How beautiful was every object! the Port de Neuilly, the hills along the Seine, the rainbows of the machine of Marly, the terras of Saint-Germains, the chateaux, the gardens, the [statues] of Marly. . . . Every moment was filled with something agreeable. The wheels of time moved on with a rapidity of which those of our carriage gave but a faint idea, yet in the evening, when one took a retrospect of the day, what a mass of happiness had we travelled over!" [11]

Jefferson was completely infatuated with Maria, so much in love, his letters to her suggest, that he no longer felt middle-aged. At the height of his exhilaration he was led into "one of those follies from which good cannot come, but ill may," as he expressed it. Strolling along a promenade by the Seine, he attempted to jump over a fence, came crashing to the ground, and dislocated his right wrist. [12] The wrist was poorly set, and he was still suffering painfully from it when the Cosways left to return to London some two weeks later on October 5. Still, he accompanied them outside Paris to Saint-Denis, shared a farewell meal, and saw them off in their carriage. "More dead than alive," he returned to Paris. [13]

There, writing tediously with his left hand, he penned one of the most remarkable letters of his long life. Addressed to Maria and filling twelve laboriously transcribed pages, the letter took the form of a dialogue between his head and his heart. When his heart spoke, it expressed his joy in throwing reason to the wind and pursuing the fleeting days of happiness with Maria. He confessed his follies but admitted that he cherished the memories. On the days that they had passed together, he wrote,

> the sun shone brightly! How gay did the face of nature appear! Hills, vallies, chateaux, gardens, rivers, every object wore it's liveliest hue! Whence did they borrow it? From the presence of our charming companion. They were pleasing, because she seemed pleased. Alone, the scene would have been dull and insipid: the participation of it with her gave it relish. Let the gloomy Monk, sequestered from the world, seek unsocial pleasures in the bottom of his cell! Let the sublimated philosopher grasp visionary happiness while pursuing phantoms dressed in the garb of truth! Their wisdom is supreme folly: and they mistake for happiness the mere absence of pain. Had they ever felt the solid pleasure of one generous spasm of the heart, they would exchange for it all the frigid speculations of their lives. [14]

When his head spoke, it reminded him of its warning that "you were imprudently engaging your affections under circumstances that must cost you a great deal of pain," that he might never see Maria again, and that his dream that he might show her the sights of America was fanciful. "The art of life is the art of avoiding pain," his reason told him. "The most effectual means of being secure against pain is to retire within ourselves, and to suffice for our own happiness. Those, which depend on ourselves, are the only pleasures a wise man will count on. . . . Hence the inestimable value of intellectual pleasures." It was his heart, however, that had the last word. "I feel more fit for death than life," he wrote. "But when I look back on the pleasures of which it is the consequence, I am conscious they were worth the price I am paying." He hoped that Maria would return to Paris in the spring.[15]

If Maria could not be quite certain from Jefferson's lengthy and complex dialogue whether the head or the heart had won the argument, so too have historians seen the dialogue in different lights. Julian Boyd was convinced that the letter demonstrated that "reason was not only enthroned as the chief disciplinarian of his life, but also . . . was itself a sovereign to which the Heart yielded a ready and full allegiance, proud of its monarch and happy in his rule." On the other hand, Dumas Malone wrote that "the most significant conclusion that emerges from the dialogue is that this highly intellectual man recognized in human life the superior claims of sentiment over reason."[16] The words of the dialogue support Malone's conclusion, but the outcome of the relationship demonstrated that reason ultimately prevailed in ordering Jefferson's life.

When he closed the dialogue, he seemed determined to pursue the relationship with Maria. "God only knows what is to happen," his heart told him. "I see things wonderfully contrived sometimes to make us happy." His letters to her were affectionate and warm, though none was so long, so ebullient, nor so introspective as his initial dialogue. On Christmas Eve of 1786 he wrote her that if he could fly, he would fly to her side and not wish to leave. "If I cannot be with you in reality, I will in imagination," he said.[17] By then he had received three letters from Maria since her return to London. She seems to have been taken aback by his dialogue and found herself so uncomfortable in trying to express herself in English that she reverted to writing in Italian. The modern reader may sense that her letters conveyed to Jefferson less reason for encouragement than his letters to her, but he refused to give up hope of seeing her in the spring.[18] "I had rather be deceived, than live without hope," he confessed. "Think of me much, and warmly. Place me in your breast with those who you love most: and comfort me with your letters." Maria responded with a long letter holding out hope that she would be able to visit Paris in the summer.[19]

Carrying on a correspondence with Maria presented problems to Jefferson that Maria never fully appreciated. All letters of the

American minister sent through the mail were opened by the French post office before they left France and read by British officials before they were delivered in England. Thus Jefferson had to find trusted private persons, such as John Trumbull, to carry his letters to London and deliver them to Maria, and he could only have been disappointed that she devoted so much space in her letters to reproaching him for neglecting to write to her. But if their trans-Channel communications were less than satisfying to either of them, Jefferson eagerly looked forward to Maria's return to Paris, and she, often melancholy during the bleak winters of London—"the air darkened by the fog and smoke"—was anxious to return to the sunshine of Paris. After Jefferson received Maria's letter indicating that it would be summer before there was any prospect of her getting to Paris, he left on a trip to the south of France and northern Italy at the end of February and did not return to Paris until June. It was July 1 before he wrote to Maria, who was clearly upset by his long silence, though his letter was a warm one. "Why were you not with me?" he asked. "So many enchanting scenes which only wanted your pencil to consecrate them to fame." When was she coming to Paris? he wanted to know.[20]

After scolding him for neglecting her, Maria replied that she feared she would be unable to come. "My husband begins to doubt it, just at the time when one should begin to prepare to leave. You cannot believe how much this uncertainty displeases me, when I have everything to fear against my desire." The next reference to Maria's summer plans found in Jefferson's papers is in a letter from Trumbull to Jefferson from London on August 28, saying that "before this reaches you, Mrs. Cosway will be with you." Trumbull was sorry that he could not be there at the same time. Shortly afterward Jefferson confirmed that Maria had arrived in Paris.[21] She had come alone. What had happened in the Cosway household is not known. Under what circumstances she left or what her husband thought of it is not known. But she was in Paris, and both she and Jefferson must have anticipated repeating the joys of the preceding summer. This was not to be. We can only speculate as to the reasons.

We know that she spent time with Jefferson and that they returned to some of the places they had visited the year before. There is also the hint in one of her notes to him before leaving Paris that Jefferson had discreetly sought to arrange for them to be alone when she had visited him at his house. But something went wrong that second summer; whether it was from Jefferson's recovery from his earlier infatuation or from Maria's unwillingness to pursue the relationship further can only be surmised. In November Jefferson confided to Trumbull that he had not seen Maria as much as he had expected. "From the meer effect of chance, she has happened to be from home several times when I have called on her, and I, when she called on me." Maria herself told Jefferson that "if my inclination had been your law I should have had the pleasure of seeing you more than I have." Jefferson on the other hand felt that she was putting obstacles to their seeing each other in private. She was staying with her friend Princess Lubomirski, whose house was some distance from Jefferson's Hôtel de Langeac, and she seemed more interested in being a part of a fashionable salon than escaping with Jefferson to Saint-Cloud. Jefferson later referred to her being "surrounded by a numerous cortege" and his being able to see her "only by scraps." "The time before we were half days, and whole days together, and I found this too little," he wrote her after she returned to London.[22]

Jefferson's sense of a growing gulf between them may be explained by Maria's own ambivalence about what she was doing. There seems little doubt that her marriage to Richard Cosway was an unhappy one, but she was totally dependent upon him for financial support, and she was a devout Catholic who had earlier considered becoming a nun. She might have grasped Jefferson as a replacement for her father, and when it was clear that Jefferson would not be satisfied with such a relationship, she was unsure of herself. Marie Kimball saw Maria Cosway's letters as evidence of "a spoiled, egocentric young woman, with a very limited emotional capacity." Fawn Brodie, willing to carry speculation even further, guessed "some kind of crucial failure for Maria in the act of love."[23] Historians do not have enough evidence to probe very deeply into the intimate relationship between Jefferson and Maria Cosway, but after she left Paris in December, 1787, Jefferson would never see her again. Some letters passed between them, and she implored him to come to London, but he never did. He had let his heart reign for a period; now his head reclaimed its dominance.

When Jefferson left Paris on the last day of February, 1787, on his long-delayed trip to the south of France, he did not intend so extensive a tour as he ultimately made. On the way he decided to go on to northern Italy and did not return to Paris until the second week of June. It turned out to be the longest trip he ever took. The immediate occasion—or at least official justification—for the journey was to try the mineral waters at Aix-en-Provence to strengthen his crippled right wrist. Concerned that, five months after his accident, he could not use his wrist for anything except writing, Jefferson was ready to follow the advice of his surgeon to try the waters, though he placed no great faith in their restorative powers. Indeed, he chose Aix-en-Provence from several places suggested to him because it was located near Marseilles—close enough "to take the tour of the ports concerned in commerce with us, to examine on the spot defects of the late regulations respecting our commerce, [and] to learn further improvements which may be made on it." Promoting American trade with France had the highest priority in his diplomacy. In his view "nothing should be spared on our part to attach this country to us. It is the only one on which we can rely for support under every event." When Jefferson's daughter Martha told him that she was inclined to think that his trip was more for pleasure than for health, she was only partly correct.[24] Had she been aware of her father's diplomatic efforts, she would have included commerce as a reason more compelling than the hope of restoring strength to his wrist.

Heading southeast from Paris through Fontainebleau and Sens to Dijon, where he stopped for two days, Jefferson turned south toward Lyon.[25] The weather was miserable. Pelted with rain, hail, and snow, with only "a few gleamings of sunshine to chear me by the way," he welcomed a stop at the Chateau de Laye-Epinaye, and he was glad to reach the Hôtel du Palais Royal in Lyon for a four-day stay. He had left Paris without a servant, planning to hire one at each principal city to accompany him to the next. He believed that "having servants who know nothing of me, places me perfectly at ease," and it also helped him avoid the official recognition and entertainment that his identity as the American minister to France would have produced. He had been unable to get a servant at Fontainebleau as he had intended, but at Dijon he got one who pleased him so much that he decided to retain him throughout the journey. He traveled in his own carriage and used post horses, stopping along the way to see the sights and only occasionally visiting the chateau of a French nobleman to whom he carried an introduction. "To make the most of the little time I have for so long a circuit, I have been obliged to keep myself rather out of the way of good dinners and good company," he wrote after five weeks on the road. "Had they been my objects, I should not have quitted Paris. I have courted the society of gardeners, vignerons, coopers, farmers etc. and have devoted every moment of every day almost, to the business of enquiry." He had found particularly useful his letters of introduction to abbés. "They are unembarrassed with families, uninvolved in form and etiquette, frequently learned, and always obliging," he told Chastellux, who had furnished him with many of his letters of introduction.[26]

In his first report on his travels to William Short, written from Lyon, he said that he had derived as much satisfaction and delight from his journey as he could have anticipated. "Architecture, painting, sculpture, antiquities, agriculture, the condition of the labouring poor fill all my moments." He was a close observer of the countryside, constantly comparing it with Virginia. He thought Burgundy "resembles extremely our red mountainous country, but is rather more stony, all in corn and vine." In Beaujolais, he felt "nature has spread it's richest gifts in profusion." The plains of the Saone were the richest country he had ever seen.[27]

From Lyon to Nîmes the classical-trained Virginian was "nourished with the remains of Roman grandeur," as he wrote excitedly from Nîmes, where for the first time he saw the Maison Carrée. "Here I am, Madam, gazing whole hours at the Maison quarrée, like a lover at his mistress," he wrote to Madame de Tessé.[28] Jefferson had fallen in love with that ancient Roman structure from drawings and paintings. He considered it as "the best morsel of ancient architecture now remaining" and had copied it for the plans of the Virginia State Capitol. The year before visiting Nîmes, he had had a plaster model made and shipped to Virginia. At the very moment that he stood in awe before the original building, construction of the Capitol in Richmond was under way.[29]

Jefferson reached Aix-en-Provence on March 25 and decided after four days that the waters were not helping his wrist. He was, however, delighted with the climate. "I am now in the land of corn, wine, oil, and sunshine," he wrote. "What more can man ask of heaven?" Being able to receive the waters of Aix in Marseilles daily, he proceeded on to the coast. He found Marseilles charming. "All life and activity, and a useful activity like London and Philadelphia." Still, he preferred the countryside. "In the great cities, I go to see what travellers think alone worthy of being seen; but I make a job of it, and generally gulp it all down in a day," he admitted to Lafayette. "On the other hand, I am never satiated with rambling through the fields and farms, examining the culture and the cultivators, with a degree of curiosity which makes some take me to be a fool, and others to be much wiser than I am."[30]

The American minister reported to Jay from Marseilles that he had informed himself about all matters that might be interesting to

American commerce and that he had also sought to discover why Piedmont rice was preferred over Carolina rice. He had heard in Paris that the Italians used a different cleaning machine that left their grain less broken than the American product. His inquiries in Marseilles led him to believe that he would find the Piedmont rice fields just beyond the Alps and be able to see the machines used for cleaning. He thus decided to extend his journey to include northern Italy. When he got to Nice, he learned that the rice fields were farther away than he thought, and he ultimately discovered that Piedmont rice was actually grown in Lombardy. Once he had committed himself to the venture, he never turned back, however, and he set out to cross the Maritime Alps—an adventure this lover of the mountains of Virginia would never forget.[31] Jefferson was overwhelmed by the grandeur of the Alps, and he urged other American travelers to discover the majesty of the crossing through the Tende Pass. In his notes Jefferson described the setting of the Chateau of Saorgo as "the most singular and picturesque I ever saw. The castle and village seem hanging to a cloud in front. On the right is a mountain cloven through to let pass a gurgling stream; on the left a river over which is thrown a magnificent bridge. The whole forms a bason, the sides of which are shagged with rocks, olive trees, vines, herds etc."[32]

Jefferson stopped in Turin and in Milan, but in his travel notes he recorded, as he had in France, his most detailed observations about the countryside. He showed nearly as much interest in cheese-making in Italy as he did in wine-making in France, though he did not neglect Italian wine either. When the Virginia farmer reported on his trip to George Wythe in Williamsburg, he said that he found much pleasure in Italian architecture, painting, and sculpture "but more than all in their agriculture, many objects of which might be adopted with us to great advantage."[33] In the neighborhood of Vercelli he found the rice fields and was able to inspect the rice-cleaning machines. To his surprise, he discovered that they were like the machinery that Edward Rutledge had described to him as being in use in South Carolina. Only one conclusion was to be drawn: the rice was of a different species. Despite a law that prohibited the exportation of seed rice on pain of death, Jefferson was determined to smuggle some out of the country, and he paid a muleteer to run a couple of sacks across the Apennines to Genoa. Having no faith that he would ever see this, however, he filled his own coat pockets with rice from Vercelli—the best grown—and carried it out himself.[34]

As he did in all the cities that he visited, Jefferson bought a guidebook to Milan and saw the sights. He was particularly impressed by the architecture and embellishments of several impressive houses and said that the salon of the Casa Belgioioso was superior to anything else that he had seen.[35] He pronounced the Cathedral of Milan "a worthy object of philosophical contemplation, to be placed among the rarest instances of the misuse of money. On viewing the churches of Italy it is evident without calculation that the expence would have sufficed to throw the Appennines into the Adriatic and thereby render it terra firma from Leghorn to Constantinople."[36]

Jefferson returned to France by way of Genoa. "I scarcely got into classical ground," he wrote. "I calculated the hours it would have taken to carry me on to Rome. But they were exactly so many more than I had to spare." He had to be content with "a peep only into Elysium." Journeying along the Italian Riviera between Luano and Albenga, he reflected that "if any person wished to retire from their acquaintance, to live absolutely unknown, and yet in the midst of physical enjoiments, it would be in some of the little villages of this coast, where air, earth and water concur to offer what each has most precious."[37]

By May 4 Jefferson was back in Marseilles ready to continue his tour of the principal French seaports with which Americans traded. Before returning to Paris he planned to visit the Atlantic ports of Bordeaux, Nantes, and Lorient. Another long-projected plan—to inspect the canal of Languedoc—fitted neatly into this itinerary. That complicated waterway, built during the reign of Louis XIV to connect the Mediterranean with the Atlantic, had long been an object of great interest to him. Even before dislocating his wrist, he had planned a trip to southern France to see the canal in order to gather information for Americans who might undertake canal building.[38]

Jefferson entered the waterway at Cette (Sete) on the Mediterranean and followed it the entire two hundred miles by water to the canal's western terminus at Toulouse, where the Garonne River connected it to the Atlantic. He spent nine days on the trip, minutely examining the canal and making elaborate notes, with details on the locks, their distances from each other, their fall of water, and other information.[39] It was a trip that this observant traveler enjoyed intensely. He had the wheels removed from his carriage, placed the carriage on the deck of a light canal barge, and was towed along the canal, proceeding at his own speed and sleeping ashore. "Of all the methods of travelling I have ever tried this is the pleasantest," he reported. "I walk the greater part of the way along the banks of the canal, level, and lined with a double row of trees which furnish shade. When fatigued I take seat in my carriage where, as much at ease as if in my study, I read, write, or observe. My carriage being of glass all round, admits a full view of all the varying scenes thro' which I am shifted, olives, figs, mulberries, vines, corn and pasture, villages and farms." At one point, he was treated to a double row of nightingales in full song along the banks of the canal.[40]

From Toulouse, Jefferson traveled to Bordeaux through wine country that attracted the same close attention as his trip through Burgundy. His detailed notes show that he had become an expert on almost every aspect of wine production. As he continued on from Bordeaux to Nantes and into Brittany to visit the seaport at Lorient, he persisted, as he had throughout his long journey, in recording detailed notes on the geography, the soil, the crops, and the conditions of the laboring men and women. When he reached Paris on June 10, he had enough notes to write a book. He had enjoyed the adventure tremendously, and he told his secretary, William Short, that the fellow Virginian should not think of returning to America without taking such a tour.[41] Jefferson said he had "never passed three months and a half more delightfully. . . . I was alone thro the whole, and think one travels more usefully when they travel alone, because they reflect more."[42] One surmises that the satisfaction that he received from the months of roaming alone through France and Italy must have played some part in the more restrained attitude that he displayed toward Maria Cosway after he returned to Paris. The long journey may not have helped Jefferson's injured wrist, but it raised his spirits immensely.

X
Witness to Revolution in France

Less than three weeks after returning to Paris—and before he had caught up on all of his work—Jefferson received word from Abigail Adams that his younger daughter, Mary (then called Polly), had arrived safely from Virginia and was waiting for him at the Adamses' house in London.[1] This was an event to which Jefferson had been looking forward for nearly two years. After he succeeded Franklin as minister to France in 1785 and could expect to remain in Europe beyond the two years of his original commission, he wrote to Virginia for Polly to be sent to him. His instructions, designed to ensure the best and safest possible voyage for the child, were explicit. She should sail from Virginia aboard a good vessel during the months of April, May, June, or July only. The ship must have made at least one Atlantic crossing and not be more than five years old. Most ships that were lost at sea, Jefferson believed, were either on their first voyage or over five years old. Polly might be entrusted to the care of "some good lady" coming to France or England or to "a careful gentleman" who would superintend her passage. In the latter case she must be attended by some woman who had had the smallpox. He mentioned one of his slaves, Isabel, as the type of "careful negro woman" who might make the voyage with Polly. "My anxieties on this subject could induce me to endless details," he concluded after composing this list of specific instructions, and he left other arrangements to Elizabeth and Francis Eppes, his sister-in-law and her husband, in whose home Polly was living.[2]

In writing to Polly, Jefferson addressed her in much the same vein that had characterized his earlier letters to her sister. His expressions of love were coupled with admonitions that she must endeavor to merit his love. He even reminded her not to go out in the sun without her bonnet "because it will make you very ugly and then we should not love you so much." Polly, who was four when her mother died, had been living with the Eppes family since then. When she received her father's request to come to Paris, she was seven and had not seen him for two years. That Polly was not eager to leave her aunt, uncle, and cousins in Virginia to join her father in a distant country is not surprising, and she wrote him frankly: "I am very sorry that you have sent for me. I don't want to go to France, I had rather stay with Aunt Eppes."[3]

Jefferson had hoped that his daughter might make the voyage during the summer of 1786, but he said that he would rather wait a year than to trust her to any but a good ship and a summer passage. It was thus 1787 before arrangements were made for her trip, and throughout the months of preparation Polly remained adamant against going to France. "We have made use of every strategem to prevail on her to consent to visit with you without effect," Elizabeth Eppes wrote to Jefferson, hoping that he would countermand his orders.[4] But he had no intention of doing so, convinced that Polly's continued separation from him and her sister would make them strangers throughout life. In May, 1787, Polly was lured aboard ship with her cousins, who stayed and played with her for several days. Then they slipped away while she slept, and the ship set sail. The child was left under the charge of the ship's captain, Andrew Ramsay, to whom she became so attached during the five-week voyage that she cried when she had to leave him. Instead of the mature woman that Jefferson had wanted to accompany her, a fourteen-year-old slave girl, Sally Hemings (whose brother James had accompanied Jefferson to Paris), was sent as her servant and companion.[5]

Polly was met in England by Abigail Adams, to whom she became so attached during her three-week stay with the Adamses that she had to be pried away from her. Mrs. Adams was nearly as taken with the amiable child, who was not yet nine. "I never felt so attached to a child in my Life on so short an acquaintance," she wrote to Polly's father. Jefferson did not ease the trauma of the young girl's adjustment to a new environment, sending a French servant to London to accompany her to Paris instead of going himself, as he had earlier said he would do if she landed in England. When Polly finally reached Paris in July, 1787, she did not recognize either her father or her sister, but Jefferson was soon reporting that she had "renewed her acquaintance and attachment." Placed in the convent school with Patsy, she would make visits to her father once or twice a week. Having her sister to ease the adjustment to the new school, Polly was soon "perfectly happy," her father observed, but he also noticed that "her face kindles with love" at the mention of her Aunt

Eppes. Within a year she was speaking French easily, but her father noted that her thoughts were about Virginia. Polly's coming to Paris and her closeness to family in Virginia no doubt rekindled her father's attachments to home, for he was soon noticing that daughter Patsy, approaching sixteen, might learn from her Aunt Eppes "things which she cannot learn here, and which after all are among the most valuable parts of education *for an American*."[6] By the summer of 1788 Jefferson was thinking about returning to America, but it would be another year before those plans matured.

It is impossible to find in Jefferson's voluminous papers any indication that the arrival of Sally Hemings in Paris with Polly made any difference in his life. Abigail Adams guessed Sally to be about fifteen or sixteen years of age but quite a child and reported that Captain Ramsay was of the opinion that she would be of so little service to Jefferson that he had better carry her back with him. Abigail felt that Jefferson must be the judge of this, but she did note that Sally seemed fond of Polly and appeared good-natured.[7] There is no reason to assume that Jefferson thought of Sally in any other way than as the child that Mrs. Adams saw, and there would be no need to introduce Sally into an account of Jefferson's life at this point had not some writers charged that she became Jefferson's mistress in Paris and remained so through the remainder of his life. Not only is there no valid historical evidence to support this, but the weight of evidence against it is also preponderant. The origins of the charges can be found in the attacks first made while Jefferson was president by James Thomson Callender, a scurrilous writer and disappointed office seeker—a most unreliable source. The pieces of the historical record seized upon by Fawn Brodie in her *Thomas Jefferson: An Intimate History* to indicate a passionate relationship between Jefferson and Sally in Paris fail the test of objective analysis. Brodie suggested that Jefferson's frequent use of the word *mulatto* to describe the soil in Holland and Germany during his trip there in 1788 indicated a preoccupation with Sally Hemings. But as one reviewer pointed out, Brodie did not apply a similar interpretation to Jefferson's repeated reference to red or reddish soil during his trip through southern France. Under Brodie's method, that would have revealed some subconscious sexual preoccupation with his daughter Patsy who had reddish hair. Equally unconvincing is Brodie's emphasis on the fact that Jefferson bought new clothes for Sally Hemings in Paris, for Jefferson would hardly allow his daughter to be escorted in Paris by a shabbily dressed servant. Indeed, the first thing Mrs. Adams did when

Polly and Sally arrived in London was to outfit both of them in new clothes proper for their new environment.[8] The defects of Brodie's work having been fully examined elsewhere, it is unnecessary to dwell upon them here. The evidence indicates that any Paris romance between Jefferson and Sally Hemings belongs in a work of fiction, not of history.[9]

When Jefferson returned from his trip to southern France and northern Italy in June, 1787, he found waiting for him in Paris letters from America reporting the activities under way that would lead to the Constitutional Convention in Philadelphia. By this time the convention was already in session and hard at work. Having been absent from America since 1784, Jefferson had played no part in the events that led to the Philadelphia convention, but he was supportive of the movement to reform the Articles of Confederation. He said that he would not go as far in reforms as some of his correspondents in America, but he was prepared to accept such changes as the members of the convention thought necessary.[10] He was less alarmed by Shays's Rebellion than many of his countrymen. Madison saw the turbulent scenes in Massachusetts as portending a crisis in civil government and feared the Confederation was "tottering to its foundation."[11] Jefferson, on the other hand, wrote: "God forbid we should ever be 20 years without such a rebellion. . . . What country can preserve it's liberties if their rulers are not warned from time to time that their people preserve the spirit of resistance? . . . The tree of liberty must be refreshed from time to time with the blood of patriots and tyrants." But if Jefferson thought the fears of anarchy exaggerated and saw the government of the Confederation as "the best existing or that ever did exist," he still recognized the need to reform its imperfections. His experience as minister to France especially demonstrated the difficulties resulting from Congress' lack of control over commerce and the problems created by its attempts to conduct foreign affairs.[12]

While the convention was sitting, Jefferson wrote to Washington, who presided, that the great objects of the new federal Constitution should be "to make our states one as to all foreign concerns, preserve them several as to all merely domestic, to give to the federal head some peaceable mode of enforcing their just authority, [and] to organize that head into Legislative, Executive, and Judiciary departments." At that time Jefferson knew that the members of the convention were empowered to make a thorough reform in the Confederation, but he had no idea what shape the Constitution was taking. Because the convention held its deliberations behind closed doors and swore its members to secrecy, months passed before Jefferson learned of its outcome and received a copy of the proposed Constitution. Deploring the secrecy, he waited impatiently for news from Philadelphia. With the end of the convention in sight, Madison on September 6 sent him his first report on the proceedings, confident that the convention would have adjourned before the letter reached Paris. It was in fact three months before Jefferson read that letter. Meanwhile, in early November he received his first copy of the Constitution from John Adams in London.[13]

Jefferson's immediate reaction after reading the document was that "there are very good articles in it: and very bad. I do not know which preponderate."[14] In a letter to Madison he elaborated on what he saw as the principal strengths and weaknesses of the new instrument.

> I like much the general idea of framing a government which should go on of itself peacefully, without needing continual recurrence to the state legislatures. I like the organization of the government into Legislative, Judiciary and Executive. I like the power given the Legislature to levy taxes; and for that reason solely approve of the greater house being chosen by the people directly. . . . I am captivated by the compromise of the opposite claims of the great and little states, of the latter to equal, and the former to proportional influence. I am much pleased too with the substitution of the method of voting by persons, instead of that of voting by states: and I like the negative given to the Executive with a third of either house, though I should have liked it better had the Judiciary been associated for that purpose, or invested with a similar and separate power.[15]

Among the things that he did not like, Jefferson emphasized two major defects. First, he objected to the omission of a bill of rights. He told one correspondent that he was astonished by its absence. Second, he deplored the abandonment of the principle of rotation in office, particularly in the case of the president's unrestricted eligibility for reelection. He feared that without a restriction the president would always be reelected and hold office for life.[16]

After studying the document closely and reading detailed commentaries from Madison on the proceedings of the convention, Jefferson concluded: "Were I in America, I would advocate it warmly till nine [states] should have adopted, and then as warmly take the other side to convince the remaining four that they ought not to come into it till the declaration of rights is annexed to it. By this means we should secure all the good of it, and procure so respectable an opposition as would induce the accepting states to offer a bill of rights. This would be the happiest turn the thing could take." This advice, which became known in America before ratification was completed, caused some embarrassment to supporters of the Constitution in the Virginia ratifying convention. Eight states had ratified when that convention met on June 2, 1788, and a ninth ratification was expected from New Hampshire. Patrick Henry, leading the opposition to ratification, appealed to the convention to follow Jefferson's advice and reject the Constitution until amended. Madison, who led the proponents of ratification in the Virginia convention, argued that it was improper to introduce the opinions of men who were not members of the convention, but his acquaintance with Jefferson's views compelled him to say that he believed that if Jefferson were present on the floor he would favor adoption.[17]

Jefferson's own papers indicate that Madison was correct in this opinion. Near the end of May, 1788, Jefferson had written to Edward Carrington: "I learn with great pleasure the progress of the new Constitution. Indeed I have presumed it would gain on the public mind, as I confess it has on my own." He said that he had rejected his earlier proposal that four states should withhold ratification until amendments were added and now favored the plan followed by Massachusetts of ratifying the Constitution and proposing amendments at the same time. This letter had not yet reached Virginia before that state ratified the Constitution on June 25, but it shows that Jefferson was fully in accord with the decision of his native state. In July he told Madison: "I sincerely rejoice at the acceptance of our new constitution by nine states. It is a good canvas, on which some strokes only want retouching."[18]

With the adoption of the Constitution and the steady progress toward the establishment of a new federal system of government in the United States, Jefferson's attention increasingly focused on the rapidly moving events in France, where before his tour of duty ended he would witness some of the most momentous happenings in the history of France. Early in 1787, before Jefferson left on his trip to the south of France, Louis XVI, facing an acute financial crisis, summoned an Assembly of Notables—the first to meet in 160 years. Jefferson saw great hope for change when the Notables gathered, and he watched their proceedings with great interest. By the time he got back to Paris, major forces of change were at work in the country, and by August he was reporting that "the spirit of this country is advancing towards a revolution in their constitution." He placed great faith in the establishment of provincial assemblies that promised "to be the instrument for circumscribing the power of the crown and raising the people into consideration." He marveled at the freedom with which the government was allowing criticism. Caricatures and placards were all over Paris. In a confidential letter to John Adams in London he described the period following the meeting of the Notables as "perhaps the most interesting interval ever known in this country" and went so far as to say that "in the course of three months the royal authority has lost, and the rights of the nation gained, as much ground, by a revolution of public opinion only, as England gained in all her civil wars under the Stuarts." [19]

That was an optimistic view, colored by his own experience in America, his faith in human nature, and his belief in the inevitable spread of liberty.[20] He was no doubt also influenced by his discussion of the principles of government with French intellectuals and his friendship with some of the French leaders, especially Lafayette, who was a member of the Assembly of Notables. With the French ministry engrossed in the internal crisis, Jefferson found fewer opportunities to press American discussions of commercial regulations and more time to watch the changing scene in France. His observations would afford posterity the unique opportunity to view the coming of the revolution in France through the eyes of the author of the American Declaration of Independence.

Early in 1788, however, the immediate problems of the financial affairs of the United States pressed more heavily upon the American minister than the happenings in France. Under the Articles of Confederation the Congress had been so unsuccessful in raising revenue that it had had to borrow money in Holland even to pay interest on its debt held there. While stationed at the Hague, John Adams had received general authority to borrow sums necessary to pay the interest on the debt and maintain the diplomatic establishment in Europe, and he had continued to exercise that authority while minister to England. When Adams began making arrangements to return to the United States in 1788, his duties seemed destined to fall on Jefferson, who regarded himself as "the most unfit person living" to assume such responsibilities.[21]

In December, 1787, the commissioners of the Treasury notified bankers in Amsterdam that they would not be able to pay anything until the new government got into operation in the United States and that the payment of Dutch interest would have to come from the unsubscribed portion of the last loan negotiated by Adams.

The Dutch bankers immediately wrote to Jefferson that there was no probability of raising enough money to meet the next interest in June and indicated that a single day's default would have serious consequences on American credit. At the same time, they presented a scheme in which they agreed to take all the unsubscribed loan in return for being allowed to retain from it the payment of one year's interest on domestic American debt that they held. When Jefferson reported the proposal to Adams, the New Englander was both amused and indignant at its disingenuousness. "I feel no Vanity in saying that this Project never would have been suggested, if it had not been known that I was recalled," he confided to Jefferson. Were he to continue in Europe, he would go to Amsterdam and open a new loan with another banking house rather than submit to this plot. The bankers were buying up immense quantities of American domestic debt, selling at a large discount, and trying to establish the precedent of having the interest on that debt paid in Europe. Jefferson seems not to have suspected this scheme when he wrote to Adams, who had a word of advice for his harassed friend. "I have been constantly vexed with such terrible Complaints and frightened with such long Faces these ten years," he wrote. "Depend upon it, the Amsterdammers love Money too well, to execute their Threats. They expect to gain too much by American Credit to destroy it." [22]

Jefferson was still reluctant to assume Adams' role, believing that he did "not understand bargaining nor possess the dexterity requisite to make them." Thus, when he learned that Adams was going to the Hague for an official leave-taking, he immediately set out for Holland. "Our affairs at Amsterdam press on my mind like a mountain," he wrote to Adams. "I am so anxious to confer with you on this, and to see you and them together, and get some effectual arrangement made in time that I determine to meet you at the Hague." When it took him longer on the road than he had calculated, he nearly panicked, as he envisioned Adams on the packet sailing back across the Channel. Happily, Adams was still at the Hague when Jefferson arrived. The New Englander completed his leave-taking, and together they proceeded to Amsterdam. There they negotiated a new loan that not only ended the immediate crisis but also provided funds to meet the demands of interest and the needs of the diplomatic missions in Europe through 1790. By that time it was expected that the machinery of the new government would be in operation. [23] The loan also provided enough money to pay the interest on debts to French officers who had fought in

America during the Revolutionary War, the neglect of which by the Confederation government had been a source of acute embarrassment to the American minister. The outcome of the frantic journey was such a relief to Jefferson that he lingered to see the sights in Holland, then took a leisurely route back to Paris, traveling along the Rhine through Cologne, Bonn, and Wiesbaden and on to Strassburg, before turning west toward Paris. He spent nearly four weeks on the return trip, reaching Paris on April 23, 1788.[24]

Jefferson found the city in the state of "high fermentation" that prevailed when he left, observing that the "gay and thoughtless Paris is now become a furnace of Politics."[25] Summing up the situation for Jay on May 23, he reported that the king had been called upon to summon the Estates General immediately, that some leaders were maneuvering to get a declaration of rights, and that there was uncertainty about the role and loyalty of the army. "There is neither head nor body in the nation to promise a successful opposition to 200,000 regular troops." His opinion was that a firm but quiet opposition would be the most likely to succeed. "Whatever turn this crisis takes, a revolution in their constitution seems inevitable, unless foreign war supervene, to suspend the present contest." By July he was describing rioting, yet still hoping that changes would come without convulsions. Early in September he reported popular demonstrations in Paris, the deaths of several participants when Paris guards charged with bayonets, and escalating violence until martial law was imposed.[26]

A period of calm returned to Paris after the government consented to summon the Estates General to meet early in 1789. Jefferson repeatedly commented on the "internal tranquillity." Even while following the controversies regarding the composition of the Estates General, he remained exceedingly optimistic about the chances for successful reform of the French government. As he saw it, the king's need for money would create an alliance between the crown and the people, represented by the Third Estate, against the clergy and the nobles, who controlled the wealth of the nation. This would begin a process by which the Estates General would gradually come to share power in the government. He thought the first goals of that body should be to establish the precedent of periodic meetings, the exclusive right of taxation, and the authority to register laws and propose amendments to them. "This would lead, as it did in England," he wrote, "to the right of originating laws." If the Estates General stopped with those gains, future reforms would follow. "But it is to be feared that an impatience to rectify every thing at once, which prevails in some minds, may terrify the court, and lead them to appeal to force, and to depend on that alone." Such an argument for gradual change from this American revolutionary seems uncharacteristically conservative. Jefferson, however, did not believe the mass of French people were prepared for republican government. "They are not yet ripe for receiving the blessings to which they are entitled," he told Madison. At the same time, he had faith in the ultimate progress of French society toward self-government. "The nation has been awakened by our revolution, they feel their strength, they are enlightened, their lights are spreading, and they will not retrograde."[27] Overly optimistic, he either ignored or failed to recognize the rising tide of aristocratic resurgence and continued to trust the nobility to accept enlightened change after many other observers had abandoned this wishful expectation. Indeed, he so much expected a period of gradual change that in November, 1788, he requested permission to return home in the spring for a six-month leave of absence.[28]

There were, it is true, more immediate and personal considerations that prompted the request. Just prior to seeking leave, he had successfully concluded a consular treaty with France that had been in the process of negotiation for some time, leaving him with no major diplomatic problems that required his continuing supervision.[29] After nearly five years in France his lands and affairs in Virginia needed his attention. Above all, he thought it was time to take his two daughters back to America. Sixteen-year-old Martha (Patsy) had spent her teenage years in a convent school, and her father was anxious to get her home in the environment of Virginia where she could meet eligible young men. He had delayed their return because he wanted his younger daughter, Polly, to perfect her French before going home, but now, as he wrote to Elizabeth Eppes, "their future welfare requires that this should no longer be postponed."[30] What he did not tell his sister-in-law was that Martha was giving serious thought to becoming a nun. A year earlier the papal nuncio in Paris, a good friend of Jefferson's, had written to John Carroll of Baltimore that Martha was inclining toward the Catholic religion. "Her father, without absolutely opposing her vocation, has tried to distract her," he wrote, adding that Jefferson hoped that she would wait until she was eighteen until she made a decision.[31] Though Jefferson's desire to remove his daughters from the environment of a convent was not the only reason for his request to return home, it was no doubt a compelling one.

He hoped to sail from France in April, 1789, and to return in November, but his request for leave came at the time of transition from the old government under the Articles to the new one under the Constitution, and he did not receive authorization to leave his post until August. Had his application been acted upon promptly and had he sailed for America in April, he would not have been witness to those dramatic events that shook France and all of Europe in the late spring and summer of 1789.

Jefferson's optimism about the movement of events in France was tempered by the unusual severity of the winter of 1788–1789, when temperatures in Paris dropped to nine below zero, increasing the problems of the government. "They had before to struggle with the want of money, and want of bread for the people, and now the want of fuel for them and want of emploiment." Nevertheless, he continued to send encouraging long-range predictions back to his own government. "Every body here is trying their hands at forming declarations of rights," he wrote to Madison in January, sending him two examples. One of them was written by Lafayette, whose draft, Jefferson said, "contains the essential principles of ours accomodated as much as could be to the actual state of things here."[32] Though Jefferson did not elaborate on his association with Lafayette, he was in close contact with him and other reform-minded French leaders and met regularly with some of them. Moreover, his own assessments of events were often shaped by Lafayette's views. At the beginning of March, Jefferson took note of a recent riot in Brittany and rising opposition in several other provinces, but he still reported that "the revolution is going on quietly and steadily." His expectations for the meeting of the Estates General remained high.[33]

When the Estates General assembled in Versailles on May 4, 1789, the American minister was present for the imposing and dramatic opening meeting, and he continued to be a frequent visitor. By June so absorbed was he in the proceedings that he went to Versailles almost every day. Jefferson was also giving advice to Lafayette and meeting privately with him and others, and in doing so he was departing from the established code of diplomatic conduct. Indeed he went so far as to draft a charter of rights to be proclaimed by the king and sent copies to Lafayette and Rabaut de St. Etienne.[34] Jefferson's high expectations for "the progress of reason" were shaken by the deadlock over whether voting would be by estates or persons. For the first time he began to express concern that the steady process of revolution would receive a serious check. He admitted that the "progress of light and liberality" among the nobles had equaled his expectations only in Paris and its vicinities. "The great mass of deputies of that order which come from the country show that the habits of tyranny over the people are deeply rooted in them." Jefferson had been slow in recognizing the resistance of the nobles, partly, perhaps, because of his personal contacts with Lafayette. But once he sensed the probability that "the Noblesse will go wrong," he advised Lafayette to repudiate his instructions and join the Third Estate.[35]

On June 10 the members of the Third Estate invited the nobles and clergy to meet with them in a common assembly and announced that they would proceed with or without the cooperation of the other estates. A week later, on June 17, the Third Estate proclaimed itself to be the National Assembly of France and moved immediately to deal with the question of taxation. Jefferson was hopeful of the outcome. "The Commons have in their chamber almost all the talents of the nation," he believed. "They are firm and bold, yet moderate. There is indeed among them a number of very hot headed members; but those of most influence are cool, temperate, and sagacious. Every step of this house has been marked with caution and wisdom. The Noblesse on the contrary are absolutely out of their senses."[36]

On June 20 the National Assembly found the doors of their chamber locked by royal orders, moved to a nearby indoor tennis court, and took an oath not to separate until they had given France a constitution. In his reports on these momentous events and others in late June, Jefferson provided Jay with day-by-day accounts of the rapidly changing scene. He believed that the fear that the army would side with the people in any confrontation with the crown was responsible for Louis XVI's decision to allow the Assembly to proceed by requesting the nobles and clergy to take their seats with the Third Estate in the National Assembly. When they did so on June 27, amidst demonstrations of popular joy in Versailles and Paris, Jefferson thought the revolution had succeeded. "This great crisis being now over," he reported to Jay, "I shall not have matter interesting enough to trouble you with as often as I have done lately."[37]

Jefferson's analysis was obviously premature, and it reflected more his own hope of the outcome of the Revolution than the reality of the French political situation. Though the king had appeared to side with the people, he in fact was siding with the nobility and was soon assembling troops, mainly foreign mercenaries, in Versailles and Paris. Even while observing the massing of troops, Jefferson still trusted Louis XVI and blamed the nobles for the military measures. Three days before the storming of the Bastille, Jefferson assured Thomas Paine that the National Assembly was in command. "The executive and the aristocracy are now at their feet," he said. "The mass of the nation, the mass of the clergy, and the army are with them. They have prostrated the old government, and are now beginning to build one from the foundation." [38] But on the same day that he wrote to Paine, the popular finance minister Jacques Necker was dismissed and ordered to leave the country. When word of this circulated in Paris, mobs poured into the streets and detachments of royal troops took up positions in the city. Before the day was over, a mob had stoned a detachment of German cavalry. Jefferson hurried off a note to Paine to update his recent letter, but he did not yet recognize the full meaning of the events. "The progress of things here will be subject to checks from time to time of course," he advised Paine. "Whether they will be great or small will depend on the army. But they will be only checks." [39]

By the time Jefferson sent his next report to his own government on July 19, the Bastille had been stormed, and Paris had been through a violent convulsion. Lafayette was now in command of the Paris Guard, and foreign mercenaries had been withdrawn. A humbled Louis XVI recalled Necker and rode to Paris to make peace with his disaffected subjects. On the outskirts of the city he was met by Lafayette and escorted into the city. The streets were lined with French Guards and thousands of citizens "armed with guns, pistols, swords, pikes, pruning hooks, scythes, and whatever they could lay hold of." Shouts of *"Vive la nation!"* greeted the king. At the Hôtel de Ville, he was presented with a red and blue cockade, and after a series of ceremonies he appeared on a balcony wearing the cockade in his hat. The crowd responded at last with *"Vive le roi et la nation!"* [40] Once more, as Paris returned to normal, Jefferson thought the Revolution was over—at least in Paris, for he suspected that the whole country would pass through the paroxysm that city had endured. He had not yet sensed the full scope of the French Revolution, but he knew that he had witnessed "such events as will be for ever memorable in history." By now Jefferson— who in the spring had his baggage packed and was waiting anxiously for permission to return home—was no longer eager to depart. The scene was "too interesting to be left at present," he thought, noting his singular fortune "to see in the course of fourteen years two such revolutions as were never before seen."[41]

In truth, Jefferson was more than an observer in France. As an adviser to Lafayette, he was, to an extent not ordinarily permitted a representative of a foreign nation, a participant in the events. The times were, of course, not ordinary times, and Jefferson, who perceived the rights of man in universal terms, had no qualms about contributing to their advancement in a foreign country, especially one that had played such an important role in the success of the American Revolution. Lafayette consulted closely with Jefferson in drafting a declaration of rights to submit to the National Assembly. Prior to introducing it, he specifically requested his American friend to "send me the Bill of Rights with Your Notes," and Jefferson promptly responded. Just before presenting it to the Assembly, Lafayette asked Jefferson to consider it again and offer his observations.[42] It is impossible to establish Jefferson's precise influence on the declaration of rights that Lafayette presented to the National Assembly on July 11, and many others would have a hand at drafting such a declaration before the Assembly adopted the Declaration of the Rights of Man and the Citizen on August 26, 1789.[43] Only parts of the final Declaration resembled Lafayette's draft, but the influence of the American Declaration of Independence on the French Declaration was evident.

The American minister's most overt involvement in the affairs of France came while the National Assembly was engaged in trying to work out the principles of a constitution. He turned down an invitation from the archbishop of Bordeaux on July 20 to meet with the drafting committee, but he could not refuse a later request from Lafayette that would intimately involve him in French matters. On August 25 Jefferson received an urgent note from Lafayette pleading "for liberty's sake" that he break every engagement and host a dinner for eight members of the National Assembly the next day. Lafayette feared that if some compromises were not made and a coalition formed, the Assembly would never agree on a new government. He saw the proposed gathering as "the only Means to prevent a total dissolution and a civil war."[44] Jefferson consented to the request and hosted the dinner. He described his guests as "leading patriots, of honest but differing opinions sensible of the necessity of effecting a coalition by mutual sacrifices." At the end of the dinner, about four in the afternoon, the tablecloth was removed, wine set on the table, and discussions continued until ten in the evening, by which time the French leaders had worked out their differences and agreed on a plan that Jefferson thought decided the fate of the constitution. In his autobiography he remembered sitting as "a silent witness" to the proceedings, but at the time he was so concerned about overstepping the boundaries of diplomatic propriety that the next morning he went immediately to the French foreign minister to explain his actions. Comte de Montmorin had already heard of the gathering and went so far in sanctioning it that Jefferson was convinced that he must have known about it in advance. Others were less tolerant. The Spanish ambassador, Comte Fernan Nunez, commented sarcastically on the use of Jefferson's house as a rendezvous for radicals.[45]

All the drafting of bills of rights and constitutions prompted Jefferson to speculate upon the question whether one generation had the right to bind another. That question he thought had not been raised either in Europe or America, and it led him into one of the most theoretical discussions of political principles in which he ever engaged. In the first week of September, 1789, while confined to his chambers by a sudden illness—perhaps one of his periodic violent headaches—Jefferson committed his thoughts to paper. It may be that he intended the commentary initially for friends in France, but he put it into final form in a letter to Madison (though he did not place it in Madison's hands until January, 1790, after his return to America). The composition of the letter suggests that Jefferson was thinking primarily of France when he drafted it, and he gave a copy of it to Dr. Richard Gem, an English physician of philosophical mind and republican principles, who attended him during his illness and with whom he discussed the question.[46]

Jefferson reasoned that "the earth belongs always to the living generation," not to the dead, and that one generation did not have the right to bind a subsequent generation. No society, he argued, could make a perpetual constitution or even a perpetual law. He moved from the statement of general principle to the elaboration of its application. Though he regarded the principle as being of extensive application, it was France that was uppermost in his mind when he wrote: "It enters into the resolution of the questions Whether the nation may change the descent of lands holden in tail? Whether they may change the appropriation of lands given antiently to the church, to hospitals, colleges, orders of chivalry, and otherwise in perpetuity? Whether they may abolish the charges and privileges attached on lands, including the whole catalogue ecclesiastical and feudal? It goes to hereditary offices, authorities and jurisdictions; to hereditary orders, distinctions and appellations; to perpetual monopolies in commerce, the arts and sciences; with a long train of et ceteras." [47]

These were for the most part questions he had not had to face in America, where the absence of a feudal past distinguished Americans from Europeans. Yet, he sought universal application for the principle. Studying the mortality data compiled by Buffon, he calculated with mathematical precision that nineteen years represented the span of a generation and that every law and every constitution naturally expired at the end of that period. Furthermore, no nation could contract a debt that could not be repaid within nineteen years. He thought that this was an application particularly appropriate for the United States. "It would furnish matter for a fine preamble to our first law for appropriating the public revenue." He feared that at first blush his idea might be ridiculed as theoretical speculation, but he expected that closer examination would prove it "solid and salutary." He urged Madison to apply his cogent logic to the proposition. [48]

Madison responded by approving the general principle but challenging on practical grounds virtually every specific application that Jefferson suggested. Madison pointed out that "if the earth be the gift of nature to the living," as Jefferson argued, "their title can extend to the earth in its natural State only. The *improvements* made by the dead form a charge against the living who take the benefit of them." He noted that debts may be incurred for the benefit of posterity, and here he cited the debts from the Revolutionary War as an example. He was also concerned about the instability that Jefferson's proposition would produce, and he pointed to the impracticability of implementing his ideas when generational lines changed daily and hourly as individual members of society came of age. In his enthusiasm for his new idea, Jefferson had not sufficiently examined the difficulties posed by its practical application. Adrienne Koch concluded after a searching examination of the celebrated exchange that Jefferson was "more speculative and more daring in putting forward dynamic generalizations" and that Madison was "the more astute politician." [49]

By the time Jefferson received permission in August to return home, he was again convinced that the revolution in France was over. The good harvest would remove the danger of the want of bread. The National Assembly was "wise, firm and moderate" and would establish the English constitutional system purged of its defects. America would continue to supply the model for France to follow. "It is impossible to desire better dispositions towards us, than prevail in this assembly," he wrote to Madison. With calm returning to France and future prospects promising, Jefferson prepared to depart as soon after the first of October as he could get passage on a ship bound for Virginia. Before he left Paris, he would recognize that events were not moving forward as smoothly as he had anticipated, but expecting to return, he did not wish to delay his departure.[50]

On September 6 Jefferson sent thirty-eight boxes, hampers, and bales of baggage to Le Havre to await his sailing. There were boxes of books, a harpsichord, works of art, furniture, plants, hampers of wine, and sea stores for the voyage. One of the boxes contained six muskets made with interchangeable parts—an innovation whose potential the inventive-minded Jefferson had recognized immediately when he first learned of it. He was eager to introduce it in America.[51] Boxes of pictures for Monticello may have contained copies of portraits that he had asked Trumbull to purchase for him in England of Bacon, Locke, and Newton—"the three greatest men that ever lived, without any exception," Jefferson said. He also brought with him or had shipped later from France portraits of Columbus, Americus Vespucius, Cortez, and Magellan that he had had copied in Italy. "Our country should not be without the portraits of it's first discoverers," he explained.[52] Before leaving Paris, Jefferson paid Houdon one thousand livres for several works, which probably included the busts of Washington, Franklin, and Lafayette; he also had obtained busts of Voltaire, Turgot, and John Paul Jones by Houdon. At least some of these were among the boxes that accompanied him, and he may also have included one or more of the plaster busts of himself executed by Houdon, for whom Jefferson had sat in 1789. Houdon had exhibited one of these in the summer Salon of 1789 in Paris.[53] Houdon's superb likeness of Jefferson would provide posterity with one of the most important images of the American who so much admired Houdon's genius and played such an important role in promoting Houdon's work in America.

Because he had so much baggage, two children, two servants, and two carriages, Jefferson hoped to find a ship sailing from Le Havre to Virginia. If not, he sought one leaving from England that would stop on the French coast to pick him up and spare him an extra seasickness. As the first weeks of September passed without finding a suitable ship, Jefferson began to despair about booking a passage before winter. When he left Paris on September 26 for Le

Havre, he still had not received word that a ship had been found for him. Fortunately, John Trumbull—who did all sorts of errands for Jefferson in England—engaged a ship sailing from London for Virginia. Although the captain refused to make a stop at Le Havre, he agreed to board Jefferson on the English coast at Cowes. By the time Jefferson received word of this, he was so relieved to have a good ship with suitable accommodations that he was willing to endure the seasickness of another Channel crossing.[54]

Arriving in Le Havre on September 28, Jefferson discovered that his baggage sent from Paris three weeks earlier had not yet reached there, and he spent two days worrying about its fate before it finally arrived. Then a period of "the most tempestuous weather ever seen" set in, preventing the Channel boat from sailing for a week. It was not until the night of October 7 that the vessel slipped out of Le Havre. Jefferson and his two daughters were soon "exceedingly seasick." After a two-week wait at Cowes, the Jeffersons on October 22 embarked at noon on board the *Clermont*, bound for Norfolk. Anchoring at evening off Yarmouth, the *Clermont* weighed anchor at daylight. Jefferson was at last on his way to Virginia. He expected to return to Paris in the spring.[55]

XI
First Months at the State Department

On November 23, 1789, one month after weighing anchor at Yarmouth, the *Clermont* arrived in Norfolk, and Jefferson set foot on American soil for the first time in over five years. The voyage had been far quicker than he had anticipated. Experienced sea captains at Cowes told Jefferson to expect a nine-week passage by the planned southern route, but unusually fine weather in the Atlantic prompted Captain Nathaniel Colley to sail directly to Virginia. A native of Norfolk, Colley was a bold yet judicious seaman, Jefferson said. His ship, only two years old, was "uncommonly swift, insomuch that we passed every thing most rapidly that we came in sight of." After the usual period of seasickness at the beginning of the voyage, the American travelers found the passage exceptionally pleasant. Thick mist and heavy winds off Virginia, however, threatened disaster and required all of Captain Colley's boldness and knowledge of the coast to bring the *Clermont* into Norfolk with only the loss of topsails and some rigging. An hour after Jefferson left the ship, and before his baggage had been unloaded, a fire broke out and for a time threatened to destroy the vessel. But the fire was brought under control, and Jefferson's baggage miraculously escaped harm.[1]

Upon going ashore, Jefferson learned for the first time that President Washington had named him secretary of state in the new government under the Constitution and that the Senate had already confirmed his nomination. Washington's official letter of notification would not catch up with him for another two weeks, but in a welcoming address the city officials of Norfolk thanked Jefferson for his services in France and wished him well in his new post. In his reply Jefferson gave no hint whether he would accept the position.[2] He was not yet prepared to say what he would do. Intending to return to France, he had not anticipated the appointment, though with John Adams now vice-president, Jefferson must have realized that he was the most experienced American diplomat available for the post. While Washington hoped that Jefferson would join his official family, he assured him that he would not nominate a successor to the court at Versailles until he learned of his decision Pressure on Jefferson to accept was more direct from others. Madison wrote that he wanted to talk with him in person before he made up his mind. Meanwhile he urged him to make no hasty decision confiding that the president would not expect him to assume the post until after his visit to Monticello. "It is of infinite importance that you should not disappoint the public wish on this subject," Madison insisted, adding that "the Southern and Western Country have it particularly at heart."[3] Jefferson would not receive this letter until after he had made his decision, but it may be assumed that Madison made the same arguments when he saw him in person at Monticello.

On the road between Norfolk and Monticello, the Jeffersons visited with family and friends. They stopped long enough in Richmond for Jefferson to receive and reply to addresses from both houses of the Virginia Assembly, and he got his first look at the progress of construction on the new State Capitol. It promised to be "an edifice of first rate dignity," he thought, and, when finished with the proper ornamentation, would be "worthy of being exhibited along side the most celebrated remains of antiquity."[4]

Washington's letter offering him the office of secretary of state reached Jefferson on December 11, and he replied a few days later expressing his appreciation for the president's confidence in him but indicating his concern about the scope of the office. Congress initially had set up a Department of Foreign Affairs but later, after establishing the Treasury and War departments, decided to combine the administration of all other domestic affairs with foreign affairs under a Department of State. "When I contemplate the extent of that office, embracing as it does the principal mass of domestic administration, together with the foreign, I cannot be insensible of my inequality to it," the secretary-designate wrote the president. Yet, while expressing his personal preference to return to France, he indicated his willingness to accept whatever assignment the president decided was best for the public interest.[5]

Washington declined to make the final determination, insisting that the choice between the two posts was up to Jefferson. Nevertheless, he waited to reply to Jefferson's letter until after he had an opportunity to confer with Madison, who visited Jefferson at

Monticello soon after Jefferson reached home on December 23. Madison was disappointed to find Jefferson not more inclined to accept the secretaryship, but he reported to the president his opinion that Jefferson's reluctance sprang primarily from his concern about the domestic duties attached to the office. Madison regarded this fear as unwarranted, and we may suppose that he sought to reassure Jefferson on that point. Once Madison returned to New York for the second session of the First Congress, where he was a member of the House of Representatives, he reported directly to the president. Washington wrote immediately to Jefferson, assuring him that it was not expected that the domestic duties of the State Department would be burdensome and that if they should become so, he was convinced that Congress would separate them from foreign affairs and create a new department. Still claiming that the final choice was in Jefferson's hands, he nonetheless left no doubt as to his preference, telling Jefferson that "so far as I have been able to obtain information from all quarters, your late appointment has given very extensive and very great satisfaction to the Public."[6] Washington's letter left Jefferson little choice, unless he was willing to ignore the president's wishes, the advice of Madison, and the expectations of many of his fellow citizens. He still waited a week to reply after a special messenger delivered Washington's letter to him at Monticello. On February 14 he informed the president of his acceptance.

That Jefferson's decision had been made earlier in his own mind can be seen in his response two days before to an address of the citizens of Albemarle County welcoming him home. His brief address, published in newspapers throughout the nation, was one of the most memorable that Jefferson ever delivered. In a moving and succinct way, Jefferson expressed the political philosophy that had guided him throughout his adult life and would continue to direct him until the end of his days. He addressed his Albemarle neighbors as "fellow-labourers and fellow-sufferers" in "the holy cause of freedom" and told them:

> It rests now with ourselves alone to enjoy in peace and concord the blessings of self-government, so long denied to mankind: to show by example the sufficiency of human reason for the care of human affairs and that the will of the majority, the Natural law of every society, is the only sure guardian of the rights of man. Perhaps even this may sometimes err. But it's errors are honest, solitary and short-lived.—Let us then, my dear friends, for ever bow down to the general reason of the society. We are safe with that, even in it's deviations, for it soon re-

turns again to the right way. These are lessons we have learnt together. We have prospered in their practice, and the liberality with which you are pleased to approve my attachment to the general rights of mankind assures me we are still together in these it's kindred sentiments.[7]

Compressed into this short passage was Jefferson's basic political creed: his belief in reason, natural law, and the rights of man; his commitment to majority rule; and his faith in the wisdom of the majority, even when it erred, for it would always return to the right way. America had taken the lead in "the holy cause of freedom" and must continue to set the example for mankind. With a new government struggling to establish itself under the Constitution, he could not refuse to serve "wherever I may be stationed, by the will of my country." No doubt remained that the will of his country was that he assume the duties of the first secretary of state.

In his letter of acceptance Jefferson informed the president, who was anxious for him to join the administration at once, that circumstances beyond his control—which he would explain when he saw him—prevented him from leaving immediately for New York. The explanation that Jefferson chose not to reveal in his letter was the approaching marriage of his eldest daughter, Martha, who had turned seventeen the previous September. Nathaniel Cutting, a young American who had become acquainted with the Jeffersons while they waited out the stormy weather at Le Havre and crossed the Channel with them to Cowes, had been much impressed with Miss Jefferson. He described her as "amiable," "tall and genteel," and despite her exposure to the habits of France, possessed of "all that winning simplicity, and good humour'd reserve that are evident proofs of innate Virtue and an happy disposition"—characteristics that Cutting saw as distinguishing American women from those of any other country. Yet he also thought he detected behind her "happy serenity" some chagrin at being separated from her European friends.[8]

Whatever apprehensions Martha may have had about leaving familiar surroundings to return to a place she had not seen since she was twelve, she could never have anticipated how quickly her life would change after she reached home. Two months after returning to Virginia, she was engaged to be married. Three months to the day after arriving in Norfolk, she became the wife of Thomas Mann Randolph, Jr., a third cousin whom she had known as a child but had not seen for years.[9] Randolph, twenty-one, had studied in Edinburgh but was still unsure of his future course. Jefferson in a letter to Madame de Corny in Paris explained: "My daughter, on her arrival in Virginia, received the addresses of a young Mr. Randolph, the son of a bosom friend of mine. Tho' his talents, dispositions, and connections and fortune were such as would have made him my own first choice, yet according to the usage of my country, I scrupulously suppressed my wishes, that my daughter might indulge her own sentiments freely. It ended in their marriage."[10] This brief account is the most detailed record that survives of their courtship. That Jefferson was pleased with the match is evident, and it is unlikely that Martha failed to sense this, despite his efforts to remain neutral.

Thomas Mann Randolph, Sr., and Jefferson had spent much of their childhood together at Tuckahoe, the Randolph plantation where Peter Jefferson moved his family for some six years to look after the lands and the children of his deceased friend William Randolph. In writing to his lifelong friend and second cousin, Jefferson said that "the marriage of your son with my daughter cannot be more pleasing to you than to me. Besides the worth which I discover in him, I am happy that the knot of friendship between us, as old as ourselves, should be drawn closer and closer to the day of our death."[11]

In anticipation of the marriage, Randolph deeded his son a tract of 950 acres, called Varina, in Henrico County, together with forty slaves. Jefferson settled on his daughter 1,000 acres of his Poplar Forest tract in Bedford County, together with twenty-seven slaves. At Jefferson's initiative a marriage settlement was signed at Monticello on February 19, 1790.[12] Of the six families of slaves transferred to Martha, five were already living on the land given to her, and the other family lived on adjoining acreage. However much Jefferson disapproved of slavery, by transferring the ownership of these slaves to his daughter and her descendants, Jefferson was helping to perpetuate the system that he deplored.

With Jefferson anxious to get off to New York to assume his new duties, Martha Jefferson and Thomas Mann Randolph, Jr., were married at Monticello on February 23, 1790. On March 1, Jefferson left for New York. The relationship between Jefferson and his eldest daughter was close, and Jefferson would feel the separation keenly. Since the death of his wife, Jefferson had taken Martha with him on his public assignments and closely directed her education. With his younger daughter, Maria, he never developed the same bonds that existed with Martha. After he reached New York, he wrote to Martha that "having had yourself and dear Poll to live with me so long, to exercise my affections and chear me in the intervals of business, I feel heavily the separation from you." But he said he found consolation in Martha's happiness and the prospects for its continuance. "Your new condition will call for abundance of little sacrifices," he advised the young bride. "But they will be greatly overpaid by the measure of affection they will secure to you. The happiness of your life depends now on the continuing to please a single person. To this all other objects must be secondary; even your love to me, were it possible that that could ever be an obstacle." In reply Martha wished for her father to visit Virginia in the fall and assured him that "my happiness can never be compleat without your company. Mr. Randolph omits nothing that can in the least contribute to it. I have made it my study to please him in every *thing* and do consider all other objects as secondary to that *except* my love for you." [13] There is no evidence that Martha ever departed from this commitment.

On the way to New York Jefferson spent a week on business in Richmond, was delayed by a snowstorm in Alexandria, stopped in Philadelphia to see Benjamin Franklin (then in his final illness), and did not reach New York until March 21. It seemed to him the most laborious journey he had ever made. He had hoped to find a house on Broadway, where the president's house and the State Department offices were located, but none was available, and he took a small house at 57 Maiden Lane. He considered the dwelling an "indifferent" one and did not expect to remain there long, but he nonetheless extravagantly built a windowed gallery across the back of the house to accommodate his books, papers, and plants. He was soon sending detailed instructions to William Short in Paris for procuring household goods and shipping his belongings from France.[14]

When Jefferson arrived in the temporary capital, the new government had been in operation for nearly a year. "The opposition to our new constitution has almost totally disappeared," he observed, and he believed that if Washington lived a few years to establish the authority of the government, the republic would be secure. The first session of Congress had created the structure of governance, and President Washington was in the process of devising the procedures to make the machinery work. Many of the mechanisms of the executive branch were still evolving when Jefferson appeared on the scene, but in matters of social style the patterns of Washington's administration had largely been set. Washington had no desire to become a king, but he wanted to make the presidential office one of dignity and authority. His personality and bearing conveyed an impression of aloofness. He had been accustomed to command and had no inclination to pose as a man of the people. Washington presided ceremoniously over a formal weekly levee, or reception, and on official public appearances rode in a carriage drawn by four or six horses, followed by his official family in other coaches.[15] Jefferson later would be critical of Washington's "court," and he himself could never be comfortable in such a role. But he had great respect for the president and did not initially appear to have been disturbed by Washington's ceremonial role.

The administration that Jefferson joined as the ranking department head was small—only three departments and the attorney general, who served as the counsel for the government but headed no department. When he went to his new office, Jefferson found the entire staff of the State Department consisted of two chief clerks, two assistant clerks, and a translator. His total budget, not including the diplomatic establishment abroad, was less than $8,000, of which $3,500 was his own salary.[16] Jefferson's colleagues—Alexander Hamilton at the Treasury, Henry Knox at the War Department, and Attorney General Edmund Randolph—all had had time to settle into their jobs before Jefferson assumed his duties, and Hamilton's first report on the public credit was already before Congress. There is nothing in the record to indicate that Jefferson anticipated any difficulties in working with the other members of the administration.

President Washington looked to his department heads and the attorney general for advice and at times also sought the opinions of Vice-President John Adams and Chief Justice John Jay. He regarded the department heads as his assistants, not as independent ministers, in administering the laws, and from the outset he made it clear that he was in charge of his administration and expected that all policy matters be presented to him for approval.[17] The mechanism of the cabinet was not initially employed, but it gradually evolved from the president's regular practice of consultation with the members of his administration. As the commanding general under whom Knox had served during the Revolution, Washington dominated the War Department. He exercised less control over the Department of State but retained the final authority in all foreign policy decisions. Less sure of himself on financial matters, Washington allowed Hamilton more freedom to formulate policy than he permitted to any other member of his administration.

Jefferson reported to the president on his first day in New York—

a Sunday—and plunged immediately into his duties. Within six weeks, however, he was stricken with one of his periodic headaches that immobilized him for a week and stayed with him for over a month.[18] At times during this period he was able to do some work, and in fact he drafted his famous report to Congress on weights and measures—a report that one scholar has called "an almost perfect embodiment of his dual allegiance to Newtonian physics and to Lockean concepts of government."[19] The problem of deriving a universal standard from nature was one that interested many men of the Enlightenment, and Jefferson drew on their theories and experiments in arriving at his recommendation: "Let the Standard of measure then be an uniform cylindrical rod of iron, of such length as in lat. 45.° in the level of the ocean, and in a cellar or other place, the temperature of which does not vary thro' the year, shall perform it's vibrations, in small and equal arcs, in one second of mean time."[20] Most modern readers will hardly be more interested in the explanation of how Jefferson arrived at this proposed standard than were most members of Congress, but every reader will be intrigued by the second aspect of Jefferson's proposal. Here he proposed to apply the decimal system to weights and measures just as Congress had earlier done, at his recommendation, in regard to coinage. For measures of length the rod used for the standard was to be divided into five equal parts, each to be called a *foot* (about one quarter of an inch shorter than the present foot). Each foot was to be divided into ten inches, each inch into ten lines, and each line into ten points. Ten feet would make a decad, ten decads a rood, ten roods a furlong, and ten furlongs a mile. He provided similar details for measures of capacity and for measures of weight. His system, he said, had the advantage of "bringing the calculation of the principal affairs of life within the arithmetic of every man who can multiply and divide plain numbers."[21] Congress was not ready for such a revolutionary step, and Jefferson's report languished without action, leaving it to revolutionary France to introduce the metric system.

Before he had fully recovered from his disabling headache, Jefferson made his first appearance before a Senate committee, to testify in behalf of the president's authority to conduct foreign relations. That authority included, he insisted, determining rank and assignments of diplomats, their pay, and other details that Congress under the Confederation had prescribed. The occasion provided the opportunity for Senator William Maclay to record a detailed description of the forty-seven-year-old secretary of state. In his diary for May 24, 1790, Maclay wrote:

When I came to the Hall Jefferson and the rest of the Committee were there. Jefferson is a slender Man. Has rather the Air of Stiffness in his Manner. His cloaths seem too small for him. He sits in a lounging Manner on one hip, commonly, and with one of his shoulders elevated much above the other. His face has a scrany Aspect. His whole figure has a loose shackling Air. He had a rambling Vacant look and nothing of that firm collected deportment which I expected would dignify the presence of a Secretary or Minister. I looked for Gravity, but a laxity of Manner, seemed shed about him. He spoke almost without ceasing. But even his discourse partook of his personal demeanor. It was loose and rambling and yet he scattered information wherever he went, and some even brilliant Sentiments sparkled from him.[22]

By the time the secretary of state was back to full-time work, the new government was at an impasse that threatened to stall its progress, and Jefferson was soon deeply involved in working out a political solution. Since Hamilton had presented his report on the public credit to Congress in January, 1790, Congress had become sharply divided over his proposals to fund the national debt and assume the debts incurred by the states during the Revolution. No differences existed over making provision to fulfill all foreign obligations, a fact that Jefferson relayed to William Short in Paris to reassure French officials. But in regard to the domestic debt, some members of Congress opposed allowing speculators who had bought up depreciated securities to make windfall profits under Hamilton's plan to fund the debt at par value with arrears of interest. Madison proposed in the House of Representatives that Congress discriminate between original holders and subsequent purchasers, but his proposition was voted down. Even more controversial was Hamilton's proposal for the assumption of state debts, which pitted states with large debts against those with small debts and threatened to deadlock Congress. Jefferson came to fear that if some compromise were not worked out, the funding bill would not pass, and the nation's credit would "burst and vanish and the states separate to take care everyone of itself."[23]

As he later recounted his role in the events, he met Hamilton one day outside the president's door, and the secretary of the treasury brought up the subject of the assumption of state debts. He thought Hamilton looked "sombre, haggard, and dejected beyond description" as the Treasury chief expressed his concern about the threat to the Union. Arguing that members of the administration should support each other, Hamilton urged Jefferson to use his influence among southern members in Congress to help break the impasse. Refusing to intercede directly, Jefferson agreed to invite Hamilton and Madison to dinner at his house the next day to discuss the issue. The outcome of that dinner, according to Jefferson, was the bargain that led to the passage of the assumption act and a bill to locate the national capital on the Potomac. While Madison would not consent to vote for assumption, it was agreed that two Virginia members whose districts lay along the Potomac would be approached with the proposal. It was also necessary that Pennsylvania members be party to the agreement, the understanding being that the temporary capital would be transferred to Philadelphia for ten years.[24] The question of the site of the capital, one of the most sensitive issues before the First Congress, had become deeply divisive. The scheme to combine the assumption proposal and the residence bill in a legislative compromise would end what Jefferson saw as the spectacle of a Congress "unable to get along as to these businesses, and indisposed to attend to any thing else till they are settled."[25]

A compromise along the lines that Jefferson described was accomplished when in July, 1790, the funding, assumption, and residence measures all passed Congress. Scholarly investigations show that not all of the provisions of the agreement were worked out at Jefferson's famous dinner. Two Maryland members as well as two Virginia members of Congress switched their votes on assumption, and other persons were also involved in the bargain, both before and after the dinner. Indeed the understanding between southerners and Pennsylvanians may have been worked out before the dinner, and the main task was to keep it from unraveling while the assumption measure was enacted.[26] Still, Jefferson played an important role in the business, and he later would confess regret at ever having contributed to advancing one of Hamilton's measures. Two years afterward, when Hamilton's program had been more fully revealed, Jefferson looked back on his cooperation as the greatest error of his political life. He felt that he had been "duped" by Hamilton and "made a tool for forwarding his schemes, not then sufficiently understood by me." At the time he acted, however, his differences with Hamilton had not yet become sharp, and in the summer of 1790 he argued for compromise as necessary to preserve the Union.[27]

Jefferson spent part of his first months as secretary of state sparring with Congress over the size and expense of the diplomatic establishment. He shared a widely held belief that a large diplomatic establishment was unnecessary, but he did not agree with Senator William Maclay that there should be none. Maclay thought all money spent on posts abroad was wasted. "I know not a single thing that we have for a minister to do in a single court in Europe," he said. "Indeed, the less we have to do with them the better." [28] Jefferson thought it wiser to economize by having lower grades of diplomatic officers and restricting them to countries with which the United States had important concerns. France was the key post for an American minister, Jefferson believed, because it was at the crossroads of Europe where the diplomatic corps was largest. He initially favored a minister plenipotentiary only for that post but, after consulting with Washington, decided that England should receive equal treatment, if and when that nation named a minister to the United States. The diplomatic establishment that he proposed, and which Congress ultimately approved, provided for ministers in Paris and London, chargés d'affaires at Madrid and Lisbon, an agent at the Hague, and a consul in Morocco, at a total annual cost of forty thousand dollars. [29]

The first major crisis in foreign affairs that Jefferson faced as secretary of state was the threat of war between England and Spain following the Spanish seizure of British ships in Nootka Sound off Vancouver Island. Two weeks after William Pitt publicly disclosed the war crisis in early May, 1790, Gouverneur Morris, the agent of the president in London, had an interview with Pitt and the Duke of Leeds, the foreign secretary. After the conference, Morris reported to Washington that if war came, both England and Spain would pay a price for American neutrality and recommended the moment for immediate negotiations with Spain in regard to the Mississippi. [30]

Meanwhile, the British ministry instructed Lord Dorchester, governor general of Canada, to collect information on the expected American reaction to war. Dorchester dispatched his aide Major George Beckwith, an intelligence officer, to New York, where he arrived at the beginning of July. On earlier information-gathering missions to the United States Beckwith had talked with Hamilton, though the secretary of the treasury had not reported these contacts to either the president or the secretary of state. On this occasion Hamilton informed Washington of his conversation with Beckwith and reported on it in a meeting attended by the secretary of state. [31]

The supposition that Beckwith, in the absence of any official British diplomatic mission to the United States, was an unofficial envoy has been shown to be unfounded by Julian Boyd, who demonstrated that Beckwith was in fact a secret agent. Boyd also argued that Hamilton, whom Beckwith designated as "Number 7" in his reports to his superiors, did not accurately present to the president the contents of Beckwith's communication in July, 1790. It is a matter of interpretation whether Hamilton deliberately misinterpreted the instructions that Beckwith showed him (as Boyd believed) or unwittingly saw in them what he wanted to believe: that the British were suggesting the possibility of an alliance.[32] The details of Hamilton's relationship with Beckwith need not be pursued here, but it is essential to an understanding of Jefferson's tenure as secretary of state to recognize that the secretary of the treasury was intimately involved in matters of foreign affairs, and Hamilton's view of what the policy of the United States should be was diametrically opposed to that of the secretary of state, to whom the idea of an alliance with England suggested not the opportunity for peaceful growth that Hamilton envisioned but renewed subjugation to a former master.

In a memorandum to the president on July 12, 1790, worked out after conferring with Madison, Jefferson outlined a proposed American policy in the event of war between England and Spain. He directed his attention largely to the most threatened interest of the United States: the navigation of the Mississippi River and access to the sea. What should the United States do if Great Britain attempted the conquest of Louisiana and the Floridas? Jefferson assumed that France would join Spain against England. If not, England would prevail and render the situation of the United States worse. Summarizing the dangers of a successful British conquest of Louisiana, the secretary of state stressed that "instead of two neighbors balancing each other, we shall have one, with more than the strength of both." British control of the Mississippi River and of a territory half the size of the United States on the west bank would put that powerful nation in a position to seduce the whole area of the United States west of the mountains and dependent upon the waters of the Mississippi. The young republic would be encircled by the British—by land and by sea. Jefferson's memorandum made it clear that the United States could not stand by and allow this to happen but concluded that there was no need for the United States to take speedy action. Great Britain might decide not to attack Louisiana and the Floridas, or fail in the attempt, or France and Spain might recover them. "If all these chances fail, we should have to re-take them." But delay would allow the United States time to become better prepared and also provide an opportunity to obtain concessions in return for American assistance.[33]

Jefferson's fear of the threat to the territorial integrity of the Union posed by a British presence on the Mississippi was not without foundation. Had he had access to the minutes of the Committee of the Privy Council for Trade, he would have been struck by its report of April 17, 1790, declaring that "in a commercial view, it will be for the benefit of the country to prevent Vermont and Kentucky and all the other Settlements now forming in the interior parts of the great Continent of North America from becoming dependent on the Government of the United States, or on that of any other foreign country, and to preserve them on the contrary in a state of Independence and to induce them to form Treaties of Commerce and Friendship with Great Britain."[34]

For immediate policy, Jefferson advised the president that the United States seek to encourage Spain to view giving independence to Louisiana and the Floridas as preferable to allowing conquest by the British. Britain should be informed through Beckwith that the United States would look with favor on a commercial treaty based on "perfect reciprocity," that the objects of any alliance would have to be made known before the United States could respond, and that such objects could not be inconsistent with any existing arrangements (*i.e.*, the alliance with France). In case of war between Great Britain and Spain "we are disposed to be strictly neutral," but "we should view with extreme uneasiness any attempts of either power to seize the possessions of the other on our frontier, as we consider our own safety interested in a due balance between our neighbors."[35]

After conferring with Jay and Hamilton, Washington decided not to deliver Jefferson's warning to Beckwith but to instruct the secretary of the treasury to extract as much information as he could from the British agent without committing the United States in any way, "leaving it entirely free to pursue, unreproached, such a line of conduct in the dispute as her interest (and honour) shall dictate."[36] On the subject of an alliance, Hamilton was to tell Beckwith that the precise objects of the British government could not be discerned from his communication.

In the report that he made to Lord Dorchester on his interview with Hamilton, Beckwith said that Hamilton assured him:

> There is the most sincere good disposition on the part of the government here to go into the consideration of all matters unsettled between us and Great Britain, in order to effect a perfect understanding between the two countries, and to lay the foundation for future amity;

this, particularly as it respects commercial objects, we view as conducive to our interest.

In the present stage of this business it is difficult to say much on the subject of a Treaty of Alliance; Your rupture with Spain, if it shall take place, opens a very wide political field; thus much I can say, we are perfectly unconnected with Spain, have even some points unadjusted with that Court, and are prepared to go into the consideration of the subject.[37]

While both the president and the secretary of state favored the negotiation of a commercial treaty with Great Britain and were also prepared to use the war crisis to press Spain for concessions, the impression that Beckwith gained from his interview with the secretary of the treasury indicated a more conciliatory stance than either Washington or Jefferson was displaying at this time. This suggests that Hamilton did not accurately convey to Beckwith the position of his government. Even more exceptional was what Hamilton said to Beckwith about the secretary of state with respect to any negotiations between the two countries. Not wanting to leave negotiations to Gouverneur Morris in London, Hamilton preferred that they take place in the United States. Such a course posed one difficulty, as he explained to Beckwith.

If it shall be judged proper to proceed in this business by the sending or appointing a proper person to come to this country to negotiate on the spot, whoever shall then be our Secretary of State, will be the person in whose department such negotiation must originate, and he will be the channel of communication with the President; in the turn of such affairs the most minute circumstances, mere trifles, give a favorable bias or otherwise to the whole. The President's mind I can declare to be perfectly dispassionate on this subject. Mr. Jefferson our present Secretary of State is I am persuaded a gentleman of honor, and zealously desirous of promoting those objects, which the nature of his duty calls for, and the interests of his country may require, but from some opinions which he has given respecting Your government, and possible predilections elsewhere, there may be difficulties which may possibly frustrate the whole, and which might be readily explained away. I shall certainly know the progress of negotiation from the president from day to day, but what I come to the present explanation for is this, that in any case any such difficulties should occur, I should wish to know them, in order that I may be sure they are clearly understood, and candidly examined.[38]

The secretary of the treasury was in effect offering to assist the negotiator of a foreign power to counteract the efforts of the secretary of state. Jefferson, of course, did not know what Hamilton told Beckwith, but the incident shows that the resentment Jefferson would display over Hamilton's meddling in his department was well founded. Almost from the outset, Hamilton made Jefferson's job as secretary of state more difficult.

Although the president chose not to convey Jefferson's proposed warning to Britain through Beckwith, he approved the basic policy of the secretary of state. This can be seen in Jefferson's instructions to Gouverneur Morris, which according to routine the president reviewed before they were sent. Writing to Morris on August 12, Jefferson said that British actions indicated the likelihood of war and of British designs on Spanish possessions bordering the United States. He instructed Morris, if war came, to intimate to the British government that the United States could not remain indifferent and would "contemplate a change of neighbours with extreme uneasiness; and that a due balance on our borders is not less desireable to us, than a balance of power in Europe has always appeared to them."[39] War did not come, and Morris did not deliver the warning. But had hostilities begun, Hamilton's conversations with Beckwith could only have served to undermine the administration's policy.

As Washington contemplated the possibility of a war between England and Spain, it appeared to him more and more likely that the British would attack Louisiana by an operation from Detroit. In a secret memorandum he asked his principal advisers for their opinions as to what his answer should be if Lord Dorchester requested permission to march troops through United States territory to the Mississippi or, as was more likely, if he moved his troops through American territory without asking leave.[40]

Jefferson prefaced his reply by stating that the dangers to the United States posed by the possible addition of Louisiana and the Floridas to the British Empire were so great that the United States should go to war if that were the only means of preventing the calamity. Nevertheless, he favored preserving neutrality as long as possible and entering the war as late as possible. Neutrality could be maintained if Britain were allowed to move troops through American territory, so long as Spain were allowed the same privilege. If Britain were refused permission and moved its troops anyway, there was no choice but to go to war. Jefferson's recommendation was that the United States avoid any answer to a request from Britain to cross American soil. Should they proceed nevertheless, or march without asking for leave, the United States should remonstrate and keep the issue alive to be used as a cause for going to war if events dictated that course.[41]

General agreement prevailed among the president's other advisers that maintaining neutrality was the best policy, but only John Adams and Henry Knox believed that it was necessary to deny passage to the British to remain neutral. Hamilton offered far more qualified answers than Jefferson but ultimately concluded that the United States ought not to refuse passage. Jefferson was the only person to advise the president to evade the issue by not responding. To Hamilton, evasive conduct indicated timidity. Jefferson, however, saw his proposed evasion as a way to play for time, allowing the United States the opportunity to choose the circumstances for entering the war, should that become necessary.[42]

Jefferson never lost sight of his first priority: to secure for the United States unhampered navigation of the Mississippi River. Eager to use the threat of war to pressure Spain for concessions, he secretly dispatched David Humphreys to Madrid with instructions for William Carmichael to bring up the navigation of the Mississippi with the Spanish foreign minister. Carmichael should "impress him thoroughly with the necessity of an early and even an immediate settlement of this matter," Jefferson said. It should be made clear that the United States was not interested in a negotiation unless Spain was prepared "in the first opening of it, to yield the immediate and full enjoyment of that navigation." With this concession achieved at the outset, the United States would then press negotiations for the use of a port at the mouth of the Mississippi. The secretary of state expected war between Spain and Great Britain to have begun before Humphreys reached Madrid. But should some accommodation have taken place, Carmichael was to press, more softly, for the same objectives, "which we are determined in the end to obtain at every risk."[43]

As it turned out, the war crisis of 1790 provided only a hypothetical exercise for American policy makers. When France failed to support Spain in the Nootka Sound dispute, Spain backed down and came to terms with England. Yet, by directing the secretary of state's attention to the Mississippi question, the crisis led to the formulation of clear foreign-policy goals that would play a key role in the years ahead. The events demonstrated that Jefferson was prepared to seize opportunities provided by European disputes to advance American interests and to move promptly and decisively when those interests were at stake. He showed himself to be a tough-minded diplomat, ready to play foreign powers against one another, determined to hold as many options in his own hands for as long as possible, and wary of being caught in a position that demanded the defense of honor without clear benefits to the national interest.

In his early months as secretary of state, Jefferson showed again, as he had as governor of Virginia, that he was a careful administrator who instituted systematic procedures that promoted efficiency and competence. He organized his small staff to perform specialized duties relating to the foreign and domestic functions of his office and established careful practices of record keeping. He had always been ahead of his time in retaining copies of his own correspondence, and he made multiple copies a routine practice in the State Department. He made a study of the time it took for him to receive communications from American diplomatic posts in Europe and devised routes and schedules to speed this essential communication.[44] Although he gave the highest priority to formulating foreign policy, he was a working administrator as well as a policy maker.

In mid-August after Congress adjourned, Jefferson accompanied Washington on a short sailing trip to Rhode Island, where the president went to welcome the state into the Union after its belated ratification of the Constitution. After a pleasant sail of two days, they visited Newport and Providence, where the president was received with great cordiality, and were back in New York within a week.[45] Jefferson had paperwork to finish and arrangements to make for the removal of his department to Philadelphia before he could get away to Virginia, all of which he hoped to complete by the time the president left for Mount Vernon at the end of the month.

On September 1 a tired secretary of state, accompanied by Madison, set out in his phaeton for Monticello. They stopped for several days in Philadelphia, where Jefferson completed arrangements for his office and living quarters for when the government moved from New York. An even more important stop was in Georgetown to inspect lands for the site of the future capital and to confer with neighboring landholders. Washington, too, stopped in Georgetown on his way to Mount Vernon, but he deferred his inspection tour until the following month and left it to his secretary of state to make the preliminary contacts and tour the potential sites. The speed with which the president and the secretary of state moved to implement the residence bill is of considerable interest. Before Washington left New York, Jefferson prepared a memorandum, which, despite his later penchant for strict construction, proposed that the president interpret the law with as much latitude as the language of the act would support. He urged the president to act promptly to obtain the land for the capital, appoint the commissioners to lay out the city, and begin the construction of public buildings. He was convinced that "if the present occasion of securing the Federal seat on the Patowmack should be lost, it could never be regained." He also believed that it would be dangerous to rely on Congress or the legislatures of Virginia and Maryland for assistance and that measures should be taken to carry the residence bill into execution without recourse to any of these bodies.[46]

Madison also had drawn up a memorandum on the residence act for the president before leaving New York. Having fought the residence battle in Congress, he, too, was anxious that the president proceed quickly.[47] Many members of Congress, especially those from Pennsylvania, were convinced that once the capital returned to Philadelphia, it would never be moved. As long as no town or buildings on the Potomac could accommodate the government, the capital would remain at Philadelphia. Both Jefferson and Madison recommended that the construction of the government buildings be financed by selling lots in the new city from lands donated by landowners who would profit from the rise in the value of adjoining lands. This would avoid going to Congress for appropriations that might provoke debates to obstruct or delay moving forward with construction.[48] The details of the locating of the District of Columbia and the construction of the capital need not concern us, but it is important to recognize the role that Washington, Jefferson, and Madison played in pushing ahead immediately to implement the residence bill, for without their efforts the new capital might never have become a reality.

After visiting Georgetown, Jefferson and Madison stopped briefly at Mount Vernon to report to the president. They reached Montpelier on September 18, and Jefferson was back home the next day. After six months of pressure in his new job, he was ready for a respite at Monticello. While at home Jefferson had business affairs to attend to, but he gave the highest priority to efforts to situate his newly married daughter and son-in-law nearby. Once Thomas Mann Randolph, Jr., indicated a preference to establish himself in Albemarle County instead of developing his Varina property (where Martha was not eager to live), his father-in-law moved immediately to help him secure a portion of the Edgehill tract owned by his father across the Rivanna River from Monticello. He wrote to the elder Randolph about the matter from New York, and after

ιe got home, he made a special trip to Tuckahoe to make an ar-
angement with his old friend. He was overjoyed when he and
Randolph reached an agreement, but almost immediately Randolph, who had recently remarried, began to have second thoughts
ιnd wanted to revise the understanding. Jefferson advised his son-
ιn-law to release his father from the agreement, but at the same
ime he patiently continued to seek to persuade the elder Randolph
ιo proceed with it by revising its terms. Jefferson was unable to
:omplete the negotiations while in Virginia, but the young couple
·emained at Monticello in his absence, and he continued to hope
hat some arrangement could be reached. The elder Randolph and
ιis quick-tempered son were not able to continue the negotiations
ωith Jefferson's calm approach. Such hard feelings developed on
ιoth sides that the younger Randolph began looking for other suit-
ιble property in Albemarle County. Ultimately, however, father
ιnd son became reconciled, and in January, 1792, the elder Randolph sold his son 1,523 acres of the Edgehill property, together
ωith the slaves living there, thus pleasing Martha and fulfilling
Jefferson's wish that she and her family (which by then included his
ϊrst grandchild) live near him.[49]

Jefferson stayed longer at Monticello in the fall of 1790 than he
ιad intended and did not leave home until November 8. He had
delayed his journey to Philadelphia to travel with Madison, and on
he way the two men stopped at Mount Vernon to confer with President Washington. At this time both Jefferson and Madison were in
:he close confidence of the president, and their trust in him was
ιnreserved. We can be sure they talked about plans for the new
:apital, the latest intelligence from Europe, and the upcoming session of Congress, which would convene on December 6. The president would follow the secretary of state and the congressional
leader to the capital a week later. The winter campaign—as Jefferson came to call the meetings of Congress—was about to begin.

XII
Conflict in Washington's Cabinet

The chill of winter was in the air on November 20, 1790, when Jefferson and Madison arrived in Philadelphia and took rooms at Mrs. Mary House's boardinghouse at Fifth and Market streets. Madison always stayed there when in Philadelphia and had done so since entering the Continental Congress in 1780. Jefferson, however, had expected the dwelling that he had rented from Thomas Leiper to be available by October. That it was not ready was partly because of his own requests for changes to be made in the three-story house, which was under construction when he leased it. He ordered a room built across the back at the second level to shelve his books, a carriage house for three carriages, and stables for five horses. In addition, he offered such detailed directions concerning the interior of the dwelling that Leiper dispatched his master carpenter to confer with him in person.[1]

The attention that Jefferson devoted to the finishing of a house that he was expecting to rent for only a few years was extraordinary but fully in harmony with his habit of seeking to establish himself in comfortable, convenient, and pleasing surroundings wherever he lived. In this instance he had to suffer considerable inconvenience before he could enjoy the results of his efforts. Three weeks passed before he could vacate his room at Mrs. House's and move into the two rooms on the third floor of Leiper's still-unfinished dwelling on December 11. It was another eight days before he got possession of his bedroom on the second floor and not until January 8 that the drawing room and parlor could be used and he was able to dine at home, though not yet in the dining room. On January 20 he recorded in his account book that he had taken possession of the dining room and front room on the first floor.[2] The house was his at last.

Meanwhile, seventy-eight large crates of furniture, household

Thomas Jefferson. Marble bust by Jean-Antoine Houdon, 1789. Taken
from life while Jefferson was minister to France.

Courtesy Museum of Fine Arts, Boston, George Nixon Black Fund

A Declaration by the Representatives of the UNITED STATES OF AMERICA, in General Congress assembled.

When in the course of human events it becomes necessary for one people to dissolve the political bands which have connected them with another, and to assume among the powers of the earth the separate and equal station to which the laws of nature & of nature's god entitle them, a decent respect to the opinions of mankind requires that they should declare the causes which impel them to the separation.

We hold these truths to be self-evident, that all men are created equal, that they are endowed by their creator with inherent & inalienable rights, that among these are life, & liberty, & the pursuit of happiness; that to secure these ends, governments are instituted among men, deriving their just powers from the consent of the governed; that whenever any form of government shall becomes destructive of these ends, it is the right of the people to alter or to abolish it, & to institute new government, laying it's foundation on such principles & organising it's powers in such form, as to them shall seem most likely to effect their safety & happiness. prudence indeed will dictate that governments long established should not be changed for light & transient causes: and accordingly all experience hath shewn that mankind are more disposed to suffer while evils are sufferable, than to right themselves by abolishing the forms to which they are accustomed. but when a long train of abuses & usurpations [begun at a distinguished period & pursuing invariably the same object, evinces a design to subject reduce them under absolute Despotism, it is their right, it is their duty, to throw off such government & to provide new guards for their future security. such has been the patient sufferance of these colonies; & such is now the necessity which constrains them to expunge their former systems of government. the history of the present king of Great Britain is a history of unremitting injuries and usurpations, among which appears no solitary fact to contradict the uniform tenor of the rest but all have in direct object the establishment of an absolute tyranny over these states. to prove this, let facts be submitted to a candid world, for the truth of which we pledge a faith yet unsullied by falsehood.

First page of Jefferson's original rough draft of the Declaration of Independence

Thomas Jefferson Papers, Manuscripts Division, Library of Congress

The Declaration of Independence. Painting by John Trumbull. The artist painted Jefferson's portrait from life during the winter of 1787–1788 in Paris. Jefferson's portrait was the second to be painted on the canvas, which Trumbull would not finish until 1820.

Miniature of Jefferson painted by John Trumbull
for Maria Cosway, 1788
Courtesy White House Collection

Martha Jefferson.
Miniature of Jefferson's daughter
by Joseph Boze, 1789.
Diplomatic Reception Rooms, United States
Department of State.
Photograph by Will Brown

Maria Cosway.
Painting by Richard Cosway.
Courtesy Cincinnati Art Museum

Jefferson as secretary of state. Painted from life by Charles Willson Peale
in Philadelphia, 1791.
Courtesy Independence National Historical Park Collection

Jefferson on the eve of his presidency. Painted from life by Rembrandt
Peale in Philadelphia, 1800.
Courtesy White House Collection

Courtesy Museum of Fine Arts, Boston

Courtesy National Portrait Gallery, Smithsonian Institution, Washington, D.C.

The Peale portrait (opposite page) became the major source of popular
images of Jefferson during his presidency, including the two on this page.
At the top is the engraving by David Edwin published in 1800. The other
engraving is by Cornelius Tiebout. It was published in Philadephia in
1801 and offered for sale to the public for two dollars soon after
Jefferson's inauguration as president.

Plaster model of the Virginia state capitol, sent in 1786 by Jefferson from
Paris to Richmond
Courtesy Virginia State Library, Richmond

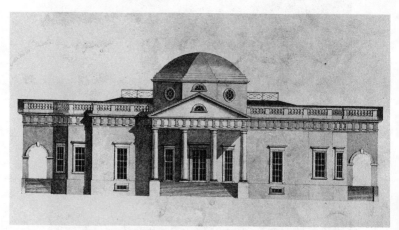

Monticello. Drawing attributed to Robert Mills, about 1803.
Courtesy Massachusetts Historical Society, Boston

furnishings, books, and other belongings shipped from France arrived in Philadelphia. He paid a "monstrous bill of freight"—$544.53—for the shipment from Le Havre, and on December 22, draymen delivered the first load of crates from the wharf. Twenty-six more loads arrived before the end of the month, filling the house with crates and littering it with packing materials as the carefully packed containers were opened—all while workmen were trying to put the finishing touches on the house's interior.[3]

What a shipment of goods from Paris it was! Packed among numerous mattresses, blankets, and pillows were enough chairs to fill a mansion, as indeed they had in his Paris residence. One crate after another was filled with chairs: 10 crimson ones (2 of them armchairs), another set of 8 covered in crimson velvet, 6 in red morocco, and 12 in blue. There were also 2 blue easy chairs, a blue silk ottoman, and a red morocco ottoman. Other crates contained 7 mahogany tables, 4 marble tops with gilt borders, 4 floor-length mirrors with gilt borders (still to be seen at Monticello today), 14 blue damask curtains, 22 bell pulls, and 145 rolls of wallpaper. There were 3 gaming tables, 2 daybeds, a library ladder, and also porcelain dishes, crystal goblets, silver candlesticks, and brass andirons. There were figurines, epergnes, vases, clocks, and fine writing paper. Even 6 stoves were crated, and among numerous kitchen utensils could be found a waffle iron and four molds for ices. Nor did his packers in Paris fail to send the fountain and its basin from his anteroom. In addition, they shipped a dozen cases of wine and 2 cases of macaroni.[4] Then, of course, there were his books.

Fifteen of the 78 crates shipped to Philadelphia were packed with books, and it was a magnificent library indeed that he had collected during his five years in France. Years later when he sold his collection to Congress for its library, he said, "While residing in Paris, I devoted every afternoon I was disengaged, for a summer or two, in examining all the principal bookstores, turning over every book with my own hands, and putting by everything which related to America, and indeed whatever was rare and valuable in every science." He also added that he had standing orders with booksellers in major European cities for books relating to America not found in Paris. Not immodestly he concluded that "such a collection was made as probably can never again be effected, because it is hardly probable that the same opportunities, the same time, industry, perseverance, and expense, with some knowledge of the bibliography of the subject, would again happen to be in concurrence." Jefferson had taken special precaution to secure the safe shipment of these treasures, having instructed that each book be wrapped separately in paper and each box wrapped in oilcloth.[5] When the books were finally unpacked and shelved, he had at hand a library to serve his needs as secretary of state as well as for his own enjoyment.

Two months after arriving in Philadelphia, half of the crates had not been opened, and Jefferson did not get his household affairs fully in order until Adrien Petit, the trusted and efficient maître d'hôtel who had managed his house in Paris, arrived in Philadelphia in July, 1791.[6] He had tried to get Petit to join him in New York, but the Frenchman preferred to stay in Paris, hoping that Jefferson's successor as minister would employ him. Not until after moving to Philadelphia did Jefferson succeed in changing Petit's mind. By then Jefferson was willing to offer higher wages, and Petit had tired of waiting for Jefferson's replacement.[7] Jefferson was delighted when Petit finally decided to come. Besides getting his house in order, Petit's arrival made it easier for him to bring his daughter Maria (Polly), now thirteen, back with him after his trip home in the fall of 1791. Petit would remain in his service as long as Jefferson was secretary of state, even though the debts that Jefferson accumulated during that period show that he could hardly afford to employ him.[8]

When everything was uncrated and in place, Jefferson had established himself in elegant and convenient surroundings. His residence, the fourth west of Eighth Street on the south side of Market, was near the building that he had rented for the State Department offices on the northwest corner of Market and Eighth streets. At first, Jefferson had thought of renting two adjoining houses, using the top two floors for his apartment and the first floor of both houses for department offices, but he found that the funds allowed for his office rent were insufficient to permit this. Though he had a secretary's room in the modest State Department offices, he did most of his serious work in his better-appointed residence, with his library close at hand.[9] His house was convenient to the president's residence, formerly occupied by Robert Morris, about three blocks away on the same street. He was also close to Congressional Hall and to the nearby American Philosophical Society, whose members earlier had chosen him as a councillor and in January, 1791, elected him one of the three vice-presidents of the society. Philadelphia was the American city that Jefferson liked best, and one reason was the circle of friends he had there, especially in the American Philosophical Society. At this moment, however, the duties of his office left him little time to devote to scientific enterprises.

From the convening of the final session of the First Congress on December 6, 1790, until its adjournment on March 3, 1791, Jefferson was unusually pressed with preparing reports for Congress and the president. Indeed, during much of the period he completed a major report nearly every week. A few days after Congress assembled, Washington asked the secretary of state to review the correspondence relating to Gouverneur Morris' mission to London and to recommend measures to be pursued. After studying the record, Jefferson concluded that the British had decided not to evacuate the posts still occupied on United States soil and that they did not intend to negotiate a commercial treaty unless the United States would agree to an alliance undermining American obligations to France. He recommended, and the president agreed, that Morris' mission be ended and that any further initiative for negotiations come from England.[10]

The adoption of this policy did not mean abandoning efforts to push the British toward reciprocity, as demonstrated in Jefferson's report on cod and whale fisheries, submitted to the House of Representatives on February 1, 1791. His exhaustive analysis of the depressed state of the fisheries concluded by drawing attention to the obligation of the government to promote free world markets and indicated that markets for the products of American fisheries could be maintained "by friendly arrangements towards those nations whose arrangements are friendly to us." While Jefferson spoke of developing markets in France, he saw no disposition on the part of England "to arrange this or any other commercial matter to mutual convenience. The exparte regulations which they have begun for mounting their navigation on the ruins of ours, can only be opposed by counter-regulations on our part."[11] Jefferson's views coincided with Madison's legislative efforts to enact navigation and trade measures that would "meet the regulations of foreign nations on terms of reciprocity." The First Congress failed to act on Madison's navigation bill before adjourning, but after the end of the session Jefferson sent copies of the proposed measure to diplomatic representatives William Short in Paris, David Humphreys in Lisbon, and William Carmichael in Madrid suggesting that they work to encourage France, Portugal, and Spain to enact similar laws. The proposed act, he said, "is perfectly innocent as to other nations, is strictly just as to the English, cannot be parried by them, and if adopted by other nations would inevitably defeat their navigation act and reduce their powers on the sea within safer limits."[12]

Convinced that British trading restrictions could be successfully countered by retaliations in trade policies by other countries, Jeffer son saw concerted action as the most effective tactic. Yet, he wa prepared for the United States to act alone. That stance clearly placed him on a confrontation course with Hamilton, who opposed any discrimination against England. When Jefferson's report on fisheries was presented to Congress and published in the news papers, Hamilton did not publicly respond, but he continued to oppose Jefferson's policy within the administration. At a cabinet meeting in December, 1791, when Jefferson indicated that he was planning to recommend retaliation against Great Britain in a re port to Congress, Hamilton argued vigorously against it, insisting that any such proposal would undermine the chances of obtain ing the British evacuation of the western posts through negotia tions with the recently arrived British minister, George Hammond Hamilton's reasoning persuaded Jefferson to hold back his report as long as there was any hope that the British intended to sur render the posts. By the time he discovered that Hammond had no authority to negotiate on that subject, it was too late to submit his report to Congress. Jefferson blamed Hammond's delaying tactics on Hamilton's revealing to him the cabinet discussions. Even with out Hamilton's interference it is not at all clear that Jefferson's and Madison's proposed policy of commercial retaliation against Britain would have worked. Britain was indeed concerned about the threat of American retaliation, but there is considerable evidence that the British were prepared to retaliate against the United States in re turn.[13] No immediate settlement of the disputes with Britain was reached.

Meanwhile, the leading objectives of the secretary of state's for eign policy were becoming clear in other areas. One of the first sub jects that Jefferson had discussed with the president after joining the cabinet concerned Americans being held captive by the Al gerines, and one of the first matters referred to him by the House of Representatives was a petition from those same captives. Not un til the next congressional session, however, did Jefferson complete his report on the subject, submitting it to Congress on December 30, 1790. The delay may have resulted from secret negotiations under way for release of the Americans or from Jefferson's desire to connect the question of the Algerine captives with the broader issue of American commerce in the Mediterranean. His slow re sponse certainly did not indicate any lack of interest in the mat ter on his part. On the contrary, the problem of the capture of American seamen by Mediterranean pirates had long concerned him. He had devoted considerable attention to the issue as minister to France, at which time he had favored using naval force, preferably in league with other states, to suppress piracy rather than paying ransom. Secretary of State Jefferson still held the same opinion when he reported to Congress on the American captives and trade in the Mediterranean. "Upon the Whole, it rests with Congress to decide between War, Tribute, and Ransom, as the Means of reestablishing our Mediterranean Commerce," he concluded. But his report and the documents accompanying it left little doubt as to the course that he believed should be followed. Senator Maclay thought the papers "seemed to breathe resentment, and abounded with martial estimates in a naval way."[14] Such a position was consistent both with the policies Jefferson had pursued as minister to France and with the larger objectives of his foreign policy as secretary of state. Protection of American trade in the Mediterranean would promote American commerce and simultaneously strike against British commercial supremacy.

Britain was willing to pay tribute and allow the Barbary pirates to prey on the ships of smaller states because there was more to be gained by this policy than by keeping the Mediterranean free of pirates for the ships of all countries. It was this aspect of the issue that may explain why Jefferson's proposal did not attract greater support from the advocates of commerce and naval power and why Hamilton was not an ally in the business. The secretary of the treasury was more interested in not offending England and in drawing the United States closer to that commercial power than in advancing the growth of independent American commerce or freedom of the seas. The result was that though a Senate committee, whose members included some of Hamilton's most influential supporters, reported that the "trade of the United States to the Mediterranean cannot be protected but by a naval force," it also equivocated by saying "it will be proper to resort to the same as soon as the state of public finances will admit." After a Senate resolution to this effect was allowed to die in committee, the Senate resolved that the president be authorized to spend forty thousand dollars to redeem citizens of the United States held in captivity in Algiers.[15] Congress thus chose to pay ransom and delay confrontation. Jefferson would have to wait until he became president to employ naval power to end the paying of tribute in the Mediterranean.

Foreign-policy differences between the secretary of state and the secretary of the treasury were evident in regard to France as well as Britain. When the French protested that Congress' failure to ex-

empt France from the higher tonnage duties levied on foreign vessels contradicted the treaty of amity and commerce, Jefferson rejected the argument. But he recommended that, considering the
value of the interests at stake and the small amount of money involved, the concession to France be made. Hamilton opposed the
proposal, and it failed to win support in Congress, which earlier
had rejected Madison's effort to impose higher duties on ships of
countries not having a commercial treaty with the United States.
While Jefferson sought to nurture relationships with France and to
counter commercial subservience to England, Hamilton looked for
opportunities to lessen ties with France and to develop links with
England. "In the case of the two nations with which we have the
most intimate connections, France and England," Jefferson explained, "my system was to give some satisfactory distinctions to
the former, of little cost to us, in return for the solid advantages
yielded us by them; and to have met the English with some restrictions which might induce them to abate their severities against our
commerce." This policy, he believed, had the support of the president. "Yet the secretary of the treasury, by his cabals with members of the legislature, and by high-toned declamation on other
occasions, has forced down his own system, which was exactly
the reverse."[16] This bitter protest, which Jefferson penned amid
heightening clashes between the two cabinet officers, reveals how
important foreign-policy matters were in producing the deep an-
tagonisms between the two men.

By 1791 foreign affairs and domestic policy intertwined to end
the earlier cooperation that Jefferson had extended to Hamilton
on funding and assumption. After the secretary of the treasury
submitted his proposal for a national bank to Congress in December, 1790, Jefferson privately began to express his concerns about
Hamilton's policies.[17] In Congress Madison openly led the opposition to the bank bill but failed to block the measure, which passed
both houses in February, 1791, and was sent to the president. Before deciding whether to sign the bill, Washington sought opinions
on its constitutionality, first from Attorney General Randolph and
then from both Jefferson and Hamilton. These confidential memoranda prepared for the president's use were not made public. Nonetheless, they were immensely important papers and in time became
known. Their importance lies less in the evidence of the emerging
split between the two cabinet members than in the constitutional
interpretations advanced. The reasoning of each officer would
have far-reaching influence in American history. Jefferson's argu-

ments for strict construction laid the foundation for the states' rights interpretation of the Constitution, while Hamilton's opinion served as the model that Chief Justice John Marshall would later follow in giving judicial sanction to the doctrine of implied powers.

Jefferson's concise brief arguing that the bill to charter a national bank was unconstitutional rested on the dictum of the still-unratified Tenth Amendment that "the powers not delegated to the United States by the Constitution, nor prohibited by it to the States, are reserved to the States respectively, or to the people." Jefferson insisted that "to take a single step beyond the boundaries thus specially drawn around the powers of Congress, is to take possession of a boundless field of power, no longer susceptible of any definition." The incorporation of a bank had not been delegated to the United States by the Constitution. He first examined the specially enumerated powers of Congress, particularly the powers to tax, to borrow money, and to regulate commerce, and concluded that the chartering of a bank was not included among any of the enumerations. He then considered the general phrase of the Constitution that identified the purpose of the taxing power as "to pay the Debts and provide for the common Defence and general Welfare of the United States." Congress, he said, was to levy taxes only for these purposes, not for any purpose they pleased. "In like manner they are *not to do anything they please* to provide for the general welfare, but only *to lay taxes* for that purpose." To interpret this provision in any other way would reduce the Constitution to "a single phrase, that of instituting a Congress with power to do whatever would be for the good of the U.S. and as they would be the sole judges of good or evil, it would be also a power to do whatever evil they pleased." [18]

Jefferson next turned to the constitutional provision giving Congress the authority to make all laws necessary and proper for carrying into execution its enumerated powers. He insisted that this key clause be read strictly. A bank was not necessary for Congress to carry into execution any of its enumerated powers and therefore was not authorized by the Constitution. It mattered not how useful or convenient a bank might be in collecting taxes or borrowing money; Congress was restricted to only that which was necessary. Otherwise there was nothing "which ingenuity may not torture into a *convenience, in some way or other, to some one* of so long a list of enumerated powers." Congress, he concluded, was limited to "those means without which the grant of the power would be nugatory." In offering his opinion to the president, Jefferson also gave a strict reading to the president's veto power and advised Washington that if he were not clearly convinced in his own mind that the measure was unauthorized by the Constitution, "a just respect for the wisdom of the legislature would naturally decide the balance in favour of their opinion."[19]

The strict construction of the Constitution that Jefferson here advocated would remain his fundamental view of the Constitution throughout his life. Even when he allowed himself to be a party to actions that he considered outside the scope of the Constitution— as in the purchase of Louisiana—he never justified it on a loose reading of the Constitution but on the necessity of implementing the will of the people in exceptional circumstances in which time did not permit constitutional amendments. As president, Jefferson would follow the rule he advocated to the first president in regard to the use of the veto power, and in eight years he would never employ the executive veto.

Jefferson had not seen Randolph's opinion when he drafted his memorandum for the president, but the attorney general also viewed the bank as unconstitutional. With two opinions against the bank bill, Washington wanted the arguments on the other side and sent both papers to Hamilton with a request for his views.[20] With their opinions before him when he prepared his lengthy exposition, Hamilton directed much of his argument to answering his colleagues. He began by asserting "that every power vested in a Government is in its nature *sovereign*, and includes by *force* of the *term*, a right to employ all the *means* requisite, and fairly *applicable* to the attainment of the *ends* of such power; and which are not precluded by restrictions and exceptions specified in the constitution." He then went on to challenge the specific arguments of the attorney general and the secretary of state. Disputing Jefferson's interpretation of the necessary and proper clause, he insisted that "it is essential to the being of the National government, that so erroneous a conception of the meaning of the word *necessary*, should be explored. It is certain, that neither the grammatical, nor popular sense of the term requires that construction. According to both, *necessary* often means no more than *needful, requisite, incidental, useful,* or *conducive to.*" Jefferson, he said, was interpreting *necessary* as if it were prefixed by the word *absolutely* or *indispensably.* We need not follow all of Hamilton's detailed argument, but it is important to note his conclusion. What he wrote would be convincing not only to Washington but also to John Marshall, who later would use much the same language in the famous case of *McCulloch* v. *Maryland* (1819) to uphold the constitutionality of the second Bank of the

United States, thereby establishing the judicial interpretation of the implied powers clause. The criterion of what is constitutional and what is not, Hamilton wrote, "is the *end* to which the measure relates as a *mean*. If the end be clearly comprehended within any of the specified powers, and if the measure have an obvious relation to that end, and is not forbidden by any particular provision of the constitution—it may safely be deemed to come within the compass of national authority." [21]

Hamilton's persuasive arguments prevailed over Jefferson's rigid interpretation and in the course of time sustained an expansion of national authority that Jefferson's strict construction would never have permitted. Jefferson's answer to the problem of adjusting government to changing times was that expressed in his belief that "the earth belongs always to the living," which encouraged the periodical drafting of new constitutions. It was not change he opposed but altering the powers of government without returning to constituent authority. Hamilton, he thought, was trying to alter the government without consulting the people.

Jefferson objected to the creation of a national bank not only on constitutional grounds but also as a matter of public policy. He saw the bank as a tool of special interests and an unhealthy concentration of economic power, part of a design to promote moneyed interests at the expense of farmers. When the bank bill was before Congress, he confided to George Mason that "the only corrective of what is amiss in our present government will be the augumentation of the numbers in the lower house, so as to get a more agricultural representation, which may put that interest above that of the stockjobbers." [22] This was an early indication of Jefferson's recognition of the need to marshal political opposition in Congress against Hamilton's programs, but he was reluctant to move openly to organize such a movement. Indeed, his first major appearance in the public press as a dissenter within the administration resulted from an inadvertent act on his own part. In returning a borrowed copy of Thomas Paine's *Rights of Man* to the Philadelphia printer who was planning to publish the pamphlet, he enclosed a brief note in which he remarked that he was extremely pleased that the work was to be reprinted in Philadelphia and that "something is at length to be publicly said against the political heresies which have sprung up among us. I have no doubt our citizens will rally a second time round the standard of Common Sense." [23] To his astonishment an extract from the letter was published at the head of Paine's pamphlet when it appeared in early May, 1791. John Adams took great offense at the publication—and justly so, because Jefferson confessed to Madison that he had had Adams' "Discourses on Davila" in mind when he wrote the comments. "I tell the writer freely that he is a heretic, but certainly never meant to step into a public newspaper with that in my mouth."[24] Jefferson was less forthright in his explanations to Adams, but he tried to smooth the matter over and placate his old friend, though he did not attempt to do so in regard to Hamilton, who, Jefferson said, was "open-mouthed" against him.[25] As newspaper editors throughout the country reprinted Jefferson's comment and joined in the controversy, Jefferson came more and more to appear in the public mind as the champion of republicanism and increasingly to be seen as the opponent of Hamilton.

Just as the controversy was beginning to swirl, Jefferson and Madison set out on a trip to New York and New England. Their itinerary took them to Lakes George and Champlain and back through Bennington, Vermont, western Massachusetts, Connecticut, and Long Island. Political observers immediately saw partisan motives in the journey. One of Hamilton's allies in New York reported "every appearance of a passionate courtship" between the Virginia travelers and Chancellor Robert R. Livingston and Aaron Burr while they were in New York, and he concluded that Hamilton was the target of their plans.[26] Such observations fostered the suspicion that the two Virginians used the trip to build a political alliance with New Yorkers. But all evidence indicates that the journey was primarily what they said it was—a vacation and a tour to study the flora and fauna of the region. Jefferson's notes written along the way offer abundant descriptions of trees, flowers, wildlife, lakes, rivers, and related matters, and not a word on politics. Madison's notes on the journey are crowded with comments on farmland, crops, and the price of wheat and likewise are devoid of politics.[27] While sailing on Lake Champlain, Jefferson wrote his daughter Martha about the previous day on Lake George. That lake, he said, was "without comparison the most beautiful water I ever saw: formed by a contour of mountains into a bason 35 miles long, and from 2 to 4 miles broad, finely interspersed with islands, its waters limpid as chrystal and the mountain sides covered with rich groves of Thuya, silver fir, white pine, Aspen and paper birch down to the water edge, here and there precipices of rock to checquer the scene and save it from monotony. An abundance of speckled trout, salmon trout, bass and other fish with which it is stored, have added to our other amusements the sport of taking them."[28] Not much political onspiracy here! The two men no doubt talked of politics, and indeed they made contacts in New York and elsewhere that later would be politically useful, but Jefferson and Madison were not yet in the business of organizing a political party.[29]

Nonetheless, they had taken steps in that direction by seeking to persuade Philip Freneau to establish a newspaper in Philadelphia. That move was not part of any conscious plan to organize a political party—for both Jefferson and Madison still saw parties as divisive. It was prompted by their desire to get a fairer and wider hearing for their political views. Yet, once Freneau's paper was established, it would contribute to the growth of parties. Freneau, who had gained something of a reputation as a poet during the Revolution, was writing for a New York newspaper when Henry Lee, a former classmate of Freneau's at Princeton, interested another Princetonian, James Madison, in Freneau's less-than-prosperous situation and his desire to relocate. The State Department then had an opening as a translating clerk, and Jefferson offered him the part-time job, which paid only $250 a year but also gave "so little to do as not to interfere with any other calling the person may choose," so long as he stayed in Philadelphia.[30] Although Freneau at first declined this offer, Madison kept in contact with him and, after various negotiations and considerable indecisiveness on Freneau's part, worked out an arrangement under which the New York printing firm of Childs and Swaine took Freneau into a partnership to establish a paper in Philadelphia, and Freneau agreed to become the editor.[31]

Although Madison took the lead in making the arrangements with Freneau, Jefferson regarded it as a joint enterprise and, besides the small salary in his department, promised the editor "the perusal of all my letters of foreign intelligence and all foreign newspapers; the publication of all proclamations and other public notices within my department, and the printing of the laws."[32] Both Jefferson and Madison were active in soliciting subscriptions for Freneau's paper, especially in Virginia, for one of their purposes was to see a paper established that would circulate nationally. The name *National Gazette*, under which Freneau began to publish his paper on October 31, 1791, reflected that aim.

A nationally circulating newspaper was not, however, the only object of Freneau's sponsors. They also wanted a paper that would "furnish a whig-vehicle of intelligence" to counteract the influence of John Fenno's *Gazette of the United States*—a publication Jefferson regarded as "a paper of pure Toryism, disseminating the doctrines of monarchy, aristocracy, and the exclusion of the influence of the

people." Jefferson expected that Freneau "would give free place
to pieces written against the aristocratical and monarchical principles." But the poet-editor was even more spirited than his backers
anticipated and launched a bold attack on Hamilton's policies as
well. Jefferson insisted that he had not expected Freneau to go that
far. "My expectations looked only to the chastisement of the aristocratical and monarchical writers, and not to any criticisms on the
proceedings of the government," he said.[33]

Jefferson regarded his employment of Freneau and other favors
to him as support for a man of genius, but Hamilton and his
friends were unwilling to be so generous, charging that Freneau
was the paid tool of the secretary of state. In a piece in Fenno's
paper, Hamilton himself pointed to the salary that Freneau received from the government and asked whether it was paid for
translations or publications designed to oppose the government's
measures, vilify its officers, and disturb the public peace.[34] Hamilton followed with more detailed charges of "a news paper instituted by a public officer, and the Editor of it regularly pensioned
with the public money, in the disposal of that officer." He said that
the whole complexion of Freneau's paper was "an exact copy of the
politics of his employer foreign and domestic, and exhibits a decisive internal evidence of the influence of that patronage under
which he acts."[35] This attack, which came some nine months after
Freneau began his paper—and while Jefferson, Madison, and Washington were all away on vacation in Virginia—rapidly escalated into
bitter exchanges between Freneau and Fenno, prompting further
anonymously published accusations by Hamilton.[36] Freneau coun-
terattacked with charges that Fenno, who received the considerable
printing business of the Treasury Department, was "a vile syco-
phant" who obtained "emoluments from government, far more lu-
crative than the salary alluded to," while "disseminating principles
and sentiments utterly subversive of the true republican interests
of this country."[37]

Hamilton, who published pieces under various pseudonyms, assumed that Jefferson was doing the same. But Jefferson assured the
president that he "never did by myself or any other, directly or indirectly, write, dictate or procure any one sentence" to be published
in Freneau's paper or in any other gazette, to which he had not
signed his name, with the exception of a paragraph about the Algerine captives that he once put into Fenno's paper. There is no evidence to dispute Jefferson's affirmation that he never wrote anything anonymously for Freneau's gazette, and technically he may

ever have procured pieces for publication. But he was not being candid in his assurances to the president, for he had encouraged others to contribute to Freneau's paper. More important, Jefferson gave Freneau access to a wide variety of materials from the Department of State that he did not make available to other editors—foreign newspapers, official pamphlets, letters, documents, American consular reports, and other foreign intelligence that he supplied selectively. He did not open up his files to Freneau. Indeed, he was careful to guard the confidentiality of diplomatic and other correspondence. But he did select items that he wanted to see published, and he held back others that he did not want Freneau to see. Madison was more direct in his contributions to Freneau. Eighteen unsigned pieces published in the *National Gazette* have been identified as from Madison's pen.[38] Neither Jefferson nor Madison was involved as directly as Hamilton in the newspaper war between Freneau and Fenno. Yet their role in attracting Freneau to Philadelphia, putting him on the payroll of the State Department, and giving him privileges denied to other editors left Jefferson vulnerable to charges difficult to refute no matter how circumspect he tried to be in his relations with the editor.

Ultimately the president hinted to Jefferson that he should intervene in some way to restrain Freneau, perhaps by withdrawing his appointment as translating clerk. Jefferson would not do so. In his view Freneau's paper had "saved our constitution which was galloping fast into monarchy." He believed that "the President, not sensible of the designs of the party, has not with his usual good sense and sang froid, looked on the efforts and effects of this free press, and seen that tho' some bad things had passed thro' it to the public, yet the good have preponderated immensely."[39] Jefferson's fears of a monarchical party appear overblown, but Freneau's paper played a major role in promoting republican views and in presenting Jefferson before the public as a champion of republicanism and the arch foe of the Hamiltonian system. Before Freneau's paper folded after two tumultuous years, it did much to speed the development of national political parties.

When the First Congress ended in March, 1791, political parties had not yet formed either in Congress or in the electorate, but during the Second Congress two opposing political blocs began to coalesce in the legislature and increasingly came to dominate its proceedings. Madison, who emerged in the First Congress as the principal leader of the opposition to Hamilton's policies, headed one group; the opposing bloc comprised supporters of Hamilton.

Less than half of the members of Congress aligned themselves with either group, so that it can hardly be said that Congress was rigidly divided into parties, but such voting blocs had not been evident in the First Congress. Moreover, the new party blocs were observable in Congress before equally clear divisions were found among the electorate. The first national political parties in the United States thus developed at the national center of government and from there spread into the broader political arena, carrying the issues that divided Congress to the electorate, which tended to align along the lines that their representatives in Congress had marked out.[40]

Jefferson's early role in the formation of the Republican party that he would lead to victory at the polls in 1800 must be viewed more broadly than as part of the split in the cabinet. He shared the leadership of the early Republican interest with Madison, whose activities in Congress were more important in an organizational sense than his. Jefferson's role was most important as the symbol of Republicanism, but he was not aloof from the business of politics and was more active in working with Madison in Congress than has sometimes been recognized.

In the spring of 1792 Jefferson for the first time began to talk about the "heats and tumults of conflicting parties." Soon afterward Alexander Hamilton charged that the last session of Congress had convinced him that "Mr. Madison cooperating with Mr. Jefferson is at the head of a faction decidedly hostile to me and my administration, and actuated by views in my judgment subversive of the principles of good government and dangerous to the union, peace and happiness of the Country." Hamilton found it difficult to understand how Madison, who had earlier agreed so fully with him and joined him in writing the *Federalist* papers, could now be so much in opposition, and he was inclined to explain it on personal and partisan grounds. He viewed Jefferson's actions in much the same way. In various conversations that had been reported to him, Jefferson had "thrown censure on my *principles* of government and on my measures of administration," he observed. "In the question concerning the Bank he not only delivered an opinion in writing against its constitutionality and expediency, but he did so *in a stile and manner* which I felt as partaking of asperity and ill humour towards me." In regard to foreign policy he accused both Jefferson and Madison of having "*a womanish attachment to France and a womanish resentment against Great Britain*" and predicted that "if these Gentlemen were left to pursue their own course there would be in less than six months *an open War between the United States and Great*

Britain." He also accused Jefferson of being motivated by presidential ambitions. Marshalling evidence from Freneau's paper, reports from informants, and his own observations, he was convinced that Jefferson and Madison were conspiring to drive him from his Treasury post.[41]

By late summer of 1792 the growing controversy in the press led by Fenno's *Gazette of the United States* and Freneau's *National Gazette* had focused so much public attention on the disputes between Jefferson and Hamilton that President Washington wrote a confidential letter to each of them expressing his concern and urging them to reconcile their differences. It was regrettable, he said, that while the new nation was surrounded by enemies "internal dissensions should be harrowing and tearing our vitals." If this continued, he feared it would destroy the Union. The letters were couched in similar language but contained enough variation to show that the president had the particular individual in mind as he drafted each letter. He mentioned to Jefferson the danger of one officer of government pulling one way and another the other way after measures had been decided and urged "more charity for the opinions and acts of one another." He told Hamilton that political differences were unavoidable, perhaps necessary, but it was to be regretted "that subjects cannot be discussed with temper on the one hand, or decisions submitted to without having the motives which led to them improperly implicated on the other." While not specifically mentioning the press to Jefferson, Washington in his letter to Hamilton referred to the "irritating charges, with which some of our Gazettes are so strongly impregnated." Despite the shadings, his plea to both men was the same, "that instead of wounding suspicions, and irritable charges, there may be liberal allowances, mutual forbearances, and temporising yieldings on *all sides*."[42]

In a lengthy response to the president, Jefferson acknowledged the dissensions within the administration and expressed his regret at being a part of them, but he placed most of the blame on the secretary of the treasury. Upon taking office as secretary of state, he had determined not to intermeddle at all with the legislature, he said, and as little as possible with other departments. In regard to Congress, he had departed from the rule only once, and that was in connection with the assumption business. As for the Treasury, he had never swerved farther from his rule than "the mere enunciation of my sentiments in conversation, and chiefly among those who, expressing the same sentiments, drew mine from me." He admitted that in his private conversations he had utterly disapproved of the system of the secretary of the treasury, and he pronounced Hamilton's policies as based on principles "adverse to liberty" and "calculated to undermine and demolish the republic, by creating an influence of his department over the members of the legislature." Nevertheless, he flatly declared that "if it has been supposed that I have ever intrigued among the members of the legislatures to defeat the plans of the Secretary of the Treasury, it is contrary to all truth."[43]

Jefferson contrasted this with Hamilton's cabals with members of the legislature, his interference in the conduct of foreign affairs, and his attacks on him in the press. There was not the least doubt that Hamilton was the author of the pieces signed "An American" appearing in Fenno's *Gazette of the United States*, Jefferson told the president. (We know today that Hamilton was indeed the author of those pieces.) It astounded Jefferson that anyone who was shuffling millions of dollars backward and forward from money to paper and back and forth between Europe and America while dealing out Treasury secrets among his friends could charge him with unethical conduct in hiring Freneau as a translating clerk at $250 a year. He went to great pains to defend his relationship with the editor. He also answered Hamilton's charges that he had no desire to see the public debt paid by saying that the difference between Hamilton and himself was that "I would wish the debt paid tomorrow; he wishes it never to be paid, but always to be a thing where with to corrupt and manage the legislature."[44] Jefferson closed his letter with an announcement of his determination to retire from office at the end of Washington's first term.

Hamilton said in his reply to the president that he considered himself the deeply injured party. "I *know*," he wrote, "that I have been an object of uniform opposition from Mr. Jefferson, from the first moment of his coming to the City of New York to enter upon his present office. I *know*, from the most authentic sources, that I have been the frequent subject of the most unkind whispers and insinuating from the same quarter." He also charged that a party had been formed in the legislature under Jefferson's auspices, bent upon his subversion. He admitted taking part in retaliations, but he said that he could not for the present recede from that course. Suggesting that it might be necessary for the president to replace the differing members of his administration, he indicated that he would cheerfully acquiesce in such a plan.[45] Hamilton may have considered himself indispensable and have seen this offer as a way to get Jefferson out of the government, not knowing that his rival had already told the president of his plans to retire. Hamilton's letter was far less detailed and explanatory than Jefferson's, but it left the distinct impression that he had little intention of altering his ways.

The bitterness that Jefferson and Hamilton displayed toward each other in their letters surprised Washington. He told Jefferson that he had been aware of their political differences but "had never suspected it had gone so far in producing a personal difference." He still hoped, however, to act as a mediator and urged Jefferson to stay in office as a check within his administration.[46] If Washington fully recognized the depth of their ideological differences and conflicting principles of administration, he could not realistically have hoped to reconcile the two principal officers of his government, especially after Hamilton had indicated that he could not alter his course for the present. At the same time, the president could hardly have been prepared for the escalation of the public dispute that ensued.

Hamilton's attacks on Jefferson in the newspapers continued, increased in volume and intensity, and along with the responses they provoked, they kept the war of words raging in the press until the end of the year. Jefferson, as he had assured the president, never directly entered the fray, but his friends did, and he supplied them with materials for responding. "Aristides" (probably Edmund Randolph) replied to Hamilton's "An American," charging the author with "the basest calumny and falsehood" and speculating that "a certain head of a department is the real author or instigator of this unprovoked and unmanly attack on Mr. Jefferson."[47] "Aristides" reasoned that if opposition to the funding system, the national bank, and other measures of the secretary of the treasury made Jefferson a patron of disunion, national insignificance, and public disorder, as "An American" indicated, then "a great majority of the independent yeomanry of our country" were equally guilty. "Aristides" prompted a response from Hamilton using the signature "Catullus." "Mr. Jefferson," he said, "has hitherto been distinguished as the quiet modest, retiring philosopher—as the plain simple unambitious republican." It was time that he be recognized as "the intriguing incendiary—the aspiring turbulent competitor." It had been amply demonstrated that "Mr. Jefferson's politics, whatever may be the motives of them *tend* to national disunion, insignificance, disorder and discredit." As Jefferson's defenders entered the contest, Hamilton continued the Catullus series in the *Gazette of the United States* through six installments that did not cease until late December.[48]

Jefferson's principal defense came from Madison and Monroe, who together prepared a series of six essays appearing under the title "Vindiction of Mr. Jefferson" in *Dunlap's American Daily Advertiser*, published in Philadelphia. Monroe did the bulk of the work, being the principal author of five of the six pieces, but Madison was an active collaborator. Besides defending the hiring of Freneau, the essayists answered Hamilton's charges that Jefferson had been hostile to the Constitution before its adoption. They published excerpts from letters that Jefferson had written to Madison from France expressing his reservations about the absence of a bill of rights but indicating his general approval.[49]

The months during which newspaper editors unfolded the rivalry between Jefferson and Hamilton before readers throughout the country coincided with the congressional and presidential elections of 1792. Washington had contemplated retiring after four years in office, and in May, 1792, he went so far as to persuade a reluctant Madison to draft a farewell message for him.[50] Meanwhile, he came under increasing pressure to stand as a candidate for another term. Madison appealed for "one more sacrifice, severe as it may be, to the desires and interests of your country." Jefferson wrote a long and impassioned plea proclaiming Washington's services to be indispensable to preserving republican government and preventing the breakup of the Union. He feared that a "corrupt squadron" in Congress aimed at getting rid of the constitutional limitations on its power and changing the republican form of government into a monarchy modeled on the English constitution. It was essential that Washington remain in office a few years longer until the republican character of the legislature could be established. Hamilton, seeing enemies of a different stripe trying to take over the government, also appealed to the president not to leave office.[51] In response to these pleas, Washington delayed his announcement of retirement, but he held back from committing himself to a second term until late in the fall of 1792, believing that a month before the election was ample time to announce his decision.

Meanwhile, elections for the House of Representatives were under way in different states at different times, and there was significant political maneuvering in regard to the vice-presidential election. Jefferson had little part in the measures relating to the election of 1792, but his close friends and political allies Madison and Monroe were actively involved. They played a major role in the arrangements worked out with Pennsylvania and New York Republican leaders to organize support for Governor George Clinton of New York for vice-president in the place of John Adams. John Beckley, the clerk of the House of Representatives and one of the most ingenious and effective party managers of the early republic, was the leading intermediary in the behind-the-scenes activities that produced the cooperation. The principals were Aaron Burr in New York and Madison and Monroe in Virginia, but Jefferson clearly was aware of what was going on, for on a trip to New York in September, 1792, Beckley carried a letter from Jefferson's good friend Dr. Benjamin Rush introducing Beckley as having "the confidence of our two illustrious patriots Mr. Jefferson and Mr. Madison." Rush urged Burr "to take an active part in removing the monarchical rubbish of our government." This early interstate cooperation among Republican leaders was remarkably successful in producing unanimous electoral votes for Clinton in New York, Virginia, North Carolina, and Georgia, giving him 50 electoral votes to 77 for John Adams. That showing against the incumbent vice-president gave notice of the rising strength of the Republican opposition and the beginnings of a political alliance between New York and Virginia Republicans.[52] Unchallenged in the presidential contest, Washington received the unanimous vote of all 132 electors.

Jefferson assessed the results of the congressional elections, which he regarded as critical, to be "generally in favor of republican and against the aristocratical candidates." Despite all of Hamilton's efforts in the newspapers, the Treasury head lost support. Counting "a decided majority in favor of the republican interest" in the next Congress, Jefferson predicted that the government would soon return to "the true principles of the Constitution."[53] It would be nearly a year, however, before that Congress met in December, 1793. By that time Jefferson would be counting the days until he left the cabinet to return to Virginia.

XIII
A Trying Year

Jefferson planned to resign as secretary of state at the end of Washington's first term as president. He gave up the lease on his house in Philadelphia effective in mid-March, 1793, began packing his considerable belongings for shipment to Monticello, and said he contemplated his approaching retirement "with the fondness of a sailor who has land in view."[1] But early in February he told the president that he would stay on for a while longer, at least until summer or fall. His concern that leaving office would be seen as retreating under attack from Hamilton and other writers in the press weighed heavily in making that decision. He confided to his daughter Martha that he feared resigning would injure him in the eyes of the public, who would suppose that he "withdrew from investigation" or "had not tone of mind sufficient to meet slander."[2]

In the months ahead Jefferson may have wondered whether he had made the right decision, for his final year as secretary of state turned out to be one of the most arduous of his many years in public life. The year 1793 was a difficult one in world affairs—a time of general war in Europe, terror in France, and uncertainty throughout the Western world. The president suggested that Jefferson return as minister to France in the critical times, but Jefferson protested that he would never again cross the Atlantic and insisted that when he left the State Department it would be to retire to Monticello.[3] At home, political divisions grew sharper and the administration more divided. In addition, the scourge of yellow fever spread through Philadelphia in late summer and forced the government to flee the capital. It was a trying year.

When the new year opened, domestic politics more than foreign affairs loomed uppermost in Jefferson's mind. His Virginia friends in Congress, led by Representative William Branch Giles, pressed an investigation into the Treasury Department that seemed aimed at driving Hamilton from his post. Jefferson's role in this is not clear, but a draft in Jefferson's handwriting of Giles's resolutions censuring the conduct of the secretary of the treasury suggests that Jefferson was a party to the business and that he was not so aloof from the proceedings of Congress as he claimed to be.[4] In the closing days of the Second Congress, the resolutions were soundly defeated, and as members scattered to their homes in early March, public interest in disputes about Treasury policies faded, while news from Europe seized the attention of most Americans.

Since his return from France, Jefferson had watched the events in that troubled country with equanimity. He had difficulty in getting information about what was happening there, and the reports he received were always six to eight weeks old. Whatever the news, he never wavered in his optimism about the ultimate success of the Revolution. As time passed, he came to see the French Revolution as essential to the spread of liberty not only in Europe but also in the United States. He wrote privately in 1791 that "a check there would retard the revival of liberty in other countries. I consider the establishment and success of their government as necessary to stay up our own and to prevent it from falling back to that kind of Half-way-house, the English constitution." Although he had approved of the constitution that established a constitutional monarchy in France, he accepted the overthrow of the king as necessary to maintain the Revolution and was prepared to condone considerable turmoil to preserve that advance. When the violent events in Paris caused William Short, Jefferson's protégé and former private secretary now at the Hague, to turn against the Revolution, Jefferson wrote him a long letter defending the events in France. He deplored the violence and loss of lives, but he said, "The liberty of the whole earth was depending on the issue of the contest, and was ever such a prize won with so little innocent blood?"[5]

Gouverneur Morris, who succeeded Jefferson as minister to France, never shared Jefferson's support for the French Revolution, and after the overthrow of the king, the secretary of state felt compelled to instruct him on the question of what kind of government he should do business with. "It accords with our principles," Jefferson wrote in a historic formulation of recognition policy, "to acknowledge any government to be rightful which is formed by the will of the nation substantially declared."[6] In a subsequent letter he elaborated: "We surely cannot deny to any nation that right whereon our own government is founded, that every one may govern itself under whatever forms it pleases, and change these forms at it's own will, and that it may transact it's business with foreign nations through whatever organ it thinks proper, whether King, convention, assembly, committee, President, or whatever else it may chuse. The will of the nation is the only thing essential to be regarded."[7]

Jefferson was convinced that most Americans shared his view of the French Revolution, and he reported to Short the "universal feasts and rejoicings" with which Americans greeted the arrival of the news of the French victories over Prussia and the establishment of the French republic.[8] The latter event, proclaimed in September, 1792, became known in America in December and provoked a tremendous outpouring of enthusiasm. The new year began with numerous toasts to the French republic and its future. Celebrations reached new heights when the first minister of the French republic, Edmond Charles Genet, arrived in Charleston, South Carolina, on April 8, 1793. By this time, however, the news had arrived that Louis XVI had been executed on January 21, and on the day before Genet landed in Charleston, Jefferson informed the president that at the beginning of February France had declared war against England and Holland. These developments deeply affected Americans, who remembered the aid of Louis XVI during their own revolution and the treaty of alliance signed with France in 1778.

In reporting the outbreak of war between England and France to the president, the secretary of state advised that the United States "take every justifiable measure for preserving our neutrality."[9] Earlier, as war clouds darkened in Europe, Jefferson had written American envoys and consuls that the United States expected to be neutral. "We wish not to meddle with the internal affairs of any country, nor with the general affairs of Europe. Peace with all nations, and the right which that gives us with respect to all nations, are our object." He instructed agents to be vigilant in securing for American vessels all the rights of neutrality and preventing foreign vessels from usurping the flag of the United States. Jefferson's commitment to neutrality is clear enough in the historical record, but contemporary perceptions of his policy were clouded by partisanship. At almost the same time that Jefferson penned the above letter, Oliver Wolcott was writing to his son, the comptroller of the treasury and a strong Hamiltonian supporter, expressing his hope that the president would closely watch the secretary of state so that his "indiscretion" would not involve the United States in "the vortex of European politics." Whatever the fears of some of his contemporaries, as long as he remained secretary of state, Jefferson pursued a policy of neutrality. He believed in the French cause, but he placed the interests of his own country first, and those interests dictated a policy of peace. At the same time, Jefferson did recognize that this course would benefit France more than England, because the United States would be more useful as a neutral supplying France with provisions than as a militarily weak ally. He admitted that Americans could not suppress their affections for France, but he promised that they would "suppress the effects of them so as to preserve a fair neutrality."[10]

The opening of hostilities between France and England, followed a month later by France's declaration of war on Spain (March 7), made it urgent that the administration define a clear policy. On April 18, President Washington, returning from a brief spring vacation at Mount Vernon cut short by the news of the war, sent a list of questions for consideration to all members of the cabinet and called a meeting at his house at nine o'clock the next morning. He asked his advisers to consider whether a neutrality proclamation should be issued, whether a minister from the French republic should be received, and, if so, whether without reservations. He also posed a series of questions relating to the alliance with France, the critical issue being whether the treaties of 1778 with France were still valid in light of the change of government in France. When he read the president's memorandum, Jefferson was convinced that, though the handwriting was Washington's, the language was Hamilton's and "the doubts his alone."[11] There was no doubt in the mind of the secretary of state that the treaties with France were still valid and that Genet ought to be received.

At the cabinet meeting on April 19, Jefferson argued that the president had no authority to issue a declaration of neutrality or to do anything more than declare the actual state of things to be that of peace. He also thought "that it would be better to hold back the declaration of neutrality, as a thing worth something to the powers at war, that they would bid for it, and we might reasonably ask a price, the *broadest privileges* of neutral nations."[12] Jefferson's views did not prevail in the cabinet or with the president. There is no evidence that, had they been followed, Great Britain would have been willing to pay the price Jefferson suggested for neutrality. Out of deference to Jefferson's opinions, the cabinet agreed not to employ the term *neutrality*, and the secretary of state joined in the unanimous recommendation that the president issue a proclamation warning American citizens against becoming involved in the hostilities.[13] The declaration, drafted by Attorney General Randolph and proclaimed by the president on April 22, 1793, thus never used the word *neutrality*, but that intent could not be mistaken. The preamble stated that the United States would "pursue a conduct friendly and impartial towards the belligerent Powers," and the main body of the proclamation admonished all citizens to avoid any actions that might contravene this policy, specifically forbidding any involvement in hostilities or the carrying of contraband goods to warring nations.[14]

The cabinet next took up the question of receiving a minister from the Republic of France. It was unanimously agreed that Genet should be received, but Jefferson recorded that Hamilton did so reluctantly, expressing great regret that any incident had obliged the United States to recognize the new French government.[15] Considerable debate followed regarding whether Genet should be received without qualifications. Hamilton took up the whole issue of the treaties with France, arguing that they had been signed when France was a monarchy, that France had now proclaimed itself to be a republic, that tomorrow it might be something else, and that the treaties should be suspended until it was clear what form the government would take. The United States could then decide whether the treaties should be reinstated or abrogated.[16]

Jefferson's position was that treaties were made between nations and that the people, as the source of all authority in a nation, had the right to change their agents at any time. This did not affect the acts of a nation. Thus the treaties between the United States and France were still valid though both nations had changed their forms of government since making the treaties. Hamilton maintained that if Genet were received without qualification, it would amount to electing to continue the treaties with France, and if it later developed that this was dangerous to the United States, the United States would not then be free to renounce them. Jefferson countered that if carrying out a treaty becomes self-destructive, the law of self-preservation overrules the laws of obligation to others. The provision of the treaties with France that raised the greatest concern was the clause guaranteeing France assistance in defense of its West Indies. Jefferson questioned whether this guarantee would inevitably require the United States to go to war and listed a series of questions that offered grounds to doubt that the guarantee clause would draw the United States into war.[17]

After the cabinet meeting adjourned without deciding the issue, Jefferson, Randolph, and Hamilton each supplied the president with written opinions. Washington confided to Jefferson that he had felt all along that the French treaties were valid, and after weighing the opinions from his advisers, he confirmed that view. He also believed that he should receive Genet, though he decided that it should be done "not with too much warmth or cordiality, so only as to be satisfactory to him." Jefferson convinced himself that this was a small sacrifice to the opinion of Hamilton. Washington accordingly received the French minister on May 18, two days after Genet finally reached Philadelphia following an exuberant over-land journey from Charleston.[18]

Determining the lines and limits of fair neutrality was difficult. "Cases are now arising which will embarrass us a little till the line of neutrality be firmly understood by ourselves and the belligerent parties," Jefferson wrote to Madison less than a week after the neu-trality proclamation. The unneutral actions of many Americans complicated the problem. When a French frigate brought a British prize into the port of Philadelphia, thousands of the yeomanry of the city flocked to the wharves and "burst into peals of exultation," Jefferson reported, when the British colors were seen reversed and the French flying above them. "I wish we may be able to repress the spirit of the people within the limits of a fair neutrality," he said, while admitting that he feared that "a fair neutrality will prove a disagreeable pill to our friends." When it turned out that the French prize that aroused such celebration in Philadelphia had been taken in American waters in the Delaware Bay, the American government ordered the liberation of the crew and the restitution of the ship and cargo.[19]

Despite the cool correctness of his reception by the president, Genet was enthusiastically feted by the citizens of Philadelphia. The secretary of state was also caught up in the warmth of the occa-sion and in private observed extravagantly that it was "impossible for anything to be more affectionate, more magnanimous than the purport of his mission." When Genet met with him for the first time, he told the secretary of state that France would not call upon the United States to guarantee the French West Indies, vindicating Jefferson's judgment on that matter. Genet also announced that France was throwing open all its colonies to American trade and produced his authority to negotiate a new commercial treaty. After the meeting Jefferson told Madison that Genet "offers everything and asks nothing." In his own mind Jefferson contrasted that with Great Britain's "sullen silence and reserve," which had not even inti-mated a wish that the United States remain neutral. "Our corre-spondence with her consists of *demands* where she is interested, and *delays* where we are." Jefferson did not expect to find much support in the cabinet for negotiating a treaty with Genet, and he complained that Hamilton and Knox "under pretence of avoiding war on the one side have no great antipathy to run foul of it on the other, and to make a part in the confederacy of princes against human liberty."[20] As it turned out, Jefferson could be glad that there was no rush by the cabinet to embrace Genet, for it would be only a matter of weeks before Jefferson himself was becoming disillusioned with the ebullient French minister. He had been overly generous in his initial reaction to Genet's mission, but he was not long misled.

In view of the broad public sympathy for France that Genet's arrival in Charleston and his journey to Philadelphia demonstrated and the known French sympathies of the secretary of state, Genet discounted the reserved reception by the president and believed that he need not interpret the neutrality proclamation strictly. While in Charleston, he had begun fitting out privateers and recruiting Americans for military service both at sea and on land against Spanish territory in Florida. Before he reached Philadelphia, these French privateers were already bringing English prizes into American ports, and in Charleston the French consul, under instructions from Genet, had assumed the authority of selling prizes. The secretary of state protested these actions as violations of American sovereignty, but Genet refused to accept his interpretation of the treaties of 1778. The French minister construed a treaty provision that prohibited the enemies of France from fitting out privateers or selling prizes in American ports to mean that such a privilege was granted to France. He also justified consular sale of prizes on the ground that captured ships were French property.[21]

Jefferson saw no validity in Genet's claim for consular sales of prizes, which he regarded as a clear violation of national sovereignty, but he understood Genet's argument that the provision making it unlawful for enemies of France to fit out privateers implied that it was lawful for France. Though he did not reveal to Genet his sympathy for this line of reasoning, he in fact had employed it in the cabinet to argue that privateers fitted out in Charleston before the French were informed of the American interpretation of the treaty should not be ordered out of American ports. No one in the cabinet had agreed with his position, and the president decided to order out such privateers.[22] Jefferson fully accepted that decision, and his position on that specific issue in no way affected his opinion on the broader rights and treaty obligations of the United States. He believed that the treaty provision prohibiting the enemies of France from fitting out privateers or selling their prizes in American ports left the United States "free to refuse the same thing to France, there being no stipulation to the contrary, and we ought to refuse it on principles of fair neutrality."[23] He explained to Genet that "it was the *right* of every nation to prohibit acts of sovereignty from being exercised by any other within its limits, and the *duty* of a neutral nation to prohibit such as would injure one of the warring powers."[24] He thus let stand his protest that consular sales of prizes violated the sovereignty of the United States, warned Genet against granting military commissions and fitting out privateers, and repeated the president's order that all previously equipped vessels depart from American ports.

Genet rejected Jefferson's definition of fair neutrality and continued to challenge the administration's decisions and actions. In a less tolerant tone than he had used earlier, Jefferson wrote to Genet on June 17, repeating that the arming of vessels in American ports was incompatible with the sovereignty of the United States. He added that this was not, as Genet seemed to think, contrary to the principles of natural law, the usage of nations, the treaties between the United States and France, or the proclamation of the president. Jefferson's style of communicating these positions to Genet as the opinions of the president—the proper form for the secretary of state—may have caused Genet to think that Jefferson was transmitting views that he did not fully endorse. Genet would later charge that Jefferson misled him. However, the record shows that once the president decided an issue, Jefferson gave it his full support. Moreover, on the key question of denying France the privilege of fitting out privateers in American ports, Jefferson had advised that course prior to the president's decision. Jefferson's early cordiality toward Genet, his undisguised attachment to France, and his openness in admitting divisions within the administration may have led the French minister to believe that Jefferson was the passive instrument of the president.[25] But that the secretary of state deliberately misled Genet is not supported by the evidence.

At the same time, Jefferson's attitude toward Genet's intrigues against Spanish territory in Louisiana could hardly have been regarded by the French minister as discouragement, however carefully the secretary of state emphasized his determination to maintain neutrality. When the French minister privately revealed to Jefferson that he was planning to recruit troops in Kentucky to attack Louisiana, Jefferson himself recorded: "I told him that his enticing officers and souldiers from Kentucky to go against Spain, was really putting a halter about their necks, for that they would assuredly be hung, if they commenced hostilities against a nation at peace with the U.S. That leaving out that article I did not care what insurrections should be excited in Louisiana."[26] This reply may be partly explained by Jefferson's belief that Spain was picking a quarrel with the United States, but it hardly seems the language of fair neutrality.[27]

It is unnecessary to examine the various incidents that produced clashes between the secretary of state and the French minister. They filled much of Jefferson's time from Genet's arrival in Philadelphia in May until the administration made its final decision on what to do about him in August. Jefferson said that he found himself "worn down with labours from morning to night, and day to day," and he placed much of the blame on Genet.[28]

Jefferson's position was also made more difficult by the mounting party conflict and the concern among his own political friends about the administration's policy. To many of them the president's neutrality proclamation had the mark of Hamilton's pro-British proclivities. Madison thought the proclamation "a most unfortunate error. It wounds the national honor, by seeming to disregard the stipulated duties to France. It wounds the popular feeling by a seeming indifference to the cause of liberty. And it seems to violate the forms and spirit of the Constitution, by making the executive Magistrate the organ . . . of the Nation in relation to War and peace." Jefferson assured his friend that he had argued against it in the cabinet but to have opposed the final decision would have hazarded an even more critical question—whether the treaties with France would be suspended. He also privately defended Washington's role. He said that "every inch of ground must be fought in our councils to desperation in order to hold up the face of even a sneaking neutrality." Hamilton was "panic-struck if we refuse our breach to every kick which Great Britain may chuse to give." If the United States preserved even a sneaking neutrality, the country would be indebted to the president. The main factor preventing the neutrality policy from becoming a mere English neutrality, Jefferson thought, was that the penchant of the president was not in that direction.[29]

The extent to which the events in Europe aroused the public surprised Jefferson, who sensed a spirit of 1776 rising again against England. He also believed that the war had "kindled and brought forward the two parties with an ardour which our own interests merely, could never excite." Into this atmosphere Hamilton released his letters of "Pacificus," published in the *Gazette of the United States* beginning on June 29, 1793. The Treasury head insisted that he wrote to counteract attempts being made "very dangerous to the peace" and "not very friendly to the constitution." He began by charging that criticisms of the neutrality proclamation were designed to promote opposition to the government by weakening the confidence of the people in the president. Then he proceeded to defend the proclamation in what was primarily a political tract, despite his expositions on the Constitution and his citations of writers on international law.[30]

Jefferson immediately recognized "Pacificus" as coming from Hamilton's pen. The day after the first number appeared he told Madison that the piece contained the same arguments that Hamilton had made in the cabinet and expressed concern that these "heresies" might go unanswered. Lest Madison fail to take the hint, Jefferson wrote again after two more numbers of "Pacificus" came off the press, saying that no one was answering Hamilton and exclaiming: "For God's sake, my dear Sir, take up your pen, select the most striking heresies and cut him to pieces in the face of the public. There is nobody else who can and will enter the lists with him." Madison, at home in Virginia, was reluctant to accept the challenge, but Jefferson pressed him with materials to use, and the congressman forced himself to the task that he found "the most grating" that he had ever experienced.[31] The result was a series of five letters of "Helvidius" that appeared in the *Gazette of the United States* in August and September in which Madison directed his replies primarily to the ideas of executive power advanced by Hamilton.[32] The "Pacificus" and "Helvidius" exchange attracted extraordinary interest because there was little doubt about the identity of the authors. Five years earlier they had collaborated to write the *Federalist* papers.

Meanwhile, the problem of Genet became critical. By July, Jefferson had decided that "never . . . was so calamitous an appointment made." He exploded to Madison that the French minister was "hot headed, all imagination, no judgment, passionate, disrespectful and even indecent towards the President in his written as well as verbal communications, talking of appeals from him to Congress, from them to the people, urging the most unreasonable and groundless propositions, and in the most dictatorial style." He was certain that if he ever had to lay Genet's communications before Congress, they would excite "universal indignation." He hardly needed to add that Genet "renders my position immensely difficult."[33]

This outburst from Jefferson was provoked by a meeting that he had just come from with the French minister. It was Sunday, July 7. Only a few days before, Jefferson had learned that the *Little Sarah*, a British merchant ship taken prize by the French and renamed the *Petite Democrate*, had been equipped as a privateer and its armament secretly augmented. When a crew went aboard, its departure from Philadelphia appeared imminent. As soon as Jefferson heard this, he hurried into the city from his house on the Schuylkill (which he had rented after giving up his Market Street residence) and called on the French minister, asking him to detain the ship pending the return of the president from Mount Vernon. In a highly emotional harangue, Genet refused to promise to do so, but he indicated that the *Petite Democrate* was not ready to put to sea. Genet's look and gesture in making the latter statement led the secretary of state to interpret it as a commitment to keep the ship at anchor until the president's return. The belief that he had an understanding with Genet induced Jefferson to oppose the opinions of Hamilton and Knox to establish a battery on Mud Island in the Delaware River to prevent the departure of the ship. Jefferson was fearful that such an action might touch off a larger conflagration, since he was convinced that the crew of the *Petite Democrate* would resist. With a large French fleet daily expected at Philadelphia, the incident might easily lead to an expanded conflict. Only the president should make such a crucial decision.[34]

The secretary of state well knew that Genet might be deceiving him, but under the circumstances he regarded the risks of military confrontation as unacceptable. Nor did he disguise his true feelings. He wondered if his colleagues in the cabinet would be equally ready to fire on British vessels violating American neutrality, and he admitted that he himself "would not gratify the combination of kings with the spectacle of the two only republics on earth destroying each other." Hamilton at the same time was insisting that not to act with decision would prostrate the government and "that nothing is so dangerous to a Government as to be wanting either in self-confidence or self-respect."[35] Jefferson was outvoted in the cabinet, which met in the president's absence, but before Secretary of War Knox could establish a battery on Mud Island, the *Petite Democrate* dropped down the river to Chester on July 9 and positioned itself to put out to sea. On the same day Genet informed the secretary of state that the vessel, now anchored beyond the range of shore batteries or militia, would sail when ready.[36]

Such was the state of affairs when Washington arrived back in the capital on July 11 to find a packet of papers from the secretary of state marked "instant attention." He read them immediately and called a cabinet meeting for the next morning. Upset to find such a crisis awaiting him and unaware that Jefferson was at home ill with a fever, he was irritated that his secretary of state was not in the city. The letter that he sent off to Jefferson by special messenger showed it. "Is the Minister of the French Republic to set the Acts of this Government at defiance, *with impunity?*" he asked, "and then threaten the Executive with an appeal to the People? What must the World think of such conduct, and of the Goverment . . . submitting to it."[37]

Washington had calmed down by the time Jefferson joined Hamilton and Knox in the cabinet meeting the following morning. Still, Jefferson sensed that the president wished that the *Petite Democrate* had been detained by military force, but he did not believe that Washington would have ordered it himself had he been on the scene. Now it was too late for military action, and the cabinet turned its attention to what to do about Genet and to the broader problem of defining more clearly what the neutrality proclamation meant. With his department heads divided, Washington accepted Jefferson's suggestion to ask the Supreme Court for an advisory opinion on the validity of the principles of neutrality. This move produced a remarkable formulation of the problem of neutrality in the series of questions posed by Hamilton and Jefferson to be answered by the justices, but when the justices declined to consider the issue, the cabinet was forced to formulate the rules of neutrality itself.[38] The outcome was a set of "Rules Governing Belligerents," approved on August 3. Thus, with Congress never called into session and the Supreme Court demurring, the cabinet, pressed by Genet's vexing actions, took the unprecedented step of implementing the president's neutrality proclamation with a body of regulations.[39]

Meanwhile, the cabinet decided Genet's fate. Hamilton and Knox had been urging the recall of the French minister since Washington's return to the capital, and on August 2 the cabinet unanimously agreed to demand Genet's recall and to send copies of his correspondence to Gouverneur Morris in Paris to support the demand. Hamilton urged that Genet's correspondence also be made public and harangued his colleagues for three-quarters of an hour in a speech Jefferson called "as inflammatory and declamatory as if he had been speaking to a jury." The opposition of both Randolph and Jefferson blocked the proposal, but Jefferson was well aware of the political repercussions of such a move and wrote immediately to warn

Madison that Genet "will sink the republican interest if they do not abandon him."[40]

In the midst of the final turbulence of the Genet mission, the secretary of state informed the president on July 31 that he planned to resign at the end of September. The circumstances that had led him to postpone his retirement at the beginning of the year no longer existed, he believed. He could now leave office without exciting adverse opinions or conjectures. He may also have chosen this moment to exert pressure on the president to handle the recall of Genet in a manner that would not be offensive to France.[41] A few days later the president rode out to Jefferson's house on the Schuylkill to appeal to him to delay the date of his departure until the end of the year. He reminded him, as he had earlier when Jefferson wanted to leave the government, that the secretary of state had been one of those who had persuaded him to continue for a second term. He talked about the difficulties of finding a capable replacement, and he reflected on the uncertainties of the times—"the fermentation which seemed to be working in the mind of the public" (which Jefferson understood to mean the rising Republican party) and the new Congress that would assemble in December. He also revealed that the secretary of the treasury had indicated his intention to resign at the end of the next session of Congress, and he suggested that it would make it easier, especially with regard to geographical considerations in the composition of his cabinet, if he could fill both vacancies about the same time. Jefferson assured the president that nothing was to be feared from the Republican party, which was firm in its support of the government, and that the next Congress would attempt nothing more than to render the legislature independent of the executive. He expressed his own uncomfortableness in being in a post that required him "to move exactly in the circle which I know to bear me peculiar hatred, that is to say the wealthy aristocrats, the merchants connected closely with England, the new created paper fortunes," and he stressed how much his affairs in Virginia needed his attention. Still, he agreed to reconsider. Whether he was moved by Washington's plea or his handling of Genet's recall, he informed the president a few days later that he would stay on until the last of December, when his and Hamilton's expected departures would be nearer together.[42] It would, however, be necessary for him to make a trip home in the fall.

The cabinet decision to demand Genet's recall did not immediately lessen the public controversy surrounding the minister, for that decision was not made public, and Genet himself would not be notified of it for six weeks. Time was required for the secretary of state to prepare the detailed summary of Genet's actions for transmittal to Gouverneur Morris. Weeks would elapse before the document reached Paris. Meanwhile rumors filled the newspapers that Genet had threatened to appeal over the president to the people of the United States. Public demonstrations of support for the president's neutrality proclamation were organized, including a public meeting in Richmond, arranged by John Marshall, where Jefferson's mentor George Wythe was prevailed upon to preside. In response Madison and Monroe began organizing other public meetings throughout Virginia to counteract the Federalist efforts to gain partisan advantage from Genet's indiscretions.[43]

Jefferson's concern about the political effects of the Genet affair on the Republican party is evident in his correspondence. While encouraging Republican friends to take up their pens in the cause, he also began plotting Republican strategy. In a confidential letter to Madison he noted that Genet's conduct was exciting public indignation and urged Republicans to support the president's policy. Looking ahead to the assembling of Congress, he advised that "it will be true wisdom in the Republican party to approve unequivocally of a state of neutrality, to avoid little cavils about who should declare it, to abandon Genet entirely, with expressions of strong friendship and adherence to his nation and confidence that he has acted against their sense. In this way we shall keep the people on our side by keeping ourselves in the right." This letter that Jefferson cautioned Madison to share only with Monroe offers one of the clearest records of the leadership role that Jefferson played in the Republican party while still secretary of state. Besides recommending the Republican course in regard to Genet and neutrality, he also outlined a plan to divide the Treasury Department between two equal chiefs of customs and internal taxes and proposed a congressional declaration of the true sense of the Constitution on the national bank. He thought the latter, even if passed by only the House of Representatives, would serve to divorce the bank from the government.[44]

Before the hot summer of 1793 passed, another crisis more threatening than Genet or Hamilton's bank descended on Philadelphia—the plague of yellow fever. Breaking out in August and spreading rapidly, the epidemic stilled the controversy over Genet and made all disputes of government seem unimportant. "Everybody who can, is flying from the city," Jefferson wrote to Madison on September 1. But he himself was still going into the city to his office every day and playing down the danger of the peril that would leave more than five thousand Philadelphians dead in a city of forty-four thousand before it ran its deadly course in November.[45] Fortunately Jefferson had moved outside the city when he gave up his residence in town in March, and he removed his daughter Maria from the city when the fever began. He had planned to work at his country house after Washington left for Mount Vernon on September 10, delaying his own trip to Monticello until October following the president's return. However, he soon changed his mind. When he went to his office on the day Washington left the city, he found only a single clerk. Hamilton, who had contracted the fever and was recovering, was planning to go to New York as soon as he was able to travel. With government offices decimated and the affairs of state at a standstill, Jefferson cleared out his correspondence file and left for Monticello on September 17.[46]

On the way home he stopped to see the president at Mount Vernon and to visit with Madison at Montpelier, arriving back on his own hilltop before the end of September. He was there a month before setting out again on October 25 for the temporary seat of government at Germantown, where the president had directed the officers of government to assemble until it was safe to return to Philadelphia.[47] By the time Jefferson arrived in Germantown on November 1, the yellow fever was abating, but the town was crowded with refugees from the city. The only lodging Jefferson could find was a bed in the corner of the public room in the King of Prussia Tavern and that, he said, only "as a great favor, the other alternative being to sleep on the floor in my cloak before the fire." Just how long it was before Jefferson was able to obtain better accommodations is not known, but Philadelphians soon began returning to the city, and by the middle of the month he had been able to reserve a room for Madison and Monroe for their arrival for the convening of Congress at the beginning of December. Washington had earlier sought advice as to whether he should summon Congress to meet at Germantown rather than Philadelphia, but Jefferson and Randolph convinced him that he had no constitutional authority to change the meeting place of Congress. Washington himself decided to keep the executive officers at Germantown until Congress convened.[48]

Preparing for the meeting of Congress, the president and his cabinet gave particular attention to drafting his annual message. In view of the extraordinary events that had transpired since Congress had adjourned in March, that address and its accompanying documents would be of immense interest. An explanation of the neutrality proclamation, a review of relations with England and France, and the whole history of the Genet mission headed the list of matters that the legislators would expect to hear explained. They would also want to know what progress had been made in getting the British to evacuate the posts that they still occupied in the Northwest ten years after the signing of the peace and about the recent orders-in-council directed against American trade with French colonies. In his brief oral address the president would be unable to go into detail on any of these matters, but he would be expected to elaborate in accompanying documents and subsequent communications.

Jefferson was deeply involved in the discussions over the content and wording of the president's address and in the preparation of the papers that would accompany it. The cabinet spent hours debating how the record should be presented and interpreted, rehashing many of the arguments aired in earlier discussions and in the press.[49] What emerged was a presidential report that neither Jefferson nor Hamilton alone would have devised but that balanced their conflicting assessments of the past and their projections of the course to be charted through the troubled waters of world affairs.

With the danger of yellow fever over and Congress about to assemble, the president moved back to Philadelphia on the last day of November. On the same day Jefferson took temporary lodgings at the corner of Seventh and Market streets. Among the unfinished business that the secretary of state pressed to complete before his last month in office ended was a paper on the privileges and restrictions on American commerce in foreign countries, submitted to the House of Representatives on December 16, 1793. Congress had requested this report earlier, and Jefferson had it ready by the end of the Second Congress. But he had asked and received permission to present it at the beginning of the next Congress.[50] Now, with the end of his tenure as secretary of state in sight, there was no longer time for delay, and mounting British efforts to cut off American trade with the French West Indies made it a propitious time to put the report before the public.

In the long course of preparation and revision Jefferson had employed the help of Tench Coxe and others in assembling data, but the report reflected the approach to commerce that had characterized his own policies and actions when he was minister to France and to which he had continued to adhere. He affirmed his belief in

free trade—that "every country be employed in producing tha
which nature has best fitted it to produce, and each be free to ex
change with others the mutual surplusses for mutual wants"—bu
he recognized that this was a distant hope and placed his emphasi
on the principle of reciprocity. Friendly arrangements with othe
nations were to be preferred, but if they could not be negotiated
counterdiscriminations, prohibitions, protective duties, and othe
regulations should be imposed. The report affirmed that America
commerce was vital to the progress of the nation and also acknowl
edged the need to encourage household manufactures. Because
England more than any other country had shown no inclination to
negotiate reciprocal commercial arrangements with the United
States, the report lent support to Madison's longstanding efforts to
induce Congress to discriminate against that dominant commer
cial power. Soon after Jefferson left office, Madison would use
Jefferson's report to introduce new resolutions for discrimination.[5]

Jefferson would not be involved in that new move. Soon after
submitting his report to Congress, he began packing his book:
and remaining belongings in Philadelphia for shipment to Vir
ginia. On December 21 the president made his last effort to per
suade Jefferson to continue in office but found him immovable
Jefferson himself confided to a friend that he was determined "to
be liberated from the hated occupations of politics, and to remain
in the bosom of my family, my farm, and my books."[52] On the last
day of 1793, he resigned his office into the hands of the president
Writing to his daughter Maria that he expected to be home by the
middle of January, he said that he hoped "no more to leave you."[5
Once more Jefferson seemed determined never again to return to
public life.

XIV
Renewal at Monticello

The fifty-year-old Virginian had looked forward to the tranquil enjoyment of his family, his farm, and his books, but after a month at home he was complaining of his isolation and the dearth of news. He had not seen a Philadelphia newspaper since he left the city, and only one letter from there had reached him. He said that he "could not have supposed, when at Philadelphia, that so little of what was passing there could be known even at Kentucky, as is the case here." A harsh and lingering winter kept him indoors, and without his books, which had not yet arrived from Philadelphia, Jefferson was depressed. When spring came, his spirits brightened. Soon he was writing friends that he had returned to farming with an ardor that he had scarcely known in his youth. "Instead of writing 10 or 12 letters a day, which I have been in the habit of doing as a thing of course, I put off answering my letters now, farmer-like, till a rainy day, and then find it sometimes postponed by other necessary occupations." A year later he remarked that he had become "the most ardent and active farmer in the state. I live constantly on horseback, rarely taking a book and never a pen if I can avoid it." [1]

After being away from Monticello for ten years, leaving farming operations to overseers, Jefferson found his lands far more depleted by ill-usage than he had expected. His first priority was to restore their productivity, and he immediately implemented an elaborate system of crop rotation that he had been formulating for some time. Dividing his tillable acreage into seven fields, he settled on a rotation of wheat; peas and potatoes; corn and potatoes; peas and potatoes; rye; clover; and clover. His lands, he concluded, were so worn out that they required such gentle treatment to renew them. He preferred wheat to tobacco culture because wheat preserved fertility and offered greater social benefits, supplying food and requiring less labor for cultivation. To provide beauty as well as fruit, he directed the planting of nearly nine hundred peach trees as dividing lines to mark the fields.[2]

Of the over 5,500 acres of land that Jefferson owned in Albemarle County—at Monticello and neighboring farms—only about 1,100 to 1,200 acres were under cultivation. The crop system employed reveals that a large portion of the farm production went to sustain those who lived there. When Jefferson made a census of his slaves in November, 1794, he listed 64 slaves living at Monticello, 15 at Tufton, 11 at Shadwell, and 15 at Lego, for a total of 105 slaves on the lands in Albemarle that constituted his seven-field system. In addition, he had 49 slaves on his lands in Bedford County.[3] Whether slavery was profitable for Jefferson is no easier to determine than the broader question of the profitability of slavery. Jefferson himself, in compiling data on capital invested in Virginia agriculture for the English agriculturalist Arthur Young, reached the conclusion that slave labor was cheaper than free labor in England, but Young challenged some of his figures. Slavery sustained Jefferson's comfortable life style, and he employed an unusually large number of slaves in household duties and as craftsmen. But he never grew wealthy on slave labor. Nonetheless, he did at times sell slaves to pay his creditors.[4] Even then, he died deeply in debt.

Under his rotation system the only cash crop—wheat—was not produced in sufficient volume to support him. In searching for supplemental income until his lands could be made more productive, Jefferson set up a shop to manufacture nails at Monticello, employing a dozen slave boys, aged ten to sixteen, and supervising the details of the business himself. "What with my farming and my nail manufactory I have my hands full," he wrote to John Adams. "I am on horseback half the day, and counting and measuring nails the other half."[5] By 1796 he was turning out a ton of nails a month but finding it difficult to sell his production. He believed that local merchants were unwilling to take his nails because import merchants refused to handle them "from a principle of suppressing every effort towards domestic manufacture." Local merchants, reluctant to alienate their suppliers, took nails from the importers along with other goods. Jefferson thus set up his own retailers under a consignment system, which obligated him to carry the full burden of capitalization.[6] Even more difficult was the task of collecting receipts due him from his agents.

His limited income from farming encouraged the efficiency-minded Jefferson to try to increase crop production by better organization of his labor force and greater use of labor-saving devices.

He first recorded his idea of improving the moldboard plow while in France, and he now worked out a design of least resistance and began testing it at Monticello.[7] He continued to perfect his invention, which he had no thought of patenting, and in time his improvement attracted considerable attention from scientists and agriculturalists, including a gold medal from the Société d'agriculture du départment de la Seine in 1805. Always interested in agricultural machinery, Jefferson also directed the building of a threshing machine at Monticello from a model sent to him from England by Thomas Pinckney. He built the horse-powered works compact enough to be portable from field to field on a wagon and first used it in the harvest of 1796.[8]

In addition to improving his lands and farming operations, Jefferson turned to rebuilding his house. He once remarked that "architecture is my delight, and putting up, and pulling down, one of my favorite amusements." Nowhere is this better illustrated than in the years following his retirement as secretary of state, when he directed his attention to remodeling and enlarging Monticello, beginning the transformation that gave the mansion the character it retains today. After completing the first version of the house, Jefferson had been much influenced by the new architecture he saw in France, returning home with his Palladian views much altered by the Louis XVI style. He was especially enthralled by Paris' beautiful *hôtels* (mansions or townhouses) designed by leading architects during a period of great architectural creativity. He said that he lacked words to describe how much he enjoyed French architecture, and he was so "violently smitten" by the Hôtel de Salm in Paris that he went almost daily to watch its construction. The style that impressed him most was the one-story mansion. In the French countryside all the good houses built within the past twenty or thirty years were single story, and the trend was spreading to the cities, he observed. "In Paris particularly all the new and good houses are of a single story—that is of the height of 16 or 18 feet generally, and the whole of it given to the rooms of entertainment; but in the parts where there are bedrooms they have two tiers of them from 8 to 10 feet high each, with a small private staircase. By these means great staircases are avoided, which are expensive and occupy a space which would make a good room in every story."[9]

Jefferson employed this style in remodeling and expanding Monticello. Doubling the exterior dimensions of the house and adding a dome modeled on that of the Halle aux Bleds in Paris, he gave the house a one-story appearance while hiding its second story, which was reached by narrow, private staircases. He had begun planning and assembling materials for the reconstruction while still secretary of state, and he put men to making bricks during the first year of his retirement. But he did not begin the construction work until 1796, and he would not complete the project before his return to public life in 1797. Isaac Weld, seeing Monticello in its unfinished state in the spring of 1796, predicted that when completed it would be "one of the most elegant private habitations in the United States." The Duc de La Rochefoucauld-Liancourt, visiting there the same year, went further and said "his house will certainly deserve to be ranked with the most pleasant mansions in France and England." To achieve that distinction Jefferson and his family would have to endure much inconvenience before the work was completed and the house free of the noise, confusion, and discomfort that Jefferson said required all of one's patience to endure.[10]

By late summer of 1797 Jefferson was planning to unroof the still-livable portions of the original dwelling and to send his family elsewhere for shelter, but apparently this was delayed, for his daughter Maria was married there in October, 1797, to John Wayles Eppes. By this time Jefferson was vice-president, and when he was not on the scene, the work moved slowly. He wrote from Philadelphia in May, 1798, that he hoped to find the house nearly roofed by summer and to be able to reunite his family under shelter. But he returned home to find that nothing had been done because the sheeting and shingles had not been delivered as promised. When he left for Philadelphia in December, the roof was still not completed. The north end would remain open for a second winter. Upon his return in March he found "scarcely a stroke" had been done in his absence. "It seems as if I should never get it inhabitable," he wrote to Maria.[11] He apparently got the roof finished that spring, flooring put down in the summer, and enough work completed to make the house usable again. It is uncertain when the dome was built. Regardless, much work remained to be done. The house was still unfinished when Jefferson assumed the presidency in 1801.[12] Its builder had a vision that he would one day achieve, but few men would have had the patience and optimism to persist through so many years. Building was a creative effort to which Jefferson turned when freed of other duties. When he started the reconstruction, he had no intention of ever again leaving Monticello.[13] Had he known that he would be elected vice-president and president, Jefferson might not have begun the project when he did, though he was always overly optimistic about how much time construction required.

After retiring from Washington's cabinet, Jefferson considered his political career at an end. Unlike Hamilton, who continued to advise Washington and influence cabinet members long after he left the government, Jefferson shunned such a role. "I cherish tranquillity too much, to suffer political things to enter my mind at all," he told the president a few months after leaving office, and he wrote to Edmund Randolph, his successor as secretary of state, that "no circumstance will ever more tempt me to engage in anything public." [14] Nor did he try to manage the Republicans in Congress from behind the scenes, as some political opponents charged. Madison, not Jefferson, was the party leader during these years. When Jefferson's name was brought forward in 1796 as a candidate for president, some even referred to him as the candidate of Madison's party.

For a while, the newly retired secretary of state ceased reading newspapers. He told Tench Coxe in 1795 that he had "interdicted to myself the reading of newspapers, and thinking or saying anything on public matters beyond what the conversation of my neighbors draws me into." However, letters from Madison and William B. Giles reported regularly on proceedings in Congress, and John Beckley kept him supplied with political pamphlets. Madison and Giles both visited him at Monticello, as did other political leaders, including Aaron Burr, who journeyed there in the fall of 1795, when politicians were turning their thoughts to the approaching presidential election. By 1796 Jefferson was reading newspapers again and asking Madison to send him a weekly report of what was happening in government "behind the curtain." [15] Both the content and tone of his letters in 1796 showed more interest in politics than those written in the first year or so of his retirement.

Despite his disclaimers Jefferson, in fact, had never lost interest in national affairs. He shared his views only with friends, but he did not refrain from commenting privately on the course of events. He wrote feelingly about what he considered to be an excessive use of military force to put down opposition to the excise tax in Pennsylvania. He expressed alarm at the denunciation of the Democratic Societies. He thought the Jay Treaty was an "infamous act, which is really nothing more than a treaty of alliance between England and the Anglomen of this country against the legislature and people of the United States." He gave his support to efforts of Republicans in the House of Representatives to block its implementation, arguing that the House had a constitutional right to refuse the means dependent on them to carry it into effect. He did not hesitate to urge Madison to take up his pen to reply to Hamilton in the press.

"When he comes foward," he told his long-time political ally, "there is nobody but yourself who can meet him." Jefferson had withdrawn from public office but not from the world of political affairs, which he repeatedly confessed to dislike but could never block from his thoughts. Still, he insisted that he would never accept office again. When his friends talked about who might succeed Washington as president, Jefferson declared firmly that his retirement was "from all office high or low, without exception" and said that the question was forever closed. "The little spice of ambition which I had in my younger days has long since evaporated," he told Madison, whom he considered to be the person Republicans should support as Washington's successor.[16]

Jefferson's opposition to becoming a contender for the presidency did not deter his supporters from promoting him as a candidate, but they were obliged to do so without his approval or cooperation. In late February, 1796, Madison told Monroe that it was pretty certain that Washington would not seek a third term, though the president had made no announcement. Until Washington revealed his intentions, party leaders were unwilling to put candidates before the public, but both Federalist and Republican leaders expected the president to retire and acted accordingly. Madison indicated to Monroe that it was expected that Adams would be the candidate of the Federalists—"the British party," Madison called them—and he said that "the Republicans, knowing that Jefferson alone can be started with hope of success, mean to push him."[17] Madison, however, did not tell Jefferson this, because the Albemarle farmer had already firmly told his friend that the question of his becoming a candidate for any office was not open to reconsideration. Madison and other party leaders thus proceeded without Jefferson's knowledge. Though Madison spent the summer in Virginia, he did not even visit Jefferson, in order to give him no opportunity to protest against being embarked in the contest. Jefferson later avowed that his name was brought forward "without concert or expectation on my part."[18]

The campaign of 1796 did not get under way until September, when Washington released to the press his now famous farewell address. Some Republicans saw this delay as a Hamiltonian scheme "designed to prevent a fair election, and the consequent choice of Mr. Jefferson." Although off to a late start, the campaign was nonetheless vigorous. It was the first party contest for the presidency. As newspapers filled with electioneering pieces, political announcements, and campaign reports, Jefferson obviously knew that he was being "pushed" by the Republicans. He did not request that they cease their activities, but neither did he move to promote his own election. Adams, likewise, was inactive, believing it improper to seek office. Yet, while neither of the two principal candidates was pursuing the office, the campaign was hard fought, and the election close. Among those most completely engaged in Jefferson's behalf was John Beckley, clerk of the House of Representatives, who organized one of the party's most advanced and aggressive campaigns in Pennsylvania. There Republicans would win fourteen of the fifteen electoral votes in a striking demonstration of the value of effective party management and organization.[19] In a growing number of states, candidates for presidential electors pledged in advance whether they would vote for Adams or Jefferson.

The Jay Treaty was a key campaign issue in 1796, but the characters of the two candidates furnished the major subject for campaign literature and newspaper debate. Republicans extolled Jefferson as the "steadfast friend to the Rights of the People" and "the uniform advocate of equal rights among citizens," while charging Adams with being the "advocate for hereditary power" and "the champion of rank, titles, and hereditary distinctions."[20] One Republican handbill told voters that "Thomas Jefferson is a firm Republican, John Adams is an avowed monarchist." Another said the election was to decide "whether the Republican Jefferson, or the Royalist Adams, shall be President of the United States."[21] Republican writers pointed out that Adams had sons who might aim to succeed their father, while Jefferson, like Washington, had no son. Voters were reminded that "Jefferson first drew the declaration of American independence" and were told that Adams was "a fond admirer of the British Constitution." Republicans described Jefferson as combining "every requisite qualification for the Presidency—a consistent uniformity of conduct, firmness and intrepidity, with an unconquerable love of liberty . . . [and] a profound knowledge of politics." Jefferson's supporters defended him against charges that he had mismanaged the office of governor of Virginia, opposed the Constitution, quit his post as secretary of state at a critical moment, and headed a French party determined to alter the whole system of government.[22]

The description of Jefferson that Congressman Robert Goodloe Harper provided his constituents in a circular letter written shortly after the election is indicative of the image that Federalists attempted to paint of the Republican candidate. Harper said that Jefferson possessed "much knowledge, chiefly however of the scientific kind, the least useful for a statesman; whose business it is to judge an act, not to write books." Harper was willing to concede Jefferson's "considerable literary genius" and even skill in diplomatic writings. "But from his public conduct, I take him to be of a weak, weavering, indecisive character; deliberating when he ought to act, and frequently acting, when he does attempt it, without steadiness, judgment or perseverance . . . always pursuing certain visionary theories of the closet, which experience constantly contradicts; like most literary men, greatly liable to flattery." He thought Jefferson "fit to be a professor in a College, President of a Philosophical Society, or even Secretary of State; but certainly not the first magistrate of a great nation."[23] This was a Federalist image of Jefferson that would die hard, if ever, and throughout the rest of his public life he would be challenged to contradict it.

The question of Jefferson's sympathy toward France was ominously thrust forward late in the campaign by the actions of the French minister in the United States, Pierre Adet. At the end of October—a week before the Pennsylvania voting—Adet delivered a note from his government to Secretary of State Timothy Pickering announcing that henceforth all American ships would be treated by France in the same manner as Americans allowed the English to treat them. Then Adet released the notice to the press. Two weeks later, he sought to produce an even greater shock by announcing the suspension of his duties as minister to the United States "as a mark of just discontent, which is to last until the Government of the United States returns to sentiments, and to measures, more conformable to the interests of the alliance, and the sworn friendship between the two nations."[24] Adet was trying to influence the election by creating fears of a confrontation with France, which Jefferson would be seen as the more likely candidate to resolve peacefully. The French minister's reports to his own government leave no doubt of his purposeful interference in the election.

If Adet believed he was helping Jefferson, he was mistaken. Although some Federalists thought the alarm provoked by Adet influenced the election in Pennsylvania in Jefferson's favor, the reaction of Republican leaders was one of deep concern about the adverse effect of Adet's interference in American politics. Madison lamented that Adet's note was "working all the evil with which it is pregnant. Those who rejoice at its indiscretions, and are taking advantage of them, have the impudence to pretend that it is an electioneering manoeuvre, and that the French Government have been led to it by the opponents of the British Treaty." Charges that Re-

ublicans were behind Adet's movements were as unfounded as his
ctions were unwelcome. In a nation still studying the words of
Vashington's farewell address warning against "the insidious wiles
f foreign influence," Republicans could only suffer in the long run
rom Adet's actions. Secretary of the Treasury Oliver Wolcott was
lready saying that should Jefferson be elected, it would be "fatal to
ur independence, now that the interference of a foreign nation in
ur affairs is no longer disguised."[25] It is impossible to measure the
ffects of Adet's actions, which may have come too late in the cam-
aign to alter the outcome of the election. But the incident in-
reased the burden of Republicans in defending their party against
harges of French influence.

Because neither the Constitution nor Congress prescribed the
nanner of choosing presidential electors, each state determined
or itself the method of selection. In 1796 six states permitted
opular election, either by districts or on a general ticket; in seven
tates, the legislature made the choice; and three states had mixed
ystems. With the election of electors taking place in various states
t different times, Jefferson kept track of the contest as the reports
lowly reached Monticello. By December he was aware that the
lection would be close. Writing to Madison that "there is nothing I
o anxiously hope, as that my name may come out either second or
hird," he said that the latter would leave him at home the whole
ear, the other two-thirds of it. In case of a tie in the electoral col-
ege, which he then thought possible, he authorized Madison, on
is behalf, to urge preference for Adams. "He has always been my
enior, from the commencement of my public life, and the expres-
ion of the public will being equal, this circumstance ought to give
im the preference."[26]

By the end of December, Jefferson believed that Adams had the
otes to win, and he was saying that he had never doubted that out-
ome. He said that he would not have refused election, but he re-
oiced at escaping, being convinced that no man would ever leave
he presidency with the reputation that he carried into it. "I have
o ambition to govern men; no passion which would lead me to de-
ight to ride in a storm," he mused. "The newspapers will permit
ne to plant my corn, peas, etc., in hills or drills as I please . . . while
ur Eastern friends will be struggling with the storm which is gath-
ring over us; perhaps be shipwrecked in it. This is certainly not a
noment to covet the helm."[27]

When the electoral votes were counted, Adams, with 71 electoral
otes, won the presidential office by the narrow margin of 3 elec-

toral votes over Jefferson's 68. Thomas Pinckney received 59 votes
Aaron Burr 30, and the remainder were widely scattered. Adams
carried all of New England, New York, New Jersey, and Delaware
and won in seven out of ten districts in Maryland. Jefferson won 14
out of 15 electoral votes in Pennsylvania, 20 out of 21 in Virginia,
11 out of 12 in North Carolina, and shut out Adams completely in
South Carolina, Georgia, Kentucky, and Tennessee. A glance at the
electoral returns showed that Adams' margin of victory rested on
the single electoral votes he received in three states that otherwise
were unanimous for Jefferson—Pennsylvania, Virginia, and North
Carolina. The meaning of this would not be lost on party leaders as
they prepared for the next presidential contest.

Until 1804 the Constitution did not provide for separate balloting for president and vice-president, specifying instead that the
candidate with the second-highest number of electoral votes assume the second office. Under this provision Jefferson was elected
vice-president. The possibility of choosing a president from one
party and a vice-president from another had not worried the fram-
ers, because they were not anticipating the rise of political parties.
When that occurred, the Twelfth Amendment (1804) was required
to revise the rules and make such a circumstance unlikely.

Many people wondered whether Jefferson would accept the second office. It was generally assumed that after two terms as vice-
president, Adams would not have taken the post again. Some feared
that Jefferson also might decline. Before the final outcome was
known, Madison sought to persuade Jefferson that he must not refuse the vice-presidency if it fell to him. Madison need not have argued the case, for Jefferson had already decided to accept the
lesser station. He also was willing to work with Adams. This may
seem surprising in light of the growing political distance between
the two men while Jefferson was secretary of state and the heated
rhetoric of the election campaign. But Jefferson at Monticello had
been isolated from the campaign and had not yet lost faith in his
Massachussetts colleague of revolutionary days. Moreover, he saw
greater threats to the republic than Adams. "If Mr. Adams can be
induced to administer the government in it's true principles, and to
relinquish his bias to an English constitution," Jefferson confided to
Madison, "it is to be considered whether it would not be on the
whole for the public good to come to a good understanding with
him as to his future elections. He is perhaps the only sure barrier
against Hamilton's getting in."[28] To another correspondent he suggested that there was reason to believe that Adams was "detached

from Hamilton, and there is a possibility he may swerve from his politics in a greater or less degree." He thus thought it advisable for Republicans to be silent until they saw what turn the new administration would take. Jefferson was successful in circulating the word that he was willing to work with Adams, and Adams was soon saying that he felt no apprehensions from Jefferson and was looking forward to administering the government with him.[29]

Jefferson at first thought that it would not be necessary to be present in Philadelphia for the inauguration. Not having been more than seven miles from home since he settled into his retirement, he dreaded a February journey to Philadelphia. But he decided to go as a mark of respect to the public and in order to dispel any rumors that he considered the second office beneath him. When he set out for the capital on February 20, he may not have envisioned the scope of the new political role that was opening before him or the higher office to which it would lead, but in returning to the world of politics, he did so without reservations. Before leaving Monticello, he wrote to George Wythe saying that it had been so long since he sat in a legislature that he was rusty in the parliamentary rules and asked Wythe, whom he considered the best-versed man in America on the subject, to loan him some notes.[30] Presiding over the Senate would be a new challenge to which he would respond with system and energy. He would be less attracted to the unavoidable role of party leader that his earlier leadership and recent election thrust upon him, but he would not shrink from that task either. When he arrived in Philadelphia on March 2, 1797, after an absence of over three years, a new era was opening in his political career and in the life of the nation.

XV
Vice-President

Jefferson spent ten days on the road from Monticello to Philadelphia. Traveling by public stage from Alexandria, the newly elected vice-president hoped to slip into the city without ceremony. But his arrival two days before the inauguration did not pass unnoticed. An artillery company was on hand to fire a welcoming salute, and enthusiastic supporters raised a banner proclaiming JEFFERSON THE FRIEND OF THE PEOPLE.[1] He went immediately to pay his respects to John Adams, who returned the call the next day at the Madisons', where Jefferson stopped for one night before taking lodging at Francis' Hotel on Fourth Street. The president-elect shared with Jefferson reports of deteriorating relations with France and discussed the composition of the mission he proposed to send to negotiate with the Directory. He talked about including Jefferson or Madison on the commission, an assignment Jefferson thought inappropriate for the vice-president, though he welcomed the bipartisan sentiment of the proposal.[2]

The inauguration on March 4, 1797, took place in an atmosphere of mutual goodwill, without any display of party differences between the new Federalist president and his Republican vice-president. Jefferson—soon to be fifty-four years of age—took the oath of office as vice-president in the Senate chamber and presented a brief address. He then proceeded to the House chamber where Adams, resplendent with a handsome sword strapped to his side, took the presidential oath and delivered a moderate and conciliatory inaugural address. The burying of party differences, however, did not last long. Two days after the inauguration, when Jefferson reopened the subject of the French mission that Adams had earlier discussed with him, he got the distinct impression that the president did not want to talk about it. Jefferson surmised that Adams had decided to abandon his initial moves to forget party division after meeting with his cabinet—a Hamiltonian clique that Adams inherited when he chose to retain Washington's advisers. The vice-president was soon writing friends that he considered his office as constitutionally confined to legislative functions and that he could not take part in executive consultations even if such were proposed. According to Jefferson, Adams never again consulted him about any measure of his administration.[3]

To Jefferson a more memorable occasion than his inauguration as vice-president may have been his installment as president of the American Philosophical Society on the evening before the inauguration. Soon after learning the outcome of the presidential vote, he had received notice of his election to succeed the late David Rittenhouse, successor to Benjamin Franklin, as president of the nation's most important scientific and philosophical organization. Its chair was an honor that he cherished and a post that he did not relinquish until 1815. A week after his installation, Jefferson presented a paper on the fossil remains of a huge animal recently discovered in the western part of Virginia. The audience, which included the English scientist and theologian Joseph Priestley and the French social philosopher Comte de Volney, made for the kind of winter "philosophical evening" that he had contemplated enjoying in Philadelphia, while the vice-presidential office left him free to enjoy rural, summer days at Monticello.[4]

Jefferson preferred the "tranquil pursuits of science," for which he believed nature had intended him, to politics, but he soon found the world of politics commanding his prime attention.[5] Remaining in Philadelphia little more than a week following the inauguration, he returned in May for the special session of Congress called by President Adams to deal with the crisis caused by France's refusal to receive Charles Cotesworth Pinckney as American minister. In normal times Congress would not have convened until December, and Jefferson would have had no reason to return to the capital until then. Instead, only two months into the new administration, he was presiding over the Senate and back in the center of national politics and political controversy.

Jefferson arrived in Philadelphia to find that one of the most sensational topics in the public press was a private letter that he had written to his old friend Philip Mazzei more than a year earlier during the contest over the Jay Treaty. Mazzei had released the letter to a Florentine paper for publication. It was soon translated from Italian into French and published in the Paris *Moniteur*, from which it was converted back into English and appeared in New York in

Noah Webster's *Minerva*. Jefferson had unfolded to Mazzei a harsh and partisan assessment of American politics. He indicated that in place of the love of liberty and republican government that had carried Americans through the Revolution, "an Anglican monarchical, and aristocratical party has sprung up, whose avowed object is to draw over us the substance, as they have already done the forms, of the British government." The mass of Americans were still republican, but all the officers of government, merchants trading on British capital, speculators, bankers, and all who preferred "the calm of despotism to the boisterous sea of liberty" were striving to assimilate the Republic to the British model. "It would give you a fever were I to name to you the apostates who have gone over to these heresies," he confided, "men who were Samsons in the field and Solomons in the council, but who have had their heads shorn by the harlot England."[6]

This was strong enough, but successive translations made some passages even stronger, and Jefferson's meaning was especially altered when *forms* became *form*. By the *forms* of the British government Jefferson meant the levees, celebration of the president's birthday, "inauguration pomposities," and other ceremonies. *Form* implied that he was hostile to the Constitution itself. Even more serious was the addition of a long sentence that Jefferson had not composed at all. This was not in the Italian version, but it appeared in the French version and in the English translation.[7] In his original letter to Mazzei, Jefferson had not mentioned France, but the added sentence had him charging his countrymen with ingratitude and injustice toward France and accusing the pro-British party with seeking to alienate Americans from France in order to bring the United States under British influence.[8] Jefferson saw this interpolation as the passage most seized upon by his critics and "made the subject of unceasing and virulent abuse." Yet, had the letter as Jefferson composed it been published, the effect would have been little different. Readers still would have concluded that he included Washington among the apostates to republicanism. Years later Jefferson said he was talking about the Society of the Cincinnati, but he did not say so at the time.[9]

As the controversy spread in the press, Jefferson remained silent and cautioned his correspondents not to let any of his letters get out of their hands lest they find their way into the newspapers. He felt he could not deny the letter because the substance of it was his, even though altered by the various translations. At the same time, he could not avow it in its published state, and any comments would only draw him into public controversy. When he sought advice from Madison and Monroe, the latter thought Jefferson should acknowledge the letter and say publicly that he believed that the government was swerving from the principles of the Revolution and republican government.[10] The more experienced Madison advised against such a course, considering it "a ticklish experiment" to reply to "the interrogatories of party spirit" and warning of unforeseen dilemmas and disagreeable explanations. He also cited the precedent of Washington's remaining silent about letters imputed to him. Jefferson never publicly acknowledged the letter nor responded to attacks on him in the press. But Republican editors replied, among them Benjamin Franklin Bache, whose Philadelphia *Aurora* voiced strong support for the views expressed in the letter, no matter who wrote it.[11]

At another time, such a controversy in the press might have repelled the sensitive Virginian from a further activist role in politics, but such was not now the case. With Madison, who had not stood for reelection to Congress, home in Virginia, Jefferson was thrust into a position of party leadership that he had shunned during the recent presidential campaign. Despite his reluctance to return to political life, once back in Philadelphia Jefferson did not hesitate to take up the leadership of the Republican party. He may have been more comfortable in other roles, but he did not draw back from the party role for which he seemed destined. He never admitted liking the task of party leader, but he exercised that role with skill until he left the presidency twelve years later.

Jefferson's assumption of party leadership is nowhere better revealed than in a letter he wrote in June, 1797, to the leading Republican activist in New York, Aaron Burr. The New York–Virginia alliance had recently been strained by the weak support given Burr in Virginia for the vice-presidency in 1796, and Jefferson's letter to Burr was warm and confiding. Revealing his disappointment with the new administration, he said he feared that the future character of the Republic was at stake. He shared his concern about the loss of Republican strength in Congress and sought Burr's help in "the penetration of truth" into the eastern states. "But will that region ever awake to the true state of things?" he asked. "Can the middle, Southern and Western states hold on till they awake? These are painful and doubtful questions: and if, in assuring me of your health, you can give me a comfortable solution of them, it will relieve a mind devoted to the preservation of our republican government." Pleased with Jefferson's display of friendship and confidence, Burr responded promptly, agreeing that "the moment requires free communication among those who adhere to the principles of our revolution." But the cautious Burr suggested that it would not be easy or discreet to respond to Jefferson's questions in a letter and arranged to meet the vice-president in Philadelphia on the following Sunday.[12] No more striking a vignette of Jefferson as a party leader can be found than that meeting with Burr, held when the Adams administration had not yet completed its fourth month.

While Burr was in Philadelphia, Jefferson also brought him together with Albert Gallatin, who succeeded Madison as the Republican leader in Congress, and with James Monroe, recently dismissed as American minister to France, who had just arrived home. In an open display of support for the recalled diplomat, Jefferson, Gallatin, and Burr boarded Monroe's ship to greet him and spent two hours in a consultation that had all the appearances of a conclave of party leaders. When a few days later Jefferson attended a public dinner given by Republicans to demonstrate support for Monroe, he provided an even clearer signal of his return to partisan politics.[13] More visibly than ever before, Jefferson was acting as a party leader.

After stopping to visit Madison on his way home not long afterward, Jefferson invited both Madison and Monroe to visit him at Monticello. Among important things to be discussed was a recent presentment by the grand jury of the federal circuit court at Richmond. In May that jury, presided over by Associate Justice James Iredell of the Supreme Court of the United States, presented "as a real evil" the circular letters of several members of Congress, particularly those of Samuel J. Cabell, who was accused of disseminating "unfounded calumnies" against the government of the United States, thereby alienating the people from their government, and increasing "a foreign influence ruinous to the peace, happiness and independence of these United States."[14]

The presentment touched off a storm of controversy in Virginia. Cabell indignantly replied that he would not be intimidated from corresponding with his constituents. Other Virginia members who were in the habit of addressing circular letters to their constituents also joined in the attack on the grand jury and Justice Iredell. Jefferson, too, was alarmed over the Federalist use of the judiciary. He believed that "the charges of the federal judges have for a considerable time been inviting the grand juries to be inquisitors on the freedom of speech, of writing and of principle of their fellow-citizens."[15] His indignation was even greater because he lived in Cabell's congressional district. Upon his return to Monticello, he drafted a petition for his neighbors to present to the Virginia House of Delegates. The petition protested the grand jury's action as a violation of the natural right of free communication between citizens and called upon the legislature to impeach and punish the jury members for "a great crime, wicked in its purpose, and mortal in its consequences unless prevented." He sent the draft to Madison for his opinion and revisions, consulted with political friends in Albemarle County, and took the lead in making arrangements to have the petition submitted to the legislature without his authorship becoming known. He even concerned himself with the timing of the presentation of the petition, so that it would coincide with the convening of the next session of Congress. His Republican friends in the House of Delegates not only arranged this but also succeeded in getting the House to approve the printing and distribution of a thousand copies of the petition. Over Federalist opposition the House approved the Republican resolution denouncing the grand jury's action but took no action against the jurors. Meanwhile, the charges against Cabell were never pressed.[16]

Jefferson's role in the Cabell incident provides evidence of his energetic assumption of party leadership. While showing his concern for civil liberties, the episode also reveals his willingness to use the legislature of a state to criticize the Federalist-dominated judiciary, setting a precedent for the challenges to a Federalist Congress a year later in the Kentucky and Virginia Resolutions. Indeed, his reasoning for directing the petition to the Virginia Assembly rather than to Congress, as Monroe suggested, foreshadowed his more systematic formulation of states' rights doctrines in the Kentucky Resolutions of 1798. He believed that petitioning Congress would only make matters worse and that a majority in the House of Representatives would rebuff the protest. "The system of the General Government is to seize all doubtful ground," he told Monroe. "We must join in the scramble, or get nothing. . . . It is of immense consequence that the States retain as complete authority as possible over their own citizens."[17]

After Monroe took up residence in Albemarle County in late summer of 1797 and with Madison not very distant in neighboring Orange County, Jefferson's closest political advisers were near at hand, restoring the inner circle of party leadership. Before returning to preside over the Senate at the second session of the Fifth Congress, Jefferson advised Monroe on the publication of his defense of his conduct as minister to France, and he stopped to visit with Madison again on his way back to Philadelphia.[18]

When the vice-president arrived in the capital on December 12,

Congress had been in session for several weeks and would sit until the middle of July in the longest session yet under the new Constitution. Although Jefferson would not stay until the very close, leaving at the end of June to return to Monticello, he would still find the session a long and difficult one. As the crisis with France deepened, it widened party divisions, raising issues that Jefferson saw as critical to the survival of the Republic.

For weeks that turned into months Congress did very little while waiting impatiently for news from the envoys—Charles Cotesworth Pinckney, John Marshall, and Elbridge Gerry—sent to Paris to negotiate. Jefferson expected the mission to be successful. He believed that France wanted peace with the United States, that Adams had overreacted to the earlier French refusal to receive Pinckney by summoning the special session of Congress the previous May, and that Adams' call for defense preparations was unnecessary. As time passed with no report from the envoys, Jefferson came to believe that no news was good news and even began to suspect that the administration was holding back dispatches. There was, in fact, little basis for Jefferson's optimism. At about the same time, Andrew Jackson, then a member of the Senate with no sources of information any better than the Senate's presiding officer, wrote that reports were circulating in Philadelphia that the envoys were returning without having been admitted.[19]

Jefferson certainly was not the only person unprepared for what was to follow. On the evening of March 4, 1798, Secretary of State Timothy Pickering finally received a bundle of dispatches from the American commissioners. As soon as he read enough of them to sense their content—it would take days to decipher the coded dispatches—he rushed them to the president. The next day Adams sent Congress the most recent report from the envoys, which indicated that there was no hope of their being received by the French government or accomplishing the objects of their mission. The president also reported an impending French order for the seizure of all neutral ships carrying any goods produced in England or its possessions.[20]

As Adams read more of the dispatches, he learned that French agents had demanded an apology for his references to France in his message to Congress in May, 1797, asked for a large loan to their government, and sought a substantial bribe for French officials before even opening negotiations. Adams' initial reaction was that the conduct of the Directory demanded a declaration of war. But without spreading the dispatches before Congress—which he thought might endanger the envoys—Congress would not be ready to take that step. He thus recommended a more limited response, calling upon Congress to take measures to protect shipping and defend the coasts, while replenishing arsenals, manufacturing arms, and raising revenue to pay for these extraordinary expenses. He told Congress that, after examining the dispatches, he saw no ground for expecting the mission to France to succeed "on terms compatible with the safety, honor or essential interests of the nation," and he announced that he was rescinding an order of President Washington forbidding the arming of American ships.[21]

One Republican member of Congress called Adams' message "a declaration of war as far as the President's *ipse dixit* can go." Jefferson called it "insane." Like many Republicans, he wondered what revelations the dispatches contained, and he believed that "if Congress are to act on the question of war, they have a right to information." Republican demands for disclosure were supported by extreme Federalists, who had gained some idea of the contents of the papers, and the House on April 2 by a vote of 65 to 27 called for the papers. The next day Adams sent Congress transcripts of all the dispatches, substituting the letters W, X, Y, and Z for the names of the French agents who had communicated with the American envoys.[22] As the dispatches were read behind closed doors, Republican members were stunned, and as portions leaked to the press, so too was the public. Soon afterward Congress voted to publish the documents, and as their contents became known, a wave of pro-administration and anti-French sentiment spread across the land.

Some Republican congressmen, such as Virginia's Samuel J. Cabell, tried to calm the rising fever against France and the talk of war by pointing out the lack of evidence incriminating the French government in the "nefarious scheme to swindle" by the unauthorized French spokesmen. A Republican colleague told his North Carolina constituents that it was to be regretted that the information in the dispatches was not more favorable but pointed out that the greatest part of their contents reported conversations of unofficial and unauthorized persons. Jefferson took a similar position. In sending his nephew Peter Carr a copy of the envoys' dispatches, he noted, "You will perceive that they have been assailed by swindlers, whether with or without the participation of Talleyrand is not very apparent." Knowing the character of that French minister, Jefferson thought it very possible that Talleyrand expected to share in the bribe demanded, but he believed it was neither proved nor probable that the Directory knew anything about it.[23]

Jefferson's analysis of the dispatches placed the primary blame for the French actions on President Adams. In his opinion Adams' insult to the French at the opening of the special session of Congress in May had prevented negotiations. In reacting to France's refusal to receive Pinckney as minister, Adams had accused the French of treating the United States "neither as allies nor as friends, nor as a sovereign state" and said that the United States should show France that they were not "the miserable instruments of foreign influence, and regardless of national honor, character, and interest." Jefferson thought the content of the dispatches from France showed that Adams' speech was the only obstacle to accommodation and the real cause of war, if war came.[24] But most Americans did not draw this conclusion and saw the French rather than their president as offering the greater insult.

Jefferson viewed the public reaction with alarm, fearing that the administration would now find support for a war against France that he suspected the Federalists of favoring all along. The dispatches did not offer any new motive for going to war, he told Madison on the day the House voted to publish the paper. "Yet such is their effect on the minds of wavering characters, that I fear, that to wipe off the imputation of being French partisans, they will go over to the war measures so furiously pushed." The vice-president did not know that Secretary of State Pickering was sending bundles of the pamphlets containing the XYZ papers to correspondents all over the country with instructions for their extensive distribution, even into the backcountry.[25] But all around him was evidence of the impact of the disclosures on the public mind. In Philadelphia the excitement over the XYZ dispatches had been maintained, and war addresses were "showering in from New Jersey and the great trading towns." The growth of Republicanism in the eastern states had been checked. In his view the dispatches from France had "carried over to the war-party most of the waverers in the House of Representatives," giving the Federalists a strong majority to carry what they pleased.[26]

Military measures came first. Congress provided for building a navy, created the Navy Department, increased coastal fortifications, and authorized the capture of French armed ships operating off American shores. The legislators expanded the regular army, authorized the president to raise a provisional army of ten thousand men and to accept volunteer companies, and passed measures for obtaining quantities of arms, munitions, and supplies. To pay for these extensive measures, Congress imposed a direct tax on land, houses, and slaves. As one discouraged Republican representative wrote his constituents at the end of the session, "the conduct of the French government . . . have irritated the public mind very much against them, and cause the adoption of measures which I fear place us in a state of war." [27]

But military preparations were only the beginning. Jefferson had early heard rumors that the Federalists planned to pass a citizen bill, an alien bill, and a sedition bill, and he was soon reporting to Madison the proceedings on these Federalist measures to tighten internal security. First came a proposal to modify the naturalization act. Next came proposals regarding aliens. Finally Jefferson wrote to Madison that "they have brought into the lower house a sedition bill, which among other enormities, undertakes to make printing certain matters criminal, though one of the amendments to the Constitution has so expressly taken religion, printing presses, etc. out of their coercion." He was convinced that the object was the suppression of Republican presses, and especially Benjamin Franklin Bache's *Aurora*, Philadelphia's leading Republican newspaper. The alien and sedition bills, Jefferson said, "are so palpably in the teeth of the Constitution as to show they mean to pay no respect to it." [28]

Jefferson did not remain in Philadelphia to see the last of these measures adopted in a Senate over which he presided, but he did delay his departure for a week when he learned of John Marshall's arrival in New York from France. He was not among the officials led by Secretary of State Pickering who went to greet the envoy when he reached Philadelphia, and he thought the procession was circuitously paraded through the streets to draw crowds, which he admitted were immense. He had stayed less to see Marshall than to hear the news from France, and he was relieved to learn that Marshall had told Robert R. Livingston in New York that they had no idea in France of a war with the United States. But he heard nothing like that circulating in the streets of Philadelphia. On the other hand, he could not avoid hearing the reports of the welcoming banquet the Federalist members of Congress hosted for the returning envoy, at which his exuberant admirers drank the toast "Millions for defense, but not one cent for tribute." [29]

As the crisis with France unfolded, Jefferson counseled, "A little patience, and we shall see the reign of witches pass over, their spells dissolved, and the people recovering their true sight, restoring their government to its true principles." [30] The optimistic Virginian still held to that opinion when he left the capital on June 27 for Monticello. But by patience he did not mean inactivity, and in the

months ahead he would take the lead in trying to move the people
to restore the government to those true principles that he cherished. Arriving back on his mountaintop on July 4, he found that
the remodeling of his house took so much of his time that there was
little left to spend at his writing desk. But when copies of the alien
and sedition acts reached him, he knew he would have to find some
time and some way to answer them.

The first alien act (June 25, 1798) empowered the president to
order the deportation of any alien he judged "dangerous to the
peace and safety of the United States" or had reasonable grounds
to suspect was involved in any treasonable intrigue against the government. It was up to the president to determine what constituted
a danger. Only after receiving a deportation order would the alien
have an opportunity to present evidence in his own behalf or, as
one Republican pointed out, to prove that the president was wrong
in deciding that he was dangerous. The second alien act (July 6,
1798) was a permanent statute permitting the president in time
of war to imprison or deport alien subjects of an enemy power.
Operative only in war time, it raised no controversial constitutional
questions. The first alien law, on the other hand, was a temporary
peacetime measure designed for the crisis with France and limited
to two years. It gave the administration power to deal with objectionable aliens, especially those who supported the Republicans,
whether war came or not.[31]

Even more sweeping and more objectionable to Republican opponents of the administration was the sedition act (July 14, 1798).
Passed in the final days of the session, after Jefferson had left for
Virginia, the act made it unlawful for any persons to combine or
conspire together to oppose any lawful measure of the government, to prevent any officer of the United States from performing
his duties, or to aid or attempt to procure "any insurrection, riot
unlawful assembly, or combination." Furthermore, it provided for
the punishment of any person writing, uttering, or publishing "any
false, scandalous and malicious writing" against the president, the
Congress, or the government of the United States, made with the
intent to defame them or to excite against them "the hatred of
the good people of the United States." Underscoring the blatant
political purposes of the measure, the act was to expire on March 3
1801, the last day of President Adams' term of office.[32]

Jefferson saw the alien and sedition laws not only as attempts to
silence Republican newspapers and drive Republican-minded aliens
from the country but also as "an experiment on the American

mind, to see how far it will bear an avowed violation of the constitution." When he took up his pen to reply, he would direct his attention to the basic constitutional issue. Because he was vice-president and the head of the Republican party, to which the acts were largely directed, his response would be secretly composed and indirectly put before the public. In October he remarked causally to one Virginia correspondent that he fancied that some of the state legislatures would take strong ground in response to the alien and sedition acts.[33] Before then he had already initiated the process to make certain that would happen.

By October he had finished the final draft of a set of resolutions protesting the unconstitutionality of the acts and sent them to Wilson Cary Nicholas, a Republican member of the Virginia Assembly, to arrange their introduction in the legislature of neighboring North Carolina. By a fortuitous coincidence former Virginian John Breckinridge, a member of the Kentucky House of Representatives, was visiting in Nicholas' neighborhood, and Nicholas arranged for him to carry the resolutions to Kentucky (where opposition to the alien and sedition laws was already stirring) and to sponsor them in the Kentucky legislature. Nicholas revealed Jefferson's authorship of the resolutions to Breckinridge, who pledged himself to secrecy and abandoned an intended visit to Monticello to avoid possible speculation. Sharing Nicholas' confidence in Breckinridge, Jefferson fully approved of the arrangements. He also urged Nicholas to discuss the resolutions with Madison, from whom he had no secrets.[34] Just how much Jefferson had already conferred with Madison regarding the resolutions is unclear, but Madison visited Jefferson at Monticello in October, and they consulted on a similar set of resolutions that Madison secretly was drafting for presentation to the Virginia Assembly by John Taylor of Caroline County.[35]

Jefferson stated the theoretical basis of the Kentucky Resolutions in the opening sentence affirming: "*Resolved*, That the several States composing the United States of America, are not united on the principle of unlimited submission to their general government; but that, by a compact under the style and title of a Constitution for the United States, and of amendments thereto, they constituted a general government for special purposes,—delegated to that government certain definite powers, reserving, each State to itself, the residuary mass of right to their own self-government; and that whensoever the general government assumes undelegated powers, its acts are unauthoritative, void, and of no force."[36] He went on to say that the general government was not made the final or exclusive judge of its powers and that each party to the compact had an equal right to judge for itself infractions of the Constitution. Subsequent resolutions specified the provisions of the Constitution violated by the alien and sedition acts and declared that because they were unconstitutional, the acts were void and of no effect.

The resolutions as adopted by the legislature of Kentucky in November, 1798, affirmed these principles, essentially in Jefferson's own words, but they departed from Jefferson's draft in regard to the means of redress. The supposition is that Breckinridge toned down Jefferson's draft before submitting it to his colleagues in the Kentucky legislature. In his draft Jefferson stated that "where powers are assumed which have not been delegated, a nullification of the act is the rightful remedy: that every State has a natural right in cases not within the compact . . . to nullify of their own authority all assumptions of powers by others within their own limits." Jefferson's draft had not gone so far as to proclaim the nullification of the alien and sedition acts, but he had employed the word and affirmed the right. The resolutions that came from the Kentucky legislature in 1798 did not contain this passage and did not use the word *nullification*.[37] The Kentucky Resolutions followed Jefferson's draft in concluding with a call to all other states to express their sentiments in regard to the alien and sedition laws. Framed with the hope that other states' views would coincide with those of Kentucky, the resolutions urged all states to concur in declaring the acts void and of no force. But the Kentucky protest dropped Jefferson's further appeal to each state to "take measures of its own for providing that neither of these acts, nor any others of the General Government, not plainly and intentionally authorized by the Constitution, shall be exercised within their respective territories." In place of this extreme proposition, Breckinridge or other Kentucky revisers substituted a call for all states to unite in requesting the repeal of the alien and sedition laws at the next session of Congress.[38]

Influenced by the more cautious Madison, Jefferson was prepared to accept this more moderate approach. To John Taylor, who was to shepherd Madison's milder resolutions through the Virginia Assembly, Jefferson wrote in late November, 1798, "For the present I should be for resolving the alien and sedition laws to be against the constitution and merely void, and for addressing the other States to obtain similar declarations; and I would not do anything at this moment which should commit us further, but reserve ourselves to shape our future measures or no measures, by the events which may happen." Jefferson did make a last-minute effort to strengthen the language of Madison's resolutions, but in the end Madison's more moderate stance prevailed.[39]

In response to the passage of the Kentucky and Virginia Resolutions, a number of states replied unfavorably to the arguments advanced, and no state voiced support. A disappointed Jefferson strongly favored a rebuttal of these negative responses. "That the principles already advanced by Virginia and Kentucky are not to be yielded in silence, I presume we all agree," he wrote to Madison, outlining the main points he thought should be emphasized in their reply. In these suggestions he went so far as to propose a threat "to sever ourselves from that union we so much value, rather than give up the rights of self government which we have reserved, and in which alone we see liberty, safety and happiness." Again Madison's moderating influence prevailed. When Jefferson sent a similar outline to Nicholas, who was to convey his views to Breckinridge in Kentucky, he was more cautious and eliminated the idea of threatening secession. He also specifically declined to prepare any draft of new resolutions to be transmitted to Kentucky to avoid suspicions, which he thought had been strong in some quarters in the preceding year.[40]

The resolutions adopted by the Kentucky legislature in 1799 thus were not of Jefferson's composition. Breckinridge or some other person revived the word *nullification*, which had been edited out of Jefferson's draft of the preceding year, and incorporated it into the new resolutions. Jefferson never objected to this restoration, but he did not initiate it. The Kentucky Resolutions of 1799 justified nullification as a rightful remedy, but the claim was not pressed. The resolutions concluded by issuing only a "solemn protest."[41] The more moderate Virginia response directed by Madison, who had returned to the Virginia House of Delegates, did not raise the specter of nullification and emphasized that the Virginia Resolutions were an expression of opinion only.[42]

In the course of time the Kentucky and Virginia Resolutions became famous for their systematic formulation of the doctrine of states' rights and for the germ of nullification. At the moment when they were written, they were most important as a political protest in defense of civil liberties. It was Jefferson's deep concern for the protection of those rights that moved him to take up his pen in their behalf. The resolutions that Jefferson and Madison authored were more than expositions of constitutional theory. They were also political statements directed against unpopular measures of a Federalist-controlled Congress and the Federalist administration of John Adams. Indeed, they were the opening guns of the election campaign of 1800.

XVI
The Election of 1800

Vice-President Jefferson took his job as presiding officer of the Senate seriously. Except at the very beginning and the end of sessions, when he was not always present, he occupied the chair daily and wielded the gavel with an authority backed by careful regard for parliamentary rules. With his usual attention to system, his orderly mind was troubled by the fact that the legislative practices of the body over which he presided were not more regularized. Finding no authority to which to turn for the fine points of procedure, he began preparing a manual of parliamentary practice. Published in 1801, the manual has ever since been the fundamental guide to Senate procedures, and the House of Representatives also later adopted applicable portions of the work.[1]

While conscientiously performing his duties as president of the Senate, Jefferson also filled the role of Republican party leader in preparing the party and the electorate for the election of 1800. Chafing powerlessly under a Federalist administration, the vice-president, unlike the reluctant candidate of 1796, was ready to run for president in 1800. Midway through Adams' presidency he began laying the groundwork for the campaign. Presidential candidates were expected to refrain from openly campaigning for office, and Jefferson would not challenge that tradition. But he would do all that he could to advance his own election and a Republican victory in 1800 by writing letters, supporting Republican newspapers, circulating political pamphlets, urging supporters to write pieces for the press, and generally encouraging Republican party activity.

Early in 1799 Jefferson wrote from Philadelphia to Madison in Virginia that the coming summer was "the season for systematic energies and sacrifices. The engine is the press. Every man must lay his purse and his pen under contribution." He urged Madison to set aside a portion of every post day to write something for the newspapers and to send it to him in Philadelphia. "When I go away I will let you know to whom you may send," he instructed, "so that your name shall be sacredly secret."[2] Jefferson similarly enlisted other Republicans to write for the press, while he himself adhered to his own proscription against writing anything for publication to which he did not sign his name.

Jefferson also gave aid and encouragement to newspaper editors and writers suffering under the sedition act. Among them was James Thomson Callender, whose abusive attacks on John Adams Jefferson later said he had not intended to encourage. After the election Jefferson said that "no man wished more to see his pen stopped" but that he had considered him "a proper object of benevolence." Justifying the two occasions on which he had given Callender fifty dollars, he insisted that the gifts were "mere charities, yielded under a strong conviction that he was injuring us by his writings." This recollection is inconsistent with what Jefferson wrote to Callender during the campaign. After Callender sent him some proof sheets of his *The Prospect Before Us*, Jefferson responded by telling the writer that "such papers cannot fail to produce the best effect. They inform the thinking part of the nation; and those again, supported by the taxgathers as their vouchers, set the people to rights." Some of Jefferson's political friends tried to warn him that Callender was not to be trusted, but no evidence has been found that the candidate heeded their advice.[3]

During the campaign of 1800 Jefferson personally took a hand in the distribution of political pamphlets favorable to the Republican cause. In sending a dozen such pamphlets to Monroe in February, 1799, he instructed him to give them to "the most influential characters among our country-men" who were still open to conviction and might have the most effect on their neighbors. "It would be useless to give them to persons already sound," he wrote. "Do not let my name be connected with the business." Throughout the campaign Jefferson continued to direct the distribution of such material. In the spring of 1800 he sent eight dozen copies of Thomas Cooper's *Political Arithmetic* to the chairman of the recently created state Republican committee, asking him to send one copy to each county committee. "Tho' I know that this is not the immediate object of your institution," he wrote, "yet I consider it as a most valuable object, to which the institution may most usefully be applied." Trusting the Virginia party chairman with the secret that the pamphlets came from the vice-president, he explained: "You will readily see what a handle would be made of my advocating their contents. I must leave to yourself therefore to say how they come to you." In *Political Arithmetic* Cooper argued that the cost of building and maintaining a navy to protect American commerce far exceeded the profit from shipping. The merchants did not assume the burden of the added taxes but passed them on, he explained. "The consumer, the farmer, the mechanic, the labourer, they and *they alone* pay."[4] Jefferson's agency in the circulation of such pamphlets shows how different his role was in the election of 1800 from that in 1796. In 1800, Jefferson was more actively engaged in the presidential campaign than any previous presidential candidate had ever been.

Jefferson's greatest contribution to the campaign of 1800 was in defining the issues before the voters and developing the Republican platform, though that term was not then in use. In letters to friends and party leaders throughout the country Jefferson spelled out his own political principles and what he believed the Republican party stood for. Writing to Elbridge Gerry of Massachusetts early in 1799, the candidate summarized those beliefs, which he affirmed were "unquestionably the principles of the great body of our fellow citizens." He began by declaring his commitment to preserving the Constitution "according to the true sense in which it was adopted by the States" and preventing the "monarchising" of its features. He was "for preserving to the States the powers not yielded by them to the Union" and "not for transferring all the powers of the States to the general government, and all those of that government to the Executive branch." He stressed that he was "for a government rigorously frugal and simple, applying all the possible savings of the public revenue to the discharge of the national debt." Addressing the military buildup following the XYZ affair, he said he opposed a standing army in time of peace and would rely solely on the militia for internal defense until an actual invasion. He favored only such naval force as necessary to protect the coasts and harbors, fearing the expenses of a larger navy and "the eternal wars in which it will implicate us, grind us with public burthens, and sink us under them."

Jefferson emphasized that the United States should stay out of the quarrels of Europe. "I am for free commerce with all nations; political connection with none," he wrote, "and little or no diplomatic establishment." Responding to recent challenges to the First Amendment, the Republican leader affirmed his support for freedom of religion and freedom of the press. No one could have failed to recognize that he had the sedition act in mind when he said that he was "against all violations of the constitution to silence by force and not by reason the complaints or criticisms, just or unjust, of our citizens against the conduct of their agents." Always more than politician, he added that he was "for encouraging the progress of science in all it's branches; and not for raising a hue and cry against the sacred name of philosophy."[5]

The Republican candidate expected the views that he expressed in this and other letters to circulate beyond the persons to whom they were addressed, and there is ample evidence that they did so. The principles and issues that he stressed appeared repeatedly in Republican newspapers, broadsides, and party leaflets throughout the campaign. The Republican party took a clear stand on the issues in 1800, and it was Jefferson more than anyone else who articulated the positions that his supporters readily embraced. Jefferson's leadership in directing opposition to the principles and policies of the Federalist administration rather than to the character of President Adams was widely followed but not entirely accepted. Adams again was accused of being a monarchist, though the issue played far less a role in the 1800 campaign than it had in 1796. Adams' policies provided more ample grounds for Republican assaults. Still, some Republicans were less concerned than Jefferson about emphasizing principle. One Virginia Republican argued that there was too much talk of principle and that Republicans should bring their arguments home to the voters' feelings. The Philadelphia *Aurora*, the nation's leading Republican newspaper, declared that under a Federalist president there would be war, but with Jefferson there would be peace. "Therefore the friends of *peace will vote for Jefferson*—the friends of war will vote for *Adams* or for *Pinckney*."[6]

Federalists employed similar tactics. Fisher Ames of Massachusetts advised Federalists to "sound the tocsin about Jefferson" in a series of papers designed "to prove the dreadful evils to be apprehended from a Jacobin President." Among such consequences, he listed war with Great Britain, an alliance with France, plunder, and anarchy. "Surely we have enough to fear from Jefferson," he reasoned. Jefferson's opponents depicted him as a threat to the stability of the government and as one who would undermine the morals of the people. "Can serious and reflecting men look about them and doubt, that if Jefferson is elected, and the Jacobins get into authority, that those morals which protect our lives from the knife of the assassin—which guard the chastity of our wives and daughters from seduction and violence—defend our property from

plunder and devastation, and shield our religion from contempt
and profanation, will not be trampled upon and exploded?" exclaimed "A Christian Federalist." The Federalist *Gazette of the United
States* posed the key question of the election, "to be asked by every
American, laying his hand on his heart," as: "Shall I continue in allegiance to God—and a Religious President; Or impiously declare
for Jefferson—and No God!!!"[7]

Federalist attacks on Jefferson on religious grounds caused Republicans more discomfort than any other charge. Though reared
in the Anglican church, Jefferson was a man of the Enlightenment
who accepted deism as the natural religion that the application of
reason to society dictated. Seeking to exploit the religious issue,
Federalists cited passages in his *Notes on Virginia* to prove his "dis-
belief of the Holy Scriptures; or, in other words, his rejection of the
Christian Religion and open profession of Deism," as the Reverend
William Linn, a New York clergyman, proclaimed. Linn insisted
that "the election of any man avowing the principles of Mr. Jefferson would . . . destroy religion, introduce immorality, and loosen
all the bonds of society," and he warned that "the voice of the nation in calling a deist to the first office must be construed into no
less than a rebellion against God."[8]

Republican defenders of Jefferson responded by also quoting
from his *Notes on Virginia*, which showed, one claimed, "that there is
not a single passage in the Notes on Virginia, or any of Mr. Jefferson's writings, repugnant to Christianity; but on the contrary, in
every respect, favourable to it." Republicans further charged that
Jefferson was being attacked "because he is not a fanatic, nor willing that the *Quaker*, the *Baptist*, the *Methodist*, or any other denominations of Christians, should pay the pastors of other sects; because
he does not think that a Catholic should be banished for believing
in transubstantiation, or a Jew, for believing in the God of Abraham, Isaac, and Jacob." What stood highest in Jefferson's favor was
his clear record of opposition to state-supported churches and his
defense of religious freedom. It was Jefferson's opposition to a religious establishment that made such an important churchman as Isaac Backus an admirer of Jefferson, and it was a stand that could be
widely appreciated throughout the growing Baptist movement
stimulated by the Second Great Awakening.[9]

As they had in 1796, Federalists tried to arouse suspicions against
Jefferson as a radical philosopher. A North Carolina planter warned
against "the dangerous principle of Mr. Jefferson's philosophy,"
linking it to the "horrid government" of France and praying, "From

the government of such philosophers, may the beneficent father o
the universe protect us." Republicans often countered with ex
travagant praise of their candidate. One lauded him as a man o
"an enlightened mind and superior wisdom; the adorer of ou
God; the patriot of his country; and the friend and benefactor o
the whole human race." Republicans repeatedly reminded voter
that Jefferson was the author of the Declaration of Independence
and one writer urged support for the man "whose whole life ha
been a comment on its precepts, and an uniform pursuit of the
great blessings of his country which it was first intended to estab
lish." In more restrained language the state Republican committe
of Virginia in its official address to the voters affirmed, "As a frienc
to liberty, we believe Jefferson second to no man, and the experi
ence of no man has afforded better lessons for its preservation."[1]

Enjoying the advantages of the party in power, the Federalist
in their campaign literature attributed the prosperous situation o
the country to "the sage maxims of administration established by
the immortal Washington, and steadily pursued by his virtuou
successor." Federalist spokesmen saw no reason to change course
The Federalist state committee in Virginia reminded voters tha
the country had remained free, independent, and at peace. Why
embark with Jefferson on "the tempestuous sea of liberty? . .
Let us be content to take a lesson, on this head, from the Frencl
Republic."[11]

As the party out of power, the Republicans sought to overcome
their disadvantage by giving attention to party organization, elec
tion laws and procedures, campaign methods, and getting out the
voters. Federalists commonly followed Republican examples, bu
Republicans tended to be the innovators in creating party ma
chinery and in implementing new campaign techniques. Jefferson
recognized the value of these activities but was not directly involved
in their management, which was largely in the hands of state anc
local party leaders with the aid and sometimes the prodding of
members of Congress. In Virginia the Republican-controlled legis
lature changed the election law from a district system of electing
presidential electors to a general ticket. Four years earlier Jeffer
son had lost one district in his home state. Under a general-ticke
system, he would be assured of the entire electoral vote of the na
tion's largest state. Virginia Federalists protested the Republicar
action, but elsewhere Federalists used the same tactic when it was tc
their advantage. In John Adams' home state of Massachusetts, the
Federalist-controlled legislature transferred the election of electors
from popular election by districts to the state legislature.[12]

After all the changes in election laws had been completed, presidential electors were popularly chosen in 1800 in only five of the sixteen states: Rhode Island, Maryland, Virginia, North Carolina, and Kentucky. Thus, as Thomas Boylston Adams, the president's youngest son, observed, "the trial of strength between the two Candidates for the chief magistracy of the Union is to be seen, not in the choice of electors by the people, but in the complexion and character of the individual legislatures."[13] Because elections for state legislatures came at different times, the presidential contest would extend through most of the year.

The first trial of strength between Jefferson and Adams was in New York City, but the principal contenders were Aaron Burr, who managed the Republican campaign, and Alexander Hamilton, who led the Federalists. The objective was to win control of the state legislature, which would choose the presidential electors. Jefferson himself believed that New York, which Adams had carried in 1796, was critical to Republican success. In the heated contest in New York City, Burr skillfully put together a Republican slate that included a number of prominent Republicans as candidates for the state assembly. The strategy succeeded decisively. The victory in New York City tipped the balance in the legislature to the Republican side, and the newly elected Assembly could be counted upon to choose presidential electors pledged to Jefferson. Hamilton, however, saw one way to avoid such an unwelcome result. Writing promptly to Governor John Jay, he urged him to call a special session of the old assembly before the terms of the Federalist majority expired on July 1. The purpose would be to change the state's method of electing presidential electors, substituting popular election by districts in place of selection by the legislature. "In times like these in which we live, it will not do to be overscrupulous," Hamilton wrote the governor. "It is easy to sacrifice the substantial interests of society by a strict adherence to ordinary rules. . . . They ought not to hinder the taking of a *legal* and *constitutional* step, to prevent an *Atheist* in Religion and a *Fanatic* in politics from getting possession of the helm of the State."[14] Jay, who had resigned as chief justice of the United States to become governor of New York, refused to be a party to the scheme, thus assuring that the Republican legislature would select Republican electors.

Coming at the end of April, the New York election gave the Republicans an important early campaign victory that they hoped would influence elections in other states. It gave a great psychological boost to Republicans, and enthusiastic Republicans widely credited Burr with the success. "He deserves anything and everything from his country," one New York admirer exclaimed.[15] Burr's reward came quickly. A week after news of the New York results reached Philadelphia, Republican members of Congress caucused and nominated Burr for vice-president. Jefferson by consensus was already the Republican candidate for president, and the caucus did not place his name in nomination. But the absence of a similar consensus regarding the second place prompted the Republican members of Congress to assume a nominating role. In doing so, they set the precedent for presidential nominations that would be followed by the Republican party until 1824.

The New York election also had its effect on the Federalists in Congress. Caucusing immediately after the New York returns reached Philadelphia, they recommended that John Adams and Charles Cotesworth Pinckney be supported equally as the Federalist candidates. With presidential electors not permitted to distinguish between presidential and vice-presidential candidates in casting their votes, the strategy was designed to give the Federalists two chances to win the presidency. It depended on the possibility that electors in some states might cast their votes for Jefferson and one of the Federalist nominees. "To support *Adams* and *Pinckney*, equally, is the only thing that can possibly save us from the fangs of *Jefferson*," Hamilton wrote privately after the New York election.[16] While this was the proclaimed rationale, the caucus decision masked a deeper strategy—the design to promote the election of Pinckney over Adams. This scheme, of which Hamilton was the principal architect, rested primarily on the prospect that in South Carolina the presidential electors might cast their votes for Jefferson and Charles Cotesworth Pinckney, a native son, in the same way they had voted for Jefferson and Thomas Pinckney in 1796. In May, 1800, Hamilton was not prepared to oppose openly the incumbent Federalist president, but he was already saying privately that he would "never more be responsible for him by my direct support—even though the consequence should be the election of *Jefferson*. If we must have an *enemy* at the head of the Government, let it be one whom we can oppose."[17] This division in the Federalist ranks would be exacerbated when Hamilton came out publicly in opposition to Adams in October. The split was less important in the outcome of the election, however, than might appear, because Hamilton's open attack came after many contests had already been decided and because Hamilton's own influence was considerably weakened by his failure to carry New York for any Federalist candidate.

The presidential contest throughout the nation was close enough that the final outcome of the election could not be determined until the returns from the last state to choose its presidential electors had been reported. Throughout the long months from April to early December, as national attention shifted from one state to another and as returns drifted in, Jefferson waited anxiously, keeping a running tally on results and prospects. During these months the Republican candidate was extremely cautious about writing letters, fearful that something that he wrote in a private letter might get into the newspapers and be used against him as the Mazzei letter had been. On the eve of the election year, in fact, he had said that he was ceasing to write political letters, "knowing that a campaign of slander is now to open upon me, and believing that the post-masters will lend their inquisitorial aid to fish out any new matter of slander they can gratify the powers that be."[18] But he found that he could not adhere rigidly to the rule and resorted to sending letters by private conveyance and leaving letters to Madison, Monroe, and other friends unsigned.

As party leaders on both sides tallied results and calculated prospects, they came to similar conclusions that the election was very close and the outcome uncertain. When Jefferson analyzed the results as he knew them at the end of November, he found the outcome still in doubt in three states: Pennsylvania, Rhode Island, and South Carolina. In Pennsylvania a Republican House of Representatives and a Federalist Senate remained deadlocked over the method to be used to choose presidential electors, and it appeared that the state would not cast a vote. A few days later Jefferson learned that the Federalists had carried Rhode Island, and he now accurately calculated the electoral vote as standing at fifty-eight for Adams and fifty-seven for Jefferson.[19] If Pennsylvania did not vote, the eight electoral votes of South Carolina would decide the election. With South Carolina being the South's most strongly Federalist state, where Charles Cotesworth Pinckney was being aggressively pushed, many Federalists were now more optimistic about the final outcome of the election than Jefferson had reason to be.

All the details will never be known about what happened in Columbia, South Carolina, when the legislature met at the end of November to choose the state's presidential electors on December 2. There is, however, ample evidence to show that Charles Pinckney, who managed the Republican effort, played a crucial role. Pinckney, a United States senator from South Carolina and cousin of the Federalist candidate, outmaneuvered the Federalists, even with Charles Cotesworth Pinckney himself on the ground, and carried the day for the Republicans. Pinckney was soon writing to Jefferson urging him not to make any arrangements about appointments in South Carolina before he had a chance to talk with him, strongly implying that he may have made some commitments about appointments that were critical to the Republican success.[20]

By the time the South Carolina result became known, the two houses of the Pennsylvania legislature had reached a compromise to divide that state's electoral vote, eight votes going to Jefferson and seven to Adams. Thus the effect of the South Carolina vote in deciding the election remained unaltered. First reports from South Carolina indicated that the vote there would be eight for Jefferson, seven for Burr, and one for George Clinton. The coeditor of the Charleston *City Gazette* had reliable sources for reporting from Columbia to his partner in Charleston that one vote was to be withheld from Burr because "it is not the wish to risque any person being higher than Jefferson."[21] But his report turned out to be inaccurate. When the South Carolina electors met to cast their votes, no vote was withheld. All eight electors voted for Jefferson and Burr.

With all states accounted for, the Federalists carried all of New England, New Jersey, and Delaware. The Republicans won the entire electoral vote of New York, Virginia, South Carolina, Georgia, Kentucky, and Tennessee. The two parties divided the vote in Pennsylvania, Maryland, and North Carolina. The Federalists would have denied Jefferson the presidency had they carried New York, but to emphasize that point can be misleading. It ignores the impressive Republican victory in the congressional elections, which gave the Republicans 67 out of the 106 seats in the House of Representatives. It also ignores the strength that Jefferson had in Pennsylvania that was not reflected in the compromise electoral vote from that state.

To many Federalists, some of whom had prematurely celebrated "the non-election of (*Citizen*) Jefferson," the final returns from South Carolina came as a jolt. "I have never heard bad tidings on anything which gave me such a shock," the Reverend Thomas Robbins recorded in his diary upon hearing the news. To this staunch Massachusetts Federalist, who had earlier declared that he did "not believe that the Most High will permit a howling atheist to sit at the head of this nation," the election of Jefferson was unthinkable.[22] But before Federalists sank too deeply into despair, the results of the elections in all the states became known and revived a glimmer of Federalist hope. Jefferson had not won after all. He had tied with Aaron Burr. The final count was Jefferson 73, Burr 73, Adams 65,

Pinckney 64, and Jay 1. The contest was not over. Under the provisions of the Constitution, the election would go to the House of Representatives for final resolution.

This news that revived Federalist spirits deprived Republicans of savoring the joys of victory. "The Feds in the legislature have expressed dispositions to make all they can of the embarrassment," Jefferson wrote of the upcoming contest in the House of Representatives, "so that after the most energetic efforts, crowned with success, we remain in the hands of our enemies by the want of foresight in the original arrangement." The lack of foresight that Jefferson bemoaned was the Republican failure to prevent a tie by making provisions to withhold one vote from Burr, in the same manner that Adams' supporters had given one vote to Jay. Republicans had certainly been aware of the possible problem. Withholding a vote from Burr had been considered in the Virginia college of electors, where Madison, one of the electors, told his colleagues that he had received assurances from a confidential friend of Burr that in "a certain quarter" votes would be thrown away from Burr to assure a majority for Jefferson. Only this assurance overcame the anxiety of George Wythe, also an elector, "whose devoted regard for Mr. Jefferson made him nearly inflexible," Madison later recalled. Jefferson himself accepted some of the responsibility for Virginia's not withholding a vote from Burr. He later said that he had taken some measures to procure the unanimous vote of Virginia for Burr because he thought any failure there might be imputed to him.[23] The special concern that Burr receive the full Virginia vote is explained by the electoral vote in 1796, when Virginia electors gave the New Yorker but one vote. In 1800 Burr privately warned his Virginia allies that "after what happened at the last election . . . it is most obvious that I should not choose to be trifled with." Just what assurance Madison received from Burr's confidential friend has never been established, but there were rumors of votes being withheld from Burr in other states, including South Carolina, where one elector later reported that such a move had been proposed but could not be agreed to. What Republican leaders did not sufficiently appreciate was that loyalty to party—to be demonstrated by carrying out the recommendations of the congressional caucus— was stronger than anyone realized. In state after state, electors demonstrated their party loyalty, apparently confident that in some other state party regularity would not be so strong. Federalist Senator Uriah Tracy expressed it another way, reporting that Republicans were now indicating that "if they had not had full confidence in the treachery of the others, they would have been treacherous themselves and not acted as they promised to act at Philadelphia last winter, viz., all vote for Jefferson and Burr."[24]

What made the Republican predicament so serious was that the election was to be decided not by the newly elected House of Representatives, in which the Republicans would have a majority, but by the Federalist House elected two years earlier in the wake of the XYZ affair. One provision of the Constitution saved the Republicans from having their fate immediately determined by their opponents—the requirement that voting in the House in such circumstances be by states, with each state casting one vote. Despite their majority the Federalists controlled only six of the sixteen states. Republicans controlled eight states, and two delegations were equally divided.

In his final months as vice-president, Jefferson was in Washington presiding over the Senate when the news from South Carolina reached the new capital, to which the government had moved during the summer. Accepting the initial reports that a vote had been withheld from Burr, he wrote immediately to his running mate to congratulate him on his election to the vice-presidency. By the time Burr received Jefferson's letter, later reports indicated that the situation was not so clear as Jefferson had assumed, but Burr replied that he did not apprehend any embarrassment even if their votes came out alike. "My personal friends are perfectly informed of my Wishes on the subject and can never think of diverting a single Vote from you," he wrote. "On the Contrary, they will be found among your most zealous adherents. I see no reason to doubt of your having at least nine States if the business shall come before the House of Representatives."[25]

Meanwhile, upon hearing the early reports from South Carolina, Burr had written to Samuel Smith of Maryland, a leading Republican in the House of Representatives, constituting him his proxy in case of a tie (which he at that time thought improbable) to declare that he would "utterly disclaim all competition" with Jefferson. The New Yorker indicated that the Federalists should expect nothing from him and that his friends would dishonor him if they even suspected that he might be an instrument in counteracting the wishes and expectations of the nation. Once Burr learned that he had actually tied with Jefferson, he professed to stand by this statement, but he refused to promise that he would not accept election by the House. He told Smith at the end of December that he had declined to answer whether he would resign if chosen president. "The question was unnecessary, unreasonable and impertinent, and I have therefore made no reply," he wrote. "If I had made any I should have told that as at present advised, I should not."[26]

Burr's position placed the election in an entirely different light and gave encouragement to those who sought to elect Burr rather than Jefferson. Even though the Federalists did not have enough votes in the House to carry the election, many Federalists hoped that by supporting Burr and preventing a choice, some Republicans might be persuaded to switch their support to Burr in order to decide the contest. A few Federalists even harbored hope that some Republicans secretly favored Burr over Jefferson. Recognizing their power to prevent an election by the House, other Federalists began thinking in terms of an interim government and another election.[27] Republicans regarded all such schemes as usurpation.

One Federalist who favored neither usurpation nor the election of Burr was Alexander Hamilton, who believed that anyone would make a better president than Burr, even Jefferson. "There is no doubt that upon every virtuous and prudent calculation Jefferson is to be preferred," Hamilton declared immediately upon learning of the probability of the electoral tie. "He is by far not so dangerous a man and he has pretensions to character. As to *Burr* there is nothing in his favor. His private character is not defended by his most partial friends. . . . His public principles have no other spring or aim than his own aggrandisement."[28] As weeks passed and Hamilton recognized the strong Federalist inclination to support Burr, he wrote letter after letter to Federalist leaders, detailing the lack of private character and absence of political principles that he saw in Burr.[29] One of the Federalists with whom Hamilton pleaded not to support Burr was James A. Bayard, the sole representative from Delaware. From the beginning of the election in the House, Bayard would have it within his power to decide the election by casting his state's vote for Jefferson. Hamilton argued for Jefferson as the lesser of two evils. He still thought Jefferson's politics were tinctured with fanaticism and that he was "too much in earnest in his democracy." Jefferson was "crafty and persevering in his objects," not very mindful of the truth, and "a contemptible hypocrite." But Hamilton did not believe that Jefferson was an enemy of executive power or favored an all-powerful House of Representatives. He assured Bayard that, while working with him in Washington's administration, he had observed that Jefferson "was generally for a large construction of the Executive authority, and not backward to act upon it in cases which coincided with his views." Aware of the picture of the Republican candidate that Federalists had painted during the campaign, Hamilton suggested that Jefferson was not likely to overthrow existing systems but could be expected to follow "a temporizing rather than violent system."[30] Hamilton spent more time arguing his case against Burr than justifying Jefferson, but he failed to win over Bayard. That assured a contest in the House of Representatives.

From the outset Republicans feared the worst. Jefferson thought the Federalists were determined to prevent an election and suspected they might pass a bill giving the government to the chief justice or the secretary of state or let it devolve on the president pro tempore of the Senate. By the fourth week of January, with the election in the House three weeks away, Albert Gallatin, the Republican congressional leader, still had not fathomed the Federalists' plans, but he believed that they would attempt to prevent an election under the pretense of voting for Burr. Gallatin was certain that Republicans would stand firm and not vote for Burr and equally sure that if all Federalists voted for Burr there could be no decision. "In that case what will be the plans of the Federalists, having, as they have, a majority in both Houses? Will they usurp at once the Presidential powers?" he asked. "An attempt of that kind will most certainly be resisted. Will they only pass a law providing for a new election?" If they adopted the latter course, which seemed the most plausible, Gallatin reasoned that, by preventing an election in four states where neither party controlled both houses of the legislature, they could annul the last election while appearing not to have violated the Constitution.[31] As Gallatin's speculations indicate, the young republic faced a major constitutional crisis in the first test of transferring political power in the national government from one political party to another.

On February 9 the House agreed that in the event of a tie in the electoral vote when the ballots were counted, the House would go into continuous session until a president was chosen. Republicans were prepared to eat and sleep in the Capitol for the last three weeks of the session if necessary. If no choice were made by March 4, there would be no government—no president and no funds to run the government. By transacting no other business until the election was decided, Congress would be prevented from passing the annual appropriations bill.[32]

There were no surprises when the electoral returns were opened and counted on Wednesday, February 11. As expected, the electoral count showed Jefferson and Burr with seventy-three votes each.

The House went immediately into continuous session and began balloting shortly after one o'clock in the afternoon. On the first ballot Jefferson had the votes of eight states, Burr had six states, and the delegations of Maryland and Vermont were divided.[33] By midnight nineteen ballots had been taken, each with the same result. As balloting continued hourly throughout the night, a bed was set up in a committee room for the ailing Joseph H. Nicholson, a Maryland Republican whose vote was critical. By eight o'clock the next morning, when the exhausted members agreed to suspend balloting until noon, twenty-seven ballots had failed to produce a decision. After one more ballot with the same result in the afternoon, the House suspended voting, without adjourning, until the following day. Two ballots that day and three the next moved neither Jefferson nor Burr closer to the nine states required for election. After thirty-three ballots, the vote still stood: Jefferson eight, Burr six, and two states divided. It was then three o'clock on Saturday afternoon, and the members had been balloting since Wednesday. Without adjourning, the House decided to suspend balloting until noon Monday.[34]

After a weekend of caucusing, some members expected the balloting to end on Monday. There were rumors that Congressman Bayard of Delaware would break the deadlock by voting for Jefferson. But when balloting resumed on Monday, February 16, there was no change. The rumors, however, were not without foundation, for on that very day Bayard was writing to his father-in-law, Richard Bassett, that the Federalists would meet in the evening "to agree upon the mode of surrendering." He said the decision had already been made to give up the contest the next day. Bayard himself had forced that decision on his Federalist colleagues by indicating that he intended to switch his vote to Jefferson. Tension was high when the thirty-sixth ballot was taken on February 17. In a few minutes it was over. Jefferson received the votes of ten states and was elected president of the United States. Bayard had not voted for Jefferson but had put in a blank ballot, while the Federalist members from Vermont and Maryland had either absented themselves or cast blank ballots, giving those two states to Jefferson. On the final ballot the Federalist-controlled delegation from South Carolina also cast a blank ballot, leaving Burr with only four states, all in New England.[35] Thus, no Federalist state ever voted for Jefferson.

Why did the Federalists give in and permit Jefferson's election? Jefferson thought it was because they saw the impossibility of electing Burr and "the certainty that a legislative usurpation would be resisted by arms, and a recourse to a convention to re-organize and amend the government." He said that "the very word convention gives them the horrors, as in the present democratical spirit of America, they fear they should lose some of the favorite morsels of the constitution." Bayard's private letters lend support to Jefferson's view. "Our opposition was continued till it was demonstrated that the New England Gentlemen meant to go without a Constitution and take the risk of a Civil War," he confided.[36] Bayard also blamed Burr for the outcome. "Burr has acted a miserable paultry part," he wrote angrily on the day he decided to throw his support to Jefferson. "The election was in his power, but he was determined to come in as a Democrat, and in that event would have been the most dangerous man in the community. We have been counteracted in the whole business by letters he has written to this place." Most of those letters have not survived, and it is unlikely that it will ever be entirely clear what Burr was doing. If Bayard's suspicions were correct, Burr's strategy seems to have escaped him. Burr already had the support of the Federalists—what he needed was Republican votes.[37]

Less than a week after the final ballot, Burr wrote that the Federalists were boasting aloud that they had compromised with Jefferson "particularly as to the retaining certain persons in office." Bayard also hinted that the Federalists had received assurances from Jefferson that he would not sweep out all Federalist officeholders.[38] Five years later Bayard testified that Samuel Smith of Maryland had given him assurances from Jefferson on certain points of policy and persons. When presented with this testimony, Smith confirmed that he had given Bayard assurances but that he had not done so on Jefferson's authority. Later Smith insisted that he had conferred with Jefferson "without his having the remotest idea of my object."[39] Jefferson himself declared that Smith had never made any proposition to him and was never authorized to speak for him. He did recall that Gouverneur Morris had sought to get assurances from him but that he had told him that he would "never go into the office of President by capitulation, nor with my hands tied by any conditions." This conforms to what Jefferson told Monroe while the balloting was in progress, when he wrote: "Many attempts have been made to obtain terms and promises from me. I have declared to them unequivocally, that I would not receive the government or capitulation, that I would not go into it with my hands tied." There is no evidence that Jefferson struck a deal. At the same time, Jefferson's supporters may have given certain Federalists promises tha

appeared to come from Jefferson. What was most decisive, however, was that the Republicans stood firm in support of Jefferson.
"The federal side of the house was so vain as to think they could
force the republicans to give up the will of the people as well as
their own," wrote one Republican member determined to stand
firm. Many Federalists came to sense that the Republicans would
not yield, and when the extremists indicated their intention to prevent Jefferson's election by continuing the deadlock, moderate Federalists like Bayard were unwilling to risk a civil war.[40]

The capitulation of the Federalists in the House of Representatives permitted the implementation of the voters' decision in the
election of 1800 and allowed the transfer of the political power of
the national government from the Federalists to the Republicans to
take place peacefully. In demonstrating the young republic's capacity to effect such a change, the election of 1800 was a momentous
event. Jefferson later would look back and speak of "the revolution
of 1800," declaring that the election was "as real a revolution in the
principles of our government as that of 1776 was in its form; not
effected indeed by the sword, as that, but by the rational and peaceable instrument of reform, the suffrage of the people." The election strengthened anew Jefferson's confidence in the American
people and his faith in the pursuit of reason.[41]

XVII
A President in Command

At noon on March 4, 1801, President-elect Jefferson, escorted by a detachment of Alexandria militia officers, marshals of the District of Columbia, and a delegation of congressmen, walked from Conrad and McMunn's boardinghouse on New Jersey Avenue at C Street to the nearby Capitol. When he arrived at the entrance to the Senate chamber—the only finished part of the new Capitol—the Alexandria rifle company posted outside the door opened ranks and, as the president-elect entered, they presented arms. The scene offered a remarkable contrast to the inaugurations of his two predecessors, who rode in impressive carriages to their inaugurals. But even the military guard was more pomp than Jefferson desired, and by his dress he showed his aversion to ceremony in a republic. While both Washington and Adams had dressed elegantly and worn swords to their inaugurations, Jefferson wore neither fancy outfit nor sword. "His dress was, as usual, that of a plain citizen," one reporter noticed, "without any distinctive badge of office."[1] Jefferson's actions reflected the simplicity he had promised in government. They were also in harmony with the unpretentiousness of the new capital village, where mud streets, scattered houses, and unfinished buildings contrasted sharply with the urban settings of New York and Philadelphia, where the previous inaugurals had been held.

Only a few weeks earlier Albert Gallatin said that the new federal city was "hated by every member of Congress without exception of persons or parties." He could not have included the new president in that assessment, for the Virginian who had envisioned his own home rising on an uncleared mountaintop near the Blue Ridge shared with L'Enfant a vision of a grand capital on the banks of the Potomac. It was fitting that Jefferson should have been the first president inaugurated in Washington, and it was symbolic of the old order's bitterness over the change of administration that President Adams departed the capital at four o'clock in the morning to avoid witnessing the transition of power. If Adams and other Federalists left the city in despair, Republicans were exuberant in welcoming the new order. Mrs. Samuel Harrison Smith, wife of the editor of the *National Intelligencer*, the infant capital's major newspaper, described the inauguration as "one of the most interesting scenes, a free people can ever witness. The changes of administration, which in every government and in every age have most generally been epochs of confusion, villainy and bloodshed," she wrote perceptively, "in this our happy country take place without any species of distraction, or disorder."[2]

Mrs. Smith was one of the visitors who crowded into the Senate chamber to watch Chief Justice John Marshall administer the oath of office to Jefferson and to listen intently as the fifty-seven-year-old president delivered his carefully prepared address. Reading from a text that he had compressed to fit on two sheets of paper written on both sides, the president failed to make his weak voice audible in many parts of the chamber. However, early that morning he had sent a copy of his address to editor Smith, who had it printed and ready for distribution as members of Congress and visitors left the ceremonies.[3]

In one of the memorable inaugural addresses in American history, the new president began with an appeal for national unity after a divisive election, calling upon his fellow citizens to unite in accepting the voice of the nation. Then he reminded his hearers of "this sacred principle that though the will of the majority is in all cases to prevail, that will, to be rightful, must be reasonable; that the minority possess their equal rights, which equal laws must protect, and to violate would be oppression." Looking back at the recent election campaign, he said that every difference of opinion was not a difference of principle, and he called for the uniting of political parties. "We have called by different names brethren of the same principle. We are all republicans: we are all federalists. If there be any among us who would wish to dissolve this Union or to change it's republican form, let them stand undisturbed as monuments of the safety with which error of opinion may be tolerated, where reason is left free to combat it." Jefferson's listeners did not know that, in appealing for party reconciliation, he discriminated between Federalist leaders and the mass of their supporters. Three days after the inaugural, he told Monroe that it was impracticable to conciliate the Federalist leaders, "whom I abandon as incurables, and will never turn an inch out of my way to reconcile them. But with the main body of the federalists, I believe it very practicable."[4] What Jefferson had in mind was converting Federalists to Republicanism. When Republicans understood this, it lessened their concerns. When Federalists realized what he meant, they found little inducement in his appeal.

Jefferson devoted a major section of his address to "the essential principles of our government, and consequently those which ought to shape it's administration." Here he reiterated his basic political principles and the leading policies that he had professed as a candidate, which he now restated as the guiding principles of his administration. He began by affirming "equal and exact justice to all men, of whatever state or persuasion, religious or political." Next, compressing the warning of Washington's farewell address into a ringing phrase, Jefferson proclaimed "Peace, commerce, and honest friendship with all nations, entangling alliances with none." He then went on to affirm his commitment to the rights of the states and the preservation of the general government, to popular election, and to an "absolute acquiescence in the decisions of the majority, the vital principles of republics, from which is no appeal but to force, the vital principle and immediate parent of despotism." Continuing to intermingle general principles and specific policies, the new president declared that he favored reliance for defense on a well-disciplined militia, the supremacy of civil over military authority, economy in public expenditures, the payment of debts, and the encouragement of agriculture and of commerce as its handmaid. He did not mention the alien and sedition acts, but he emphasized "the diffusion of information, and arraignment of all abuses at the bar of public reason:—freedom of religion; freedom of the press; and freedom of person, under the protection of Habeas corpus:—and trial by juries impartially selected." "These principles" he concluded, "form the bright constellation, which has gone before us and guided our steps through an age of revolution and reformation. . . . They should be the creed of our political faith, the text of civic instruction, the touchstone by which we try the services of those we trust."[5]

Virginia Congressman William Branch Giles praised the president's speech as "the only American language I ever heard from the Presidential chair," but like many other Republicans he expressed apprehension about its moderate tone regarding the Federalists. Telling the president that he spoke for many of his firmest supporters, he said that "a pretty general purgation of office, has been one of the benefits expected by the friends of the new order of things." What Giles wrote privately to the president, other Republicans expressed openly. "It is rational to suppose that those who removed John Adams from office . . . would naturally expect the removal of the lesser culprits in office," declared the New York *American Citizen*. "If this should not be the case, for what, in the name of God, have we been contending? Merely for the removal of John Adams, that Mr. Jefferson might occupy the place which he shamefully left?" Another Republican newspaper declared that the "unequivocal wish" of Republicans was "that *the board should be swept*" and claimed that "it was as well understood previous to the elections, that men who had advocated the baleful measures of several years past . . . were to be removed and the offices filled by men of republican principles, if they succeeded in their candidates, as if it had been reduced to a written contract."[6] These comments and similar ones that came to the president's attention during the early weeks of his administration defined the issue that would pose for the new executive one of the most burdensome problems of his presidency. It was an issue that had to be faced immediately and without the benefit of precedent, for in succeeding Washington, Adams had left all officers in place, including all members of Washington's cabinet.

Although Jefferson moved promptly to form his administration as soon as the House decided the election, it took some weeks to assemble all of his official family in Washington. There were no surprises in the key posts in his administration. As widely expected, he named Madison to be secretary of state and Gallatin, the leading fiscal expert in Republican ranks, to be secretary of the treasury. With no equally obvious candidates for other positions, Jefferson recruited two New Englanders to provide geographical representation among his advisers, choosing Henry Dearborn as secretary of war and Levi Lincoln as attorney general—moves also designed to win support in the section of the country where Republicans were weakest. By inauguration day Jefferson had received three refusals of the secretaryship of the navy. By the time he assembled the rest of his cabinet, he was masking his concern about finding a qualified Republican to fill the post by jesting that he might have to advertise the opening. It was not until July, when he offered the position to Robert Smith of Baltimore, brother of Congressman Samuel Smith, that Jefferson finally received an acceptance and completed his five-member cabinet.[7]

Four days after taking office, while still lodging at Conrad and

McMunn's, the new president held his first cabinet meeting, with Gallatin, Dearborn, and Lincoln in attendance. His notes on the meeting show that they devoted their attention entirely to matters of appointments and removals. At a second meeting of the same members the next day, the cabinet agreed to halt all prosecutions pending under the sedition law and to remit the fines of those already convicted. Jefferson moved promptly to pardon all those still suffering under the law.[8] There was a break in regular meetings of the cabinet while Madison was detained in Virginia by the death of his father and Gallatin left for Pennsylvania to move his family to Washington. Meanwhile, Jefferson made his annual spring trip to Monticello.

On May 15 Jefferson held his first full cabinet meeting, with Madison, Gallatin, Dearborn, Lincoln, and Samuel Smith (who was acting as secretary of the navy) attending. Appointments and removals were not on the agenda. The subject was the first critical question of foreign policy to face the new administration. Reports that Tripoli had sent cruisers to attack American shipping in the Mediterranean had prompted Jefferson to assemble a squadron at Norfolk prepared to sail for the Mediterranean. "But as this might lead to war, I wished to have the approbation of the new administration," the president explained as he posed the question to his advisers. "Shall the squadron now at Norfolk be ordered to cruise in the Mediterranean?" If so, "what shall be the object of the cruise?"[9] At issue was the key question of how far the president's power extended to take military action on his own authority.

All members of the cabinet agreed that the squadron should be sent to the Mediterranean to protect American commerce, but they expressed varying opinions on the extent of the president's power under such circumstances. Gallatin and Smith took the broadest view—that if the United States were attacked by another nation, the president had the authority to employ military force to defend the country. Attorney General Lincoln held the narrowest position—that "our men of war may repel an attack on individual vessels, but after the repulse, may not proceed to destroy the enemy's vessels generally." His view was rejected by a majority of the cabinet, who agreed that if war existed, naval captains should be authorized to destroy the enemy's vessels wherever they found them.[10]

This decision at the outset of Jefferson's presidency to use force against the pirates in the Mediterranean reflected the position that Jefferson had favored since his years as minister to France. Although he was prepared to proceed with the payment of tribute already authorized by Congress, he was convinced that the money paid by his predecessors had been thrown away. "There is no end to the demand of these powers, nor any security in their promises," he argued. "The real alternative before us is whether to abandon the Mediterranean or to keep up a cruise in it, perhaps in rotation with other powers." This was for Congress ultimately to decide, but Jefferson left no doubt that he favored the latter course.[11]

Throughout his presidency Jefferson continued to consult his entire cabinet on foreign affairs. He worked out many other matters with the particular department head most directly involved, but he never considered foreign policy something to be decided by the president and the secretary of state alone. Nor did he believe that the responsibility should be delegated to the secretary of state. As president, Jefferson took charge of foreign affairs and included all of his cabinet in the decision-making process.[12]

The Seventh Congress would not convene until early December, 1801, permitting Jefferson time to devote the opening months of his presidency to organizing his administration, establishing its operating procedures, and formulating the policies and proposals to be presented to the legislature when it assembled. The most pressing task was making appointments and removals. After three months in office, Jefferson confessed that "it is the business of removal and appointment which presents the serious difficulties. All others compared with these, are as nothing." He would leave the presidency still feeling that this was the most dreadful burden of that office.[13]

Responding to Republican concerns that his inaugural address implied that Federalists would be left undisturbed in office, Jefferson explained privately that he did not mean there would be no removals. He condemned Adams' "indecent conduct in crowding nominations after he knew they were not for himself, till 9 o'clock of the night, at 12 o'clock of which he was to go out of office," and said he would dismiss all such officials, serving at the president's pleasure, appointed after Adams learned the outcome of the election on December 12, 1800. Adams had filled the courts with Federalist judges—many appointed under the Judiciary Act of 1801, passed during the waning weeks of his presidency. Because judges were not removable by the president, Jefferson decided to replace all Federalist marshals and district attorneys with Republicans "as a shield to the republican part of our fellow citizens," which he considered the main body of the people. In addition, he intended to remove all officers guilty of official misconduct. But otherwise, he explained in the early weeks of his presidency, "good men, to whom there is no objection but a difference of political principle, practised on only as far as the right of a private citizen will justify, are not proper subjects of removal." New appointments, however, would go only to Republicans until something like an equilibrium in office was restored.[14]

These guidelines under which Jefferson began to make the first appointments and removals of his administration did not go far enough to satisfy many of his supporters. Despite wide approval of the idea of refraining from the political intolerance of the Federalists, Republicans tended to expect political tolerance to be applied in states other than their own. "Even if it should be judged good policy in all other States, to retain the federalists in office," a group of Connecticut Republicans wrote, "yet in this State, we could contemplate, in such policy only the certain ruin of republicanism."[15] Similar pressures came from Republicans elsewhere. In June, 1801, Representative Giles reported to the president from Virginia that "the soundest republicans in this place and throughout the country are rising considerably in the tone which they think ought to be assumed by the administration."[16]

The president reacted to these mounting pressures by issuing a new public statement on his patronage policy in July, 1801. Using the occasion of a memorial from a group of New Haven merchants protesting the removal of the Federalist collector of New Haven, one of Adams' midnight appointments, he insisted that his inaugural address had been misinterpreted and that he had never suggested that tenure of offices was to be undisturbed. Was it to be imagined that the Federalist monopoly of offices was to be continued? he asked. "Is it *political intolerance* to claim a proportionate share in the direction of the public affairs? . . . If a due participation of office is a matter of right, how are vacancies to be obtained? Those by death are few; by resignation, none. Can any other mode than that of removal be proposed? This is a painful office; but it is made my duty, and I meet it as such." Had he found a moderate participation in offices in Republican hands when he took office, he would have left it to time and accident to raise the Republicans to their just share, but their total exclusion required prompter correctives.[17]

Four months in office had brought a new tone and a different meaning to Jefferson's declarations and showed that the pressures from his own party and the fading prospects of reconciling Federalists to his administration had produced a modification of his initial position. While most Republicans applauded the president's words, Federalists called them a recantation of his inaugural speech and "an expiatory sacrifice" to his supporters who resented its tolerant tone. In concluding his new statement, Jefferson promised that as soon as the Republicans had their proportionate share of offices, he would "return with joy to that state of things, when the only questions concerning a candidate shall be, is he honest? Is he capable? Is he faithful to the Constitution?"[18] During eight years in office, Jefferson would never reach the point where these were the only questions asked. He came to define the Republican share as being between two-thirds and three-fourths, and Republicans never gained that proportion of federal offices. Still, his practices never became so sweeping as his response to the New Haven merchants suggested.

Early in his presidency Jefferson said that the difficult task was deciding where to draw the line between removing all Federalists and none and suggested that the administration might follow a policy of "balancing our measures according to the impression we perceive them to make."[19] To a large degree that described the patronage policy Jefferson followed. On numerous occasions he responded to party pressures by making removals, but he never wanted to be accused of the political intolerance with which he had charged Adams. Thus, at other times he resisted local demands for changes. A record made by Jefferson of the 316 offices subject to appointment and removal by the president showed that in 1803 Republicans held 158 offices, Federalists had 132, and 26 were in neutral hands. Closer analysis indicates that Republicans were in the most influential posts in the various states, where they could be expected to be most useful to the Republican party. Nonetheless, Jefferson's actions never became sweeping enough to satisfy many of his followers, most of whom would have supported far more removals, including the dismissal of Federalist clerks from government offices, a practice that Jefferson's department heads never employed.[20]

Jefferson began planning early for the convening of the Seventh Congress in December, 1801. From the election returns he knew that the Republican party would have majorities in both houses, and he anticipated a good working relationship with them. Seeing the outcome of the election of 1800 as a mandate for changing the nation's course, he sought to put the ship of state on a more republican tack. Despite the fears of executive power that Republicans had often expressed, Jefferson believed that the president should provide leadership not only for the executive branch but also for the legislature. He respected the principle of separation of powers, but he did not think that it should prevent the cooperation of the president and the Congress.

Nearly a month before Congress was to assemble, Jefferson began circulating a draft of his annual message among members of his cabinet. Having already collected information from them about the affairs of their departments, he now sought their advice about the proposed text. The president urged them to be candid in their criticisms and suggestions, and most of them were. Secretary of the Treasury Gallatin sent him nine pages of detailed notes; Navy Secretary Robert Smith supplied six pages. After all cabinet officers had a chance to review the document, Jefferson revised his draft, making the final decisions as to which suggestions to accept or reject.[21]

Perhaps his most significant alteration was to strike out a passage in which he had invoked presidential authority to declare the sedition law unconstitutional. Claiming an executive right to exercise his free and independent judgment in interpreting the Constitution, he was prepared to announce: "I took that act into consideration, compared it with the constitution, viewed it under every aspect of which I thought it susceptible, and gave it all the attention which the magnitude of the case demanded. On mature deliberation, in the presence of the nation, and under the tie of the solemn oath which binds me to them and to my duty, I do declare that I hold that act to be in palpable and unqualified contradiction to the constitution." Both Gallatin and Smith questioned the propriety of this extraordinary declaration, and Smith said that the prevailing opinion among constitutional lawyers would be opposed to the principles advanced. Predicting that the declaration would divide Republicans, Smith warned that the claim to such an executive prerogative would not be easily assented to.[22] In accepting his advisers' recommendations, Jefferson never agreed to their constitutional arguments, but he deleted the offensive paragraph in order to avoid furnishing an issue to the opposition.[23]

The procedure of circulating the draft of his annual message among the members of his cabinet and revising it in light of their suggestions would be employed by Jefferson in every year of his presidency. Recognizing the message as a major tool of presidential leadership, Jefferson used it to report the state of the Union, to direct Congress' attention to specific issues, and to offer recommendations for legislation. He also knew it would have a wide audience, and he gave careful attention to its content and tone.

At the outset of his administration Jefferson decided to let the words of his annual message speak for themselves, and instead of appearing before Congress to deliver his address as Washington and Adams had done, he sent a written message. Some thought he made the change because he had a poor speaking voice. The president himself said he did it for the convenience of Congress. But the basic reason was more fundamental and sprang from Republican fears that the president's address and the formal reply from Congress resembled too closely the ceremonies of British monarchy. It was a concern shared by many Republicans, among them Nathaniel Macon of North Carolina, who was elected Speaker of the House of Representatives the day before Jefferson sent his first message to Congress. Months earlier, just after Jefferson took office, Macon had written to the new president offering a list of changes that he said "the people expect." High among them was that "the communication to the next Congress will be by letter not a speech." Republican expectations rather than Jefferson's public speaking ability best explain his departure from the tradition of his predecessors. One Republican congressman applauded Jefferson for dispensing with "all the pomp and pageantry, which once dishonored our republican institutions," and rejoiced that the public was to be spared a president "drawn to the Capitol by six horses, and followed by the creatures of his nostrils, and gaped at by a wondering multitude."[24] In sending his private secretary to carry his message to the Capitol, Jefferson established a new tradition that would not be challenged until President Woodrow Wilson appeared before Congress in December, 1913.

When members of Congress in December, 1801, turned their attention from the form of Jefferson's message to its content, they found an agenda for legislative action. The president recommended the repeal of all internal taxes and reductions in the army, the navy, and the civil establishment. He also suggested that Congress reexamine the judiciary act passed by the preceding Congress and urged a revision of the naturalization law. In the course of the session Congress followed the president's recommendation on all of these matters, repealing all internal taxes dating back to Hamilton's excise on whiskey, abolishing the internal revenue service employed to collect them, cutting military appropriations, and reducing the residence requirement for naturalization back to five years, from the fourteen-year requirement imposed by the Federalists. The elimination of the internal revenue service cut five hundred employees from the Treasury Department, reducing its work force outside Washington by 40 percent. Congress also enacted the plan prepared by Treasury Secretary Gallatin to pay off the entire national debt within sixteen years by annual appropriations of $7,300,000.[25]

The most controversial issue that Congress confronted during the five-month session that adjourned on May 3, 1802, was the proposal to repeal the Judiciary Act of February, 1801, passed during the final weeks of Adams' presidency. That act reduced the number of Supreme Court justices from six to five and relieved them of their circuit-court duties, while adding sixteen new circuit judges and additional marshals, district attorneys, and clerks. Many persons had recognized the need for some judicial reform, but the haste of President Adams in filling the new judgeships with Federalists gave the measure a partisan character never forgotten nor forgiven by Republicans. Some Republicans wanted to go further than simply repealing the Federalist measure and favored constitutional changes to make the judiciary more subject to popular will. Jefferson gave no encouragement to such moves and in his annual message suggested only that Congress reconsider the measure. In supplying information on the workload of the federal courts, showing that the expanded court system was unnecessary, he provided the most effective argument used to justify repeal of the measure, though the data were hastily prepared and inaccurate. The Federalist claim that the move was an attack on the independence of the judiciary concerned many Republicans, who, while resenting the blatant partisanship of the Federalists in implementing the act, questioned the efficacy of its repeal. After spending more time debating the repeal of the act than any other subject before it, Congress decided the issue less on its merits than by a party vote. A few Republicans did not go along with their party, but the repeal passed the Senate, 16 to 15, and the House, 59 to 32.[26]

The pending case of *Marbury* v. *Madison*, a by-product of the Judiciary Act of 1801, increased the partisan conflict in Congress over the judiciary. William Marbury, appointed a justice of the peace in the District of Columbia under the provisions of that act, did not receive his commission, which President Adams had signed in the waning hours of his presidency. In accordance with Jefferson's decision to nullify those of Adams' last-minute appointments that he could legally undo, the administration halted the delivery of undelivered commissions. Marbury and three other justices of the

peace whose commissions had been withheld petitioned the Supreme Court for writs of mandamus requiring Secretary of State
Madison to deliver their commissions. Their motion was presented
to the court on December 17, 1801, only nine days after the opening of the Seventh Congress. When Chief Justice Marshall agreed
to hear arguments in the case at its next term, Jefferson protested
that the Federalists "have retired into the judiciary as a stronghold
. . . and from that battery all the works of republicanism are to be
beaten down and erased." Many Republicans in Congress shared
these fears, and they played an important role in uniting the party
behind the repeal of the Judiciary Act of 1801.[27]

When the Supreme Court handed down its decision in February,
1803, Marshall lectured the administration for not delivering the
commissions, but he said that it was not within the court's jurisdiction to issue a writ of mandamus, because the law giving it that authority was unconstitutional. While resenting Marshall's criticism of
the president, Republicans were relieved that the court had not assumed the requested prerogative, and there was little criticism that
in deciding the case the court had held an act of Congress unconstitutional. Neither Jefferson nor most Republicans were prepared
to deny the right of the Supreme Court to review for itself an act of
Congress, but they claimed an equal and independent right in the
other two branches of the government. In the mind of Jefferson
and most of his contemporaries, Marshall's decision in *Marbury* v.
Madison did not establish the exclusive and superior power of judicial review, and, in fact, Marshall did not assert that claim.[28] Jefferson's hostility toward the court would become more manifest as
time passed. At this time his opposition to Marshall was more on
political than constitutional grounds.

Most Federalists thought that Jefferson's influence had determined not only the agenda but also the outcome of the first legislative session of his presidency. Connecticut's Senator James Hillhouse insisted that "never were a set of men more blindly devoted
to the will of a *prime Mover* or *Minister* than the Majority of both
houses to the will and wishes of the Chief Magistrate." Similar complaints would be voiced throughout Jefferson's presidency. At the
next session, North Carolina Federalist Archibald Henderson, a
member of the House, declared: "The President has only to act and
the Majority will approve. I do not believe that in any Country
there ever was more implicit obedience paid to an administration
than in this. I do not mean to say that Mr. Jefferson has this uncon-
trolled authority, but that when the Cabinet determines on mea-

sures they will be passed." In 1806 Senator Timothy Pickering, a bitter Massachusetts Federalist, went even further and proclaimed that Jefferson "*behind the curtain*, directs the measures he wishes to have adopted; while in each house a majority of puppets move as he touches the wires." Even John Quincy Adams, a moderate Federalist, recorded in his diary that the president's "whole system of administration seems founded upon this principle of carrying through the legislature measures by his personal or official influence" and noted that some members of both houses had no other question than what was the president's wish.[29]

How are we to evaluate these contemporary charges? The record indicates that the Federalists exaggerated the degree of Jefferson's influence over Congress, but it also shows that there was a basis for the Federalists' accusations. Jefferson did seek to lead Congress, to get the measures that he proposed enacted, and to work with his party in Congress to implement Republican promises to the voters. From the outset of his presidency Jefferson tried with varying degrees of success to maintain a congressional spokesman with whom he could share his views and confidential information. Explaining what he expected of such an administration leader in trying to recruit Barnabas Bidwell, a Massachusetts representative, he said: "I do not mean that any gentleman relinquishing his own judgment, should implicitly support all the measures of the administration, but that, where he does not disapprove of them he should not suffer them to go off in sleep, but bring them to the attention of the house and give them a fair chance." Jefferson tried to develop such a relationship with John Randolph after Speaker Macon named the Virginia congressman as chairman of the Ways and Means Committee, but the independent Randolph was uncomfortable in such a role and ultimately broke with the president. On the floor of the House in 1806, Randolph denounced the "back-stairs influence—of men who bring messages to this House, which, although they do not appear on the Journals, govern its decisions." An offended president mused that "we never heard this while the declaimer was himself a backstairs man as he called it, but in the confidence and views of the administration as may more properly and respectfully be said." He insisted that if the members of Congress were "to know nothing but what is important enough to be put into a public message, and indifferent enough to be made known to all the world, if the Executive is to keep all other information to himself, and the house to plunge on in the dark, it becomes a government of chance and not of design."[30]

Although Jefferson was never successful in establishing a continuing working relationship with one chief congressional leader, he did have close contacts with a number of Republican members in both houses and supplied them with information and legislative proposals. Indeed, in an era when presidents were not expected to draft legislation, Jefferson personally prepared a number of bills and sent them to friendly members to introduce. He often requested the return of his original draft because, as he told Senator John Breckinridge, "you know with what bloody teeth and fangs the federalists will attack any sentiment or principle known to come from me."[31] In sending his proposals to members, Jefferson was also careful to point out that his drafts were only suggestions for Congress to consider and that he was not attempting to interfere in legislative business. But as a president whose wide popular support gave him immense power, his proposals obviously carried great weight.[32]

Members of Jefferson's cabinet also drafted bills for Congress, supplied congressional committees with all matter of information, testified before committees, and informally influenced the legislative process. Indeed, the structure of the government was such that the executive branch inevitably exerted considerable influence on legislation. Aside from the clerk's office, Congress had no staff. Neither did members, who did not even have offices—only a desk on the floor of their legislative chamber. Thus, all gathering of information and other staff work had to be done by department offices. When congressional committees called on department heads for information, they commonly also asked for recommendations. The legislators did not always follow the advice of the executive officers, but the administration was in a position to wield considerable influence and, under Jefferson, did so. Congressmen felt other pressures besides those coming from the administration, and few fitted the Federalist picture of men bending to the president's every wish, but Jefferson exerted strong presidential leadership through most of his presidency, faltering only as he approached the end of his second term.[33]

Jefferson was a working administrator as well as a political leader. Throughout his presidency he spent long hours at his desk and kept a close watch on the operation of the executive branch. Describing his administrative routine as "a steady and uniform course," he said, "It keeps me from 10 to 12 and 13 hours a day at my writing table, giving me an interval of 4 hours for riding, dining and a little unbending."[34] It also kept him in Washington except for a visit to Monticello for two or three weeks in the spring after Congress adjourned and a regular summer recess, when he moved the presidential office to Monticello during August and September of each year.

Convinced that the coastal lowlands in late summer were a threat to health, he encouraged his officers also to take those months for their own affairs. When important matters were pending, at least one cabinet official remained in the capital, but the administration of department offices was left largely in the hands of the chief clerks. The postmaster general arranged a special mail service by which the president could get information from Washington in two days and have an answer back within a week, and Jefferson carried on correspondence with his department heads wherever they might be. With Madison thirty miles away at Montpelier, he had his closest adviser nearby. When Federalists criticized the absence of so many members of the administration from the capital during his first summer recess, Jefferson reacted indignantly. "I consider it as a trying experiment for a person from the mountains to pass the two bilious months on the tide-water," he declared. "I have not done it these forty years, and nothing should induce me to do it. As it is not possible but that the Administration must take some portion of time for their own affairs, I think it best they should select that season for absence. General Washington set the example of those two months; Mr. Adams extended them to eight months. I should not suppose our bringing it back to two months a ground for grumbling, but, grumble who will, I will never pass those months on tide-water."[35] Throughout eight years in office, Jefferson never wavered from this resolve.

As president, Jefferson made it clear that he intended to be in charge of his administration and to take the responsibility for its actions. To do so he stayed remarkably well informed about departmental business and was able to respond knowledgeably to department heads when they brought matters to him. The notion that Jefferson was a philosopher who had no interest in the mundane tasks of administering the government derives from images created by his partisan opponents, not from the historical record. Early in his presidency in a memorandum to all department heads Jefferson asked them to send him a daily packet of letters received, together with drafts of their answers. This did not apply to routine matters, but to all subjects requiring a judgmental response. He said that he expected to be "always in accurate possession of all facts and proceedings in every part of the Union, and to whatsoever department they related."[36] Such procedures required steady application and considerable presidential paperwork.

Part of Jefferson's time-consuming labor resulted from his practice of writing all his own letters and drafting his own state papers, while employing his private secretary more as an aide than as a scribe. In appointing young army lieutenant Meriwether Lewis as his first private secretary, Jefferson told him that he would be "one of my family." Lewis and the secretaries who succeeded him were primarily employed in greeting visitors to the President's House, carrying messages to Congress, communicating occasional confidential communications to members, reporting on congressional proceedings, and in other ways serving as an aide-de-camp. Jefferson's secretary did transcribe his annual messages to Congress from his revised drafts and sometimes copied other papers, but Jefferson did the bulk of his own writing and made copies of his letters and other papers in a letterpress. After the invention of the polygraph, he enthusiastically adopted that device, leaving for historians a record fuller than that of any other early president.[37]

Jefferson employed no speech writers. He systematically circulated the draft of his annual messages to Congress to all members of his cabinet for their suggestions for revisions, but he never asked an adviser to prepare the first draft. Although President Washington had on occasion sent a bundle of papers to Hamilton asking him to draft a message to Congress and called on both Madison and Hamilton in drafting the farewell address, Jefferson did nothing similar while president.

Jefferson made the cabinet the principal policy-making mechanism of his presidency. "The ordinary business of every day is done by consultation between the President and the Head of the department alone to which it belongs," he explained in describing his administrative system. "For measures of importance or difficulty, a consultation is held with the Heads of departments, either assembled, or by taking their opinions separately in conversation or in writing." The practice that Jefferson most commonly followed was to assemble his advisers in a cabinet meeting—not on a regularly scheduled basis but whenever needed. The government was small; departmental offices were all located close to the President's House, and the president could quickly assemble his cabinet. He resorted to separate consultations primarily when he anticipated "disagreeable collisions."[38]

There were, in fact, few frictions within Jefferson's cabinet; he looked back at his administration as "an example of harmony in a cabinet of six persons, to which perhaps history has furnished no parallel." This may put too heavy a gloss over the clashes between Treasury Secretary Gallatin and Navy Secretary Smith, but Jefferson kept their differences under control. Jefferson's system aimed at developing a consensus within his cabinet. "We sometimes met under differences of opinion," he said, "but scarcely ever failed, by conversing and reasoning, so to modify each other's ideas, as to produce an unanimous result."[39] This was not always the case, for Jefferson recorded some divided votes in his notes on cabinet meetings. But in contrast to the cabinets of his predecessors, it was a harmonious group that shared the same political outlook. As a former member of the first president's cabinet, Jefferson was well aware how deep the divisions had been in Washington's administration, and as vice-president he had watched his predecessor face a cabinet more loyal to Hamilton than to the president. Thus, he had reason to remark on the unity of his own administration. Jefferson never had to worry about loyalty and rarely about turnover in his cabinet. His four principal department heads stayed with him throughout his eight years in office; the only changes were in the office of attorney general.

Jefferson's strong popular support was an important factor in making the cabinet system work, as was his own clear sense of being in command in his administration. While he spoke of his vote counting as one in the cabinet, he knew that was only technically true and doubted that the unanimity in the cabinet would have been the same had each member possessed equal and independent powers. He admitted that "the power of decision in the President left no object for internal dissension."[40] Yet his style of leadership was one of persuasion rather than dictation, and there is ample evidence to show that his advisers felt free to speak their own minds without fear of retribution. They also knew that the president relied on their advice and had no advisers outside the cabinet whom he regularly consulted.

Attention to administrative demands led Jefferson to organize his time carefully. He rose regularly at five in the morning and worked on his paperwork until nine, when he began receiving cabinet officers or others who had business to discuss with the president. Members of Congress were free to drop in without appointments. He commonly scheduled cabinet meetings for noon. At one in the afternoon, Jefferson normally went for a ride on horseback—his principal form of exercise. At three-thirty he had dinner, and sometimes invited a guest to arrive a half hour earlier for a private consultation before dinner.[41]

President Jefferson used the dinner hour as his main social activity and as an important tool of governing. While Congress was in session he held dinner parties three times a week, inviting members in small groups (generally about twelve), seating them around an oval table with no place of command or honor, offering them good cuisine and fine wines, and engaging them in conversation. When one member implied this was improper executive influence, Jefferson responded, "I cultivate personal intercourse with the members of the legislature that we may know one another and have opportunities of little explanations of circumstances, which, not understood might produce jealousies and suspicions injurious to the public interest." He also said that he depended heavily on members of Congress to provide him with information from throughout the country and help him to sense public opinion. Early in his administration when he still had hopes of reconciling parties, he did not consider party affiliation in issuing invitations. But as time passed, he tended to invite Federalists and Republicans on different days. A number of guest lists for these dinners survive among the meticulous records that Jefferson maintained, and they show that he invited Republican congressional leaders more frequently than others, but most members received at least one invitation during a session. In keeping with his republican informality, Jefferson used for his invitations a printed form that contained no emblems of the presidential office and began "Th: Jefferson requests" rather than "The President requests."[42]

New York Congressman Samuel L. Mitchill, describing a dinner party in 1802 as "easy and sociable," commented that no toasts were drunk and thought the president's French cook "understands the art of preparing and serving up food, to a nicety." Mitchill was particularly impressed by ice-cream balls enclosed in warm pastry. As a scientist, he also enjoyed the after-dinner conversation, in the course of which Jefferson showed his guests a piece of homemade silk cloth from silk produced in Virginia. Talking about a process of waterproofing cloth developed in Europe, the president brought out a treated coat made in England, gathered a pocket of cloth, and poured water into it to prove that no water seeped through. In late 1804 both Mitchill and Senator William Plumer, dining with the president on different evenings, reported that their host treated his guests to water from the Mississippi River and the famous "mammoth cheese." That giant round of cheese, weighing 1,200 pounds, had been presented to him as a gift from a Baptist congregation in Cheshire, Massachusetts, on his first New Year's Day as president in 1802. In accordance with his rule of accepting no gifts, he paid two hundred dollars for it and was still trying to give it away more than two years later. Plumer judged it "very far from being good."[43]

The hospitable president kept careful records of the cost of his entertaining, all of which he paid out of his salary of $25,000. During his first year in office, his wine bill alone was nearly $2,800, and all of his household and office expenses totaled over $16,000. When the year was over, he had to borrow $4,000 to balance his personal budget.[44] These expenditures did not cause him to curtail his entertaining, however, because he regarded it as essential to the governmental process.

After dining, guests were free to linger for awhile, and sometimes other members of Congress dropped by to join in the hospitality. But the president expected everyone to be gone by six o'clock, when he then returned to his writing desk. He usually stayed busy with his paperwork until ten, and let it be known that he would accept no evening social invitations.[45]

It was during such after-dinner work sessions that Jefferson, toward the end of his first term, spent several evenings clipping passages from the Gospels of Matthew, Mark, Luke, and John and pasting them onto blank pages to produce, for his own use, "The Philosophy of Jesus." "It was the work of 2 or 3 nights only at Washington, after getting thro' the evening task of reading the letters and papers of the day," he later recalled, though he surely must have spent hours previously deciding what passages to select.[46] It was, in fact, a subject of great interest to him and one to which he would later return to compile a similar but more extensive work entitled "The Life and Morals of Jesus."[47] Though the actual preparation of "The Philosophy of Jesus" was completed in a remarkably short time in February or early March, 1804, Jefferson's thoughts had repeatedly turned to religion since the attacks made upon him in the election of 1800. These attacks continued in Federalist publications after he became president.[48] The charges that he was an irreligious enemy of Christianity concerned him, and in 1803, after reading Joseph Priestley's *Socrates and Jesus Compared*, he composed a brief, two-page summary of his religious faith that he titled "Syllabus of an Estimate of the merit of the doctrines of Jesus, compared with those of others." He sent copies to Benjamin Rush, to his two daughters, and to at least two members of his cabinet. Influenced by Joseph Priestley's *An History of the Corruptions of Christianity*, he continued his quest to define his religious beliefs and became convinced that the early Christians held a Unitarian concept of God that was compatible with his own views. He thus sought to identify

the authentic teachings of Jesus, the result of which was his compilation of "The Philosophy of Jesus." [49] Excising from the Gospels
the supernaturalism that he was convinced was added by later cor-
ruptors of the simple moral teachings of Jesus, he left what he regarded as Jesus' authentic words. "There will be found remaining,"
he told John Adams, "the most sublime and benevolent code of
morals which has ever been offered to man. I have performed this
operation for my own use, by cutting verse by verse out of the
printed book, and arranging the matter which is evidently his, and
which is as easily distinguishable as diamonds in a dunghill. The
result is an 8vo. of 46 pages of pure and unsophisticated doctrines,
such as professed and acted on by the *unlettered* apostles, the Apos-
tolic fathers, and the Christians of the lst century." [50]

Most of President Jefferson's evenings were devoted to less philosophical enterprises. Though this project had been forming in his
mind since the issue of his religion was raised in the campaign of
1800, it had to wait until 1804, while he spent long evenings poring
over letters of recommendation for office, drafts of congressional
bills, foreign dispatches, and all matter of problems brought to him
by his department heads. Yet, even during such busy times of his
presidency, Jefferson continued a wide correspondence that kept
alive his many intellectual interests and allowed him momentary es-
capes from the pressures of political life. The duties of the presidency, however, always commanded his prime attention, and there
were few lulls during his eight years in office.

Jefferson brought to the presidency an informality that reduced
the ceremonial role of the presidency initiated by Washington and
continued by Adams. He ended the levees—formal receptions—
that Washington and Adams had presided over, and much to the
discomfort of foreign diplomats, he abandoned the formal rules of
diplomatic etiquette. "When brought together in society, all are
perfectly equal, whether foreign or domestic, titled or untitled, in
or out of office," he wrote in a memorandum for the members of
his administration. [51] Some foreign diplomats were dismayed at the
president's style. When Anthony Merry arrived at the executive
mansion in full diplomatic uniform to present his credentials as
British minister to the United States, he considered himself in-
sulted when Jefferson received him in casual dress, wearing slippers without heels. When invited to dine with the president, Merry
was offended when Jefferson offered his arm to Mrs. Madison instead of Mrs. Merry to escort to the dinner table and followed his
usual practice of allowing his guests to find seats at the table pell-

mell—a practice that Jefferson also recommended to the member of his cabinet.[52] Merry nearly made an international incident out of what he saw as an affront to his nation, but more perceptive diplomats would find that the republican president was very accessible to foreign ministers, who could call informally at his residence and converse directly with the head of state.

Foreign diplomats were not the only persons shocked at the dress of the president. Senator Plumer, on his first call upon the president, was surprised to find that "he was drest, or rather *undrest* with an old brown coat, red waistcoat, old corduroy small clothes much soiled—woolen hose—and slippers without heels." But when Plumer was invited to dinner, he found the president "well dressed— A new suit of black—silk hose—shoes—clean linnen, and his hair highly powdered." Plumer judged the dinner elegant, the eight kinds of wine very good, and the president, though in low spirit that day, "naturally very social and communicative."[53] From all reports Jefferson dressed for comfort while working in the large, drafty, and still-unfinished President's House, and he considered his personal appearance of less importance than the affairs of state or his hospitality to his guests. Many Federalists thought he was playing a role in trying to appear a man of the people, but his republicanism was far deeper than the manner of his dress.

XVIII
Presidential Zenith

The most serious problem and the major triumph of Jefferson's first term as president resulted from the crisis over Louisiana. In his first message to Congress in December, 1801, Jefferson hardly referred to foreign affairs except to report the naval actions against the Tripolitan cruisers. By that time, however, the president had received reliable, though still unconfirmed, reports of the secret treaty between Spain and France for the retrocession of Louisiana to France. After learning of the rumored agreement from Rufus King in London in May, 1801, the president and the secretary of state had promptly launched a diplomatic campaign against the retrocession.[1] Madison told Charles Pinckney in Madrid to stress America's preference for Spain over France in Louisiana and instructed Robert R. Livingston in Paris to determine what agreement had actually been made and to try to dissuade the French from carrying it through if they had not already done so. Livingston was to impress upon them how drastically such a transfer would imperil relations between the two countries. If the cession had irrevocably taken place, he was to inquire into the possibility of their ceding the Floridas, especially West Florida, to the United States, provided those areas had been included in the transfer.[2] None of these diplomatic efforts, of course, could be publicly reported to Congress.

By the spring of 1802 the administration was convinced that, despite French denials, the transfer of Louisiana was to take place, and it stepped up its diplomatic campaign. In a private letter to Livingston, the president reviewed the past friendship between France and the United States, which he now saw threatened. "There is on the globe one single spot, the possessor of which is our natural and habitual enemy," he wrote. "It is New Orleans. . . . France placing herself in that door assumes to us the attitude of defiance." While a feeble Spain might have retained New Orleans quietly for years, it was "impossible that France and the U.S. can continue long friends when they meet in so irritable a position." The day that France took possession of New Orleans would seal the union between the United States and Great Britain. "From that moment we must marry ourselves to the British fleet and nation. We must turn all our attentions to a maritime force." Lest this tactic of diplomacy be confused with a statement of policy, it should be noted that Jefferson sent this letter to France by du Pont de Nemours and left it open for him to read, telling him, "I wish you to be possessed of the subject, because you may be able to impress on the government of France the inevitable consequences of their taking possession of Louisiana."[3]

Before the United States was able to determine France's intentions in regard to Louisiana, a startling event turned the slowly developing issue into a crisis of unpredictable dimensions. In April, 1802, Jefferson may have been guilty of hyperbole when he wrote: "Every eye in the U.S. is now fixed on this affair of Louisiana. Perhaps nothing since the revolutionary war has produced more uneasy sensations through the body of the nation." But by November all eyes did focus on New Orleans, not because of French actions, but because of an unexpected move by the city's Spanish intendant. On October 18, 1802, in violation of the treaty of 1795 with the United States, the Spanish official suspended the right of deposit at New Orleans without providing, as the treaty required, an alternate place for American goods coming down the Mississippi River to be deposited while awaiting ocean transport. Jefferson learned of this in late November and was led to believe by the Spanish minister in Washington and statements from the governor of Louisiana that the intendant at New Orleans had acted without authority, though it is known today that orders had come from Madrid. Secretary of State Madison promptly dispatched instructions to Pinckney in Madrid to inform the Spanish government that "from whatever source the measure may have proceeded the President expects that the Spanish Government will neither lose a moment in countermanding it, nor hesitate to repair every damage which may result from it." Madison went on to indicate his conviction that the alarm of westerners was justified. "The Mississippi is to them everything. It is the Hudson, the Delaware, the Potomac and all the navigable rivers of the Atlantic States formed into one stream." A few weeks later Madison sounded even more belligerent when he wrote to Livingston in Paris, where he expected the real decisions to be made, that there were, or soon would be, "200,000 militia on the waters of the Mississippi, every man of whom would march at a moment's warning to remove obstructions from that outlet to the sea, every man of whom regards the free use of that river as a natural and indefeasible right and is conscious of the physical force that can at any time give effect to it."[4]

Jefferson reported none of these diplomatic moves in his second annual message to Congress in December, 1802, a message in which he proposed among other things to reduce naval expenses by building a dry dock at the Washington naval yard. His novel plan to preserve the life of naval vessels when not in use by getting them out of the water and protected from the weather met more derision than careful study, and he did not push it, though he saw it as a means of maintaining a naval force for emergencies without the burden of sustaining an active fleet. Federalists had a field day with the "visionary scheme." "What a glorious thing to have for president a visionary Philosopher, whose projects not even democratic sycophants dare approve," chortled one Federalist member when the House declined to pursue the proposal.[5]

Members were waiting to hear not about plans for dry docks but what the president planned to do about New Orleans. In regard to the expected cession of Louisiana to France, Jefferson said only that the event would produce "a change in the aspect of our foreign relations," and he did not even mention the crisis over the withdrawal of deposit at New Orleans. Disappointed members would probably have agreed with Hamilton's description of the message as a "lullaby." The House promptly passed a resolution calling upon the president for documents relating to the closing of New Orleans.[6]

While the Republican majority was inclined to follow the administration's cautious approach, the Federalists were voicing demands for action, many seeing military measures against New Orleans as the appropriate response. Jefferson opposed taking military action before attempting negotiation. Aware that a renewal of the war in Europe between France and England seemed likely and that Napoleon's effort to regain control over the island of Santo Domingo was faltering, he saw nothing to be gained by a precipitant military response. At the same time, his administration had quietly begun military preparations. Secretary of War Dearborn strengthened troops on the frontier, concentrating four infantry and three artillery companies at Fort Adams on the Mississippi just north of the Spanish border. The governor of the Mississippi Territory, William C. C. Claiborne, reported that two thousand "pretty well organized" militia were in readiness at Natchez and said that six hundred of them could take New Orleans so long as it was defended only by Spanish troops.[7] Jefferson, however, was unwilling to let the Federalists push him into war.

Compounding the closure of New Orleans with the expected cession to France—issues that the administration was endeavoring to keep separate—Federalist Roger Griswold, a representative from Connecticut, on January 4, 1803, introduced a resolution calling on the president for documents relating to the cession of Louisiana to France and for a report "explaining the stipulations, circumstances, and conditions under which that province is to be delivered up." The Republicans rallied to defeat this motion and also a series of resolutions moved by Griswold vigorously affirming the right of free navigation of the Mississippi and the necessity of maintaining that right. After a closed-door debate, the House adopted a resolution supportive of the president's policy in regard to the suspension of deposit at New Orleans. The resolution followed the president in conceding the benefit of the doubt to Spain that the closing of New Orleans was an unauthorized act of the intendant and not the breach of the treaty by the Spanish monarch. Giving the president a vote of confidence, the House promised to await the issue of presidential measures and at the same time reaffirmed its strong commitment to the rights of navigation and commerce through the Mississippi River.[8]

A few days later, on January 11, 1803, Jefferson answered his Federalist critics and calmed his Republican supporters by sending to the Senate the nomination of James Monroe as a special emissary to France and Spain to negotiate on the explosive issues. Jefferson was concerned about the way the Federalists were using the Louisiana crisis. "The fever into which the western mind is thrown by the affair at New Orleans stimulated by the mercantile, and generally the federal interest threatens to overbear our peace," he wrote to Monroe in telling him it was impossible to decline the mission for which he had nominated him without prior consultation. After the Senate speedily confirmed Monroe's nomination over Federalist opposition by a party vote of 15 to 12, Jefferson wrote to him again that the Federalists' object was "to force us into war if possible, in order to derange our finances, or if this cannot be done, to attach the western country to them, as their best friends, and thus get again into power." In the president's view some effort more visible than normal diplomacy was necessary to satisfy public concern, and Monroe, admired in the West and sharing the confidence of Republicans everywhere, was the man for the task.[9] Jefferson left his friend no avenue to decline the mission, and Monroe made immediate preparations to depart for Paris.

Although Jefferson told Monroe that his nomination had silenced the Federalists in Congress, they did not vote for his confirmation, and nowhere did Federalists remain quiet for long. Writing as "Pericles" in the New York *Evening Post*, Hamilton argued that the United States should immediately seize the Floridas and New Orleans and then negotiate. There was ample justification for hostilities, he insisted, and "not the most remote probability" that Napoleon would sell the land. Now was the time, before Monroe left for France, for the United States to occupy the territories and expand its army to hold them. "Such measures would astonish and disconcert Bonaparte himself; our envoy would be enabled to speak and treat with effect; and all Europe would be taught to respect us. . . . If the President would adopt this course," he concluded, "he might yet retrieve his character; induce the best part of the community to look favorably on his political career, exalt himself in the eyes of Europe, save the country, and secure a permanent fame. But for this, alas! Jefferson is not destined!" [10]

Jefferson indeed was not destined to achieve fame by making war on France and Spain, but the course that he was pursuing would bring a fame that Hamilton could not have imagined. What Hamilton did not know was that Jefferson had already received indications that France was willing to negotiate. Du Pont, who had carried Jefferson's strident letter of April 18, 1802, to Livingston, had replied immediately to its threatening tone by suggesting that the United States should attempt to buy New Orleans and West Florida by offering Napoleon enough money to tempt him before he took possession of Louisiana. Du Pont also recommended that the United States renounce any desire for territory west of the Mississippi. Jefferson and Madison, of course, had already thought of attempting to buy West Florida and had instructed Livingston to explore the matter, though not by offering to renounce all land west of the river. After six months in France, du Pont repeated his proposal and suggested a specific figure of six million dollars as the possible selling price for New Orleans and all the other territory east of the Mississippi. Du Pont, like others, was incorrectly assuming that the Floridas were to be included in the transfer, but his specificity suggested that he may have had some contact with high French officials. Du Pont even enclosed a brief draft of a proposed treaty. [11]

Jefferson received du Pont's letter on December 31, 1802, just ten days before he decided to send Monroe to France; in the legislation

accompanying the approval of Monroe's mission, Congress appropriated two million dollars "to defray any expenses which may be
incurred in relation to the intercourse between the United States
and foreign nations."[12] That the purpose of this appropriation was
to begin negotiations to purchase New Orleans and the Floridas
was revealed only in secret session. When Monroe departed from
New York on March 8, he carried instructions authorizing the payment of up to fifty million livres—a little over nine million dollars—for New Orleans and the Floridas.[13] Meanwhile in Paris,
Livingston had been trying without success to open negotiations
for the purchase of both territories. In one proposal he went further and suggested that France might also sell to the United States
the area of Louisiana north of the Arkansas River, arguing that this
would place an American buffer between the French in Louisiana
and the English in Canada.[14]

Before learning the outcome of Monroe's mission, Jefferson
would receive word that the Spanish government had restored deposit at New Orleans and affirmed that the right was preserved in
the treaty of cession to France. At this time Jefferson was not counting on being able to buy New Orleans from France, but he was confident that his policy of not seizing New Orleans "as our federal ma-
niacs wished" had been wise. "We have obtained by a peaceful
appeal to justice, in four months, what we should not have obtained
under seven years of war," he said. Time was on the side of the
United States, whose advantage it was to delay confrontation "till
we have planted a population on the Mississippi itself sufficient to
do its own work without marching men fifteen hundred miles from
the Atlantic shores."[15]

When Monroe arrived in Paris on April 12, events in France were
moving more rapidly than the State Department had ever imagined possible. After suffering rebuff after rebuff in his efforts,
Livingston seemed suddenly on the verge of accomplishing the
purposes of his mission. On April 11, while Monroe was en route
from Le Havre to Paris, Livingston was summoned to Talleyrand's
office, where the foreign minister startled the hard-of-hearing
American by asking if the United States was interested in purchasing the whole of Louisiana. Earlier that morning Napoleon had
summoned his finance minister, Barbé-Marbois, and told him that
he had decided to sell all of Louisiana to the United States. Having
abandoned the idea of a new French empire in America after failing to reclaim Santo Domingo, and expecting shortly to be at war
again with Great Britain, Napoleon regarded Louisiana as vulner-

able to conquest. Besides, his treasury was depleted.[16] Although Livingston resented the arrival of Monroe just when there was movement in the negotiations, the two men successfully concluded the negotiations that produced the treaty for the purchase of Louisiana. On April 30 they initialed the agreement ceding Louisiana to the United States in return for sixty million francs and the assumption by the United States of twenty million francs in claims of Americans against France—a total price of fifteen million dollars. The treaty was signed on May 2.[17] The territory was to be transferred to the United States with the boundaries that it had when conveyed from Spain to France. The Floridas were not included, but otherwise the limits were left so vague by the new treaty that there was reason to suspect that Napoleon hoped to promote a clash between the United States and Spain.

Whatever the boundaries, President Jefferson could not but be elated over a territory so vast as to more than double the size of the United States and bring the entire Missouri and Mississippi rivers within its borders. By a coincidence that again tied Jefferson to the Fourth of July, the news of the signing of the treaty reached Washington on July 3, 1803, enabling the *National Intelligencer* to announce the feat the next day and later report that the Fourth of July was "a proud day for the President," the recipient of "the widespread joy of millions at an event which history will record among the most splendid in our annals." Despite the wide popular acclaim, the president resented that the Federalists were reluctant to give him or any Republican credit for the accomplishment. They denied credit to Monroe and to Livingston, and "these grumblers too are very uneasy least the administration should share some little credit for the acquisition, the whole of which they ascribe to the accident of war," he complained. "They would be cruelly mortified could they see our files. . . . They would see that tho' we could not say when war would arise, yet we said with energy what would take place when it should arise. We did not, by our intrigues, produce the war: but we availed ourselves of it when it happened." He could not resist noting that there was a war in Europe while the Federalists were in power and asked what the Federalists had got out of it for their country.[18]

Such frustrations were expressed only in private letters. Jefferson devoted his main energies to getting the Louisiana treaty ratified and implemented. As he saw it, there was one major obstacle to Senate ratification: "The general government has no powers but such as the constitution has given it; and it has not given it a power of holding foreign territory, and still less of incorporating it into the Union." True to his convictions, he believed that a constitutional amendment was required for the annexation of Louisiana to the United States, and he drew up an amendment for that purpose. Still, the constitutional issue posed a dilemma for the strict-constructionist president. The adoption of an amendment would take time, and Monroe and Livingston were urging prompt action, warning that the French should not be given the least opening for withdrawing from the agreement. Jefferson also feared that the constitutional issue might be used by his enemies as a tactic for delaying or defeating the ratification of the treaty. He thus convinced himself that the extraordinary circumstances of the moment required that Congress act without waiting for an amendment. "The Executive in seizing the fugitive occurrence which so much advances the good of their country, have done an act beyond the Constitution," he admitted privately. "The Legislature in casting behind them metaphysical subtleties, and risking themselves like faithful servants, must ratify and pay for it, and throw themselves on their country for doing for them unauthorized what we know they would have done for themselves had they been in a situation to do it." He considered it important, however, to set an example against broad construction by subsequently appealing to the people for a constitutional amendment approving what had been done. Nonetheless, he said that if his Republican friends thought differently, he would acquiesce, "confiding, that the good sense of our country will correct the evil of construction when it shall produce ill effects." [19] When most of his fellow Republicans recognized the treaty-making power as ample to cover the Louisiana Purchase, Jefferson did not press the matter. In his message at the opening of the Eighth Congress on October 17, 1803, called into early session to ratify and implement the Louisiana agreement, he devoted most of his attention to foreign affairs and the resolution of the Louisiana crisis but did not mention the constitutional issue.

There was little doubt that the Senate would follow the president's recommendation and ratify the Louisiana treaty and that the House of Representatives would appropriate the money to pay for it. Republican majorities had increased in both houses following the midterm elections of 1802. After the new apportionment under the census of 1800 and the admission of Ohio, there were 103 Republicans and 39 Federalists in the House, and the Senate division was 25 Republicans and 9 Federalists. The treaty and conventions relating to Louisiana presented to the Senate on October 17 were

atified three days later by a vote of 24 to 7. Only 1 Federalist joined
3 Republicans in voting for the treaty; all negative votes came
rom Federalist senators. William Plumer of New Hampshire, one
f the minority, complained that the Senate had "taken less time to
eliberate on this important treaty, than they allowed themselves
n the most trivial Indian contract." He believed that had not Sen-
te rules required three readings on separate days, the treaty would
ave been ratified after the first reading.[20]

In his annual message the president alerted the legislators to be
repared to implement the treaty and to take all measures neces-
ary for the immediate occupation and temporary government of
ouisiana and for its incorporation into the Union.[21] Immediately
fter Senate ratification, the exchange of ratifications with the
rench minister took place on October 20, 1803, and the next day
he president asked Congress for the necessary enabling legisla-
ion.[22] On December 20, 1803, in a ceremony in New Orleans,
rance formally transferred Louisiana to the United States. Jeffer-
on referred to the new territory as enlarging "the empire of lib-
rty," and he told Congress that the acquisition offered "an ample
rovision for our posterity, and a widespread field for the blessings
f freedom and equal laws." Obviously, the president was speaking
nly of white Americans, for the new territory also offered a wide
rea for the expansion of slavery. That institution already existed
n the settled areas of New Orleans and lower Louisiana, and the
reaty guaranteed the inhabitants of Louisiana all the rights and
mmunities of citizens of the United States. When Senator James
lillhouse of Connecticut in 1804 offered an amendment to the bill
rganizing the territory of Louisiana to prohibit slavery in the en-
ire purchase, Jefferson refrained from supporting it. Neither Con-
ress nor the president went any further than the prohibition of
he importation of slaves into Louisiana from abroad.[23]

The annexation of Louisiana to the United States required not
nly enabling legislation but also considerable administrative ac-
ivity. In taking control of New Orleans, a city of eight thousand,
he United States had to absorb an alien population and an admin-
strative structure created by the French and the Spanish. The in-
orporation of Louisiana into the United States was a test unlike
ny previous demand on the national government. Jefferson's ad-
inistration met the challenge. Immediately upon receiving the
ews of the Louisiana Purchase, the president said, "We shall cer-
ainly endeavour to introduce the American laws there and that
annot be done but by amalgamating the people with such a body

of Americans as may take the lead in legislation and government. But as time passed, the administration more and more came to rec ognize and respect the wishes, rights, and traditions of the non American population and in 1808 accepted the *Digest of the Civil Laws Now in Force in the Territory of Orleans*, which incorporated the traditions of French and Spanish civil law into Louisiana law. This compromise brought the acceptance by the settled population of lower Louisiana of permanent American rule and elevated the level of American tolerance of foreign peoples within its borders.[24]

If the boundaries of Louisiana were vague, much of the land within those borders was unknown. By coincidence or an optimistic vision of the destiny of the United States, Jefferson, months before the purchase, initiated a project that for the first time would open up to the consciousness of Americans the vast areas of the upper reaches of the Missouri River and the Rocky Mountains. In late No vember 1802 the president inquired of the Marqués de Casa Yrujo the Spanish minister in Washington, whether his government would object if Congress authorized an expedition to explore the course of the Missouri River, having as the main object the advancement of knowledge of geography. As the Spanish minister reported the conversation to the minister of foreign affairs in Madrid, Jefferson confided that the nominal object would be the investigation of everything that might contribute to the progress of commerce in order to get funding from Congress, which had no constitutional authority to appropriate money for "a purely literary expedition." Yrujo told the president that such an expedition "could not fail to give umbrage" to his government, but Jefferson continued to argue that Spain had no reason to fear the undertaking. In his report to Madrid, Yrujo acknowledged that Jefferson was a man of letters but he also speculated that the American president might hope "to discover the way by which the Americans may some day extend their population and their influence" to the coast of the Pacific.[25]

Despite the lack of Spanish approval and the pending transfer of Louisiana to France, Jefferson pressed ahead with his plan. In a confidential message to Congress on January 18, 1803, the presi dent asked for an appropriation of $2,500 to fund a small expedi tion to explore the Missouri River to its source and search for a river flowing to the Pacific within portage of the Missouri. His mes sage emphasized expansion of trade with the Indians and recom mended that to keep the measure from attracting notice Congress designate the appropriation as being "for the purpose of extending the external commerce of the U.S." Reminding the legislators that the interests of commerce formed the principal object within their constitutional powers, he added that the prospect that the expedition might "incidently advance the geographical knowledge of our own continent can not but be an additional gratification." Congress quietly passed the requested legislation, which the president signed on February 28, 1803.[26]

Before sending the request to Congress, Jefferson had discussed the project with his private secretary, Meriwether Lewis, and he promptly named the twenty-eight-year-old army captain to command the expedition. Jefferson had chosen Lewis as his secretary partly because of his personal acquaintance as an Albemarle neighbor and partly because of Lewis' knowledge of the western country. That the president and his secretary must often have talked about the West during the many hours they spent together in the President's House seems beyond question, but that Jefferson had decided to send Lewis on a western expedition when he appointed him as his secretary in 1801 is not documented in the record.[27]

Immediately after Congress' approval, Lewis began preparations for the expedition, assembling supplies and equipment for the journey and asking William Clark to join him as coleader, promising him equality of command, as the president had authorized him to do. Jefferson himself, who had long been interested in a transcontinental expedition, prepared the detailed instructions, which he signed on June 20, 1803. By this time he knew that Talleyrand had offered to sell Louisiana, but he had not yet received the news of the signing of the treaty.[28] It would be the following spring before Lewis and Clark began their ascent of the Missouri River and another year before Jefferson, in the summer of 1805, received his first direct reports of their progress.

The widespread public approval of the transfer of Louisiana to the United States and the private satisfaction that Jefferson had in sending Lewis and Clark to explore a vast unknown territory gave an aura of success to an administration approaching a review of its record in the election of 1804. The president's great popularity, however, did not mean that Federalist opposition had disappeared or that attacks on him in the press had ceased. Indeed, Timothy Pickering and a small group of embittered Federalists convinced themselves that there was a Jeffersonian conspiracy to perpetuate the Republicans in power. After the purchase of Louisiana, they carried their opposition to the extreme of plotting the secession of New England from the Union. When Aaron Burr ran for governor of New York in 1804, they endeavored to bring him into the plot, but his defeat destroyed that prospect. From the outset the absence of support for disunion impeded their plans. In the end Jefferson's overwhelming victory in the election of 1804 exposed the total unreality of their secessionist scheme.[29]

If Jefferson ever heard any rumors of Pickering's plotting, he did not pay them any notice. But he could not bring himself to ignore all of the newspaper attacks on himself and his administration, and he departed so far from his devotion to freedom of the press as to lend his support to state actions for libel against anti-Republican editors. In February, 1803, Governor Thomas McKean of Pennsylvania wrote to the president complaining about the "infamous and seditious libels, published almost daily in our newspapers" and suggested that they might be greatly reduced by a few prosecutions. "But as the President, Congress, and several of the principal officers of the U.S. have been frequently implicated," McKean explained, "I have declined it until I should obtain your advice and consent." The president's reply, coming from one who had protested the sedition law and aided writers suffering under it, is surprising to read today. He reasoned that having failed to destroy the freedom of the press by the sedition law, the Federalists were assaulting it from the opposite side "by pushing it's licentiousness and it's lying to such a degree as to deprive it of all credit." He thought this was a dangerous trend and that the credibility of the press ought to be restored. "The restraints provided by the laws of the states are sufficient for this if applied. And I have therefore long thought that a few prosecutions of the most prominent offenders would have a wholesome effect in restoring the integrity of the presses. Not a general prosecution, for that would look like persecution: but a selected one."[30] He even enclosed a paper as an example of a case that might be pursued. That paper has not survived and the case that McKean chose to prosecute was based on writings published after Jefferson's letter was written, but Joseph Dennie, editor of the *Port Folio*, was cited for seditious libel and brought to trial, with Jefferson's apparent blessing.[31]

Jefferson cited attacks by the Federalists as the principal reason for seeking reelection in 1804. It had been his hope to retire to a life of tranquillity after one term, he said, but "the unbounded calumnies of the federal party have obliged me to throw myself on the verdict of my country for trial." Yet, it surely was not only the Federalist opposition that persuaded him to run but also his Republican supporters, who knew he was an unbeatable candidate. A week before Jefferson wrote the above letter, 108 Republican members of Congress met in a nominating caucus and unanimously renominated him for president. With equal unanimity they dropped the incumbent vice-president from the party ticket. Though they voted for six different candidates for the vice-presidential slot, New York's George Clinton had a clear majority. "Mr. Burr had not one single vote, and not a word was lisped in his favor at the meeting," one participant observed.[32]

In his first year in office Jefferson made it clear that his vice-president did not share his confidence by openly rejecting Burr's patronage recommendations for New York, and Burr was soon read out of the Republican party by national leaders.[33] By 1804 his support in New York had so eroded that he failed to win the Republican nomination for governor. Though he ran anyway, hoping to divide the Republican vote and attract Federalist votes, he suffered another blow to his declining political fortunes. In the aftermath of that defeat, he challenged Hamilton to a duel and fatally wounded his longtime foe, alienating even Republican enemies of that Federalist giant. Burr had been so completely abandoned by Republicans by 1804 that his renomination was never at issue. Clinton was a popular choice for those who wanted New York represented on the ticket and for those who saw him as too old to block a Virginia successor to Jefferson in 1808.

Jefferson did little save stand on his record to win reelection in 1804, but that record, capped by the purchase of Louisiana, was an enviable one. At the beginning of the election year Jefferson thought the Republicans could count on carrying all but four states.[34] As it turned out, Republicans carried all but two states, Connecticut and Delaware. In Maryland, Federalists won two of the state's eleven districts, but elsewhere Jefferson had the unanimous electoral vote of the remaining fourteen states. The total electoral vote was 162 for Jefferson to 14 for Charles Cotesworth Pinckney, the Federalist candidate.

Politically the year 1804 marked the zenith of Jefferson's presidency; privately it brought him great personal sorrow. In April his daughter Maria, not yet twenty-six, died in the aftermath of childbirth, in a repetition of events that must have brought back the agonizing memories of his wife's death twenty-two years earlier. Maria's death also was a poignant reminder to him that he had not carried out the small request that she had made earlier in the year that he have his portrait drawn by Saint-Mémin when the artist visited Washington to make his popular drawings and engravings. "If you did but know what a source of pleasure it would be to us while so much separated from you to have so excellent a likeness of you," Maria had written her father, "you would not I think refuse us. It is what we have allways most wanted all our lives and the certainty with which he takes the likenesses makes this request I think not unreasonable." Maria died before he could fulfill her request, but when the artist next set up his physiognotrace in Washington in November, 1804, Jefferson arranged a sitting. Saint-Mémin provided him with a life-size profile portrait, an engraved copperplate in reduced size, and twelve impressions—the artist's usual $25 package. Jefferson also paid $4.50 for an additional thirty-six impressions and was soon sending copies to relatives and distant friends. The artist himself engraved another plate for his own use and offered copies of the print for sale in Washington on the eve of Jefferson's second inauguration.[35]

The final months of Jefferson's first term prompted less exuberance than might have been expected in the aftermath of his extraordinary reelection victory. What dominated the newspapers in the months preceding his March 4 inaugural was not the anticipation of that event but the impeachment trial of Supreme Court Justice Samuel Chase. That climactic event, nearly two years in the making, was the most sensational display yet of Republican frustration over the persisting Federalist domination of the judiciary. Though he neither directed not controlled the course of events, it was Jefferson who initially set them into motion. In May, 1803, Justice Chase, whose political harangues to grand juries and his conduct of trials of Republican editors prosecuted under the sedition law in 1800 had enraged Republicans, again stirred their anger by a political tirade to a federal grand jury in Baltimore. After an irate Maryland Republican clipped Chase's charge from a Baltimore paper and sent it to the president, Jefferson reacted promptly. "You must have heard of the extraordinary charge of Chase to the Grand Jury at Baltimore," he wrote to Maryland Congressman Joseph H. Nicholson. "Ought this seditious and official attack on the principles of our Constitution, and on the proceedings of a State, to go unpunished?" Nicholson conferred with House Speaker Macon, who questioned pursuing the matter. But at the next session of Congress, John Randolph moved that the House appoint a committee to investigate Chase's conduct, and he was named to head the seven-man committee that promptly began gathering evidence. "You can scarcely conceive the mass of testimony procured against Chase," a member of the House reported a month later, estimating that it might fill as many as five hundred pages.[36] In addition to the

charge to the Baltimore jury, the investigation focused on the treason trial of John Fries in Philadelphia and the libel trial of James
Thomson Callender in Richmond, both in 1800.

The atmosphere of the expanding investigation was highly
charged because of the impeachment proceedings then in progress
against John Pickering, federal district judge of New Hampshire.
Although the cases were different, Federalists depicted both as assaults on the independence of the judiciary. Judge Pickering's misconduct on the bench was the result of his insanity, but having
failed in all efforts to get him to resign, Jefferson had presented the
case to Congress for impeachment as the only available recourse
for removal. On the same day that Pickering was convicted by the
Senate and ordered removed, March 12, 1804, the House voted 73
to 32 to impeach Justice Chase. "You may conclude he will be condemned," exclaimed Senator Timothy Pickering. "If a considerable
majority of the House were to impeach any man in the United
States, he would by the Senate be found guilty." Senator Plumer
charged that impeachment and removal had become synonymous
terms and that the independence of the judiciary was gone. "The
process of impeachment is to be considered in effect as a *mode of
removal*," he declared, "and not as a charge and conviction of high
crimes and misdemeanors."[37]

Republicans resented such criticisms, believing that had the Federalists cooperated, Judge Pickering's friends could have persuaded
him to resign. Yet, many were uneasy over whether Chase's actions,
improper as they clearly were, constituted the "high crimes and
misdemeanors" required by the Constitution for removal from
office. Republican senators had ample time to contemplate their dilemma after Chase's trial was put off until the next session of Congress. When Congress reconvened, William Branch Giles, the Republican leader in the Senate, argued that impeachment was a
means of removal and judges could be removed for errors in judgment. Senator John Quincy Adams reported that Giles told the
Senate that "impeachment is nothing more than an enquiry, by the
two Houses of Congress, whether the office of any public man
might not be better filled by another."[38] Not all Republicans shared
this view, and widening internal Republican divisions made the outcome of the trial increasingly doubtful.

Scheduled to begin on January 2, 1805, Chase's trial did not get
under way until February 4. In his last major act in office, Vice-
President Burr presided over a scene he had carefully arranged.
Empowered to make the necessary arrangements for the proceed-

ings, he transformed the Senate chamber into a setting "beyond anything which has ever appeared in this country," one senator observed.[39] The senators' desks and chairs were removed and two rows of seats covered with red baize were built on each side of the vice-president's chair. Seats covered with green cloth were arranged for the members of the House of Representatives, together with special seats for officials and an elegant gallery for ladies. The chamber, a member of the House observed, had "more the appearance of a play house than a Court." With the galleries packed, John Randolph heading the House managers, and Justice Chase attended by a battery of prominent lawyers, the scene was set for high drama. The spectators were not disappointed. But as the trial proceeded and the legislative business of Congress came to a halt, Senator Plumer observed that "all parties appear to wish it had never been commenced—I believe we shall not hear of another very soon."[40]

Jefferson, who had started it all with his letter to Nicholson nearly two years earlier, told the congressman at that time that "it is better that I should not interfere," and there is no evidence that, after his initial act, he did. Through the long months preceding the trial, he appears not to have commented on the proceedings nor to have used his office to influence the outcome, leading one scholar to conclude that the president's unwillingness to become involved was one of the decisive factors in the final verdict.[41] Jefferson, who had earlier admitted that removing judges by impeachment was a bungling way, may have wished that he had never called attention to Chase's misconduct. But we know he followed Chase's trial closely, because he left in his papers a tally sheet on which he recorded the votes of every senator on each of the eight articles of impeachment. That vote was taken on March 1, 1805. A majority of senators found Chase guilty on three of the eight articles, but no article received the two-thirds vote required for conviction. The highest vote, 19 to 15, for conviction was cast on the article relating to Chase's charge to the grand jury in Baltimore, but it was 4 votes short of the constitutional requirement.[42]

The trial was an unpropitious ending to an auspicious first term. Three days later Jefferson would stand before Chief Justice Marshall to take the presidential oath of office for the second time.

XIX
Trials of a Second Term

On Saturday March 2, 1805, in the Senate chamber, where Justice Samuel Chase had been acquitted the day before, Vice-President Aaron Burr delivered a moving farewell address to a hushed Senate. As he walked slowly from the room and closed the door behind him, he left many of the senators in tears. Washington was still buzzing with talk of Chase's acquittal and Burr's valedictory as Congress closed its harried session on Sunday. Before noon on Monday, March 4, when Jefferson rose in the same Senate chamber to repeat the oath of office as president, many members of Congress were already on their way home. No air of anticipation surrounded the event, and there was even less ceremony than marked his first inaugural. Instead of walking to the Capitol, as he had four years earlier, Jefferson came by carriage from the President's House, accompanied only by his private secretary and a groom. There was no pageantry. One British diplomat remembered that Jefferson was dressed in black and even wore black silk stockings, but neither the president's dress nor the ceremony attracted much attention in the press.[1]

In words that echoed comments on Jefferson's first inaugural, Senator John Quincy Adams recorded that the president delivered his address "in so low a voice that not half of it was heard by any part of the crowded auditory." The speech, however, was widely published. When Senator William Plumer, who took the mail stage from Washington the night before the inauguration, reached Baltimore on the afternoon of March 4, he found the president's inaugural address on the streets within an hour of his arrival and deduced that it had come on the same stage. He faulted editor Samuel Harrison Smith, to whom Jefferson had supplied an advance copy, for describing the speech as being delivered to both houses of Congress when there was not a quorum of either House left in Washington. But he welcomed the early printing and read it closely enough to find that the Republican president took a more generous view of the preceding four years than the Federalist senator.[2]

After thanking his countrymen for their new proof of confidence in him, Jefferson began his address by saying that his conscience told him that he had lived up to the principles he had declared four years before. In support of this claim he reviewed the major accomplishments of his first term. In domestic policies he emphasized the elimination of unnecessary offices and expenses, the abolition of internal taxes, and the progress in paying off the debt. He proudly pointed out that the government was supported by revenue from taxes on the consumption of foreign goods, paid by those who could afford to buy luxuries. "It may be the pleasure and pride of an American to ask," he said, "what farmer, what mechanic, what laborer, ever sees a tax gatherer of the United States?" In regard to foreign affairs he did not gloat over the acquisition of Louisiana. Instead he acknowledged that it had been disapproved by some from an apprehension that the additional territory would endanger the union. "But who can limit the extent to which the federative principle may operate effectively?" he asked. "The larger our association, the less will it be shaken by local passions."[3]

One of the longest and most philosophical passages of his address dealt with "the aboriginal inhabitants," whom he saw as "endowed with the faculties and the rights of men, breathing an ardent love of liberty and independence," but now being overwhelmed by a relentless stream of overflowing white population. "Humanity enjoins us to teach them agriculture and the domestic arts," he said, "to encourage them to that industry which alone can enable them to maintain their place in existence, and to prepare them in time for that state of society, which to bodily comforts adds the improvement of mind and morals." His administration had liberally furnished them with the implements of husbandry and household use and sent instructors to teach them the needed skills, he indicated, while acknowledging that all "endeavours to enlighten them on the fate which awaits their present course of life" and persuade them to change their ways encountered powerful obstacles.[4] Jefferson here was struggling with a dilemma that he never resolved. The Indians could be saved from extinction only by destroying their culture, for he had no doubt that their culture must ultimately bend to the rule of reason. He admitted in his own notes on his speech that he expanded upon the obstruction to change among the Indians in order to speak to a broader audience. He was not speaking only of Indians when he criticized persons who "inculcate a sanctimonious reverence for the customs of their ancestors; that whatsoever they did, must be done through all time; that reason is a false guide, and to advance under its counsel, in their physical, moral, or political condition, is perilous innovation." This passage was addressed broadly to all those responsible for "the hue and cry raised against philosophy and the rights of man," he wrote in his notes. "I have thought it best to say what is directly applied to Indians only, but admits by inference a more general extention."[5] Without mentioning the Federalist extremists, he could expect his audience to make the connection.

In light of Jefferson's encouragement of Governor McKean of Pennsylvania to check the licentiousness of the press through selected prosecutions, the eloquent disquisition on the freedom of the press that he included toward the close of his speech seems somewhat contrived. He took pride that his reelection had demonstrated that a government conducting itself within the true spirit of the Constitution could not be written down by falsehood and defamation. He said that he did not mean to infer that state laws against false and defamatory publications should not be enforced, but he indicated that his administration had left offenders to find their punishment in public indignation. "Since truth and reason have maintained their ground against false opinions in league with false facts, the press, confined to truth, needs no other legal restraint," he affirmed.[6] This he unquestionably believed, but he was having some trouble with the problem of confining the press to truth.

After the inaugural ceremonies, Jefferson held an open house similar to those he customarily hosted on New Year's Day and on the Fourth of July. One British diplomat reported "a very mixed company . . . some lolling about on couches and in dirty shoes." He also described "a collection of people on the road" as "composed of low persons, for the most part Irish labourers." What this aristocratic observer did not know was that the procession in the street, which had been formed by mechanics in the Naval Yard, had presented the president with a congratulatory address signed by more than one hundred, expressing gratitude for being able to live in "a land of equal rights and liberties, where the honest industry of the mechanic is equally supported with the splendor of the wealthy."[7]

Not long after his second inaugural, the president agreed to sit for America's most famous portrait painter, Gilbert Stuart. He had sat for Stuart in 1800 and liked the result, but he never received the portrait. What happened to that effort is not known. When Stuart requested Jefferson to sit again in 1805, the artist indicated that he was not satisfied with the 1800 portrait, but the real reason was that he had received a commission from James Bowdoin III for a portrait of the president and needed a new sitting. Jefferson yielded to the request, and Stuart drew his portrait from life, painted a replica for Bowdoin, and did another one for Madison. Madison received his portrait by 1806, Bowdoin got his canvas in 1807, but Jefferson did not get Stuart to relinquish the original portrait until 1821. Meanwhile, Bowdoin's *Jefferson* was copied and engraved by Robert Field and published in Boston in 1807 in an exceptionally fine print offered to the public for one dollar. Stuart's image soon surpassed in popularity Rembrandt Peale's portrait of 1800, which had been the major source of images of the president during his first term, and it became the preeminent icon of Jefferson for over a century.[8]

When he accepted the presidency for a second time, Jefferson had decided to follow the precedent of President Washington and retire at the end of his second term. But at the urging of his closest advisers, he refrained from announcing that intention at his inauguration. Because he had already revealed his intent privately, however, maneuvering in regard to his successor began almost immediately. A year had barely passed before John Randolph declared on the floor of the House of Representatives that in every action all eyes were fixed on the President's House. In a debate on nonimportation he said that "the question was not what we should do with France, or Spain, or England, but who should be the next President. And at this moment, every motion that is made . . . is made with a view to the occupation of that House."[9] This factor, with which Jefferson had not had to contend during his first four years, would contribute to the difficulties that beset his second term.

From the beginning of that term, Jefferson was increasingly occupied with European affairs. At the time of his inaugural Monroe was in Madrid trying to negotiate with Spain on the disputed boundaries of the Louisiana Purchase. Enraged by France's transfer of Louisiana to the United States, Spain had refused to carry through with the convention of 1802 settling spoliation claims, and the Spanish government took further umbrage at the United States' claim to the Perdido River (the present boundary between Alabama and Florida) as the eastern boundary of Louisiana. Buoyed by the Louisiana triumph, Jefferson moved pugnaciously to deal with Spain. "We scarcely expect any liberal or just settlement with Spain, and are perfectly determined to obtain or to take our just limits," Jefferson wrote to Monroe shortly after the transfer of Louisiana to the United States, while predicting that the inhabitants on the east bank of the Mississippi River would soon ask to come under American jurisdiction. At first France seemed to promise support for American efforts to obtain West Florida and persuaded Monroe to delay his mission to Madrid until Spanish tempers cooled. After being appointed to succeed Rufus King as minister to Great Britain, Monroe took up his post in London and did not set out for Madrid until the end of 1804. Meanwhile, as he discovered in a stop in Paris, the French had decided against aiding the American efforts, and Spain had been further alienated by Jefferson's establishing a revenue district in West Florida. So dominant was Napoleon's influence over his weak neighbor that Monroe's mission to Madrid had little chance of success. After nearly five frustrating months Monroe and Pinckney terminated the negotiations. Convinced that Spain would make no concessions without compulsion, they recommended to the secretary of state that the United States take possession of both of the Floridas.[10]

Jefferson learned of the failure of Monroe's mission in early August, 1805, while at Monticello, and it overshadowed the recent good news from the Mediterranean that a treaty had been signed with Tripoli bringing to an end the naval action he had launched at the outset of his presidency. He blamed Napoleon for the futile negotiations with Spain, writing Madison that he was convinced of the "hostile and treacherous intentions against us on the part of France, and that we should lose no time in securing something more than a mutual friendship with England." Spain now became the president's principal object of concern. As he sought to deal with the question of Spanish territory bordering the United States while the war in Europe was still in progress, he began thinking in terms of some kind of alliance with England to put pressure on France. "A procrastination till peace in Europe shall leave us without an ally," he told the secretary of state.[11]

By the time he had returned to Washington in October he had changed his mind on the need for even a temporary alliance with England. He now believed that the war in Europe would go on for at least another year, with probably an additional one for peace negotiations. "This gives us our great disideratum, time," he confided to Madison. There was time to make another effort at a peaceful settlement, but negotiations should not be held at Madrid. Paris was the place to negotiate—with "France as the mediator, the price of the Floridas as the means. We need not care who gets that: and an enlargement of the sum we had thought of may be the bait to France." The cabinet agreed to such a policy at a meeting on November 14 and set five million dollars as the amount the United States would be willing to pay for East and West Florida.[12] A few days later Jefferson received a letter from John Armstrong, who had replaced Livingston as minister to France, containing an unofficial proposition from Talleyrand in which the French minister had suggested a plan similar to his own. "He advises that we alarm the fears of Spain by a vigorous language and conduct, in order to induce her to join us in appealing to the interference of the Emperor," Jefferson noted in recording that Talleyrand's proposal was in accord with the cabinet's decision except as to the sum of money, which Talleyrand placed at seven million dollars.[13]

In his fifth annual message to Congress on December 3, 1805, the president offered a bleak picture of deteriorating relations with Spain, informed Congress that he had given orders to the troops on the frontier to be in readiness to protect American citizens and repel any aggressions, and promised a special message on Spanish relations.[14] In a confidential message three days later Jefferson reviewed Monroe's fruitless endeavor to reach some agreement in regard to American spoliation claims and the Louisiana boundary and concluded that "our injured citizens were thus left without any prospect of retribution from the wrongdoer; and as to the boundary each party was to take its own course." In addition to denying all American claims east of the Mississippi, Spain pressed for a western boundary that, Jefferson said, "would have left us but a string of land" on the west bank of the Mississippi. He indicated that the documents accompanying his message showed that the Spanish intended "to advance on our possessions until they shall be repressed by an opposing force. Considering that Congress alone is constitutionally invested with the power of changing our condition from peace to war, I have thought it my duty to await their authority for using force in any degree which could be avoided." The crisis in Europe offered a favorable time to press for a settlement, he believed. Formal war was not necessary, "but the protection of our citizens, the spirit and honor of our country, require that force should be interposed to a certain degree. It will probably contribute to advance the object of peace."[15]

The president included a brief analysis of France's attitude and indicated his opinion that France was disposed to effect a settlement, but he offered no details except to say that "the course to be pursued will require the command of means which it belongs to Congress exclusively to yield or to deny." Gallatin had urged Jefferson to be more specific in his message, complaining after reading the draft that it did not explicitly declare its object. He suggested that Jefferson's failure to mention Florida by name or to indicate that a large sum of money would be required might give Congress a mistaken view of his object. But Jefferson preferred to work behind the scenes and privately conveyed to Republican congressional leaders his recommendation for an immediate two-million-dollar appropriation. After the success that a similar appropriation for the Louisiana negotiations had produced, he did not anticipate any difficulty in obtaining the allocation. Here he miscalculated. When John Randolph, who had been named to head the House committee to which Jefferson's confidential message was referred, was briefed by the president and learned that he sought two million dollars for the negotiations, he announced that he would not agree to such a measure not requested in the message. Randolph accused the president of trying to shift responsibility to the House but declared that even if Jefferson had asked for the money, he would still have opposed it as a bribe to France. "After the total failure of every attempt at negotiation, such a step would disgrace us forever," he protested.[16]

Jefferson may have been astonished that Randolph chose this issue upon which to oppose him, but he could hardly have been surprised that the independent Virginian was moving to an open break. The distance between Randolph and the president began widening over the Yazoo land controversy, the settlement of which Randolph had succeeded in blocking during the two previous sessions. That issue went back to the agreement that a commission composed of Secretary of State Madison, Secretary of the Treasury Gallatin, and Attorney General Lincoln had negotiated with Georgia in 1802 for the cession of its western lands to the United States. In accepting Georgia's lands, the United States set aside five million acres to settle unresolved claims. Most of those claims grew out of the sale of thirty-five million acres of the Yazoo lands to four land companies by the Georgia legislature in 1795. In the following year the legislature rescinded the sale on the clear grounds of bribery of members of the previous assembly. Meanwhile, much of the land had been sold, leaving titles in dispute and new purchasers pressing their claims. Notable among them was the New England Mississippi Land Company, which had purchased eleven million acres on the very day the act had been repealed. The federal commissioners denied the claimants' title but proposed a compromise compensation on the ground that many were innocent parties unaware of the corruption of the legislature. By accusing anyone who was willing to approve the compromise as sanctioning corruption, Randolph blocked congressional action in 1804 and 1805 and came close to breaking with the administration over the issue.[17] Randolph's position as the Republican leader in the House was further weakened by his unsuccessful conduct of the proceedings against Justice Chase. His clash with the president over foreign policy brought an irreparable break with the administration in 1806, and Jefferson soon moved to isolate Randolph and other "Old Republicans" who followed his lead. Not only policies but also presidential politics widened the breach between Randolph and the president. Madison's name, which was being prominently mentioned as Jefferson's successor, was anathema to Randolph, who favored Monroe, whom he saw as a Republican still true to the principles of the old Republican party.

Randolph's opposition did not block Jefferson's request for the secret appropriation of two million dollars, which passed the House on January 16, 1806, by a vote of 76 to 54 and was concurred with by the Senate three weeks later. But the break in Republican ranks encouraged Federalists to join in calling the plan a disgraceful scheme to purchase peace by employing money as bribes at the French court and buying land in West Florida already paid for. Thomas Mann Randolph, Jr., the president's son-in-law and a member of the House, defended the administration against such charges in a letter to his constituents after Congress lifted the ban of secrecy. He said that the majority in the House "saw no humiliation to their country in offering to France and Spain combined, the alternative of assured peace and a generous price for Florida, or the manifest risk, from inevitable collisions, of war, with its certain consequences the invasion of Mexico and Cuba."[18]

After all the controversy at a high cost to Republican party unity, the diplomatic effort met with failure. The Spanish could not be lured to the negotiating table, and after the safeguards the administration imposed to prevent French jobbery, Talleyrand lost interest. Conditions in Europe had also changed dramatically. At the time Jefferson sent his Spanish message to Congress, he knew nothing of either Trafalgar or Austerlitz, both of which battles had already been decided. As the administration assessed those momentous events when the news did reach America, Jefferson's concern with obtaining West Florida gave way to more pressing matters.

Nelson's victory at Trafalgar broke the naval power of France and made the British master of the seas. Napoleon's victory at Austerlitz forced Austria to sue for peace and put the Russian armies into retreat. "What an awful spectacle does the world exhibit at this instant," Jefferson wrote in January, 1806, "one man bestriding the continent of Europe like a Colossus, and another roaming unbridled on the ocean. But even this is better than that one should rule both elements." [19]

Although Senator John Quincy Adams would shortly accuse the president of "unqualified submission to France and unqualified defiance of Great Britain," Jefferson regarded a balance of power in Europe as in the interest of the United States. But he also saw Great Britain as the greater menace. He had not mentioned Britain by name in his annual message, but he protested armed vessels hovering off the coasts and harbors of the United States and the new principles "interpolated into the law of nations" to curtail neutral trade. The latter was a reference to the *Essex* decision, issued in the spring of 1805, by which the British sought to end the prevailing practice allowing American merchants to import goods into the United States and reexport them as neutral cargo. The British had followed the *Essex* decision with the seizure of numerous unsuspecting American vessels. In response Jefferson recommended that Congress increase the number of gunboats to protect American seaports and informed the legislators that his government had assembled materials to build warships if Congress saw fit to authorize their construction. The day after the House passed the two-million-dollar act, which put the Spanish business out of the way for the moment, Jefferson sent Congress a special message on neutral commerce, enclosing memorials from American merchants and other papers documenting the British interference with American neutral trade and the impressment of American seamen. [20]

On the preceding day, January 16, each senator had found on his desk in the Senate a 204-page pamphlet entitled *An Examination of the British Doctrine, Which Subjects to Capture a Neutral Trade, not Open in Time of Peace*. Although the author's name did not appear on the work, there was no secret that it came from the pen of the Secretary of State. In a learned but prolix dissertation, Madison argued that there was no basis in international law for the British "Rule of 1756," which denied to neutrals in time of war a trade not open to them in time of peace. Jefferson thought Madison's pamphlet "pulverized" the rule by "a logic not to be controverted." [21] But no argument of logic would dissuade the British from trying to prevent all

trade between the West Indies and France, for the British were convinced that their survival depended on maintaining control of the
seas and strangling Napoleon by tightening their blockade of the
Continent.

The section of the president's annual message relating to the conduct of belligerent powers toward the United States had been referred to the House Committee of Ways and Means with instructions
to inquire into the violations of neutral rights and recommend counteracting measures.[22] Chairman John Randolph had already asked
Madison for information on "what new principles, or constructions,
of the laws of nations have been adopted by belligerent powers of
Europe, to the prejudice of neutral rights?" But Randolph delayed
bringing the matter before the House, and after Jefferson's special
message of January 17, 1806, the House transferred the matter to
the Committee of the Whole for consideration.[23]

In his special message of January 17, Jefferson did not recommend a specific course of action. Although he had taken the lead in
formulating Spanish policy, he now held back in regard to Great
Britain. With no administration direction and the alienated Randolph deriding the president and his cabinet, Congress floundered
in often tiresome wrangling. The House began by debating resolutions introduced by Representative Andrew Gregg of Pennsylvania
to ban all British imports until a satisfactory understanding was
reached with Great Britain on neutral commerce and impressment.
Two months later it ended up passing an act to prohibit the importation of a list of specified British goods beginning at the distant
date of November 15, 1806.[24]

Although he remained more aloof from Congress' deliberations
than usual, the president let it be known that he favored the course
adopted. Senator Adams clearly sensed that preference in conversation at the president's dinner table. Yet Jefferson did not assert
the same degree of leadership that had previously characterized his
presidency. Whether because of Republican divisions in Congress
or his own lack of urgency, he did not press for action. While Congress debated what to do, the president optimistically wrote to
Thomas Paine that he expected the difficulties with England to "be
dissipated by the disasters of her allies, the change of her ministry,
and the measures which Congress are likely to adopt to furnish motives for her becoming just to us." With Napoleon still expanding
his control of the Continent, Jefferson had no sound basis for such
optimism. Randolph in the course of the debates protested that "it
is not for the master and mate . . . in bad weather, to go below, and

leave the management of the ship to the cook and cabin boy." He denounced the measure finally adopted as "a milk-and-water bill, a dose of chicken broth to be taken nine months hence." [25] Jefferson was able to isolate Randolph politically, but Randolph sensed the beginning of a decline of the confident leadership that had characterized Jefferson's previous years at the helm of state.

Besides the nonimportation act, Congress also gave the president support for negotiations with Great Britain. Though Jefferson had favored leaving the negotiations in the hands of Monroe, he yielded to congressional pressure to name a special commission, and following the passage of the nonimportation act, he nominated William Pinkney, a Baltimore lawyer, to join Monroe as a joint commissioner.[26] While Jefferson awaited the outcome of the negotiations in London, reports reached him of a new threat to the nation in the West—not from a foreign power but from within. At the center of the suspected intrigue was his former vice-president, Aaron Burr.

Jefferson had received his first warning against Burr in December, 1805. Shortly after he entertained the ex-vice-president at dinner, an anonymous hand-printed letter arrived from Philadelphia warning of Burr's intrigues. "You admit him at your table . . . at the very moment he is meditating the overthrow of your Administration and what is more is conspiring against the State," the writer declared. "His aberrations through the Western States had no other object." He advised the president to watch Burr's connections with Anthony Merry, the British minister, "and you will find him a British Pensioner and Agent." A few days later a second letter arrived from the same writer, who described himself as a friend of Jefferson and a lover of his country and warned further of Burr's intrigues.[27]

There is no evidence that Jefferson gave any more attention to these letters than to other anonymous letters that reached his desk, though he retained them in his files, as he did all letters addressed to the president. He could not have known, as historians do today, that a month after killing Alexander Hamilton in the duel that ended Burr's political career and seven months before the end of his vice-presidential term, Burr had met secretly with the British minister. Merry reported to London an offer from Burr "to lend his assistance to His Majesty's Government in any Manner in which they may think fit to employ him, particularly in endeavouring to effect a Separation of the Western Part of the United States from that which lies between the Atlantick and the Mountains."

Nor would Jefferson have known that, soon after leaving the vice-presidential office, Burr had talked with Merry about plans to promote the independence of Louisiana. Nor would Jefferson have been aware that Burr indirectly had also been in contact with the Spanish government.[28] But Jefferson knew of Burr's trip through the West after leaving office, and he would not have failed to read an article entitled "Queries," which had been widely published in the newspapers, questioning the motives behind Burr's journey. Originally published in the Federalist *United States Gazette* in July, 1805, the unsigned communication suggested as possible motives the formation of a separate government in the West, the seizure and distribution of public lands, and the invasion and despoiling of Mexico. Because "Queries" had appeared in a rabidly Federalist paper and had been dismissed by the Republican Philadelphia *Aurora* as "imaginery" and "absurd," Jefferson probably subscribed to editor William Duane's assessment that the questions raised were unworthy of serious consideration. He certainly shared Duane's confidence in the loyalty of westerners to the Union. Before he received the warning from the anonymous "friend" in Philadelphia, the president had also read Governor William C. C. Claiborne's report that during a visit to New Orleans Burr had associated intimately with critics of the territorial government and with Juan Ventura Morales, the former Spanish intendant.[29] If these reports aroused Jefferson's suspicions, he left no record of it.

Jefferson gave more attention to a private letter that came to him early in February, 1806, from Joseph H. Daveiss, the United States district attorney for Kentucky. In a confidential report that did not mention Burr, Daveiss warned the president about Spanish intrigues and a plot against the Union. "We have traitors among us," he wrote. "A separation of the union in favour of Spain, is the object." He said that, though he did not know by what means this was to be attempted, the plot was laid wider than Jefferson could imagine. "Mention the subject to no man from the western country however high in office he may be:—some of them are deeply tainted with this Treason." Daveiss particularly cautioned the president against General James Wilkinson, commanding general of the army and governor of upper Louisiana, whom he suspected of being in the pay of the Spanish government.[30]

Jefferson shared the letter with Madison, Gallatin, and Dearborn, none of whom apparently took alarm. Though we know today that General Wilkinson was in Spanish pay, even such a hard-nosed realist as Gallatin could not believe that Wilkinson was capable of betraying his country. Nonetheless, Jefferson replied promptly to Daveiss, requesting a full communication of everything known by him, including the names of all persons involved in the combination and witnesses to any part of it. When Daveiss, a Federalist, supplied names, he listed not only Wilkinson and Burr but also a number of prominent Republicans, including Jefferson's Attorney General John Breckinridge, William Henry Harrison, and Henry Clay.[31] Daveiss later struck Breckinridge and Clay from his list, but he had already destroyed his credibility with the president, who was now disposed to doubt the reports of a Federalist appointee of John Adams. Daveiss' rambling letters also meshed Spanish intrigues of the 1790s with more recent events, and Jefferson stopped replying to his letters until Daveiss pressed him to acknowledge their receipts, which Jefferson did in September, 1806.[32]

About this time Jefferson also received reports of Burr's activities from other sources. Colonel George Morgan wrote from western Pennsylvania that Burr had tried to enlist his sons in a military expedition and had talked about the independence of the West. Jefferson later said that Morgan's letter was "the very first intimation I had of this plot." But it was not until after he received a letter from Gideon Granger, his postmaster general, that the president moved into action.[33] Granger reported from Massachusetts in a letter received by Jefferson on October 20, 1806, the information that in the previous winter Burr had offered General William Eaton the second in command, under Wilkinson, of an expedition designed to separate the western states from the Union. Granger had confirmed this with General Eaton himself before transmitting the report to the president.[34]

Two days later Jefferson assembled his cabinet and relayed this and earlier reports that both he and Madison had received regarding Burr's actions. In meetings over several days the cabinet decided to send John Graham, secretary of the Orleans Territory, who was then in Washington, on Burr's trail with discretionary powers to consult confidentially with western governors and to arrest Burr if he committed any overt act. Letters were dispatched to the governors of the Orleans and Mississippi territories to be on their guard. Orders also were prepared to dispatch Captains Edward Preble and Stephen Decatur to New Orleans but rescinded when mail arrived from the West containing no word of any movements of Burr. Jefferson reasoned that the total silence of the officers of government and the newspapers indicated that Burr was committing no overt act against the law. The cabinet also discussed what should be done in regard to General Wilkinson. Jefferson acknowledged that suspicions of his infidelity had become widespread, but the cabinet postponed action, awaiting further information.[35]

At nearly the same time that the administration was trying to decide what to do in regard to Burr and Wilkinson, the general was deciding to abandon Burr, expose his coconspirator, and present himself as the savior of his country. Because Burr presented different plans to different parties, it is impossible to say with certainty what he intended to do, but the records are convincing that he was engaged in some conspiracy and that Wilkinson, whom one leading scholar called "the most skillful and unscrupulous plotter this country has ever produced," was a party to the plotting.[36]

On October 8, 1806, Samuel Swartwout, a Burr aide, arrived in Wilkinson's headquarters at Natchitoches to deliver an unsigned cipher letter, written in late July, 1806, indicating that funds had been obtained, naval aid from England was expected, and operations were beginning. Burr was proceeding westward as of August 1. Forces would rendezvous on the Ohio on November 1, and the first five hundred to one thousand men would move rapidly from the falls at Louisville on November 15, anticipating arriving at Natchez between December 5 and 15, where they would expect to meet Wilkinson. "Wilkinson shall be second to Burr only and Wilkinson shall dictate the rank and promotion of his officers," said the letter.[37] Wilkinson identified this letter as coming from Burr, an assumption generally accepted until challenged in 1983 by the editors of Burr's papers, who posited Jonathan Dayton, another of the conspirators, as the real author of the letter.[38] While the authorship of this major piece of evidence is critical to the interpretation of Burr's role in the events, it does not lessen its importance as evidence of a conspiracy nor make any clearer the ultimate aims of the plotters.

Wilkinson waited nearly two weeks after deciphering the letter before acting. He then dispatched Lieutenant Thomas A. Smith to Washington with a packet of confidential communications for the president. First was a paper that the general identified as having fallen into his hands but that was obviously written by Wilkinson himself (and later so acknowledged). Dated October 20, 1806, the memorandum reported "a numerous and powerful association," extending from New York to the Mississippi, designed to assemble eight thousand to ten thousand men at New Orleans for an expedition against Vera Cruz. The first rendezvous would be near the rapids of the Ohio on or before November 20. The leaders of the enterprise and their source of support were unknown, the report claimed, as were their intentions in regard to the Orleans Territory. Wilkinson accompanied this communication with a confidential letter of October 21 expressing his dismay at the disclosure, which he described as perplexing, and adding, "I am not only uninformed of the prime mover and ultimate objects of this daring enterprize, but am ignorant of the foundation on which it rests." He went on to offer his opinion that a revolt of the Orleans Territory was an auxiliary step in the main design of attacking Mexico.[39]

When Lieutenant Smith arrived at the President's House on November 25 with the dispatches from Wilkinson, Jefferson could no longer afford to wait until Burr committed some overt act before issuing a public warning. He assembled his cabinet the same day, and they agreed on a presidential proclamation and orders to be sent to various military posts and civil officials to stop the enterprise wherever it might be in progress. The president issued his proclamation two days later, warning all citizens against the conspiracy. He ordered all officers of the government, civil and military, to search out and bring to justice all persons involved, and to seize all vessels, arms, and military stores employed.[40] Nowhere in the proclamation was Burr named, but there was no doubt that it was directed against him. Senator Plumer indicated that "reports have for some time circulated from one end of the United States to the other, that Aaron Burr, late Vice President, with others, in the western States are preparing gun boats, provisions, money, men, etc. to make war upon the Spaniards." Plumer believed their intention was to establish a new empire in the west, combining Spanish territory with the western states.[41]

Jefferson was confident that Burr's project would collapse with the issuance of his proclamation, believing that Burr's strength rested on men who thought the government was a party to the enterprise. Referring only briefly to his proclamation in his annual message in December, 1806, the president did not report further on the matter until requested to do so by the House of Representatives in mid-January.[42] In a special message to both houses on January 22, 1807, he then exposed "an illegal combination of private individuals against the peace and safety of the Union, and a military expedition planned by them against the territories of a power in amity with the United States." He named Aaron Burr as the prime mover and, in an extraordinary statement for the president to make, announced that Burr's "guilt is placed beyond question." By beginning his review of events in late September and ignoring the early warnings from Daveiss, he presented the record of a prompt, but not precipitate, executive response. He also gave more credit than due to Wilkinson and capped his presentation by communicating to Congress a copy of the sensational cipher letter that Wilkinson had recently forwarded to him at his request.[43] It was published in the *National Intelligencer* the next day.

At the time the president made public the revelations in the cipher letter, Burr had already surrendered to civil authorities in the Mississippi Territory, though this news had not yet reached Washington. Near the end of December, Burr had rendezvoused with Harman Blennerhassett, a major Ohio backer, at the mouth of the Cumberland River, and they had proceeded toward Natchez with a small flotilla of ten boats and some sixty men. At a stop some thirty miles above Natchez, on January 10, Burr learned for the first time that Wilkinson had betrayed him, that the president had issued a proclamation, and that the acting governor of the Mississippi Territory had ordered his arrest. A week later he surrendered. A grand jury, however, failed to indict Burr, and the territorial supreme court divided over whether Burr should be discharged from his recognizance. At this point Burr disappeared from the town of Washington and was declared a fugitive from justice. Attempting to escape from the Mississippi Territory, he headed southeast but was recognized, arrested, and made a military prisoner at Fort Stoddert on February 19, 1807. In March, he was brought under guard to Richmond for trial.[44]

On March 30, 1807, in a secluded room in Richmond's Eagle Tavern, Burr stood before Chief Justice Marshall, who presided over the federal circuit court in Richmond, for a preliminary hearing. District Attorney George Hay presented a motion that the former vice-president be committed on a charge of high misdemeanor for setting on foot an expedition against the dominions of Spain and a charge of treason for assembling an armed force for the purpose of seizing New Orleans, revolutionizing the Orleans Territory, and separating the western states from the Atlantic states. Also present were Caesar A. Rodney, the attorney general of the United States, and two leading Richmond attorneys, John Wickham and Edmund Randolph, whom Burr had retained as counsel. In view of the expected length of discussion on the motion, Marshall adjourned the hearing until the next day in the chamber of the House of Delegates in the nearby Capitol. At that time Hay opened the government's argument, and Rodney presented the closing summation in an unusual demonstration of the administration's interest in the case. Ruling that no proof had been offered to show that Burr assembled troops for a treasonable purpose, Marshall on April 1 refused to include a charge of treason in the commitment, though leaving the attorney general free to obtain such an indictment later. He then released Burr on bail of ten thousand dollars on the charge of misdemeanor to be answered at the next term of the circuit court in Richmond on May 22.[45]

Jefferson was enraged by Marshall's action and denounced "the tricks of the judges to force trials before it is possible to collect the evidence, dispersed through a line of 2000 miles from Maine to Orleans." He charged the Federalists with aiding Burr and found it ironic that those who had complained of "the supine inattention of the administration to a treason stalking through the land in open day" now protested that it had been crushed before overt acts could be produced. And he lashed out at the federal courts for "their new born zeal for the liberty of those whom we would not permit to overthrow the liberties of their country."[46]

When the court convened with the chief justice presiding on May 22, 1807, a panel of leading citizens of the state had been summoned for grand jury service, and witnesses and visitors had crowded into the city from throughout the country. After sixteen jurors were approved, Marshall named John Randolph, the leading Republican critic of the president, as foreman of the grand jury. Soon after the jury was impaneled, District Attorney Hay moved that Burr be committed for treason, which would have denied his continuing on bail. But Marshall was reluctant to rule on the motion before the grand jury acted, and he accepted the defense's offer for increased bail, raising the total to twenty thousand dollars. Further proceedings were delayed because the government's principal witness, General Wilkinson, had not appeared. The court adjourned from day to day until he arrived in Richmond on June 13.[47]

While the proceedings were at a standstill awaiting the arrival of Wilkinson, Burr asked the court on June 9 to issue a subpoena duces tecum to President Jefferson requiring him to appear before the court and produce the letter that Wilkinson had addressed to him on October 21 and his reply to it, together with the orders that he had issued to the army and navy for Burr's apprehension. Burr argued that these papers were material to his defense. After an acrimonious debate between the opposing counsel, Marshall on June 13 ordered that such a subpoena be issued to summon the president or such of the secretaries of the departments that may have the papers. But when the writ was issued, it contained an endorsement signed by Burr specifying that the transmission of the original letter of General Wilkinson and duly authenticated copies of the other papers requested would be sufficient observance of the process, without the personal attendance of any of the persons named.[48]

As soon as Hay had informed the president of Burr's request and before Marshall had made his ruling, Jefferson volunteered to send the papers. Writing to Hay on June 12, he said, "Reserving the necessary right of the President of the U.S. to decide, independently of all other authority, what papers, coming to him as President, the public interests permit to be communicated, and to whom, I assure you of my readiness under that restriction, voluntarily to furnish on all occasions, whatever the purposes of justice may require." He said that he had already turned over all of his papers relating to the case to the attorney general, and if Rodney had not left them in Hay's possession, he would immediately instruct him to forward the papers to Richmond. He indicated that more specific requests would be needed for papers from the War and Navy departments, but he made clear to Hay his willingness to provide all material pertinent to the defense.[49]

By the time Jefferson had received the subpoena, he believed that he had taken all necessary steps to supply the papers requested, and he authorized Hay to give his consent to the taking of depositions in Washington of himself or heads of the departments if the court requested. As to his personal appearance in Richmond, or that of his department heads, he indicated that "paramount duties to the nation at large control the obligation of compliance with their summons." To agree to appear in Richmond might subsequently compel attendance at trials in Ohio or the Mississippi Territory and leave the nation without an executive. Jefferson's readiness to give a deposition in Washington suggests a willingness to testify in court had the trial been in Washington, but should Marshall require him to appear in Richmond, he was prepared to exercise the independent prerogative of the executive to refuse. Though Marshall did not actually summon the president, Jefferson resented his arguments that indicated his authority to do so. "Would the executive be independent of the judiciary, if he were subject to the *commands* of the latter, and to imprisonment for disobedience," he asked, "if the several courts could bandy him from pillar to post, keep him constantly trudging from north to south and east to west, and withdraw him entirely from his constitutional duties?" Jefferson was convinced that such judicial compulsion would be contrary to the intention of the Constitution that each branch should be independent of the others.[50]

General Wilkinson finally made his appearance before the grand jury on June 15 and during fours days of testimony made several damaging admissions but escaped being indicted for misprision of treason by a vote of 7 to 9. Randolph deplored that "the mammoth of iniquity escaped" and said that "Wilkinson is the only man that I ever saw who was from the bark to the very core a villain." Jefferson, on the other hand, wrote to the general that "your enemies have filled the public ear with slanders" and assured him that "no one is more sensible than myself of the injustice which has been aimed at you." [51]

After examining some fifty witnesses, the grand jury on June 24 indicted Burr for treason and misdemeanor. He was held for trial that began on August 3 and dragged on through the remainder of a hot Richmond August. [52] The crucial point in the trial came on August 20 after the prosecution had presented its testimony regarding events on Blennerhassett's Island. Throughout the proceedings the prosecution had been guided by the opinion of the Supreme Court ordering the release of Erich Bollman and Samuel Swartwout, arrested by Wilkinson as Burr's agents and sent to Washington for trial. In that decision Marshall had written that "if a body of men be actually assembled, for the purpose of effecting by force a treasonable purpose, all those who perform any part, however minute, or however remote from the scene of action, and who are actually leagued in the general conspiracy, are to be considered as traitors. But there must be an actual assembling of men, for treasonable purpose, to constitute a levying of war." The indictment of Burr for treason had been based on the assembling of a force on December 10, 1806, on Blennerhassett's Island in the Ohio River, where Burr admittedly was not present. The prosecution sought to prove the treasonable purpose of the assemblage and the involvement of Burr as the prime mover in procuring the assemblage. As the prosecution moved beyond the events on Blennerhassett's Island to connect Burr with them, the defense objected to the presentation of collateral evidence not relating directly to the overt act, which the defense claimed had not been demonstrated. The trial was then diverted from the taking of testimony to a debate on the defense's motion to arrest the evidence. [53]

On August 31 the chief justice read his lengthy decision on the defense motion and concluded, "No testimony relative to the conduct or declarations of the prisoner elsewhere and subsequent to the transaction on Blennerhassett's island can be admitted; because such testimony, being in its nature merely corroborative and incompetent to prove the overt act itself, is irrelevant until there be proof of the overt act by two witnesses." Marshall's ruling halted the taking of evidence, and he instructed the jury that they had now heard the opinion of the court on the law of the case. The next morning Hay announced that the prosecution had no further arguments to present. The jury then retired for twenty-five minutes and returned to report that "Aaron Burr is not proved to be guilty under this indictment by any evidence submitted to us. We therefore find him not guilty." When Burr's counsel objected to the wording of the verdict, Marshall allowed it to stand but ordered that "not guilty" be entered on the record. On the same day, a frustrated George Hay wrote to the president: "The opinion of the Chief Justice is too voluminous to be generally read, and on the great question about the overt act of levying war too obscure and perplexed to be understood. The *explanation* of the opinion of the Supreme Court in the Case of Bollman and Swartwout renders it very difficult to comprehend what was before perfectly intelligible."[54]

Earlier in the summer Jefferson had written to du Pont that "Burr's conspiracy has been one of the most flagitious of which history will very furnish an example. . . . Yet altho' there is not a man in the U.S. who is not satisfied of the depth of his guilt, such are the jealous provisions of our laws in favor of the accused, and against the accuser, that I question if he can be convicted." Still, the president professed that the whole affair confirmed the innate strength of the American republic in demonstrating the loyalty of the people to their government. Once the verdict was in, however, he was not so generous. "The scenes which have been acted at Richmond are such as have never before been exhibited in any country where all regard to public character has not yet been thrown off," he wrote to Wilkinson. "They are equivalent to a proclamation of impunity to every traitorous combination which may be formed to destroy the Union." He predicted that they would produce an amendment to the Constitution that while "keeping the judges independent of the Executive, will not leave them so, of the nation."[55] Jefferson viewed Marshall's rulings at the trial as politically motivated. Never carefully weighing Marshall's arguments, he offered no objective opinion of the rigid definition of treason that Marshall applied to the Constitution—a definition that would make treason trials rare in American history. More pressing matters occupied the president by the time Burr's trial ended. The nation had escaped from the intrigues of Aaron Burr, but a new crisis of greater proportions had erupted. The United States and Great Britain again faced each other in menacing postures that threatened the peace.

XX
Closing a Political Career

In the same week that Burr was indicted for treason in Richmond, the United States frigate *Chesapeake* was fired upon by the British ship *Leopard* off the Virginia capes. Jefferson learned the news on June 25, 1807, three days after the incident had set flame to the long-smoldering controversy over the British practice of impressment. That issue had been the critical one in the negotiations that Monroe and Pinkney had begun in London the previous year. Initially Jefferson had been sufficiently encouraged by the prospects of their success to ask Congress to suspend the effective date of the nonimportation act against England, and Congress extended it to July 1, 1807.[1] But the president's early optimism was unjustified. When the text of the Monroe-Pinkney treaty reached him on the eve of the adjournment of the Ninth Congress, Jefferson was so displeased with it that he did not submit it to the Senate for consideration. Having decided in advance in the cabinet that the treaty would be unacceptable if it contained no agreement regarding impressment, the president saw no reason to seek the advice of the Senate after Monroe and Pinkney failed to get the British to yield on that key issue.[2]

With Napoleon at the height of his power, the year 1807 was an inopportune moment to expect the British to give up a practice that they regarded as essential to maintaining supremacy on the seas. To the British, who recognized no right of expatriation, the ability to impress British subjects into military service was essential to man the Royal Navy. To Americans the British claim to a right to decide who were British citizens and to impress them into service—even if found on board American ships on the high seas—was an intolerable insult to American sovereignty. Neither side was without blame in the intensifying controversy. American citizens were recklesly impressed into the British navy, while deserters from British ships could easily obtain false papers in American ports and enlist aboard American ships.

In London, Monroe and Pinkney sensed the depth of the British struggle with Napoleon, which was not well understood across the Atlantic, and believed that they had won all the concessions the British would make. In a separate note accompanying the treaty, the British promised to take the strictest care to safeguard American citizens, and the American envoys were hopeful that the United States would win in practice what the British were not willing to concede in principle. If the American diplomats in London had a better understanding of British priorities than their superiors in Washington, the British minister in Washington, David Erskine (who had replaced Anthony Merry), likewise had a clearer understanding of the American position than his superiors in London. Reporting to the foreign secretary after a conversation with Madison in February, 1807, Erskine said that "all the parties in this country take a warm interest on the point of non-impressment of sailors (claimed as British) out of American ships on the high seas, and . . . I am persuaded that no cordiality can be expected from this country whilst it is deemed necessary to His Majesty to enforce that right."[3]

That Erskine was correct about American feelings in regard to impressment was demonstrated after the crippled *Chesapeake* returned to Hampton Roads with shattered masts, tattered sails, and its battered hull filling with water. When the story of the attack by the *Leopard* was told and it was learned that the unprepared *Chesapeake* had been bombarded into striking its flag and allowing a British boarding party to carry off four sailors, the public outcry was intense. Whether the sailors taken were deserters from the Royal Navy was not the issue—the *Chesapeake* was a ship of the United States Navy, leaving its own shores for duty in the Mediterranean. American honor and sovereignty had been rudely violated. When three dead and eighteen wounded sailors were carried from the *Chesapeake*, emotions ran high in Hampton, where a mob destroyed two hundred water casks ready for transfer to the British squadron anchored in Lynnhaven Bay. As the news spread, angry citizens at public meetings in towns and cities throughout the land expressed their anger in spirited resolutions. "Such an assemblage of people I never saw," reported former Congressman Michael Leib in describing a gathering in Philadelphia, where resolutions were adopted with unaccustomed unanimity. Everywhere party divisions seemed to be forgotten. "There is no distinction permitted but between Englishman and American," exclaimed a Virginian who participated in the adoption of resolutions in Staunton after a meeting "full of indignation at the outrage." Attorney General Caesar A. Rodney, waiting for the cabinet to assemble to decide the course of action, said that the attack on the *Chesapeake* "has excited the spirit of 76 and the whole country is literally in arms."[4]

President Jefferson was calmer than most of his fellow citizens when he received the unexpected report of the attack. In the absence of Treasury Secretary Gallatin and Secretary of War Dearborn, he delayed responding until he could assemble his advisers. Summoning them to return to Washington immediately, he began working with Madison on drafting a presidential proclamation to lay before the cabinet as soon as possible.[5] "Whether the outrage is a proper cause of war," he thought, was for Congress to decide. It was the administration's duty not to commit the legislature by doing anything that would have to be retracted. However, the executive could exercise its powers to prevent future insults in American harbors and to claim satisfaction for past acts. "This will leave Congress free to decide whether war is the most efficacious mode of redress in our case, or whether, having taught so many other useful lessons to Europe, we may not add that of showing them that there are peaceable means of repressing injustice, by making it the interest of the aggressor to do what is just, and abstain from future wrong."[6] The implication of this private communication to the governor of Virginia, whose state faced the most serious threat of further British assault, was that the president favored pursuing peaceful means of obtaining redress.[7]

Assembling on July 2, the cabinet approved a presidential proclamation ordering all armed English vessels out of American ports and decided to send the schooner *Revenge* to England immediately with instructions for Monroe to demand satisfaction for the attack. The American minister was to demand a disavowal of the act and of the principle of searching public armed vessels, the restoration of the men taken, and the recall of Vice-Admiral Sir George Berkeley, who had issued the orders for the action.[8] Secretary of the Navy Smith, arguing that the British had already begun a de facto war against the United States, urged that Congress be called into session immediately. He got support from Gallatin and continued to press it upon the president, who was also under pressure from outside his cabinet to summon the Congress. Meeting four times within the week, the cabinet rejected an immediate call of Congress but agreed to an early call for October 26, unless events dictated more urgent action. Meanwhile the cabinet requested the governors to have their respective quotas of one hundred thousand militia in readiness and asked the governor of Virginia to order into active service such portion of that state's militia as necessary to defend Norfolk and the surrounding area.[9]

Jefferson considered these measures sufficient to put the country in a state of preparedness and allow American merchants time to call in their ships and seamen before hostilities might begin. While giving England a chance to redress the wrong before Congress made the decision for peace or war, he also wanted to keep the war fever alive in the United States until satisfaction had been obtained. "Altho' we demand of England what is merely of right, reparation for the past, security for the future, yet as their pride will possibly, nay probably, prevent their yielding them to the extent we shall require, my opinion is, that the public mind, which I believe is made up for war, should maintain itself at that point. They have often enough, God knows, given us cause of war before, but it has been on points which would not have united the nation. But now they have touched a chord which vibrates in every heart. Now then is the time to settle the old and the new."[10] Jefferson correctly judged the popular support for war in July, 1807, but he misjudged the likelihood of public feeling maintaining itself at the same bellicose level for months.

By the end of July, Jefferson was convinced that the British squadron in the Chesapeake was not going to attack Norfolk or commit further hostilities other than remaining in American waters in defiance of his proclamation, until orders arrived from England. He thus authorized the discharge of the militia that had been called into service at Norfolk, and after being satisfied that the necessary measures were under way for the defense of New York and other vulnerable coastal points, he set out for Monticello on August 1 to escape the sickly season that he so much feared. The postmaster general set up a special express mail, and the president spent much of August and September in correspondence with Secretary of War Dearborn, who remained in Washington through most of August, and with other members of his cabinet who had made their escape from Washington. After issuing a call for Congress to convene on October 26, he resisted pressures for an earlier date on the ground that the legislature would be unable to act until an answer was received from England. "In the meanwhile," he said, "we are making every preparation which could be made were they in session."[11]

Jefferson's reference to "reparation for the past, security for the future" and to settling old and new grievances against England

must be understood in relation to the instructions to Monroe prepared by the secretary of state with the president's collaboration
and completed on July 6, 1807. Those instructions went further
than Jefferson indicated in his notes on the cabinet meeting of July
2 and tied the settlement of the *Chesapeake* crisis to the settlement of
the impressment issue. Besides being instructed to demand disavowal of British actions in the *Chesapeake* incident, Monroe was advised that "as a security for the future, an entire abolition of im-
pressments from vessels under the flag of the United States, if not
already arranged, is also to make an indispensable part of the satisfaction." The *Revenge*, carrying these instructions to Monroe, did
not sail until mid-July. Meanwhile, learning of the attack before receiving his orders, Monroe made a premature and ill-advised protest that allowed Foreign Secretary George Canning to take the offensive. Jefferson received Monroe's report on these developments
in late September while still at Monticello. Writing before the *Revenge* had reached England, Monroe enclosed copies of his exchange with Canning in which the foreign secretary said that "His
Majesty neither does nor has it at any time maintained the pretension of a right to search ships of war, in the national service of any
state, for deserters."[12] While this appeared to offer satisfaction for
the *Chesapeake* attack, Madison observed to the president that "the
British government renounces the pretension to search ships of
war for deserters; but employs words which may possibly be meant
to qualify the renunciation, or at least to quibble away the proposed
atonement." Monroe pointed to the harsh tone of Canning's letter
and reported a strong party in England composed of shipowners,
the navy, East and West India merchants, and certain powerful
political characters who favored war with the United States. "So
powerful is this combination," Monroe concluded, "that it is most
certain that nothing can be obtained on any point but what may be
extorted by necessity."[13]

As Jefferson in the isolation of Monticello reflected on the situation of the United States in late summer of 1807, he too came to the
conclusion that Britain was not likely to meet American demands.
Resigning himself to the probability of war, he began to speculate
on how such a war might be used to gain his goal of acquiring the
Floridas. He suggested to Madison that the United States might demand the payment of spoliation claims from Spain and seize the
Floridas if they were not paid. "I had rather have war against Spain
than not, if we go to war against England," he told the secretary of
state. "Our southern defensive force can take the Floridas, volun-

teers for a Mexican army will flock to our standard, and a rich
pabulum will be offered to our privateers in the plunder of their
commerce and coasts. Probably Cuba would add itself to our con
federation." This was hardly the language of a pacifist. And as he
reflected on public sentiment, which he felt had never been more
excited since the battle of Lexington, his anti-British feelings rose
"I never expected to be under the necessity of wishing success to
Buonaparte," he wrote privately. "But the English being equally ty
rannical at sea as he is on land, and that tyranny bearing on us in
every point of either honor or interest, I say 'down with England
and as what Buonaparte is then to do to us, let us trust to the chap
ter of accidents. I cannot, with Anglomen, prefer a certain presen
evil to a future hypothetical one." [14]

With such speculations running through his mind as he walked
the grounds at Monticello, he received Monroe's first unpromising
report from London and the more discouraging news from Halifax
that court martial proceedings had been held against the four al
leged deserters removed from the *Chesapeake* and that one of them
Jenkin Ratford, had been hanged. Though even Madison acknowl
edged that Ratford was probably a British subject, both the presi
dent and the secretary of state regarded the British action as insult
ing, and it rendered impossible one of the unnegotiable American
demands for satisfaction. [15]

The initial British response increased the pessimism of the presi
dent and his secretary of state as they returned to the capital in Oc
tober to find a letter from David Humphreys, a former diploma
recently returned from London, who gave his opinion of the En
glish state of mind as being determined "to maintain the naval su
premacy or perish as a nation." He believed the British would sat
isfy American demands to refrain from searching ships of war, bu
he saw no hope that they would consent to the American insistence
that the American flag protected merchant ships from searches.
That was precisely what Jefferson and Madison were demanding

Whether because of discouraging reports, his own rising Anglo
phobia, or his belief that a war spirit must be maintained in the
United States until Britain gave satisfaction, Jefferson's draft of hi
annual message for the opening of Congress was far more bellig
erent in tone than anything that he had said publicly since the crisi
began. When Gallatin read it, he said that it seemed to be "rather in
the shape of a manifesto issued against Great Britain on the eve o
a war, than such as the existing undecided state of affairs seems t
require." In a similar vein, Navy Secretary Smith told the president

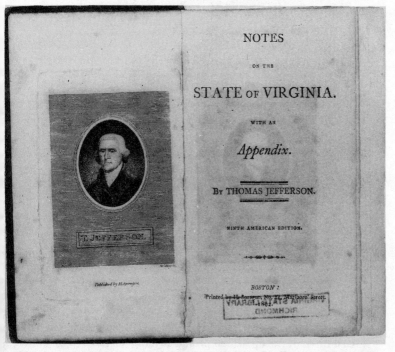

Th: Jefferson requests the favour of The Honble. Genl. Mattoon to dine with him the day after tomorrow ———— at half after three, or at whatever later hour the house may rise.

Monday Feb. 1st 1802.

The favour of an answer is asked.

Invitation to dinner at the President's House. Jefferson's invitation to Representative Ebenezer Mattoon of Massachusetts, February 1, 1802.
Broadsides Collection, Rare Book Division, Library of Congress

NOTES

ON THE

STATE OF VIRGINIA.

WITH AN

Appendix.

By THOMAS JEFFERSON.

NINTH AMERICAN EDITION.

BOSTON :
Printed by H. Sprague, No. 44, Marlboro' Street.
1802.

T. JEFFERSON.

Published by H. Sprague.

Title page and frontispiece of the 1802 edition of Jefferson's *Notes on the State of Virginia*
Courtesy Virginia State Library, Richmond

Profile of Jefferson by Charles-Balthazar-Julien Févret de Saint-Mémin.
Drawn from life using a physiognotrace, Washington, 1804.

Courtesy Worcester Art Museum, Worcester, Massachusetts

Engraving of Jefferson by David Edwin, 1809. From a drawing by William
Russell Birch of the medallion profile of Jefferson painted by Gilbert
Stuart in 1805. Jefferson himself said that this profile was the best that
had ever been taken of him.

Courtesy Manuscripts Department, University of Virginia Library

THE JEFFERSON

Engraving by Saint-Mémin of his drawing of Jefferson taken in 1804 (opposite page). Saint-Mémin offered this small print for sale to the public on the eve of Jefferson's second inaugural.

Courtesy Rare Book Room, Princeton University Library

Jefferson as president. Painted by Gilbert Stuart for James Madison from
a sitting in 1805. Madison had the portrait in his possession by 1806.

Courtesy Colonial Williamsburg Foundation

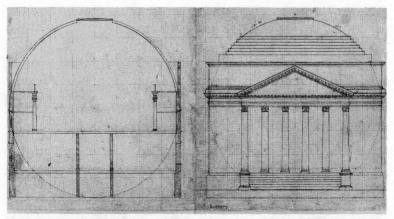

Jefferson's drawings for the Rotunda of the University of Virginia, from about 1821

Thomas Jefferson Papers, University of Virginia Library

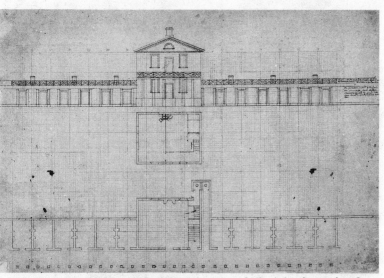

Jefferson's study for Pavilion VII, University of Virginia, drawn in 1817

Thomas Jefferson Papers, University of Virginia Library

The University of Virginia. Engraving by Benjamin Tanner, published on the 1827 Böye map of Virginia.

Courtesy Manuscripts Department, University of Virginia Library

could the dead feel any interest in Monu
-ments or other remembrances of them, when, as
Anacreon says: Ὀλίγη δὲ κεισομεσθα
Κόνις, ὀστεων λυθεντων
the following would be to my Manes the most
gratifying.
On the grave
a plain die or cube of 3.f without any
mouldings, surmounted by an Obelisk
of 6.f. height, each of a single stone:
on the faces of the Obelisk the following
inscription, & not a word more
"Here was buried
Thomas Jefferson
Author of the Declaration of American Independance
of the Statute of Virginia for religious freedom
& Father of the University of Virginia."
because by these, as testimonials that I have lived, I wish most to
be remembered. to be of the coarse stone of which
my columns are made, that no one might be tempted
hereafter to destroy it for the value of the materials.
my bust by Ciracchi, with the pedestal and truncated
column on which it stands, might be given to the University
if they would place it in the Dome room of the Rotunda.
on the Die of the Obelisk might be engraved
Born Apr. 2. 1743. O.S.
Died ———

Jefferson's design and inscription for his tombstone
Thomas Jefferson Papers, Manuscripts Division, Library of Congress

Jefferson at age seventy-eight. Painted from life by Thomas Sully, 1821.
Courtesy American Philosophical Society, Philadelphia

"As peace is our favorite object, as it is not intended to excite Congress to a declaration of war . . . I could wish the Message had less of the air of a Manifesto against the British government." [17] Even Secretary of War Dearborn, who was always the most reserved member of the cabinet in proposing alterations in the president's annual messages, thought the message contained some expressions stronger than necessary, indicating the intention of offensive operations. Gallatin, who regularly provided the most detailed critiques of the drafts of Jefferson's messages, told the president that he believed that Great Britain would go to war with the United States rather than meet American demands, and he thought it important to maintain the support of world and national opinion by not rushing into war before England had a chance to give satisfaction for the outrage on the *Chesapeake*. [18]

No notes by Madison on this message have been found, but it may be assumed that Jefferson and the secretary of state collaborated on the draft before it was circulated among the other members of the cabinet, for Madison was always the first officer to review the drafts of the president's messages. If this was the case, the chief foreign-policy makers were out of step with the rest of the cabinet and the country. Jefferson clearly sensed this and modified the tone and content of his message. Gallatin, who took the major credit for the alterations, confided to his wife that "the President's speech was originally more warlike than was necessary, but I succeeded in getting it neutralized; this between us; but it was lucky; for Congress is certainly peaceably disposed." [19]

If Jefferson, who had tried to restrain war fever in July, returned to Washington convinced that war was the only course for the nation, he now found that the mood of the country had changed and that he must adjust his policies to the new conditions. Shortly after reaching Washington in October, he wrote Thomas Paine that "all the little circumstances coming to our knowledge are unfavorable to our wishes for peace." Reflecting on the withdrawal of Russia and Prussia from the war against Napoleon, he offered his opinion that the United States might "never again have so favorable a conjunction of circumstances" to settle the issue of impressment. But before a month had passed, Jefferson wrote several correspondents that "we are all pacifically inclined here, if anything comes from thence which will permit us to follow our inclinations." [20]

At the end of November, while the president was still awaiting the return of the *Revenge* from England, Erskine received dispatches from London reporting Canning's response to Monroe's demands, and he showed Jefferson and Madison copies of the letters exchanged. Jefferson judged Canning's response to be "unfriendly, proud, and harsh" and felt that it offered little more than a disavowal of having ordered the attack on the *Chesapeake*. A piece published in the *National Intelligencer* that could have come only from the administration declared, "The letter is in a style more haughty than conciliatory, and calculated rather to increase than lessen the sentiment of indignation so generally excited by the unprincipled conduct of Great Britain towards neutrals generally, and particularly towards the United States." A few days later Jefferson received a duplicate set of the dispatches from Monroe, the originals of which were aboard the *Revenge*, and he sent them to be read behind closed doors in both houses of Congress.[21] These papers, which did not include the instructions to Monroe that would be withheld from Congress for several more months, showed that the negotiations in London had broken down and that the clever Canning had managed to transfer them to America. Canning, in replying to Monroe's demands for satisfaction, had admitted that British naval officers had committed an unauthorized hostile act and that the United States was entitled to reparation. But claiming that the United States also was guilty of hostile acts, he argued that these must be considered before the reparation could be determined. He specifically named the president's proclamation as one such act and implied that the enlistment of British deserters was another. While indicating his willingness to give further consideration to matters relating to the *Chesapeake* incident, he denied that impressment was one of them. Because Monroe had been instructed not to separate the two issues, their negotiations were thus terminated. But seizing upon Monroe's suggestion—made as instructed—that a special envoy carry the British apology and reparation to America, Canning announced that a special envoy would be sent to enter into negotiations relating to the *Chesapeake*.[22] The administration's effort to tie the impressment issue with the *Chesapeake* affair had failed and with it the effort to obtain prompt satisfaction for the outrage.

Jefferson told his son-in-law Thomas Mann Randolph, Jr., after learning of the failure of Monroe's negotiations, that Congress would have to decide between "War, Embargo or Nothing," but he gave Congress no guidance when he submitted the dispatches from Monroe on December 8. By closing his brief message of transmittal with a reference to continuing negotiations, the president left the legislators with the impression that there was no urgent need for action.[23] But ten days later the president came back to Congress with additional communications that showed, he said, "the great and increasing dangers with which our vessels, our seamen, and merchandise, are threatened on the high seas and elsewhere, from the belligerent powers of Europe." He now proposed action by recommending an embargo on the departure of all American vessels from the ports of the United States.[24]

The change in administration policy can be explained by several major developments that swallowed up the *Chesapeake* issue in the broader question of neutral trade. Suddenly, as the documents Jefferson sent to Congress showed, American commerce was faced with new threats from both England and France. On October 16, 1807, King George III issued a proclamation requiring all British naval officers to enforce impressment rigorously over neutral merchant vessels. Along with a copy of this proclamation, the president supplied Congress with documents providing evidence that Napoleon's Berlin decree of November, 1806, proclaiming a blockade of Great Britain, was now being applied to vessels of the United States. By this time he had also heard of the British response to French actions: the new orders-in-council of November 11, 1807, prohibiting trade with all continental ports from which the British flag was excluded and declaring that all vessels bound for open ports on the Continent must pass through British ports, pay taxes, and secure clearance. Jefferson did not include these orders with his message of December 18, but the news of them had been reported in the Philadelphia *Aurora* on December 17, and all evidence indicates that he knew of this latest British action at the time of the cabinet deliberations on December 17.[25]

Unfortunately, no notes such as Jefferson kept on many cabinet meetings at critical moments survive to record the deliberations that preceded the recommendation of the embargo to Congress. The few extant papers show that the subject had been under discussion for several weeks in connection with the twice-postponed nonimportation act of 1806, which became effective on December 14, 1807, but the final decision for an embargo was hastily made on December 17. All the cabinet was present and unanimously concurred in the recommendation to Congress.[26] Gallatin soon had second thoughts, however, and sent the president a memorandum the first thing the next morning recommending changes before the proposal was sent to Congress. "An embargo for a limited time will at this moment be preferable in itself, and less objectionable in Congress," he told the president. "In every point of view, privations, sufferings, revenue, effect on the enemy, politics at home, etc., I prefer war to a permanent embargo." He went on to argue that "government prohibitions do always more mischief than had been calculated" and concluded that "the measure being a doubtful policy, and hastily adopted on the first view of our foreign intelligence, I think we had better recommend it with modifications." Immediately upon receiving Gallatin's note, Jefferson called him to his office so that they could discuss his message before it left his hands.[27] But no change was made in the recommendation to Congress, which had been drafted by Madison as a substitute for a less specific text prepared by Jefferson.[28]

Madison's drafting of the message, brief though it was, and Gallatin's questioning the decision after the cabinet had acted suggest that the president had not provided the cabinet with the clear sense of direction he normally gave and that Madison, who pushed for immediate action, was the embargo's strongest advocate. This is not surprising. Since his days in Congress, Madison had been a strong proponent of commercial retaliation. Jefferson, too, had favored such tactics, and at the beginning of the *Chesapeake* crisis he seemed inclined toward some type of peaceful coercion rather than war. But the early draft of his message for the opening of Congress pointed more toward war than economic retaliation. There is nothing in the record to suggest that Jefferson seized the opportunity to try an experiment in economic coercion. Indeed, he appears to have regarded the embargo, at least at the outset, as more precautionary than coercive.[29] Nothing in Jefferson's public or private papers indicates that he initially expected the embargo to coerce England into meeting American demands.

Just what Congress expected the embargo to accomplish is not much clearer than the administration's aims, but both houses acted with unaccustomed alacrity. Senator John Quincy Adams recorded that Senator Samuel Smith, who headed the committee on the president's address, said that the president wanted the measure to aid in the negotiations with George Rose, the British envoy being sent over for the *Chesapeake* talks. Smith also suggested that it might lead to the repeal of the nonimportation act. Adams suspected there were other reasons not revealed by Smith, but he supported the measure as did the entire committee. On the same day that the president's message was read, the Senate suspended its rules and passed a bill for a general embargo by a vote of 22 to 6. Senator Samuel L. Mitchill, who voted with the majority, said that "in a choice of evils an Embargo was the least."[30] Three days later the House passed the measure by a vote of 82 to 44. When he signed the bill the next day, Jefferson observed that half of the opposition vote came from the Federalists, one-fourth from the dissident Randolph Republicans ("the little band," he called them), and the other fourth from Republicans "happening to take up mistaken views of the subject."[31] The president was too quick in discounting opposition to the embargo, and such early doubts about the wisdom of the measure would grow to haunt him in the months ahead.

Initially some members of Congress held high hopes for the success of the embargo. Congressman George W. Campbell told his Tennessee constituents that though it would be felt severely by Americans, it would work greater hardships on England and France. "We may complain because we cannot sell for a good price our surplus provisions and other productions; they will *suffer* because they cannot procure a sufficient quantity of those articles to subsist upon—*to support life*." He predicted that the United States would win recognition of its rights if the American people showed their determination to support the embargo policy.[32] In a similar vein Joseph Desha wrote his Kentucky constituents that the embargo "will not only have the effect of securing our resources but of coercing our enemies to change that nefarious policy, which has driven our commerce from the seas." But from the outset of the embargo a Federalist minority protested that it would only help Napoleon.[33]

The crisis over neutral rights came at an unfortunate time in the cycle of American politics—the eve of a presidential election. Beginning in November, 1806, a wave of Republican party meetings throughout the country began passing resolutions and sending addresses to the president pleading that he not retire from office at the end of his second term.[34] State legislatures joined in the pleas, and in time nine states and one territory urged the president to serve four more years.[35] Although the appeals began before Jefferson issued his proclamation against the Burr conspiracy, they accelerated in the months immediately following. As the crisis with England intensified, new calls rose for him to remain in office. Divisions in Republican ranks more than national crises provided the initial inspiration for the petitions, but the appeals took on increased momentum and broader support as threats to the Union and to peace unfolded. Thomas Leiper, a leading Pennsylvania Republican, wrote Jefferson during the *Chesapeake* crisis: "As matters and things now stand you cannot by any means refuse serving again as President. . . . The voice of the people were never so strong in your favour as at present." [36]

Not until December, 1807, when new movements were developing to pressure him to seek a third term, did Jefferson publicly reply to the addresses that had reached him during the preceding year. He then limited his replies to those from state legislatures, writing to each that he considered it as much his duty to lay down his charge at a proper time as to have borne it faithfully. If neither the Constitution nor practice fixed the term of the presidency, he feared the office would become one for life. "I should unwillingly be the person who, disregarding the sound precedent set by an illustrious predecessor, should furnish the first example of prolongation beyond the second term of office." Applauding the president's statement, editor Thomas Ritchie wrote in the Richmond *Enquirer* that had Jefferson consented to serve because of the emergency, a "less virtuous and more ambitious" successor might find it easy "to seize upon any lowering speck in the distant horizon, perhaps to conjure up an imaginary danger, that he might shield his ambition under a similar excuse. Mr. Jefferson's retirement wrests this plausible pretext from the hands of his successors. They will see from his example, that no crisis, however fruitful in danger or in war *can* justify the prolongation of their term of office." [37]

In taking himself irrevocably out of the contest, Jefferson removed the last restraints on the competition that was already well under way to succeed him. While Congress marked time waiting for the news from England in November, 1807, Madison was busy giving dinners and, in Senator Mitchill's view, making "generous displays" to the members. With an attractive wife to support his pretensions, Madison, in Mitchill's judgment, was well ahead of Vice-President Clinton in pursuit of the caucus nomination. [38] Busy promoting Monroe, then on his way home from England, was John Randolph, who was meeting with some success in gathering support for his candidate in Virginia. In describing the maneuvering for the presidency, Mitchill observed that Jefferson was already beginning to move his belongings to Virginia—an observation that may help to explain Jefferson's hesitant leadership in putting forward the embargo.

The embargo began with substantial public support, and the ever optimistic president even hoped that if the United States bought more time, events in Europe might still rescue the nation from its dilemma. Assuming as usual that time was on the side of the United

States, he thought the wisest policy was for the United States to isolate itself from "the present paroxysm of the insanity of Europe."[39] If he hoped that the embargo would aid Madison in his negotiations with George Rose, he was disappointed. By the end of February, 1808, those negotiations had broken down without accomplishing anything. Continuing to regard the embargo as a temporary policy, Jefferson told Madison in March that he took the universal opinion to be that "war will become preferable to continuance of the embargo after a certain time." He thought that Congress at its next session would have to decide between the embargo and war. Meanwhile, he proposed that both Britain and France be asked to lift all their decrees and orders as applied to neutrals and be given to understand that if one did and the other did not, the United States would declare war on the refuser. By June, Jefferson was saying that if the embargo was abandoned before the repeal of the orders-in-council, "we must abandon it only for a state of war. The day is not distant, when that will be preferable to a longer continuance of the embargo."[40]

The problem of the embargo dominated Jefferson's last year in office like no other issue of his presidency. While it is not necessary to follow Jefferson month by month through this travail, it is important to recognize its effects on the president and his leadership. The embargo increasingly claimed his attention in matters of administration and enforcement and led him to adopt policies of government control inconsistent with his basic philosophy of government. Yet, surprisingly, Jefferson never presented the case for the embargo either to the Congress or to the American people. As he became more and more committed to the policy, it became less a measure of precaution and more a system of coercion. Problems of enforcing the hastily drawn embargo act became obvious almost immediately, and Congress responded to the administration's requests to strengthen its enforcement by giving the president unprecedented powers to exercise control over the economic affairs of individual Americans. Dumas Malone saw Jefferson as "so obsessed with the immediate problem of making the embargo work as to be unmindful of republican theory and also of certain basic facts of human nature."[41]

As difficulties in enforcing the embargo mounted, Gallatin, whose department bore the principal responsibility of implementing the act, wrote the president from New York at the end of July that if the embargo was to be continued, more stringent enforcement would be required. He recommended that not a single vessel be permitted to move without special permission of the executive and that collectors be empowered to seize property and prevent the departure of vessels without being liable to personal suits. "I am sensible that such arbitrary powers are equally dangerous and odious," Gallatin wrote. "But a restrictive measure of the nature of the embargo applied to a nation under such circumstances as the United States cannot be enforced without the assistance of means as strong as the measure itself." His conclusion was that "Congress must either invest the Executive with the most arbitrary powers and sufficient force to carry the embargo into effect, or give it up altogether."[42] Though Jefferson did not specifically endorse the treasury secretary's proposals, he supported the main thrust of Gallatin's argument. "This embargo law is certainly the most embarrassing one we have ever had to execute," he replied from Monticello. "I did not expect a crop of so sudden and rank growth of fraud and open opposition by force could have grown up in the U.S. I am satisfied with you that if orders and decrees are not repealed, and a continuance of the embargo is preferred to war (which sentiment is universal here) Congress must legalize all *means* which may be necessary to obtain it's *end*."[43]

Still, Jefferson did not give up hope that the embargo would produce results and eagerly seized upon a report from Pinkney in London of a pending conference with Canning as a hopeful sign. In fact, he went so far as to alert the war and navy secretaries to keep an eye to the possible invasion of the Floridas in stationing troops and vessels, explaining, "Should England make up with us, while Bonaparte continues at war with Spain, a moment may occur when we may without danger of commitment with either France or England seize to our own limits of Louisiana as of right, and the residue of the Floridas as reprisal for spoliations."[44] This was wishful thinking inspired by his Florida obsession, not a likely development. Instead of favorable dispatches from London, Jefferson found himself inundated with petitions from his fellow citizens seeking repeal of the embargo. In a two-week period in late August and early September, he replied to petitions from thirty-eight towns and sent off instructions to Samuel Harrison Smith in Washington to prepare printed form letters so that he could keep up with the task of replying.[45] As counterpetitions also began to arrive, he had another form printed to respond to them. By December, the president would record the receipt of 199 petitions against the embargo and 46 counterpetitions.[46]

When Jefferson sent his eighth and last annual message to Congress on November 8, 1808, he reviewed the lack of success in getting the belligerent powers of Europe to modify or withdraw their orders and decrees. In searching for something favorable to say about the embargo, he pointed out that it had saved American seamen and property from loss and given the United States time to prepare its defenses, but he declined to express any opinion on the continuance of the controversial measure, indicating that it rested with the wisdom of Congress to decide what course to follow.[47]

Although not all presidential electors had been chosen by the time Jefferson sent his message to Congress, the unofficial returns tallied by Republican congressmen returning to Washington showed that Madison would be the next president of the United States. Madison had been Jefferson's choice as his successor, but the president had carefully refrained from participating in the campaign. While Madison received the nomination of the Republican congressional caucus, some supporters of both George Clinton and James Monroe refused to give up their candidates. Without Jefferson heading the Republican ticket and with the embargo as a divisive issue, Republican party unity was severely tested, but in the end Madison won a respectable victory with 122 electoral votes to 47 for Federalist Charles C. Pinckney and 6 for George Clinton.[48] This was not as impressive as Jefferson's trouncing of Pinckney, 162 to 14, in 1804, but it enabled Jefferson to leave the presidency with the Republican party still in control of the government and his closest political collaborator as president.

With the presidential office passing from Jefferson to his secretary of state, the transition of power should hardly have been expected to cause problems. Even though the nation was divided over the embargo and uncertain as to its future course, the longtime cooperation of Jefferson and Madison might be expected to continue to provide the leadership that had characterized Jefferson's administration. This was not the case. Before Congress assembled, Jefferson had determined that he would not recommend to Congress the choice between the embargo, war, or submission, which he said were the only alternatives. "On this occasion, I think it is fair to leave to those who are to act on them, the decisions they prefer, being to be myself but a spectator," he explained. "I should not feel justified in directing measures which those who are to execute them would disapprove." This left Congress in confusion. "The President gives no opinion as to the measures that ought to be adopted," Nathaniel Macon protested. "It is not known whether he be for war or peace." The cabinet also was rudderless and appealed to the president to give Congress direction. "Both Mr. Madison and myself concur in opinion," Gallatin wrote the president, "that, considering the temper of the Legislature, or rather of its members, it would be eligible to point out to them some precise and distinct course." Gallatin confessed that they might not all agree on that course and that he himself was still undecided between enforcing the embargo and war. "But I think that we must (or rather you must) decide the question absolutely, so that we may point out a decisive course either way to our friends."[49]

Jefferson, however, continued to resist making the decision. "I think it fair that my successor should now originate those measures which he will be charged with the execution and responsibility, and that it is my duty to clothe them with the forms of authority," he told Monroe in late January, 1809, by which time Congress had passed an embargo enforcement act but was already considering a change of course.[50] A few days later the House took the first steps toward repealing the embargo, which act Jefferson would sign before leaving office.

Jefferson's abdication of leadership during his last months as president can be explained in part by his resentment of President Adams, who at the end of his presidency filled offices and signed bills that would inhibit his successor. Jefferson himself in December, 1808, ceased filling any vacancies that could be put off until March 4.[51] But this was inadequate justification for his premature retirement from leadership in a government that was to remain under the control of many of the same people and the same political party, and it detracts from the record of his presidency. But it cannot deny to Jefferson the credit for providing strong executive leadership for Congress and the nation during most of his years in office. Addressing his constituents in Tennessee on the eve of Jefferson's retirement, Congressman John Rhea must have expressed the sentiments of many of the president's admirers.

> On the third day of next March the administration of Thomas Jefferson, president of the United States, after a duration of eight years, will terminate. During that term of time the United States (certain disagreeable occurrences arising from exterior relations notwithstanding) have been in possession of national happiness and prosperity, unexampled in the annals of nations. In that term of time, more than in any of the same duration, it hath been manifested that a government can be administered agreeably to, and consistent with the principles of moral rectitude. In that term of time, if there had been no hindrance arising from relations of the United States with foreign powers, and from the conduct of foreign powers, (particularly Great Britain) a fair experiment, so long desired, might have been made, how near to perfection a government founded on reason could be

made to approximate. To make the people of the United States respectable, happy, great and independent as possible, was the object of the administration of Mr. Jefferson.[52]

As Jefferson's political career came to an end, he could take pride that there were those like John Rhea who understood his commitment to "a government founded on reason." The pursuit of reason that had guided his life did not always provide answers to every specific problem, but on fundamental questions it served him well, and he would leave government with his faith in reason undiminished.

Ever since publicly announcing his determination to retire at the end of his second term, Jefferson had been looking forward to that day. Over a year before he would finish his term, he confided to Monroe, "My longings for retirement are so strong, that I with difficulty encounter the daily drudgeries of my duty." As the final day approached, he repeatedly expressed his growing feeling of relief. "Five weeks more will relieve me from a drudgery to which I am no longer equal, and restore me to a scene of tranquillity, amidst my family and friends, more congenial to my age and natural inclinations." Finally, on next to his last full day in office, he could write: "Within a few days I retire to my family, my books and farms. . . . Never did a prisoner, released from his chains, feel such relief as I shall on shaking off the shackles of power."[53] The agony of the embargo increased Jefferson's discontent during his final year in office, and the pull of Monticello, which had always been great, was never stronger.

On March 4, 1809, Jefferson rode up Pennsylvania Avenue with his grandson Thomas Jefferson Randolph to the Capitol to witness the inauguration of his successor. Sitting beside Madison on the dais of the newly completed hall of the House of Representatives, he looked out over a crowded audience in which, Mrs. Samuel Harrison Smith observed, "the high and low were promiscuously blended on the floor and in the galleries." Frances Few, the nineteen-year-old niece of Mrs. Albert Gallatin, visiting from New York, said it was the most numerous assembly she had ever seen and noted that "Mr. Jefferson appeared one of the most happy among this concourse of people."[54]

As he watched Chief Justice Marshall administer the oath of office to his successor, the retiring president must have thought back to his own first inaugural and reflected on the events and the changes that had since transpired. He could feel satisfied that he had been largely successful in carrying out the promises of his in-

320 IN PURSUIT OF REASON

augural address in giving a new direction to domestic affairs and putting the Republic on a more republican tack, but he could only regret that he had not ensured "peace, commerce, and honest friendship with all nations." He could lift his head with pride if he thought of his young aide Meriwether Lewis, who had carried his first annual message to the Congress and had gone on to lead the most remarkable and successful expedition in the history of North America, exploring the Missouri River to its distant source, crossing the Rocky Mountains to the Pacific, and retraversing the continent to St. Louis. In retirement the intellectually curious president would have time to assimilate the vast amount of geographical, scientific, and other information that Lewis and Clark had brought back. He had learned of their arrival in St. Louis in late October, 1806, a month after they reached the banks of the Mississippi. But before Lewis reached Washington in late December, Jefferson was so distracted by the unfolding Burr conspiracy that he could not fully revel in the triumph. Now he could anticipate a more careful study of their findings, as he carried back to Monticello some of the specimens they had brought him. If thoughts of Lewis and Clark flashed through his mind with visions of the vast expanse of land that they had revealed, he could rest confident that the sparsely settled nation of seven million would have room for expansion for generations that stretched far beyond his ability to imagine. The Louisiana Purchase had assured the continuance of the "empire for liberty."

The retiring president's countenance must have fallen if he reflected on how the events in Europe, which had worked to such advantage for his country during his first years in office, had had the opposite effect during his second term. How rewarding it would have been to be leaving office having demonstrated that patience and economic coercion might be successfully substituted for war. He must have had second thoughts about how far his administration had gone in enforcing the embargo and pondered the unhappy ending the embargo's failure had given to his long public career. If he reflected on things not done, he must have regretted that the foreign difficulties of the past two years had prevented him from ending his presidential term by implementing the forward-looking program that he had outlined in his annual message of 1806—a message soon overshadowed by the uncertainties of the Burr conspiracy. In the message of 1806 he had pointed to the reduction of the national debt and a growing surplus of revenues and encouraged Congress to consider how future revenues (all from custom duties) might be employed. He suggested their application,

after the appropriate constitutional amendment, "to the great purposes of the public education, roads, rivers, canals, and such other
objects of public improvement as it may be thought proper to add
to the constitutional enumeration of federal powers."[55] But that
prospect had been shattered by "the insanity of Europe," and he
was leaving office still unsure whether there would be peace
or war.

If he thought about the crowds along Pennsylvania Avenue that
he had seen on his ride to the Capitol, he may not have estimated
them as "thousands and thousands of people," as did Mrs. Smith,
but he could not but have been pleased with the steady growth of
the new city and could now be satisfied that it would remain the
capital of the Republic. Indeed, earlier that day in drafting a reply
to an address from the citizens of Washington—one of the many
messages of appreciation he received upon his retirement—he had
used the term "national metropolis." And in words that harkened
back to his address to his Albemarle neighbors nearly two decades
earlier upon leaving to join the new government under the Constitution, Jefferson reminded his Washington neighbors of the destiny of "this solitary republic of the world, the only monument of
human rights, and the sole depository of the sacred fire of freedom
and self-government, from hence it is to be lighted up in other regions of the earth, if other regions of the earth shall ever become
susceptible of its benign influence."[56]

After the inauguration, the retiring president was among the
large number of well-wishers who went to call at the Madisons'
home. Then he returned to the President's House to accept fare-
wells. In the evening he attended Madison's inaugural ball, where
Mrs. Smith, whose heart sank at the thought that Jefferson was
leaving Washington, described him as being in high spirits and
beaming with joy. But it was a joy dampened by the regret, as he
had recently told the General Assembly of Virginia, that he had not
left the nation assured of continued peace.[57] Ending a political career that had spanned forty years, Jefferson mused: "Nature intended me for the tranquil pursuits of science, by rendering them
my supreme delight. But the enormities of the times in which I
have lived have forced me to take a part in resisting them, and to
commit myself on the boisterous ocean of political passions."[58] Now
that tempestuous voyage was over, and he would happily return to
his Virginia mountaintop, never again to leave his native state and
never to venture far from his beloved Monticello.

XXI
The Sage of Monticello

Jefferson's Albemarle County neighbors wanted to meet the ex-president on the road home and escort him into Charlottesville—"Not only the militia companies but the body of the people," his daughter Martha informed him. "They wish it as the last opportunity they can have of giving you a public testimony of their respect and affection." Having never liked ceremonies or military escorts, Jefferson declined the tribute, explaining that the task of gathering his papers and belongings and vacating the President's House made it impossible to fix the date of his return. "It is a sufficient happiness to me to know that my fellow citizens of the county generally entertain for me the kind sentiments which have prompted this proposition, without giving to so many the trouble of leaving their homes to meet a single individual. . . . I can say with truth that my return to them will make me happier than I have been since I left them." [1]

While clearing up his paper work and packing his belongings, Jefferson paid his bills, settled his accounts, sold a carriage, and on his last day in Washington deposited in the Bank of the United States a warrant for $1,148, the balance due him on his account while minister to France, from which he had returned twenty years earlier. After sending ahead wagons loaded with his possessions, he left Washington on March 11 and arrived at Monticello on March 15, after a very fatiguing journey. Finding the roads excessively bad—though he said he had seen them worse—he rode the last three days on horseback and "travelled eight hours through as disagreeable a snow storm as I was ever in." But his rapid recovery from the fatigue of the trip renewed his confidence in the state of his health. [2] A few months earlier, when he had been confined indoors for six weeks because of an abscessed tooth and burdened by the pressures of office, the sixty-five-year-old president had been concerned about his vigor. He saw a decline in his power of walking and thought his "memory not so faithful as it used to be." Now, after suffering no ill effects from his travel he felt "more confidence in my *vis vitae* than I had before entertained."[3]

Jefferson expected his farms, gardens, and orchards to constitute his principal occupation in his retirement. Before leaving Washington, he had ordered *Hope's Philadelphia Price-Current*, and in the first letter he wrote to Madison after reaching Monticello, he talked about the late-spring damage to his wheat and the price of flour in Richmond before he mentioned public affairs.[4] It was not his interest in agriculture and horticulture alone that inspired his attention to his lands; it was also his need of money. He told one correspondent that he had added nothing to his private fortune during his public service and was leaving office "with hands as clean as they are empty." To his daughter he confided that he had contracted debts of ten thousand dollars while president and hoped to sell off detached tracts of land to pay them off and then live within the income of his Albemarle possessions. He confessed that this would require close management, but he wanted to reserve the income from his lands in Bedford County to assist his grandchildren as they grew up and needed to establish themselves. "My own personal wants will be almost nothing beyond those of a chum of the family," he told Martha, who was planning to resume management of his household at Monticello. While agreeing with her father on the necessity of retrenchment, Martha insisted that his needs should come before those of the children, who were young and healthy. "I can bear any thing but the idea of seeing you harrassed in your old age by debts or deprived of those comforts which long habit has rendered necessary to you," the devoted daughter wrote her father. "The possession of millions would not compensate for one year's sadness and discomfort to you."[5]

Ever since Martha and her husband, Thomas Mann Randolph, Jr., had built their home at Edgehill, only a few miles east of Monticello on the north side of the Rivanna River, Martha had moved easily back and forth between Edgehill and Monticello, always trying to be at Monticello when her father was home for visits. She was there with her children when her father returned from Washington to stay and immediately took over the direction of his household. Her husband apparently followed, while still maintaining Edgehill and managing his farm there. As long as her father lived, Martha remained at Monticello with a growing family of children and grandchildren, while Randolph came and went, drawn away by war and politics and by his own moods of resentment and depression. Randolph served briefly as a colonel on the Canadian front during the War of 1812 and was governor of Virginia from 1819 to 1822.[6] To a large extent he abdicated the responsibilities of providing a fatherly presence in his children's lives, a vacuum that their grandfather readily filled.

When Martha took up residence at Monticello in March, 1809, she had eight children, ranging in ages from eight months to eighteen years. The oldest child, Anne Cary, had married Charles Bankhead six months earlier, and Martha's oldest son, Thomas Jefferson Randolph, was studying in Philadelphia under arrangements made by his grandfather. The sixty-six-year-old former president, who had talked about retiring to the tranquillity of Monticello, found himself surrounded by six children under the age of thirteen.[7] But he delighted in his situation and wrote proudly to John Adams in 1812, "I live in the midst of my grandchildren, one of whom has lately promoted me to be a great grandfather." Eight years later, counting "about half a dozen" great-grandchildren, he wrote Maria Cosway, who had renewed their long-lapsed correspondence, that he lived "like a patriarch of old" among his grandchildren and great-grandchildren.[8]

The memories that his grandchildren had of growing up at Monticello indicate that they regarded their grandfather warmly and that he had an important presence in their lives. Less rigid with them than he had been with his own children, he was generous in his affection and support and respected them as individuals as they matured. He was also prone to spoil them with gifts, sometimes when the state of his finances could ill afford the costs. But he left indelible memories in the young minds of his adoring granddaughters who enjoyed the closest contacts with him in the early years of his retirement. Ellen, who was twelve when Jefferson retired, remembered, "My Bible came from him, my Shakespeare, my first writing table, my first handsome writing-desk, my first Leghorn hat, my first silk dress." And she recalled that her sisters were equally provided for. "Our grandfather seemed to read our hearts, to see our invisible wishes," said Ellen, who was married in the drawing room at Monticello in 1825 to Joseph Coolidge, Jr., of Boston—a young Harvard graduate she met when he made a pilgrimage to Monticello to see Jefferson.[9] Virginia, who also remembered her grandfather buying her and her sisters their first silk dresses, remembered their walks in the gardens, the games he taught them to play, and the footraces he conducted on the terraces and around the lawn. Positioning each child at a starting point appropriate for his or her age, he gave the starting signal by dropping his handkerchief and awarded prizes of dried fruit at the finish line. Virginia, who was nine when Jefferson returned to Monticello in 1809, recalled these details thirty years later, testifying that the loving grandfather had applied his characteristic system to whatever he did.[10]

With his eldest grandson, Thomas Jefferson Randolph, who was sixteen when Jefferson retired, Jefferson also enjoyed a close relationship, and when he saw that his grandson's interests were close to the land, he gave him increasing responsibilities at Monticello. In 1815, when he was seventy-two, Jefferson turned over to Jeff the management of Monticello and all his farms in Albemarle, and he came increasingly to rely upon this dependable namesake.[11]

A common image of Jefferson etched in the memories of his grandchildren was of him with a book in hand sitting in a chair reading. In the early years of his retirement the Sage of Monticello also shared his large library with students who sought his guidance. "A part of my occupation, and by no means the least pleasing," he said in 1810, "is the direction of studies of such young men as ask it." They found lodging nearby, and he counseled them on their reading and gave them free use of his library. In advising them on the course of their readings, he said he tried to keep their attention focused on the object of all learning: the freedom and happiness of man. Thus, if they went into government, they would understand the sole object of all legitimate governments.[12]

Even with his love of Monticello and the contentment he found among his grandchildren, Jefferson still liked to escape periodically from his usual environment and routine and sometimes also from the strain of visitors to Monticello. After leaving the presidency, he increased the frequency of his visits to his lands in Bedford County. That ninety-mile journey became more attractive after he started building a house there in 1806. He was able to stay in it for the first time in 1809. His love of building drew him back more often after that, and by 1812 he was making three trips a year there. But it was 1816—seven years after he left office—before he apparently considered the house, which he named Poplar Forest, livable enough to invite his daughter and two granddaughters to accompany him, though his grandson Jeff had accompanied him earlier. Thereafter, a couple of his granddaughters usually made the journey with him.[13]

Poplar Forest was an architectural gem, one of Jefferson's most remarkable architectural achievements. He had originally drawn the plans for his daughter Maria and her husband, John Wayles

Eppes, to be built at Pantops near Monticello, but when Maria died in 1804 before the plans were implemented, he decided to use the design for Poplar Forest. Employing an octagonal scheme, Jefferson achieved near perfection in geometric form. Within an octagonal exterior, octagonal rooms opened off a square dining room, lighted by a skylight, in the center of the house. Octagonal terraces and gardens, and even octagonal "necessaries," completed the setting. Jefferson would never tire of visiting his country retreat, making his last visit there at age eighty, not long after turning the property over to his grandson Francis Eppes, Maria's only surviving child, and his bride as a wedding gift.[14]

Jefferson's return to farming in 1809 got off to an abysmal start. Writing his grandson Jeff in Philadelphia in June, he told of a distressing drought in April and May and said that wheat and corn had scarcely vegetated and no seeds in the garden had come up. Rains but very cold weather followed, "so that prospects are disheartening for the farmer and little better to the gardener." But it would take more than bad weather to drive this man of the soil from the land, and farming soon took precedence over other pursuits. "From sunrise till breakfast only I allot for all my pen and ink work," he said. "From breakfast till dinner I am in my garden, shops, or on horse back in the farms, and after dinner I devote entirely to relaxation or light reading."[15]

By the time Jefferson retired, wheat had replaced tobacco as the main money crop on his farms in Albemarle County, though tobacco continued to be the money crop on his Bedford County lands. Though the soil in Albemarle was better suited to wheat than to tobacco, his fields were never very productive, despite his application of scientific methods of agriculture. Edmund Bacon, Jefferson's overseer at Monticello during most of his retirement years, recalled, "It was not a profitable estate; it was too uneven and hard to work." In addition to poor soil and droughts, such constant enemies as Hessian flies and wheat rusts made the yearly yield highly uncertain. The quantity of flour, into which Jefferson converted his wheat before sending it to market, ranged from a high of five to six hundred barrels to a low of two hundred, and the prices he received fluctuated widely between three dollars and fifteen dollars per barrel. Low water in the Rivanna River in times of drought and ice in winter increased the uncertainties of transporting the flour to market in Richmond. Jefferson's income from this money crop was always uncertain and generally inadequate to pay his creditors.[16]

Jefferson had long experimented with other ventures to supplement his income. His nailery was still in operation when he returned to Monticello, but it never proved too successful. His continuing difficulties in collecting accounts caused him temporarily to suspend operations in 1811 after failing to recover enough money due him from sales to buy new nailrod. Though he resumed production for a time in 1812, the war with Great Britain cut off his supply of iron from Philadelphia, and he was forced to close down until 1815. After that, the shop operated only intermittently until 1823.[17]

Jefferson was little more successful in the milling business. In 1803 he rebuilt the gristmill on the Rivanna River constructed by his father and destroyed by the freshet of 1771. This he operated only for his own use, and in 1806 he constructed a large manufacturing mill that ground grain for all comers. With two independent waterwheels, it was, he said, "finished in the best manner with every modern convenience." He invested over ten thousand dollars in the operation, which he leased out from the outset. Whether because of the poor management of the lessees, controversies with them, or the high cost of maintenance, the mill never proved profitable.[18]

In another nonfarming enterprise at Monticello, Jefferson expanded the domestic manufacture of cloth more from patriotism and necessity induced by the embargo and nonimportation acts than as a means to improve his fortunes. In 1811 he purchased a spinning jenny and a loom with a flying shuttle, and during the War of 1812 he increased production. Writing to Thaddeus Kosciusko at the beginning of the war, he said that his household manufactures were just getting into operation with a carding machine, a spinning machine carrying six spindles for wool, another with twelve spindles for cotton, and a loom, with a flying shuttle, weaving twenty yards a day. This machinery, worked by two women and two girls, could produce the two thousand yards of linen, cotton, and woolen cloth that he needed yearly to clothe his family—in which he included his slaves. By 1814 he had four spinning jennies running, three of them with twenty-four spindles and one with forty. These machines doubled the output of a common loom, although according to Jefferson they did "not perform the miracles ascribed to them."[19]

Jefferson's experience in the household manufacture of cloth at Monticello influenced his thinking on political economy, which had been changing since the last years of his presidency. After a year of the embargo he was convinced that household manufactures had increased so rapidly in his native state that Virginia would never again import one-half of the coarse goods it had imported prior to the various British and French edicts. As early as 1809 he spoke out against the growing jealousy of commercial men toward manufacturing. "My idea is that we should encourage home manufactures to the extent of our own consumption of everything of which we raise the raw material. I do not think it fair in the ship-owners to say we ought not to make our own axes, nails, etc., here, that they may have the benefit of carrying the iron to Europe, and bringing back the axes, nails, etc. Our agriculture will still afford surplus produce enough to employ a due proportion of navigation."[20]

His model included no place for a carrying trade engaged in exchanging the goods of the world. In declaring in 1809 that "an equilibrium of agriculture, manufactures, and commerce is certainly become essential to our independence," he had not abandoned his model of an agrarian republic. "Manufactures, sufficient for our own consumption, of what we raise the raw material (and no more). Commerce sufficient to carry the surplus produce of agriculture, beyond our own consumption, to a market for exchanging it for articles we cannot raise (and no more). These are the true limits of manufactures and commerce."[21]

The War of 1812 modified his thinking. He took pride not only in the spread of household manufactures but also in the establishments rising in larger cities for the production of finer goods. The war had hardly begun when he expressed the view that "nothing is more certain than that, come peace when it will, we shall never again go to England for a shilling where we have gone for a dollar's worth." As the war continued, he was glad to see commercial capital going into manufactures; when it was over, he supported the tariff of 1816, which gave protection to infant manufacturing industries. He now found himself having to refute things that he had written in his *Notes on Virginia*. When he learned that he was being quoted "by those who wish to continue our dependence on England for manufactures," he said: "There was a time when I might have been so quoted with more candor, but within thirty years which have since elapsed, how are circumstances changed! . . . We have experienced what we did not then believe, that there exists both profligacy and power enough to exclude us from the field of interchange with other nations: that to be independent for the comforts of life we must fabricate them ourselves. We must place the manufacturer by the side of the agriculturist. . . . Experience has taught me that manufactures are now as necessary to our independence as to our comfort."[22]

When Jefferson spoke of placing the manufacturer beside the agriculturist, he meant precisely that—not placing the manufacturer ahead of the farmer. He still saw American commerce as primarily exchanging surplus agricultural commodities for other needs. It was still his view that "the agricultural capacities of our country constitute its distinguishing feature; and the adapting our policy and pursuits to that, is more likely to make us a numerous and happy people, than the mimicry of an Amsterdam, a Hamburgh, or a city of London."[23]

One of the most satisfying moments of Jefferson's years of retirement from politics was the renewal of his once close friendship with John Adams. Strained by the political divisions of the 1790s, the friendship between the two patriots of the Revolution seemed ended forever by the election of 1800. Adams, humiliated by his defeat, returned embittered to Massachusetts, while Jefferson, angered by Adams' "midnight appointments," began his presidency convinced that his predecessor's actions were vengefully designed to impede his administration. Toward the end of Jefferson's first term, Mrs. Adams was moved by the death of his daughter Maria to write to the grieving father to share her affection for Maria, which reached back to Jefferson's ministership in France. Jefferson responded with warmth and took advantage of Abigail's letter of condolence to move to restore the severed bonds of friendship. He said that the only act of John Adams' life that had caused him pain was his making his last appointments to office, which he considered as personally unkind. After unbosoming himself of his resentment of that action, he said that he had forgiven Adams and would carry into private life "an uniform and high measure of respect and good will" for him and a "sincere attachment" for Mrs. Adams. There followed an exchange of letters over the next several months in which Jefferson and Mrs. Adams aired their grievances but failed to reach a common ground of understanding before she closed the correspondence. Only then did she inform her husband of the exchange.[24]

Not until after Jefferson left the presidency did another opportunity for rapprochement arise, when Dr. Benjamin Rush of Philadelphia cast himself in the role of mediator. A fellow signer of the Declaration of Independence and friend of both men, he had long been distressed by the estrangement of the two presidents. After Jefferson left office, he wrote to Adams hinting that Jefferson's retirement offered an occasion for the reopening of their correspondence. But Adams rebuffed the overture, and Rush waited over

a year before he tried again. He then wrote to Jefferson remind-
ing him of "your early attachment to Mr. Adams, and his to you"
and expressing his hope that they might renew their friendship
through correspondence. Jefferson responded by sending Rush his
exchange of letters with Mrs. Adams to demonstrate that he had
"not been wanting either in the desire, or the endeavor to remove
this misunderstanding." Declaring that he had "the same good
opinion of Mr. Adams which I ever had" and leaving to Rush to
decide whether the correspondence with Mrs. Adams warranted
his continued efforts, he made it clear that the next move was up
to Adams.[25]

While Rush contemplated his failure, an unexpected occurrence
gave new life to his efforts. During the summer of 1811 two of
Jefferson's Albemarle neighbors, Edward Coles (President Madison's
private secretary) and his brother John, were traveling in New England and had an interview with John Adams. In the course of their
conversations Adams talked about the politics of his presidency
and his differences with Jefferson and added at one point, "I always
loved Jefferson, and still love him." When Jefferson learned of
Adams' remarks, he wrote to Rush to say, "This is enough for me. I
only needed this knowledge to revive towards him all the affections
of the most cordial moments of our lives." Jefferson hoped for
some occasion that would provide the opportunity to overcome the
awkwardness of resuming their correspondence. Rush wrote immediately to Adams, quoting warm passages from Jefferson's letter
and urging him to "receive the olive branch which has thus been
offered to you by the hand of a man who still loves you. Fellow laborers in erecting the great fabric of American independence! . . .
Embrace—embrace each other!" Adams resisted no longer. He
teased Rush by telling him that he perceived plainly that Rush
had been writing Jefferson just as he had been writing him and
asked, "Of what use can it be for Jefferson and me to exchange
letters?" But he revealed his true intent by suggesting, "Time and
chance, however, or possibly design, may produce ere long a letter
between us."[26]

Adams wrote to Rush on Christmas Day, 1811, and on New Year's
Day he took up his pen to wish Jefferson "many happy New Years"
in a short letter signed, "with a long and sincere Esteem your
Friend and Servant John Adams." He told Jefferson that he was
sending him by post a package containing two pieces of homespun
that he thought Jefferson as a friend of domestic manufactures
would appreciate.[27] When Adams' letter arrived in Virginia without
the accompanying packet, Jefferson was so pleased to receive the

letter that he did not wait for the pieces of homespun to arrive before writing Adams a long and warm letter, which he began with a
brief essay on domestic manufactures in Virginia. He then went on
to reflect on the time when they were "fellow laborers in the same
cause" and on the difficulties the nation had faced in the years since
independence. "In your day French depredations: in mine English,
and the Berlin and Milan decrees: now the English orders of council." But before he got carried away, he reminded himself that he
had taken leave of politics and told Adams that he had given up
newspapers for Tacitus and Thucydides, for Newton and Euclid,
and found himself much happier. He concluded by commenting
on his health, his daily routine, and his grandchildren and solicited
similar "egotisms" from Adams. When he sent his letter to the post
office, he received in return the laggard parcel. When he tore open
the wrappings, he found not pieces of cloth but two volumes of *Lectures on Rhetoric and Oratory*, written by John Quincy Adams while a
professor at Harvard College. The delighted Virginian immediately sent off a note to Adams saying that "a little more sagacity of
conjecture" on his part would have saved Adams from reading a
dissertation on real homespun but it gave him another opportunity
to assure him of his friendship and respect.[28]

The long-broken ties of friendship were restored. The exchange
marked the beginning of one of the most remarkable literary exchanges in American history, as the two former presidents reflected
on their past experiences, their political views, their presidencies,
and their wide interests. They debated political theory and philosophy, discussed their reading, past and present, and ranged widely
over the whole of human experience. Their speculations in political theory and on the nature of man and society left for posterity
such fascinating exchanges as their discussion of aristocracy, which
drew from Jefferson an essay on natural and artificial aristocracy
and the form of government that best provided for the elevation of
the "good and wise" into office.[29] The elder statesmen could not
free themselves from the realm of politics that had engrossed their
lives, but they seemed to derive the most pleasure from discussing
historical, scientific, and religious subjects. They exchanged information and opinions on the American Indians and on their own
regions. And they bombarded each other with ideas that provoked
response. Through the last year of their lives, letters continued to
pass between Quincy and Monticello.[30]

In 1814 after the British set fire to the Capitol during the War of
1812, destroying the Library of Congress, Jefferson offered his li-

brary of nearly 6,500 books to Congress. Condemning the British action as one of the "acts of barbarism which do not belong to a civilized age," he assumed that Congress would wish to rebuild the collection. Indicating that he had planned for Congress to have first refusal of his library, at their own price, upon his death, he said he was moved by the recent loss to offer it now. In assembling his collection over a period of fifty years, he had "spared no pains, opportunity or expense, to make it what it is," he explained in sending along a catalog to show that "while it includes what is chiefly valuable in science and literature generally, [it] extends more particularly to whatever belongs to the American statesman. In the diplomatic and parliamentary branches, it is particularly strong." He made it clear that he wanted his collection to be taken as a whole. "I do not know that it contains any branch of science which Congress would wish to exclude from their collection," he wrote, employing the word *science* to embrace all knowledge. "There is, in fact no subject to which a member of Congress may not have occasion to refer." He would leave it to Congress to set the price and method of payment.[31]

Visitors to Monticello had never failed to be impressed by Jefferson's library. Francis Calley Gray, a well-educated Bostonian who visited there a few months after Jefferson offered his library to Congress, observed that the collection was strongest in books relating to North and South America. "The collection on this subject is without a question the most valuable in the world." But most members of Congress had never seen his library, and though they could examine his catalog, they had an inadequate idea of its immense value. Federalist partisanship also still lingered. "The grand library of Mr. Jefferson will undoubtedly be purchased with all its finery and philosophical nonsense," the Washington correspondent for the Boston *Gazette* reported. After escaping several crippling amendments and several motions to postpone action, a bill passed to pay Jefferson $23,950 for his 6,487 volumes. A motion was made by Representative Cyrus King to select from the collection "all books of an atheistical, irreligious, and immoral tendency" and return them to Jefferson, but the Massachusetts Federalist withdrew his motion.[3]

The ex-president personally supervised the packing of the books which were left in the pine bookcases in which they were shelved and ten wagons were required to transport them to Washington. As he bid his cherished volumes farewell, he mused that they consti tuted "unquestionably the choicest collection of books in the U.S and I hope it will not be without some general effect on the litera ture of our country."[33] His wish would not go unfulfilled. Upon this foundation would be built one of the great libraries of the world.

The sale of his books left an emptiness in Jefferson as great as that of the rooms that had housed them. The last wagon of his treasures was hardly down the hill at Monticello before he was starting to build another collection. "I can not live without books," he wrote to John Adams, while entering in his account book a payment of $187 to his grandson Jeff for books and commissioning George Ticknor, a young Boston scholar who had recently visited him and was on his way to Europe, to buy certain editions of the classics for him in Europe. Before his death, he would have collected another library of some one thousand volumes.[34]

The record of Jefferson's last months in the presidential office made it clear that he would not seek to dictate policy to his successor. At the same time, he did not isolate himself from political affairs as much as he had tried to do earlier when he retired as secretary of state. President Madison was one of the first persons to whom he wrote after reaching Monticello, and he continued to exchange letters with him throughout his presidency. He generally approved of his successor's conduct of foreign affairs and was supportive of his course as he moved the nation toward war with Great Britain. On the eve of the final decision for war he reported to Madison the volunteer companies forming in Virginia and said of the Albemarle cavalry: "The only inquiry they make is whether they are to go to Canada or Florida? Not a man, as far as I have learned, entertains any of those doubts which puzzle the lawyers of Congress and astonish common sense, whether it is lawful for them to pursue a retreating enemy across the boundary line of the Union." A week before the declaration of war in 1812, in a letter to John Adams, Jefferson expressed confidence in the conquest of Canada.[35]

While professing a preference for occupying his mind with subjects other than politics, he admitted that "although I do not often permit myself to think of that subject, it sometimes obtrudes itself, and suggests ideas which I am tempted to pursue."[36] At no time did he yield more completely to the temptation than when he turned his thoughts to the problems of financing the War of 1812. Writing to his son-in-law John W. Eppes, who was chairman of the House Ways and Means Committee, he outlined a plan for taxation and government borrowing in the summer of 1813, when government finances were in a critical state because of both the war and the ex-

piration of the charter of the Bank of the United States. Drawing
on his long-held view that the earth belongs to the living, his opposition to a permanent national debt, and his distrust of banks,
the former president proposed a system for the suppression of
bank paper and its replacement with treasury notes tied to a specific schedule of redemption provided by taxation. When Eppes requested him to develop his ideas, Jefferson did so with diligence,
providing the congressman with an elaborate proposal.[37] He shared
these ideas with Monroe, who was now secretary of state, and a few
others, thus assuring that they would reach the president, to whom
he later expanded on his plan. While he encouraged his correspondents to use his ideas, he also cautioned them not to connect his
name with them. "I am too desirous of tranquillity to bring such a
nest of hornets on me as the fraternities of banking companies," he
said, "and this infatuation of banks is a torrent which it would be a
folly for me to get into the way of. I see that it must take its course,
until actual ruin shall awaken us from its delusions."[38]

Monroe was the chief supporter of Jefferson's plan within the administration and thought it represented the only alternative to a
national bank. But the current in favor of reviving the bank was
growing, as Jefferson himself realized, and before leaving office,
Madison signed the bill to charter the second Bank of the United
States.[39] Jefferson did not press his objections upon his longtime
friend who had been his partner in opposing Hamilton's first bank,
but he did not abandon his own constitutional objections to a national bank. Marshall's decision upholding its constitutionality in
McCulloch v. Maryland (1819) increased his hostility to Marshall,
who borrowed arguments and even language from Hamilton to
sanction the bank. The court's verdict also deepened his concern
about national consolidation. He privately applauded the series
of articles by Virginia Judge Spencer Roane, published under
the name "Hampden" in the Richmond Enquirer, condemning
Marshall's sweeping assertion of the supremacy of the national government and broad construction of implied powers. "We find the
judiciary on every occasion still driving us into consolidation," he
wrote to Roane, telling him that he subscribed to "every tittle" of
his essays as containing "the true principles of the revolution of
1800." But he declined to allow his opinions to be made public, not
wishing to become embroiled in public controversy that might endanger the principal object of his life at that moment, the establishment of a university in his native state.[40]

While only an inveterate optimist would have launched the effort that he did to get a state university established in Virginia, Jefferson's fears of national consolidation began to undermine his habitual optimism. The controversy over the admission of Missouri into the Union quickened his concern, and though he welcomed the compromise, it left him disturbed. "This momentous question, like a fire bell in the night, awakened and filled me with terror," he wrote. "I considered it at once as the knell of the Union. It is hushed, indeed, for the moment. But this is a reprieve only, not a final sentence." The optimist who once was certain that the next generation would abolish the evil of slavery was no longer confident of that happening, and he feared for the survival of the Union. "I regret that I am now to die in the belief, that the useless sacrifice of themselves by the generation of 1776, to acquire self-government and happiness to their country, is to be thrown away by the unwise and unworthy passions of their sons, and that my only consolation is to be, that I live not to weep over it."[41] Jefferson was seventy-seven years of age when he wrote these words in 1820, and he did not overcome his pessimism about the course of the nation in his declining years. Six months before his death, with John Quincy Adams in the White House, he wrote that he saw "with the deepest affliction, the rapid strides with which the federal branch of our government is advancing towards the usurpation of all the rights reserved to the States, and the consolidation in itself of all powers, foreign and domestic; and that, too, by constructions which, if legitimate, leave no limits to their power."[42]

If Jefferson's last years were darkened by his concerns about the rights of states and the future of the Union, they were also brightened by the outcome of the most important enterprise that he attempted after he left the presidency. It was a project that claimed his most intense interest, effort, and devotion and one that in its fruition left to him his greatest monument: the establishment of the University of Virginia.

XXII
A Final Legacy

Despite the rejection of his plan for general education in Virginia in the early years of independence, Jefferson's interest in the establishment of a state system of education from elementary school through college never waned. He continued to insist that no republic could maintain itself in strength without the broad education of its people, and he favored beginning at the bottom with elementary schools.[1] But when renewed attempts to get the Virginia legislature to create a comprehensive educational system failed, Jefferson directed his major energies to establishing a state university, convinced that attention to lower schools would eventually have to follow. Even this more limited goal turned out to be more difficult to accomplish than he envisioned, and probably no one without his stature could have pushed ahead as he did to overcome the obstacles and ultimately achieve his objective.

Jefferson had been developing his ideas about a university in Virginia for years. As early as 1800, when some movement toward establishing a state university seemed to be emerging, he began collecting ideas about what a university should be from Joseph Priestly, du Pont de Nemours, and others, though he already had rather firm notions of the kind of university he wanted to see established. He wanted a university "on a plan so broad and liberal and *modern*, as to be worth patronizing with the public support, and be a temptation to the youth of other States to come and drink of the cup of knowledge and fraternize with us." He did not want to attempt to revitalize and expand the College of William and Mary, which in his opinion was "just well enough endowed to draw out the miserable existence to which a miserable constitution has doomed it." He also regarded Williamsburg as too isolated and its climate too unhealthy; he favored a university more centrally located in the healthy upper country—a site description that fit his own neighborhood around Charlottesville.[2]

Midway through his presidency, Jefferson outlined a plan for establishing a university to Littleton W. Tazewell, who sought his counsel at a time when he thought interest in a university was developing in the Virginia General Assembly. By then Jefferson had collected plans of study from institutions in Edinburgh and the National Institute of France, and he was expecting a response from Geneva. He regarded Oxford, Cambridge, and the Sorbonne as "a century or two behind the science of the age" and recommended that in establishing a new university its object be defined solely in general terms of "teaching the useful branches of science" (*i.e.*, knowledge), leaving specific subjects to be determined by the needs of the time. "What was useful two centuries ago is now become useless," he thought. "What is now deemed useful will in some of it's parts become useless in another century." He recommended a small board of visitors qualified "to keep their institution up in even pace with the science of the times." By 1805 Jefferson had already developed his main concept of the physical plan of the university. It should not be one large building but a village—a few years later he would call it "an academical village"—with houses containing classrooms for professors, lodgings for students between the professorial houses, and all structures connected by covered walkways. Additional units could be built as the university grew.[3]

Although a proposal to create a university was introduced in the General Assembly in 1806, nothing came of it, and interest in the project did not revive until after Jefferson left the presidency. Then it was the ex-president who was the principal mover behind the renewed effort. Named in 1814 as a trustee of the Albemarle Academy, chartered a decade earlier but never instituted, he immediately began to use this position as a base to advance his more ambitious plans. When the board of the academy, chaired by his nephew Peter Carr, asked him to prepare a plan for the institution, he could not resist including a design for a state system of education at all levels. He was not yet ready to settle for providing only for higher education, but he indicated that he had "long entertained the hope that this, our native State, would take up the subject of education and make an establishment . . . where every branch of science, deemed useful at this day, should be taught in its highest degree."[4] Along with his proposal, he prepared a petition to the legislature to change the name of Albemarle Academy to Central College.

Jefferson drafted his plan during one of the darkest periods of the War of 1812—just after the burning of Washington—when only a person of his optimism, determination, and intellectual discipline would have been able to devote himself to such a task. It would be January, 1816, a year after the war was over, before the legislature would act, passing a bill, drafted by Jefferson, creating Central College. In accordance with his views the act provided for a Board of Visitors of only six members. Following Jefferson's recommendations, his friend Governor Wilson Cary Nicholas named Madison and Monroe to the board, along with Jefferson, David Watson, John H. Cocke, and Joseph C. Cabell, the latter being the leading proponent of Jefferson's ideas in the Virginia Senate. If a state university were to be established, Jefferson was positioning Central College to receive the mission. When the first regular meeting of the Board of Visitors convened on May 5, 1817, with President Monroe and the two ex-presidents in attendance, it attracted the public attention that the Sage of Monticello wanted. The board authorized the purchase of two hundred acres of land, approved Jefferson's plan for an academical village, authorized the construction of the first professorial pavilion, and began a subscription drive for funds. Each of the visitors present at the first meeting subscribed one thousand dollars, and Jefferson was soon busy soliciting friends throughout the state.[5]

Jefferson had already assumed the role of architect, having presented the Board of Visitors with a drawing of his plan, and he now assumed the role of builder. On July 18, 1817, he surveyed the site, adjusted his plan to the lay of the land, staked out three terraces, and decided the locations of six pavilions. The idea of the academical village, with dormitories for students adjoining professorial pavilions, was, as Benjamin Henry Latrobe observed, "entirely novel." But in developing its architectural design, the seventy-four-year-old architect and builder, who had been absorbing ideas for a lifetime, must have recalled to mind the château of Louis XIV at Marly, which he had visited years before. There the Sun King had situated his pavilion at the head of a quadrangle along the two sides of which rows of six pavilions (one for each of the months) faced each other across a broad expanse of grass.[6] When Latrobe reviewed Jefferson's plan, he suggested a large building in the center of one side of the opened-ended quadrangle that Jefferson had sketched for him, and he sent along a drawing of a building with a dome. In his pocket notebook in which he sketched the plan that he laid out on July 18, Jefferson had noted a place for "some principal building" and replied promptly to Latrobe that the north end of the quadrangle would be left open and might be filled with "something of the grand kind" should the legislature decide to establish a university.[7] Thus, a larger vision was already in Jefferson's mind when he staked out the first buildings for Central College.

Jefferson lost no time in getting construction under way. The day after he staked out the site, he wrote to General John H. Cocke, one of the Visitors not at the meeting in May, "Our squares are laid off, the brick-yard begun, and the leveling will be begun in the course of the week."[8] On October 6, 1817, the cornerstone of the first pavilion was laid, with President Monroe officiating and all of the other five Visitors in attendance.

As this project got under way, Jefferson was quietly working for it to become part of a larger state system of education. In September he sent Joseph C. Cabell the draft of a bill for the establishment of elementary schools. When Cabell requested bills for academies and a university also, Jefferson followed with a comprehensive plan for a state system of elementary, secondary, and higher education. He described the bill as essentially his plan of 1779 "accommodated to the circumstances of this, instead of that day."[9] From Poplar Forest, Jefferson wrote to George Ticknor in late November that he was "now entirely absorbed in endeavours to effect the establishment of a general system of education" in his native state but that he was not very hopeful of success. He feared that the members of the Virginia legislature did not sufficiently understand "that knowledge is power, that knowledge is safety, and that knowledge is happiness." His concern about the legislators' response was not unjustified. After a long controversy over public education, no plan was adopted. Although Jefferson's bill was rejected, Cabell managed to salvage something by proposing to add to a bill appropriating funds for the education of the children of the poor an amendment providing for the establishment of a university with an annual appropriation of fifteen thousand dollars—after the legislature determined its location. The measure passed both houses in February, 1818.[10] It was a limited victory. The appropriation was embarrassingly inadequate, and the site was still undetermined. But Jefferson would make the most of it and ultimately turn it into a large triumph.

Named by Governor James P. Preston to the commission to recommend the location of the university, Jefferson arrived well prepared at the commission's meeting at Rockfish Gap in the Blue Ridge on August 1, 1818. Indeed, he came with a draft of a proposed report of the commission already written and carried the day with the commission, which represented all the senatorial districts in the state and included such well-disposed members as James Madison and Judge Spencer Roane. The members unanimously elected Jefferson president of the commission. Sixteen of the twenty-one commissioners present voted for Central College over competing proposals from Lexington and Staunton as the site of the university, and after adding minor amendments, they unanimously approved the report that Jefferson had prepared.[11]

The Rockfish Gap report contained Jefferson's final plan for the University of Virginia, spelling out in detail the arrangement of the buildings, the subjects of instruction, the composition of the faculty and its governance, the broad purposes of the institution, the specific justifications for its curriculum, and a set of bylaws for its operation. He proposed a faculty of ten professors, and though he grouped the fields of learning into ten categories, he recommended that the fields for which each professor would be responsible be left to the Board of Visitors. In conformity to the principles of religious freedom, he proposed no professor of divinity.[12] This remarkable document was the mature product of years of contemplation on the subject of education in a republic.

Jefferson's ambitions for the university were lofty. He wanted an "institution where science in all it's branches is taught, and in the highest degree to which the human mind has carried it." He did not want it to be a provincial. "The salaries of the first professors should be very liberal, that we might draw the first names of Europe to our institution in order to give it a celebrity in the outset, which will draw to it the youth of all the states, and make Virginia their cherished and beloved Alma mater." The faculty was to be of first rank. "We mean to accept for our institution no person of secondary grade in his science, if there be one of the first on either side of the Atlantic who can be tempted to come to us."[13] He wanted the architecture of the university buildings to serve as "models in architecture of the purest forms of antiquity, furnishing to the students examples of the precepts he will be taught in that art."[14] The professorial pavilions in his view should be "models of taste and good architecture, and of a variety of appearance, no two alike, so as to serve as specimens for the Architectural lecturer."[15]

Realizing his dream would be filled with difficulties. The enlightened prospectus for a university of eminence offered in the Rockfish Gap report was inadequately appreciated by the legislators whose approval was required. For a time, sectional rivalries over the location of the site threatened rejection of the recommendations, but finally in January, 1819, both houses of the General Assembly voted their approval.[16] "Your college is made the University of Virginia," Wilson Cary Nicholas wrote to him from Richmond. "I call it yours, as you are its real founder, its commencement can only be ascribed to you. To your exertions and influence its being adopted can only be attributed." Jefferson joined in the joy shared by his friends at the passage of the bill, but he feared "it will be a great measure on paper only with our present funds."[17] The struggle in the legislature had been a foretaste of the obstacles to be surmounted or finessed in the years ahead, but Jefferson would never compromise his goal.

Jefferson was named to the Board of Visitors appointed by the governor for the new University of Virginia, and at its first meeting (March 29, 1819) the board elected him rector. The board also appointed Thomas Cooper, who had earlier been engaged for the faculty of Central College, to a professorship of chemistry, mineralogy, and natural philosophy, and temporarily to a professorship of law. Cooper was to begin his duties in April, 1820, but six months later the board postponed his appointment for one year. Meanwhile, the news of Cooper's appointment raised such a storm of religious opposition that the controversial professor, whom Jefferson regarded as first in America in the powers of intellect and information, withdrew from the appointment.[18] Despite his pushing for the appointment of Cooper, to whom he felt an obligation after engaging him for Central College, Jefferson believed that the buildings for the university should be constructed before the faculty was hired. He wanted to use all funds for construction and not open the university "until we can do it with the degree of splendor necessary to give it a prominent character."[19]

By December, 1819, Jefferson reported to the governor that the walls of seven pavilions and thirty-seven dormitories (to house two students each) had been erected and that eighty thousand dollars was needed to complete them. But times were hard in Virginia, and the only help provided by the legislature was to authorize the Board of Visitors to borrow sixty thousand dollars, which was obtained from the state's Literary Fund. The next year found the legislature little more inclined to appropriate funds for the university. Reports from Richmond caused Jefferson to despair of living to see the university opened.[20] He had hoped for a remission of the loan of the previous year and additional funds to complete the buildings, including forty thousand dollars for a library building. But another loan of sixty thousand dollars from the Literary Fund was as much as the legislature was willing to approve.[21]

Building costs were running above his estimates, but Jefferson did not consider the expenditures excessive. He optimistically predicted that the construction costs, excluding the library, would be little more than $162,000 and said that no office building in Washington had cost less and that the Henrico County Courthouse in Richmond had cost nearly that much. But he was concerned about criticisms that the buildings were too ornate and the general plan too extravagant. He urged Joseph Cabell to point out privately to legislators how much more some other states were spending on education and how far Virginia was falling behind. He also began appealing not only to state pride but also to sectional prejudices. In the wake of the Missouri controversy, as the legislature continued to keep a tight grip on the purse strings, he suggested that there must be five hundred Virginians studying at northern institutions "imbibing opinions and principles in discord with those of their own country." He understood that more than half of the students at Princeton were Virginians, and he wondered how many were at Harvard "learning the lessons of anti-Missourianism." He grimaced at the thought of the University of Virginia opening with only six professors, "while Harvard will still prime it over us with her twenty professors." [22]

Still, despite growing frustrations, he was firm in his belief that the university should not open until all the buildings, including the library, were completed and paid for. Otherwise, it would never get the funds for his primary goal, a distinguished faculty. He was unwilling to compromise on either the building plans or on the faculty. "The great object of our aim from the beginning has been to make this establishment the most eminent in the United States," he wrote to Cabell in 1822. "We have proposed therefore to call to it characters of the first order of science from Europe as well as our own country; and . . . by the distinguished scale of it's structure and preparation, and the promise of future eminence which these would hold up, to induce them to commit their reputation to it's future fortunes. . . . To stop where we are is to abandon our high hopes, and become suitors to Yale and Harvard for their secondary characters." [23]

By 1821 Jefferson had drawn the plans and secured the estimates for a great domed building to house the library and serve as a unifying focal point of his grand design. Using as his model Palladio's drawings and descriptions of the Pantheon in Rome, he drew the plans for the Rotunda, making its diameter one half that of the Pantheon. Lack of funds, however, delayed beginning its construction until 1823, when the legislature authorized another loan of sixty thousand dollars to complete the buildings. Contracts were let in March, 1823, and construction began immediately. By the fall of 1823 the circular walls of the Rotunda had been completed. By that time all the other buildings were ready for occupancy, and the legislature was more favorably disposed toward the project, since it was receiving favorable reports from most of those who saw Jefferson's unique creation. In 1824 the Assembly relieved the university of its debt, while maintaining the right to reimpose it, and promised fifty thousand dollars for books and equipment.[24]

Jefferson moved quickly to acquire a faculty. With the approval of the Board of Visitors, Francis Walker Gilmer was dispatched on a recruiting mission to England. Jefferson considered Gilmer, a young lawyer who lived near Charlottesville, as the best-educated Virginian of his generation and authorized him to engage professors to fill six of the eight professorships under which the university was expected to open, though pavilions were ready for ten. The posts of law and moral philosophy were reserved for Americans, and Gilmer was offered his choice of them. After failing earlier to interest able Americans from other institutions, Jefferson considered it necessary to turn to Europe to fill the other vacancies.[25] Overcoming early discouragements, Gilmer succeeded in attracting five professors to join the new institution. "I could hear of not a single man in all Great Britain at all fit for our purpose of Natural history," he wrote, but he was successful in finding scholars in mathematics (Thomas Key), ancient languages (George Long), modern languages (George Blaettermann), anatomy and medicine (Dr. Robley Dunglison), and natural philosophy (Charles Bonnycastle). After Gilmer declined any position, the professorship of law became the last to be filled. Meanwhile, Dr. John Patton Emmet, of New York, was named professor of natural history, and George Tucker of Virginia, then a member of Congress, was appointed to the chair of moral philosophy.[26]

Jefferson was busy drafting schedules of classes, rules for student conduct, faculty bylaws, requirements for examinations and the awarding of degrees, and numerous other details, all of which went before the Board of Visitors for their approval. One basic stipulation was that "every student shall be free to attend the schools of his choice, and no other than he chooses." The board defined the subjects to be taught in each "school," which consisted of the classes held by an individual professor. In assigning to the school of law the instruction in the principles of government and political economy, the board, at Jefferson's suggestion, went so far as to mandate specific readings. Asserting a responsibility "to pay especial attention to the principles of government which shall be inculcated therein, and to provide that none shall be inculcated which are incompatible with those on which the Constitutions of this State, and of the United States were genuinely based," the board required the

use of specific texts. These included specified writings of John
Locke and Algernon Sidney, *The Federalist*, the Virginia Resolutions
of 1799, and Washington's Farewell Address.[27] Jefferson had discussed this list with Madison and Cabell, but the idea was his and
poses a contradiction to his declaration five years earlier when he
said: "This institution will be based on the illimitable freedom of
the human mind. For here we are not afraid to follow truth wherever it may lead, nor to tolerate any error so long as reason is left
free to combat it."[28] Despite this deviation, Jefferson could write
with just pride in the final year of his life that the university was
"now qualified to raise its youth to an order of science unequalled
in any other State; and this superiority will be the greater from the
free range of mind encouraged there, and the restraint imposed at
other seminaries by the shackles of a domineering hierachy, and a
bigoted adhesion to ancient habits."[29]

As Jefferson was planning for the opening of the university, he
received word, in August, 1824, of Lafayette's arrival in America,
for what would become a triumphal tour unparalleled in American
history. Along with an invitation from the town of Charlottesville to
a dinner in his honor, he sent his old friend a warm invitation to
stay with him at Monticello. After being in Yorktown in October for
the anniversary of the surrender of Cornwallis, Lafayette and his
party, which was soon joined by Frances and Camilla Wright, arrived at Monticello in November and enjoyed his hospitality for ten
days. Upon his arrival in Albemarle County, Lafayette was accompanied to Monticello by a military escort and a large procession of
citizens. When the two old patriots embraced each other outside
the portico of Monticello, it was a moment of high drama for the
crowd that had gathered on the grounds to witness the historic
event, and it was a moment of high emotion for the two men, who
had not seen each other since the opening months of the French
Revolution.[30]

Another moving event took place the following day, inaugurat-
ing to public usage the still unfinished Rotunda. In an occasion
of historic dimensions rarely again to be equaled there, Lafayette
was honored at a dinner held in the spacious circular room on
the upper floor beneath the dome. Seated between Lafayette and
Madison through a meal that lasted three hours, Jefferson not only
raised his glass to Lafayette but also heard himself toasted as the
"founder of the University of Virginia." In his own brief, prepared
remarks, which he asked to be read for him, pleading age and
a voice too weak to utter them, he praised Lafayette and thanked
his friends and neighbors for their kindnesses over many years.

Concluding what would be his last public address, he expressed his hopes for the future success of the institution where they were then gathered and affirmed his love of country and its "indissoluble union."[31]

On March 7, 1825, the University of Virginia opened without fanfare and with about thirty students in attendance. Although the interior of the Rotunda was not yet finished, one of the unoccupied pavilions was available for use as a library. The university could begin in the impressive surroundings that Jefferson had envisioned. Visiting Jefferson at Monticello in the previous December, Professor George Ticknor of Harvard described the buildings of the university as "more beautiful than anything architectural in New England, and more appropriate to an university than can be found, perhaps, in the world." It was fortunate indeed that Jefferson had been able to complete his basic plan, for at the next session of the legislature the Assembly refused to grant the university any more money. General John H. Cocke told fellow Visitor Joseph C. Cabell shortly thereafter that "the temper of the House ought to be an admonition to the Old Sachem that the state has enough of his buildings."[32]

A few weeks after the opening of the university, Jefferson wrote that he was "closing the last scenes of life by fashioning and fostering an establishment for the instruction of those who are to come after us. I hope its influence on their virtue, freedom, fame, and happiness, will be salutary and permanent."[33] He would remain active in the affairs of the university until the end of his life, attending his last board meeting only three months before his death, and he would regard his role in founding the university as one of the greatest accomplishments of his life.

Jefferson never recovered from the burden of debt with which he ended his public career. His daughter Martha's fervent wish that her father not be harassed by debt in his old age was never realized. On the contrary, nothing intruded more upon the tranquillity of his declining years. Owing to circumstances not all of his own making, the debts that he had hoped to pay off increased rather than diminished. He gained some relief in 1815 when he sold his library to Congress, using most of that money ($23,950) to reduce his debts by more than one-half. But they were never so low again. The vagaries of agriculture often left him short of cash. While he had generously subscribed $1,000 to Central College in 1817, a year later he borrowed $100 from a Charlottesville merchant to make the trip to Rockfish Gap for the meeting of the commissioners to recommend the site for the University of Virginia.[34] He never expected to earn enough from farming or other enterprises to pay off his debts but counted on selling part of his extensive landholdings to do so. Here he was thwarted by conditions beyond his control. The price of land in Virginia plummeted so low during the depression of 1819 that this was no longer a viable option. "Lands in this state cannot now be sold for a year's rent," Jefferson wrote to John Adams. That was not the only problem aggravated by the financial crisis. The Bank of the United States, which had overextended credit, began contracting it. When the bank announced a 12½ percent curtailment of all notes presented for renewal, Jefferson did not have the cash to meet the demand and had to resort to more borrowing. By the summer of 1819, this foe of banks had five loans from three banks in Richmond. Then came what Jefferson called the coup de grace. Wilson Cary Nicholas, for whom Jefferson had endorsed two notes for $10,000 each, went bankrupt, leaving Jefferson with an obligation to pay $1,200 a year in interest, which he could meet only by borrowing.[35]

Jefferson's financial situation—like his health—continued to deteriorate with each passing year, and in the final year of his life it was exacerbated by the bankruptcy of his son-in-law Thomas Mann Randolph, Jr., which left him to provide for all the expenses of his daughter and his unmarried grandchildren.[36] Early in 1826 Jefferson hit upon the idea of a lottery as a means of selling enough of his property to pay his debts. Such a scheme required the permission of the legislature, which had granted such requests in the past for various public and charitable purposes. At a time when land prices were so low as to provide little relief and buyers were few, a lottery offered a means of producing a fair return on the land offered as the prize. It was expected that lottery tickets would be sold in small denominations throughout the nation. To the aging patriarch, the plan seemed the last chance to forestall disaster. If the legislature would permit the lottery, "I can save the house of Monticello and a farm adjoining to end my days in and bury my bones. If not I must sell house and all here and carry my family to Bedford where I have not even a log hut to put my head into." When his grandson Francis Eppes heard of his application to the legislature, he offered to return the property at Poplar Forest to his grandfather, for whom he expressed his deepest affection and gratitude.[37] Jefferson refused the offer, but could not but have appreciated the sincerity with which it was made.

Jefferson was disappointed by the initial coolness of many members of the legislature to his request, but in the end a measure authorizing the lottery passed by a large majority. Only then did Jefferson learn that Monticello would have to be included in the plan to pay his debts, which were now over $100,000.[38] The shock of this was relieved only by the stipulation that he could occupy the house for as long as he lived and that his daughter Martha could remain for two years after his death. Though tickets were printed and preparations were made for the lottery, no tickets were sold before his death, which came less than four months after he made his last will on March 16, 1826.

The state of his finances ruled out providing in his will for the emancipation of his slaves had he been so inclined, but there is no indication that such a step had ever been his intention. In his will Jefferson went no further than to stipulate freedom for five of his slaves, all of whom had trades that would enable them to support themselves in a free society. He appealed to the legislature to allow them to remain within the state, since Virginia law required all manumitted slaves to leave the state within one year. In his last years Jefferson still adhered to his belief that slavery would someday be ended. He wrote to Frances Wright in 1825 that "the abolition of the evil is not impossible; it ought never therefore to be despaired of. Every plan should be adopted, every experiment tried, which may do something towards that ultimate object." It is clear that Jefferson did not fully understand Wright's plan for Nashoba when he wished her success, but in any case he refused to let her use his name in support of the enterprise.[39] At eighty-two, Jefferson pleaded old age as the reason for not participating in any new enterprises, even for bettering the condition of man. Yet, even before age had taken its toll, he had already assigned to the next generation the task of dealing with slavery. He had continued to believe, as he had when he wrote his *Notes on Virginia*, in gradual emancipation, but he had done nothing during his years of retirement to advance that cause.

On the one occasion when he was approached by a member of the younger generation, whom he counted on to end slavery, and was asked to lend his public support to the antislavery cause, he rebuffed the overture. That was in 1814, when he still had energy left to devote to educational reform but no motivation to take up an antislavery banner. Edward Coles, an Albemarle neighbor then serving as private secretary to President Madison, wrote urging him to take the lead in promoting emancipation. Coles, who had already decided to free the slaves he had inherited from his father and five years later would settle them in Illinois, suggested that it would be easier for "the revered fathers of all our political and social blessings" than for succeeding statesmen to begin the work of gradual emancipation. "And it is a duty, as I conceive, that devolves particularly on you," he told Jefferson with suitable apologies for his presumptuousness, "from your known philosophical and enlarged view of subjects, and from the principles you have professed and practiced through a long and useful life." He hoped that no fear of failing would deter Jefferson from using his pen to eradicate this remnant of British colonial policy so repugnant to the principles of the Revolution and the free institutions of the Republic.[40]

In reply Jefferson commended Coles for his views and said that he had read his letter with peculiar pleasure, but he insisted that "this enterprize is for the young; for those who can follow it up, and bear it through to its consummation." In the lengthy letter he reviewed his long opposition to slavery and restated his support for gradual emancipation but refused to accept Coles's challenge to provide public leadership. He also urged Coles to abandon his intention of leaving Virginia and instead remain to work for gradual emancipation within the state.[41] Jefferson would end his days without risking his way of life or alienating himself from the mass of his fellow Virginians by publicly planting an antislavery standard on his Albemarle mountaintop.

In the codicil to his will Jefferson left Madison his gold-mounted walking stick as a token of their long and affectionate friendship and their years of political collaboration.[42] A few weeks earlier, depressed by financial burdens and declining health, he had written to Madison that "the friendship which has subsisted between us, now half a century, and the harmony of our political principles and pursuits, have been sources of constant happiness to me through that long period. And if I remove beyond the reach of attentions to the University, or beyond the bourne of life itself, as I soon must, it is a comfort to leave that institution under your care, and an assurance that it will not be wanting." He closed the moving letter by saying: "To myself you have been a pillar of support through life. Take care of me when dead, and be assured that I shall leave with you my last affections."[43]

Jefferson had been through periods of illness and declining vigor at earlier times during his retirement, but now he seemed to sense that his life was drawing to a close. He was able to attend the meeting of the Board of Visitors of the university in early April, 1826, and in May visited his cherished academical village to decide on final instructions for the placement of the marble columns of the

Rotunda. On June 24 he wrote to decline, because of his health, an invitation from the citizens of Washington to the celebration of the fiftieth anniversary of the Declaration of Independence. In this the last letter to come from his pen, he showed that his faith in the pursuit of reason that had guided his life sustained him in his final days, as he counted among the blessings of self-government resting on the Declaration "the free right to the unbounded exercise of reason."[44]

On the same day Jefferson summoned his physician, Dr. Robley Dunglison, professor of anatomy and medicine at the university, who, seeing little hope for his recovery, remained at Monticello to be in attendance when needed. On July 2 Jefferson lapsed into unconsciousness, but aroused on one or more occasions afterward to inquire if it was the Fourth of July. He gained his wish that he might live until that day, and at fifty minutes past noon on July 4 Thomas Jefferson died.[45]

Six hundred miles away in Quincy, Massachusetts, John Adams also lay on his deathbed. About noon he aroused enough to utter "Thomas Jefferson survives," but before the sun set, Adams, who had joined Jefferson in drafting the Declaration of Independence, joined his Virginia colleague in death. "A strange and very striking coincidence," President John Quincy Adams recorded in his diary when he learned of Jefferson's death on the fiftieth anniversary of American independence, unaware of his own father's death. When he learned that his father, too, had died on the same day, he saw "visible and palpable marks of Divine favor," a feeling that was soon widely shared throughout the nation.[46]

Jefferson was buried beside his wife in the cemetery on the sloping hillside at Monticello. He had drawn the design and left the instructions for a plain obelisk of coarse stone to mark his grave and requested as his epitaph "the following inscription, and not a word more":

Here was buried
Thomas Jefferson
Author of the Declaration of American Independence
of the Statute of Virginia for religious freedom
and Father of the University of Virginia.

He explained that "because by these, as testimonials that I have lived, I wish most to be remembered."[47]

Notes

Preface

1. Samuel I. Rosenman (ed.), *The Public Papers and Addresses of Franklin D. Roosevelt, 1943* (New York, 1950), 162–64.
2. Merrill D. Peterson, *The Jefferson Image in the American Mind* (New York, 1962), 362–63, 377–78; Washington *Post*, April 30, 1962, p. B-5.
3. William Howard Adams (ed.), *The Eye of Thomas Jefferson* (Washington, D.C., 1976).
4. Jefferson to George Ticknor, November 25, 1817, in Paul L. Ford (ed.), *The Works of Thomas Jefferson* (Federal Edition; 12 vols.; New York, 1904), XII, 77–78.

Chapter I

1. Jefferson, Autobiography, in Paul L. Ford (ed.), *The Works of Thomas Jefferson* (Federal Edition; 12 vols.; New York, 1904), I, 4.
2. *Ibid.*
3. Jefferson to John Harvie, January 14, 1760, in Julian P. Boyd (ed.), *The Papers of Thomas Jefferson* (Princeton, 1950–), I, 3.
4. Jefferson to Thomas Jefferson Randolph, November 24, 1808, in Edwin M. Betts and James A. Bear, Jr. (eds.), *The Family Letters of Thomas Jefferson* (Columbia, Mo., 1966), 362–63.
5. On the other children of Peter and Jane Randolph Jefferson see Dumas Malone, *Jefferson and His Time* (6 vols.; Boston, 1948–81), I, 430.
6. Fawn Brodie speculated that Jefferson's feelings toward his mother were deeply hostile, but her use of two letters from Jefferson to John Adams, August 1, 1816, and March 25, 1826, to judge Jefferson's childhood cannot sustain her interpretation. Fawn M. Brodie, *Thomas Jefferson: An Intimate History* (New York, 1974), 46; Lester J. Cappon (ed.), *The Adams-Jefferson Letters* (2 vols.; Chapel Hill, 1959), II, 483, 614.
7. Jefferson, Autobiography, in Ford (ed.), *Works of Jefferson*, I, 5.
8. *Ibid.*
9. *Ibid.*
10. Jefferson to Giovanni Fabbroni, June 8, 1778, in Boyd (ed.), *Papers of Jefferson*, II, 196; Eleanor D. Berman, *Thomas Jefferson Among the Arts* (New York, 1947), 172; Malone, *Jefferson*, I, 47.
11. Jefferson to John Harvie, January 14, 1760 in Boyd (ed.), *Papers of Jefferson*, I, 3; Jefferson to Martha Jefferson, March 28 and May 5, 1787, in Betts and Bear (eds.), *Family Letters*, 34, 40.

12. Jefferson, Autobiography, in Ford (ed.), *Works of Jefferson*, I, 5-6. See also Jefferson to L. H. Giradin, January 15, 1815, in Andrew A. Lipscomb and Albert E. Bergh (eds.), *The Writings of Thomas Jefferson* (20 vols.; Washington, D.C., 1903), XIV, 231.

13. Jefferson, Autobiography, in Ford (ed.), *Works of Jefferson*, I, 6; Malone, *Jefferson*, I, 53; Jefferson to L. H. Giradin, January 15, 1815, in Lipscomb and Bergh (eds.), *Writings of Jefferson*, XIV, 231.

14. Jefferson to Thomas McAuley, June 14, 1819, in Boyd (ed.), *Papers of Jefferson*, I, 32n.

15. Jefferson to John Page, December 25, 1762, in *ibid.*, 5.

16. Jefferson to Page, January 20, 1763, in *ibid.*, 7.

17. Jefferson to Page, July 15, 1763, quoting Page's letter to Jefferson, May 30, 1763 (lost), in *ibid.*, 9.

18. Brodie, *Jefferson*, 65; Jefferson to Page, February 12, 1763, in Boyd (ed.), *Papers of Jefferson*, I, 8.

19. Jefferson to Page, July 15 and October 7, 1763, in Boyd (ed.), *Papers of Jefferson*, 9-11. See also Gilbert Chinard (ed.), *The Literary Bible of Thomas Jefferson: His Commonplace Book of Philosophers and Poets* (Baltimore, 1928), 22; Douglas L. Wilson, "Thomas Jefferson's Early Notebooks," *William and Mary Quarterly*, 3rd Ser., XLII (1985), 441.

20. Jefferson to Thomas Turpin, February 5, 1769, in Boyd (ed.), *Papers of Jefferson*, I, 24.

21. Jefferson to Page, December 25, 1762, in *ibid.*, 5; Jefferson to Madison, February 17, 1826, in Ford (ed.), *Works of Jefferson*, XII, 456; Merrill D. Peterson, *Thomas Jefferson and the New Nation: A Biography* (New York, 1970), 16-17. See also Jefferson to Horatio G. Spafford, March 17, 1814, in Lipscomb and Bergh (eds.), *Writings of Jefferson*, XIV, 120.

22. Gilbert Chinard (ed.), *The Commonplace Book of Thomas Jefferson: A Repertory of His Ideas on Government* (Baltimore, 1926), 67-167. See also Edward Dumbauld, *Thomas Jefferson and the Law* (Norman, 1978), 15, 171.

23. Jefferson to Thomas Cooper, February 10, 1814, in Ford (ed.), *Works of Jefferson*, I, 454n.

24. Malone, *Jefferson*, I, 435-40; Thomas Jefferson Memorial Foundation, *Report of the Curator, 1981* (Monticello, [1982]), 20-21.

25. Malone, *Jefferson*, I, 439-41.

26. Hugh Jones, *The Present State of Virginia*, ed. Richard L. Morton (Chapel Hill, 1956), 70.

27. Jefferson to William Wirt, August 15, 1815, in Ford (ed.), *Works of Jefferson*, XI, 404, 407; Edmund S. Morgan (ed.), *Prologue to Revolution: Sources and Documents on the Stamp Act Crisis, 1764-1766* (Chapel Hill, 1959), 47; Robert D. Meade, *Patrick Henry: Patriot in the Making* (Philadelphia, 1957), 169-79.

28. Jefferson to Page, May 25, 1766, in Boyd (ed.), *Papers of Jefferson*, I, 19-20.

29. Edwin Morris Betts (ed.), *Thomas Jefferson's Garden Book, 1766-1824* (Philadelphia, 1944), 1, 6, 11, 12.

30. The entry is quoted in full in Dumbauld, *Jefferson and the Law*, 89.

31. Jefferson, memoranda books, 1767-1770, 1773, in Thomas Jefferson Papers, Library of Congress; Henry S. Randall, *The Life of Thomas Jefferson* (3 vols.; New York, 1858), I, 45-48; Dumbauld, *Jefferson and the Law*, 158n.

32. Dumbauld, *Jefferson and the Law*, 89-90, 93; Malone, *Jefferson*, I, 122.

33. Edmund Randolph, *History of Virginia*, ed. Arthur H. Shaffer (Charlottesville, 1970), 182-83.

34. *Howell* v. *Netherland,* April, 1770. Jefferson's argument is in Ford (ed.), *Works of Jefferson,* I, 470–81.

35. *Ibid.,* 480–81; Dumbauld, *Jefferson and the Law,* 84.

36. Dumbauld, *Jefferson and the Law,* 89, 157n; Boyd (ed.), *Papers of Jefferson,* VI, 151–58.

Chapter II

1. Rind's *Virginia Gazette,* December 15, 1768; Charles S. Sydnor, *Gentlemen Freeholders: Political Practices in Washington's Virginia* (Chapel Hill, 1952), 20–29; memorandum or account book, 1767–1770, entries for December 5, 1768, in Thomas Jefferson Papers, Library of Congress (hereinafter cited LC).

2. Julian P. Boyd (ed.), *The Papers of Thomas Jefferson* (Princeton, 1950–), I, 26–27. See also Jefferson to William Wirt, August 5, 1815, in Paul L. Ford (ed.), *The Works of Thomas Jefferson* (Federal Edition; 12 vols.; New York, 1904), I, 466n.

3. *Journals of the House of Burgesses of Virginia, 1766–1769,* ed. John P. Kennedy (Richmond, 1906), 190–91.

4. Proceedings, May 17, 1769, in Boyd (ed.), *Papers of Jefferson,* I, 27–31; Purdie and Dixon's *Virginia Gazette,* May 18, 1769.

5. See Robert A. Rutland (ed.), *The Papers of George Mason, 1725–1792* (3 vols.; Chapel Hill, 1970), I, 94–96, 112–13.

6. Jefferson, Autobiography, in Ford (ed.), *Works of Jefferson,* I, 9; *Journals of the House of Burgesses, 1766–1769,* pp. 221, 228, 229, 262, 296, 298, 308, 317; *Journals of the House of Burgesses of Virginia, 1770–1772,* ed. John P. Kennedy (Richmond, 1906), 63, 105.

7. Other titles included William Petyt, *Jus Parliamentarium; or, the Ancient Power, Jurisdiction, Rights and Liberties, of the Most High Court of Parliament, Revived and Asserted;* William Hakewill, *Modus tenendi Parliamentum; or the Old Manner of Holding Parliaments in England;* and Ferdinando Warner, *The History of the Rebellion and Civil-War in Ireland.* Invoice enclosed in Perkins, Buchanan & Brown to Jefferson, October 2, 1769, in Boyd (ed.), *Papers of Jefferson,* I, 34; E. Millicent Sowerby (ed.), *Catalogue of the Library of Thomas Jefferson* (5 vols.; Washington, D.C., 1952–59), I, 192–93, II, 70, III, 2, 12, 20–21, 123, 177, 182, 237–38.

8. Garry Wills, *Inventing America: Jefferson's Declaration of Independence* (New York, 1978), 174; Frank L. Dewey, "Thomas Jefferson's Notes on Divorce," *William and Mary Quarterly,* 3rd Ser., XXXIX (1982), 214–15, 217, 220.

9. Sowerby (ed.), *Catalogue,* III, 12. It was also included in Locke's *Works* sold to Congress. Douglas L. Wilson, "Sowerby Revisited: The Unfinished Catalogue of Thomas Jefferson's Library," *William and Mary Quarterly,* 3rd Ser., XLI (1984), 628.

10. It is estimated that two-thirds of Jefferson's library was destroyed by fire in 1851. Sowerby (ed.), *Catalogue,* I, x.

11. This invoice, not published in Boyd (ed.), *Papers of Jefferson,* is in the Virginia Historical Society, Richmond.

12. Account book, August 4, 1773, in Jefferson Papers, LC.

13. Jefferson to John Page, February 21, 1770, in Boyd (ed.), *Papers of Jefferson,* I, 34–35.

14. Jefferson to James Ogilvie, February 20, 1771, in *ibid.,* 63; Jefferson's account book, 1767–1770, quoted in Edwin Morris Betts (ed.), *Thomas Jefferson's Garden Book, 1764–1824* (Philadelphia, 1944), 12, 16–18, 20.

15. Frederick D. Nichols, "Jefferson: The Making of an Architect," in William Howard Adams (ed.), *Jefferson and the Arts: An Extended View* (Washington, D.C.,

1976), 163; Frederick D. Nichols, *Thomas Jefferson's Architectural Drawings* (3rd ed.; Charlottesville, 1961), 34–38.

16. Thomas Jefferson, *Notes on the State of Virginia*, ed. William Peden (Chapel Hill, 1954), 152–53; Jefferson to Page, May 25, 1766, in Boyd (ed.), *Papers of Jefferson*, I, 20; Edmund Randolph, *History of Virginia*, ed. Arthur H. Shaffer (Charlottesville, 1970), 181.

17. Marie Kimball, *Jefferson: The Road to Glory, 1743 to 1776* (New York, 1943), 147; James Gibbs, *A Book of Architecture, Containing Designs of Buildings and Ornaments* (London, 1728); Gibbs, *Rules for Drawing the Several Parts of Architecture* (London, 1732); Robert Morris, *Select Architecture: Being Regular Designs of Plans and Elevations Well Suited to Both Town and Country* (London, 1755); Nichols, *Jefferson's Architectural Drawings*, 34–35; William B. O'Neal, *Jefferson's Fine Arts Library: His Selections for the University of Virginia Together with His Own Architectural Books* (Charlottesville, 1976), 136–42, 231.

18. Nichols, "Jefferson: The Making of an Architect," 164–66; Nichols, *Jefferson's Architectural Drawings*, 3, 34–35.

19. Nichols, *Jefferson's Architectural Drawings*, 3; Fiske Kimball, *Thomas Jefferson, Architect* (Boston, 1916), 24–26 and fig. 23; Marquis de Chastellux, *Travels in North America in the Years 1780, 1781 and 1782*, ed. Howard C. Rice, Jr. (2 vols.; Chapel Hill, 1963), II, 391, 575.

20. Marquis de Chastellux, *Travels in North America*, II, 391.

21. Jefferson to Maria Cosway, October 12, 1786, and Jefferson to George Gilmer, August 12, 1787, in Boyd (ed.), *Papers of Jefferson*, X, 447, XII, 26.

22. Jefferson to Thomas Adams, June 1, 1771, and Jefferson to Robert Skipwith, August 3, 1771, in *ibid.*, I, 71, 78; Kimball, *Jefferson: Road to Glory*, 173–74.

23. It was years after the incident that Walker charged Jefferson with the indiscretion and not until Jefferson became president that the story found its way into the press. Dumas Malone, *Jefferson and His Time* (6 vols.; Boston, 1948–81), I, 447–51.

24. *Ibid.*, I, 156–58, 432; Kimball, *Jefferson: Road to Glory*, 169, 176. Fawn Brodie questioned the date of John Skelton's death, but the evidence is not conclusive. Brodie, *Thomas Jefferson: An Intimate History* (New York, 1974), 86, 505.

25. Sarah N. Randolph, *The Domestic Life of Thomas Jefferson* (1871; rpr. New York, 1958), 43–44; Skipwith to Jefferson, September 20, 1771, in Boyd (ed.), *Papers of Jefferson*, I, 84.

26. Jefferson to Thomas Adams, June 1, 1771, in Boyd (ed.), *Papers of Jefferson*, I, 72.

27. Betts (ed.), *Jefferson's Garden Book*, 33; Randolph, *Domestic Life of Jefferson*, 44.

28. Kimball, *Jefferson: Road to Glory*, 156. See also Malone, *Jefferson*, I, 150.

29. *Journals of the House of Burgesses, 1770–1772*, p. 143.

Chapter III

1. Jefferson, Autobiography, in Paul L. Ford (ed.), *The Works of Thomas Jefferson* (Federal Edition; 12 vols.; New York, 1904), I, 9.

2. *Ibid.*, 9–10.

3. *Journals of the House of Burgesses, 1773–1776, Including the Records of the Committee of Correspondence*, ed. John P. Kennedy (Richmond, 1905), 28; Lawrence Henry Gipson, *The Coming of the Revolution, 1763–1775* (New York, 1954), 209–10; Jefferson, Autobiography, in Ford (ed.), *Works of Jefferson*, I, 10–11.

4. Dunmore to Lord Dartmouth, March 31, 1773, in *Journals of the House of Burgesses, 1773–1776*, x.

5. Julian P. Boyd (ed.), *The Papers of Thomas Jefferson* (Princeton, 1950–), I, 98n; Dumas Malone, *Jefferson and His Time* (6 vols.; Boston, 1948–81), I, 431, 441–45.

6. Purdie and Dixon's *Virginia Gazette* reported the news May 19, 1774. Robert A. Rutland (ed.), *The Papers of George Mason, 1725–1792* (3 vols.; Chapel Hill, 1970), I, 191n.

7. Jefferson, Autobiography, in Ford (ed.), *Works of Jefferson*, I, 11–12; Resolution, May 24, 1774, in Boyd (ed.), *Papers of Jefferson*, 105–106, 106n.

8. *Journals of the House of Burgesses, 1773–1776*, p. 132; Boyd (ed.), *Papers of Jefferson*, I, 106n, 107n; George Washington to George William Fairfax, June 10, 1774, in John C. Fitzpatrick (ed.), *The Writings of George Washington* (39 vols.; Washington, D.C., 1931–44), III, 223.

9. Association, May 27, 1774, in Boyd (ed.), *Papers of Jefferson*, I, 107–108.

10. *Journals of the House of Burgesses, 1773–1776*, p. 138; letter from Peyton Randolph and others, May 31, 1774, in Boyd (ed.), *Papers of Jefferson*, I, 111–12; see also 110n.

11. Boyd (ed.), *Papers of Jefferson*, I, 117–19.

12. Jefferson, Autobiography, in Ford (ed.), *Works of Jefferson*, I, 14–15; Boyd (ed.), *Papers of Jefferson*, I, 669–73.

13. Jefferson, Autobiography, in Ford (ed.), *Works of Jefferson*, I, 14.

14. Jefferson, *A Summary View of the Rights of British America*, in Boyd (ed.), *Papers of Jefferson*, I, 121–25.

15. Jefferson, Autobiography, in Ford (ed.), *Works of Jefferson*, I, 14.

16. Jefferson, *A Summary View*, in Boyd (ed.), *Papers of Jefferson*, I, 121–35.

17. The resolutions are in Boyd (ed.), *Papers of Jefferson*, I, 137–40.

18. *Ibid.*, I, 672.

19. Editorial work now in progress on Jefferson's notebooks by Douglas L. Wilson will aid greatly in dating the entries. See Wilson, "Thomas Jefferson's Early Notebooks," *William and Mary Quarterly*, 3rd Ser., XLII (1985), 433–52.

20. On Jefferson's reading of Montesquieu see David W. Carrithers, "Montesquieu, Jefferson and the Fundamentals of Eighteenth-Century Republican Theory," *French-American Review*, VI (1982), 160–88.

21. Gilbert Chinard (ed.), *The Commonplace Book of Thomas Jefferson: A Repertory of His Ideas on Government* (Baltimore, 1926), 18–19, 99. For Jefferson's early reading see H. Trevor Colbourn, *The Lamp of Experience: Whig History and the Intellectual Origins of the American Revolution* (Chapel Hill, 1965), 158–60.

22. On the familiarity of Virginians with Locke see Richard Beale Davis, *A Colonial Southern Bookshelf: Reading in the Eighteenth Century* (Athens, Ga., 1979), 49–50.

23. Jefferson to Mason Locke Weems, December 13, 1804, in Thomas Jefferson Papers, Library of Congress; Gilbert Chinard (ed.), *The Literary Bible of Thomas Jefferson: His Commonplace Book of Philosophers and Poets* (Baltimore, 1928), 19–20, 40–71; Jefferson to Robert Skipwith, August 31, 1771, in Boyd (ed.), *Papers of Jefferson*, I, 76–80. On Jefferson's later criticism of Montesquieu, see Joyce Appleby, "What Is Still American in the Political Philosophy of Thomas Jefferson," *William and Mary Quarterly*, 3rd Ser., XXXIX (1982), 287–301.

24. Examples from both are given in Garry Wills, *Inventing America: Jefferson's Declaration of Independence* (New York, 1978), 80–83.

25. Jefferson to William Wirt, August 5, 1815, in Ford (ed.), *Works of Jefferson*, XI, 413.

26. Chinard (ed.), *Commonplace Book*, 21–22, 172, 178, 181–82; Abraham Stanyan, *Grecian History Down to the Death of Philip Macedon* (2 vols.; London, 1739).

27. Charles Francis Adams (ed.), *Memoirs of John Quincy Adams, Comprising Portions of His Diary from 1795 to 1848* (12 vols.; Philadelphia, 1874–77), VIII, 279; Wills, *Inventing America*, 84.

28. L. H. Butterfield (ed.), *Diary and Autobiography of John Adams* (4 vols.; Cambridge, Mass., 1961), III, 335–36. Garry Wills argued that Adams was not referring to *A Summary View*, but Julian Boyd concluded that he was. Wills, *Inventing America*, 78; Boyd (ed.), *Papers of Jefferson*, I, 676.

29. A record of the vote is reproduced in Douglas Southall Freeman, *George Washington: A Biography* (7 vols.; New York, 1948–57), III, 373.

30. Boyd (ed.), *Papers of Jefferson*, I, 672–73; Marie Kimball, *Jefferson: The Road to Glory, 1743 to 1776* (New York, 1943), 242–43.

31. *Journals of the Continental Congress, 1774–1789*, ed. Worthington C. Ford *et al.* (34 vols.; Washington, D.C., 1904–37), I, 67–73.

32. Association, October 20, 1774, in *ibid.*, 75–80; Jefferson, Autobiography, in Ford (ed.), *Works of Jefferson*, I, 16; Malone, *Jefferson*, I, 192; Kimball, *Jefferson: Road to Glory*, 256.

33. Convention proceedings, in Peter Force (ed.), *American Archives*, Ser. 4, II (1839), 165.

34. Jefferson, Autobiography, in Ford (ed.), *Works of Jefferson*, I, 16; Edmund Randolph, *History of Virginia*, ed. Arthur H. Shaffer (Charlottesville, 1970), 213; Report, [March 25, 1775], in Boyd (ed.), *Papers of Jefferson*, I, 160–62.

35. William Wirt, *The Life of Patrick Henry*, ed. Henry Ketcham (1817; rpr. New York, 1903), 122; Jefferson to Small, May 7, 1775, in Boyd (ed.), *Papers of Jefferson*, I, 165.

36. Kimball, *Jefferson: Road to Glory*, 260–62.

37. Jefferson, Autobiography, in Ford (ed.), *Works of Jefferson*, I, 17; Jefferson, comments on François Soules' *Histoire des troubles de L'Amérique Anglaise*, August 3, 1786, in Boyd (ed.), *Papers of Jefferson*, X, 371.

38. Jefferson, Autobiography, in Ford (ed.), *Works of Jefferson*, I, 17; Boyd (ed.), *Papers of Jefferson*, I, 174n.

39. Virginia Resolutions, June 10, 1775, in Boyd (ed.), *Papers of Jefferson*, I, 170–74.

40. Jefferson, account book, June 17, 1775, transcript by James A. Bear, Jr., in University of Virginia library, Charlottesville.

Chapter IV

1. Jefferson to Francis Eppes, June 26, 1775, Julian P. Boyd (ed.), *The Papers of Thomas Jefferson* (Princeton, 1950–), I, 174.

2. Samuel Ward to Henry Ward, June 22, 1775, in Paul H. Smith (ed.), *Letters of Delegates to Congress, 1774–1789* (Washington, D.C., 1976–), I, 535; Adams to Timothy Pickering, August 6, 1822, in Charles Francis Adams (ed.), *The Works of John Adams* (10 vols.; Boston, 1856), II, 513–14; L. H. Butterfield (ed.), *Diary and Autobiography of John Adams*, (4 vols.; Cambridge, Mass., 1961), III, 335.

3. Adams to William Tudor, July 6, 1775, in Smith (ed.), *Letters of Delegates*, I, 587; Boyd (ed.), *Papers of Jefferson*, I, 187–219.

4. Jefferson to Gilmer, [July 5, 1775], Gilmer to Jefferson, [July 26 or 27, 1775], in Boyd (ed.), *Papers of Jefferson*, I, 185–86, 186n, 236–38.

5. *Journals of the Continental Congress, 1774–1789*, ed. Worthington C. Ford *et al.* (34 vols.; Washington, D.C., 1904–37), II, 127, 158; Jefferson, Autobiography, in Paul L. Ford (ed.), *The Works of Thomas Jefferson* (Federal Edition; 12 vols.; New York,

1904), I, 19; Virginia delegates to Peyton Randolph, July 11, 1775, in Boyd (ed.), *Papers of Jefferson*, I, 223–24.

6. Boyd (ed.), *Papers of Jefferson*, I, 225–33.

7. Convention proceedings, in Peter Force (ed.), *American Archives*, Ser. 4, III (1840), 377, 379, 383.

8. Jefferson to John Randolph, August 25, 1775, in Boyd (ed.), *Papers of Jefferson*, I, 241.

9. Boyd (ed.), *Papers of Jefferson*, I, 66–67.

10. Jefferson to Randolph, August 25, 1775, in *ibid.*, 241–42.

11. Joseph Hewes to James Iredell, November 9, 1775, Richard Henry Lee to Washington, November 13, 1775, in Smith (ed.), *Letters of Delegates*, II, 322, 335, 337n; Marie Kimball, *Jefferson: The Road to Glory* (New York, 1943), 273; Jefferson to Francis Eppes, October 24, 1775, in Boyd (ed.), *Papers of Jefferson*, I, 249.

12. Jefferson to Randolph, November 29, 1775, in Boyd (ed.), *Papers of Jefferson*, I, 269.

13. Jefferson to Eppes, November 7, 1775, in *ibid.*, 252.

14. Boyd (ed.), *Papers of Jefferson*, I, 272–73, 274–75.

15. Jefferson to Thomas Cooper, October 27, 1808, in Andrew A. Lipscomb and Albert E. Bergh (eds.), *The Writings of Thomas Jefferson* (20 vols.; Washington, D.C., 1903), XII, 180; Jefferson to Dr. Vine Utley, March 21, 1819, in Sarah N. Randolph, *The Domestic Life of Thomas Jefferson* (1871; rpr. New York, 1958), 371; Fawn M. Brodie, *Thomas Jefferson: An Intimate History* (New York, 1974), 114–15; Edmund Pendleton to Jefferson, May 24, 1776, in Boyd (ed.), *Papers of Jefferson*, I, 296.

16. *Parliamentary History of England*, XVIII (London, 1813), 696; Adams to Horatio Gates, March 23, 1776, in Smith (ed.), *Letters of Delegates*, III, 431; John R. Alden, *The American Revolution, 1775–1783* (New York, 1954), 62–67; Nelson to Jefferson, February 4, 1776, in Boyd (ed.), *Papers of Jefferson*, I, 286.

17. Page to Jefferson, April 6, 1776, James McClurg to Jefferson, April 6, 1776, Jefferson to Thomas Nelson, Jr., May 16, 1776, in Boyd (ed.), *Papers of Jefferson*, I, 287, 292.

18. Resolutions, May 15, 1776, in *ibid.*, 290–91.

19. Jefferson to Nelson, May 16, 1776, Pendleton to Jefferson, May 24, 1776, in *ibid.*, 292, 296.

20. Boyd (ed.), *Papers of Jefferson*, I, 329–86; Robert A. Rutland (ed.), *The Papers of George Mason* (3 vols.; Chapel Hill, 1970), I, 295–310.

21. Wythe to Jefferson, July 27, 1776, in Boyd (ed.), *Papers of Jefferson*, I, 476–77.

22. Boyd (ed.), *Papers of Jefferson*, I, 345–46, 415–19.

23. Jefferson's drafts and the constitution as adopted are in *ibid.*, 337–83.

24. Jefferson to Pendleton, August 26, 1776, in *ibid.*, 503.

25. Jefferson to Samuel Kercheval, July 12, 1816, in Ford (ed.), *Works of Jefferson*, XII, 4.

26. See Gordon S. Wood, *The Creation of the American Republic, 1776–1787* (Chapel Hill, 1969), 255.

27. Rutland (ed.), *Papers of Mason*, I, 289; Boyd (ed.), *Papers of Jefferson*, I, 363.

28. Wythe to Jefferson, July 27, 1776, in Boyd (ed.), *Papers of Jefferson*, I, 477; Pendleton to Jefferson, August 10, 1776, in David J. Mays (ed.), *The Letters and Papers of Edmund Pendleton* (2 vols.; Charlottesville, 1967), I, 197.

29. Boyd (ed.), *Papers of Jefferson*, I, 298.

30. Jefferson, Notes on proceedings in Congress, in *ibid.*, 313.

31. Silvio A. Bedini, *Declaration of Independence Desk: Relic of Revolution* (Washington, D.C., 1981), 5–6.

358 NOTES TO PAGES 47-55

...ms to Timothy Pickering, August 6, 1822, in Adams (ed.), *Works of John
...s*, II, 514.

33. Jefferson to Madison, August 30, 1823, in Ford (ed.), *Works of Jefferson*, I, 31n.

34. Boyd (ed.), *Papers of Jefferson*, I, 413-33. A detailed textual analysis is in
Julian P. Boyd, *The Declaration of Independence: The Evolution of the Text* (Princeton,
1945). See also Jefferson to Madison, August 30, 1823, in Ford (ed.), *Works of Jefferson*, I, 31n, and Butterfield (ed.), *Diary and Autobiography of John Adams*, III, 335-37.

35. Boyd (ed.), *Papers of Jefferson*, I, 314-15, 426.

36. Jefferson to Richard Henry Lee, July 8, 1776, Edmund Pendleton to Jefferson, August 10, 1776, in *ibid.*, 455-56, 488.

37. Boyd (ed.), *Papers of Jefferson*, I, 315, 414.

38. Jefferson to Madison, August 30, 1823, in Ford (ed.), *Works of Jefferson*, I, 31n;
Adams to Timothy Pickering, August 6, 1822, in Adams (ed.), *Works of John Adams*,
II, 514.

39. Jefferson to Henry Lee, May 8, 1825, in Ford (ed.), *Works of Jefferson*, XII, 409.

40. Rutland (ed.), *Papers of Mason*, I, 276, 283; Boyd (ed.), *Papers of Jefferson*, I,
423.

41. Garry Wills, in *Inventing America: Jefferson's Declaration of Independence* (New
York, 1978), denigrated the influence of Locke and argued for the dominant influence of Francis Hutcheson and the Scottish moral philosophers. Wills's use of evidence and his conclusions have been challenged by Ronald Hamowy in "Jefferson
and the Scottish Enlightenment: A Critique of Garry Wills's *Inventing America: Jefferson's Declaration of Independence*," *William and Mary Quarterly*, 3rd Ser., XXXVI (1979),
503-23.

42. See Boyd, *Declaration of Independence*, 22-24.

43. Boyd (ed.), *Papers of Jefferson*, I, 423; Arthur M. Schlesinger, Sr., "The Lost
Meaning of the 'Pursuit of Happiness,'" *William and Mary Quarterly*, 3rd Ser., XXI
(1964), 325-27.

44. See Chapter I.

45. Bartlett to John Langdon, July 1, 1776, in Smith (ed.), *Letters of Delegates*, IV,
351.

46. Caesar Rodney to Thomas Rodney, July 4, 1776, Adams to Mary Palmer, July
5, 1776, Adams to Abigail Adams, July 3, 1776, in *ibid.*, 388, 389, 376.

Chapter V

1. Edmund Randolph to Jefferson, June 23, 1776, William Fleming to Jefferson,
July 27, 1776, Jefferson to Edmund Pendleton, [*ca.* June 30, 1776], in Julian P. Boyd
(ed.), *The Papers of Thomas Jefferson* (Princeton, 1950-), I, 407, 474, 408.

2. Jefferson to Richard Henry Lee, July 29, 1776, Pendleton to Jefferson, August
26, 1776, in *ibid.*, 477, 508.

3. Jefferson to William Fleming, July 1, 1776, in *ibid.*, 412.

4. Pendleton to Jefferson, July 22, and August 10, 1776, in *ibid.*, 472, 489.

5. Boyd (ed.), *Papers of Jefferson*, I, 605.

6. Jefferson to Hancock, October 11, 1776, in *ibid.*, 524.

7. Boyd (ed.), *Papers of Jefferson*, I, 525-58, 605-52. On the evangelical movement in Virginia see Rhys Isaac, *The Transformation of Virginia, 1740-1790* (Chapel
Hill, 1982), 200-203, 260-95.

8. Jefferson, Autobiography, in Paul L. Ford (ed.), *The Works of Thomas Jefferson*
(Federal Edition; 12 vols.; New York, 1904), *Journal of the House of Delegates of Virginia*

(Williamsburg, 1776), October 11, 14, 1776, in William S. Jenkins (ed.), *Records of the States of the United States of America: A Microfilm Compilation* (Washington, D.C., 1949).

9. Boyd (ed.), *Papers of Jefferson*, I, 525–28, 534; Jefferson, Autobiography in Ford (ed.), *Works of Jefferson*, I, 63.

10. The conflict over religion in Virginia is summarized in Merrill D. Peterson, *Thomas Jefferson and the New Nation: A Biography* (New York, 1970), 133–44. See also Thomas E. Buckley, *Church and State in Revolutionary Virginia, 1776–1787* (Charlottesville, 1977), 17–62; Isaac, *Transformation of Virginia*, 278–95.

11. Jefferson to Adams, October 28, 1813, in Lester J. Cappon (ed.), *The Adams-Jefferson Letters* (2 vols.; Chapel Hill, 1959), II, 389. The importance of the abolition of entail and primogeniture in bringing about a less aristocratic society has been questioned by C. Ray Keim, "Primogeniture and Entail in Colonial Virginia," *William and Mary Quarterly*, 3rd Ser., XXV (1968), 545–86.

12. Jefferson, Autobiography, in Ford (ed.), *Works of Jefferson*, I, 58. Compare with the reference to natural aristocracy in James Harrington's *The Commonwealth of Oceana* (1656), quoted in Lance Banning, *The Jeffersonian Persuasion: Evolution of a Party Ideology* (Ithaca, N.Y., 1978), 26.

13. Jefferson, Autobiography, in Ford (ed.), *Works of Jefferson*, I, 66–67.

14. The act is in Boyd (ed.), *Papers of Jefferson*, I, 562–63.

15. Jefferson, Autobiography, in Ford (ed.), *Works of Jefferson*, I, 67–68; Robert A. Rutland (ed.), *The Papers of George Mason, 1725–1792* (3 vols.; Chapel Hill, 1970), I, 327, 331; Thomas Jefferson, *Notes on the State of Virginia*, ed. William Peden (Chapel Hill, 1954), 137; Boyd (ed.), *Papers of Jefferson*, II, 306.

16. Jefferson, Autobiography, in Ford (ed.), *Works of Jefferson*, I, 70; Pendleton to Jefferson, May 11, 1779 in David J. Mays (ed.), *The Letters and Papers of Edmund Pendleton* (2 vols.; Charlottesville, 1967), I, 283; Boyd (ed.), *Papers of Jefferson*, II, 329–33, 492–95, 515, 526; Jefferson, *Notes on Virginia*, 137.

17. Boyd (ed.), *Papers of Jefferson*, II, 307, 322.

18. *Ibid.*, 391–93, 535; Ford (ed.), *Works of Jefferson*, I, 77.

19. Jefferson to George Wythe, August 13, 1786, in Boyd (ed.), *Papers of Jefferson*, X, 244.

20. Boyd (ed.), *Papers of Jefferson*, II, 526–33; Jefferson, *Notes on Virginia*, 146.

21. Jefferson, *Notes on Virginia*, 146–47.

22. "A Bill for the More General Diffusion of Knowledge," in Boyd (ed.), *Papers of Jefferson*, II, 526–27.

23. Boyd (ed.), *Papers of Jefferson*, II, 535n.

24. *Ibid.*, 492–93; Peterson, *Thomas Jefferson and the New Nation*, 124–33. See also Boyd (ed.), *Papers of Jefferson*, II, 505n.

25. Madison to Jefferson, February 15, 1787, in Boyd (ed.), *Papers of Jefferson*, XI, 152.

26. Jefferson, *Notes in Virginia*, 137–38. On Jefferson's *Notes on Virginia* see Chapter VII.

27. Ford (ed.), *Works of Jefferson*, I, 77; Boyd (ed.), *Papers of Jefferson*, II, 472–73; Jefferson, *Notes on Virginia*, 214, 297.

28. Jefferson, *Notes on Virginia*, 141–43; Ramsay to Jefferson, May 3, 1786 in Boyd (ed.), *Papers of Jefferson*, IX, 441.

29. John C. Miller, *The Wolf by the Ears: Thomas Jefferson and Slavery* (New York, 1977), 52, 57. For a detailed examination of Jefferson and slavery and race see Winthrop D. Jordan, *White over Black: American Attitudes Toward the Negro, 1550–1812* (Chapel Hill, 1968), 429–81.

...n, *Notes on Virginia*, 162–63.

...dison to Samuel H. Smith, November 4, 1826, in Boyd (ed.), *Papers of ...son*, II, 313.

32. "A Bill for Establishing a Public Library," in *ibid.*, 544.

Chapter VI

1. Julian P. Boyd (ed.), *The Papers of Thomas Jefferson* (Princeton, 1950–), II, 278; Emory G. Evans, *Thomas Nelson of Yorktown: Revolutionary Virginian* (Williamsburg, 1975), 3, 82; David J. Mays (ed.), *The Letters and Papers of Edmund Pendleton* (2 vols.; Charlottesville, 1967), I, 290.

2. Page to Jefferson, June 2, 1779, Jefferson to Page, June 3, 1779, in Boyd (ed.), *Papers of Jefferson*, II, 278–79.

3. Jefferson to Baron von Riedesel, July 4, 1779, Jefferson to Lee, June 17, 1779, in *ibid.*, III, 24, II, 298.

4. Jefferson to Lee, September 13, 1780, in *ibid.*, III, 643.

5. Council to Jefferson, November 13, 1799, in *ibid.*, 183–84; Jefferson to James Barbour, January 22, 1812, in Paul L. Ford (ed.), *The Works of Thomas Jefferson* (Federal Edition; 12 vols.; New York, 1904), XI, 222–25; H. R. McIlwaine and Wilmer L. Hall (eds.), *Journals of the Council of State of Virginia* (3 vols.; Richmond, 1931–52), II, 271–75.

6. Boyd (ed.), *Papers of Jefferson*, II, 364–65, 365n, 366–67, III, 399n.

7. *Ibid.*, I, 598, II, 271–72.

8. Marie Kimball, *Jefferson: War and Peace, 1776 to 1784* (New York, 1947), 55–58.

9. Board of War to Jefferson, November 16, 1779, Jefferson to the Board of War, November 18, 1779, Washington to Jefferson, December 11, 1779, in Boyd (ed.), *Papers of Jefferson*, III, 191, 193–94, 217.

10. Madison to Jefferson, March 27, 1780, Washington to Jefferson, April 15, 1780, in *ibid.*, 335, 352–53; Dumas Malone, *Jefferson and His Time* (6 vols.; Boston, 1848–81), I, 322.

11. Boyd (ed.), *Papers of Jefferson*, III, 403n.

12. Jefferson to Samuel Huntington, June 9, 1780, Gates to Jefferson, July 19, 1780, in *ibid.*, 426, 496.

13. Jefferson to Washington, October 22, 1780, Greene to Jefferson, December 6, 1780, in *ibid.*, IV, 59–60, 183–84.

14. William Davies to Jefferson, February 1, 1781, in *ibid.*, 493–94.

15. Boyd (ed.), *Papers of Jefferson*, III, 318–19, 535, IV, 76.

16. On Jefferson's role in the war in the West see Kimball, *Jefferson: War and Peace*, 78–95.

17. Morgan to Jefferson, February 1, 1781, Jefferson to Lafayette, March 10, 1781, in Boyd (ed.), *Papers of Jefferson*, IV, 495–96, V, 113. On Virginians' attitudes toward military service see Charles Royster, *A Revolutionary People at War* (Chapel Hill, 1979), 322–25.

18. Greene to Jefferson, March 27, 1781, Jefferson to Greene, April 1, 1781, in Boyd (ed.), *Papers of Jefferson*, IV, 258, 312.

19. Jefferson's account of these events is in Boyd (ed.), *Papers of Jefferson*, IV, 258–70.

20. *Ibid.*, 263–64.

21. Jefferson to Lafayette, May 14, 1781, in *ibid.*, V, 644; Evans, *Thomas Nelson*, 99–101; John R. Alden, *The South in the Revolution, 1763–1789* (Baton Rouge, 1957), 293.

22. Boyd (ed.), *Papers of Jefferson*, IV, 260–61; see also Jefferson, Autobiography, in Ford (ed.), *Works of Jefferson*, I, 79.

23. Jefferson's account is in Boyd (ed.), *Papers of Jefferson*, IV, 260–61. See also Madison to Philip Mazzei, July 7, 1781, in William T. Hutchinson, William M. E. Rachal, and Robert A. Rutland (eds.), *The Papers of James Madison* (Chicago and Charlottesville, 1962–), III, 178.

24. Boyd (ed.), *Papers of Jefferson*, IV, 265.

25. Resolution, in *ibid.*, VI, 88.

26. Archibald Cary to Jefferson, June 19, 1781, in *ibid.*, 96–97; Robert D. Meade, *Patrick Henry, Practical Revolutionary* (Philadelphia, 1969), 245–48.

27. Jefferson to Nicholas, July 28, 1781, Nicholas to Jefferson, July 31, 1781, in Boyd (ed.), *Papers of Jefferson*, VI, 104–106.

28. Boyd (ed.), *Papers of Jefferson*, IV, 261–62, VI, 134–35, 106–108.

29. *Ibid.*, VI, 135–36.

30. See his letter to Isaac Zane, December 24, 1781, in *ibid.*, 143.

31. See Boyd (ed.), *Papers of Jefferson*, IV, 271–77; Noble E. Cunningham, Jr., *The Jeffersonian Republicans: The Formation of Party Organization, 1789–1801* (Chapel Hill, 1957), 100.

32. Boyd (ed.), *Papers of Jefferson*, VI, 94–95.

33. Jefferson to Thomas McKean, August 4, 1781, in *ibid.*, 113. See also Jefferson to Lafayette, August 4, 1781, in *ibid.*, 112.

34. Randolph to Jefferson, September 7, 1781, Jefferson to Randolph, September 15, 1781, in *ibid.*, 116–17.

35. Madison to Edmund Randolph, June 11, 1782, in Hutchinson, Rachal, and Rutland (eds.), *Papers of Madison*, IV, 333.

Chapter VII

1. Jefferson to the Chavalier D'Anmours, November 30, 1780, in Julian P. Boyd (ed.), *The Papers of Thomas Jefferson,* (Princeton, 1950–), IV, 168.

2. Sullivan to Meshech Weare, December 25, 1780, quoted in *ibid.*, 167n.

3. Jefferson, Autobiography, Paul L. Ford (ed.), *The Works of Thomas Jefferson* (Federal Edition; 12 vols.; New York, 1904), I, 94; Boyd (ed.), *Papers of Jefferson*, IV, 167n; Henry Steele Commager, "Jefferson and the Enlightenment," in Lally Weymouth (ed.), *Thomas Jefferson: The Man, His World, His Influence* (New York, 1973), 40–41; Thomas Jefferson, *Notes on the State of Virginia*, ed. William Peden (Chapel Hill, 1954), xi.

4. Jefferson to Marbois, December 20, 1781, March 24, 1782, in Boyd (ed.), *Papers of Jefferson*, VI, 141–42, 171–72.

5. Jefferson to Thomson, December 20, 1781, Thomson to Jefferson, Mar. 9, 1782, in *ibid.*, 142, 163–64; Jefferson, *Notes on Virginia*, xv. See also Marie Kimball, *Jefferson: War and Peace, 1776 to 1784* (New York, 1947), 270–74.

6. Jefferson, *Notes on Virginia*, 10, 43–65, 103–107.

7. *Ibid.*, 43–65; 268n. See also Daniel J. Boorstin, *The Lost World of Thomas Jefferson* (1948; rpr. Chicago, 1981) 100–105.

8. John C. Greene, *American Science in the Age of Jefferson* (Ames, Iowa, 1984), 31–33.

9. Jefferson, *Notes on Virginia*, 118–20.

10. *Ibid.*, 62.

11. See Chapter V.

12. Jefferson, *Notes on Virginia*, 164–65.

13. Thomson to Jefferson, March 6, 1785, in Boyd (ed.), *Papers of Jefferson*, VIII, 16. On the publication of the work see Chapter VIII.

14. Marquis de Chastellux, *Travels in North America in the Years 1780, 1781, and 1782*, ed. Howard C. Rice, Jr. (2 vols.; Chapel Hill, 1963), II, 391–92.

15. Jefferson, account book, May 8, 1782, transcript by James A. Bear, Jr., in University of Virginia library, Charlottesville.

16. The record of the Jefferson children can be found in Dumas Malone, *Jefferson and His Time* (6 vols.; Boston, 1948–81), I, 434.

17. Jefferson to Monroe, May 20, 1782, in Boyd (ed.), *The Papers of Jefferson*, VI, 186.

18. Boyd (ed.), *The Papers of Jefferson*, VI, 196n.

19. *Ibid.*, 196.

20. Sarah N. Randolph, *The Domestic Life of Jefferson* (1871; rpr. New York, 1958), 63; Boyd (ed.), *Papers of Jefferson*, VI, 199n–200n.

21. Jefferson to Chastellux, November 26, 1782, in Boyd (ed.), *Papers of Jefferson*, VI, 203.

22. The action was taken on November 12, 1782, in *ibid.*, 202.

23. Jefferson to Chastellux, November 26, 1782, in *ibid.*, 203.

24. Jefferson, Autobiography, in Ford (ed.), *Works of Jefferson*, I, 81.

25. Malone, *Jefferson*, I, 405; Jefferson to Monroe, November 18, 1783, in Boyd (ed.), *Papers of Jefferson*, VI, 355.

26. Jefferson to Marbois, December 5, 1783, in *ibid.*, 374.

27. Jefferson to Martha (Patsy) Jefferson, November 28, 1783, in Edwin M. Betts and James A. Bear, Jr. (eds.), *The Family Letters of Thomas Jefferson* (Columbia, Mo., 1966), 19–20.

28. *Ibid.*

29. Boyd (ed.), *Papers of Jefferson*, VI, 404–406, 412.

30. Robert F. Berkhofer, Jr., "Jefferson, the Ordinance of 1784, and the American Territorial System," *William and Mary Quarterly*, 3rd Ser., XXIX (1972), 230–55; William T. Hutchinson, M. E. Rachal, and Robert A. Rutland (eds.), *The Papers of James Madison* (Chicago and Charlottesville, 1962–), II, 77, 138.

31. Boyd (ed.), *Papers of Jefferson*, VI, 592, 604–605.

32. *Ibid.*, 608, 614.

33. The report is in *ibid.*, VII, 65–80.

34. Related documents and notes are in *ibid.*, 150–202.

35. *Ibid.*, 229, 239.

36. Jefferson to Edmund Pendleton, May 25, 1784, in *ibid.*, 292.

37. Boyd (ed.), *Papers of Jefferson*, VII, 303.

38. Jefferson, account book, July 5, 1784, transcript by Bear, in U. Va. library; Jefferson to David Humphreys, June 27, 1784, in Boyd (ed.), *Papers of Jefferson*, VII, 321.

39. Francis Hopkinson to Jefferson, May 30, [1784], Jefferson to Samuel Henley, March 3, 1785, in Boyd (ed.), *Papers of Jefferson*, VII, 295–96, VIII, 11; Kimball, *Jefferson: War and Peace*, 356.

40. Martha Jefferson to Eliza Trist, [1785], in Boyd (ed.), *Papers of Jefferson*, VIII, 436; Jefferson, account book, July 5–24, 1784, transcript by Bear, in U. Va. library.

41. Jefferson, account book, July 26–30, 1784, in U. Va. library; Jefferson to Monroe, November 11, 1784, Martha Jefferson to Eliza Trist, [1785], in Boyd (ed.), *Papers of Jefferson*, VII, 508, VIII, 436–37.

Chapter VIII

1. Martha Jefferson to Eliza Trist, [1785], Jefferson to James Monroe, November 11, 1784, in Julian P. Boyd (ed.), *The Papers of Thomas Jefferson* (Princeton, 1950–), VIII, 437, VII, 508; Jefferson, account book, August 6, 1784, transcript by James A. Bear, Jr., in University of Virginia library, Charlottesville; William Howard Adams (ed.), *The Eye of Thomas Jefferson* (Washington, D.C., 1976), 133.

2. Howard C. Rice, Jr., *Thomas Jefferson's Paris* (Princeton, 1976); 13; Jefferson, account book, August 6, 8, 10, 11, 1784, transcript by Bear, in U. Va. library; Martha Jefferson to Eliza Trist, [1785], Jefferson to Mary Jefferson Bolling, July 23, 1787, in Boyd (ed.), *Papers of Jefferson*, VIII, 437, XI, 612.

3. Rice, *Jefferson's Paris*, 8–9, 37–40, 51; Jefferson to John Jay, May 15, 1788, in Boyd (ed.), *Papers of Jefferson*, XIII, 162; Marie Kimball, *Jefferson: The Scene of Europe, 1784 to 1789* (New York, 1950), 10–12.

4. Jefferson to Monroe, March 18, 1785, in Boyd (ed.), *Papers of Jefferson*, VIII, 43.

5. Jefferson to Monroe, June 17, 1785, in *ibid.*, 233.

6. Jefferson to Bellini, September 30, 1785, in *ibid.*, 568–69; Helen Cripe, *Thomas Jefferson and Music* (Charlottesville, 1974), 19–20.

7. Jefferson to Eliza Trist, August 18, 1785, in Boyd (ed.), *Papers of Jefferson*, VIII, 404.

8. Boyd (ed.), *Papers of Jefferson*, VII, 463–93.

9. Jefferson to Monroe, June 17, 1785, in *ibid.*, VIII, 231. See also *ibid.*, VII, 470, 478–79, VIII, 266–67.

10. Boyd (ed.), *Papers of Jefferson*, VII, 486–87; Jefferson, Autobiography, in Paul L. Ford (ed.), *The Works of Thomas Jefferson* (Federal Edition; 12 vols.; New York, 1904), I, 96.

11. Jefferson to Chastellux, January 16, 1784, Jefferson to Madison, May 25, 1784, in Boyd (ed.), *Papers of Jefferson*, VI, 467, VII, 288–89; Jefferson, Autobiography, in Ford (ed.), *Works of Jefferson*, I, 94.

12. Louis Guillaume Otto to Jefferson, May 28, 1785, in Boyd (ed.), *Papers of Jefferson*, VIII, 169–70. See also inscription in presentation copy to Richard Price, in *ibid.*, facing p. 246.

13. Jefferson to Monroe, June 17, 1785, in *ibid.*, 229.

14. Jefferson to Chastellux, June 1, 1785, in *ibid.*, 184.

15. Jefferson to Madison, May 11, 1785, Madison to Jefferson, November 15, 1785, Thomson to Jefferson, November 2, 1785, in *ibid.*, VIII, 147–48, IX, 9, 38.

16. Jefferson to Madison, September 1, 1785, Jefferson to C. W. F. Dumas, February 2, 1786, Jefferson to Madison, February 8, 1786, Jefferson to Edward Bancroft, February 26, 1786, in *ibid.*, VIII, 462, IX, 244, 265, 267n–68n, 299; Thomas Jefferson, *Notes on the State of Virginia*, ed. William Peden (Chapel Hill, 1954), xviii.

17. Madison to Jefferson, May 12, 1786, in Boyd (ed.), *Papers of Jefferson*, IX, 517; Coolie Verner, "The Maps and Plates Appearing with the Several Editions of Mr. Jefferson's 'Notes on the State of Virginia,'" *Virginia Magazine of History and Biography*, LIX (1951), 21–25; Jefferson, *Notes on Virginia*, xix–xx; Coolie Verner, *A Further Checklist of the Separate Editions of Jefferson's Notes on the State of Virginia* (Charlottesville, 1950), 8; E. Millicent Sowerby (ed.), *Catalogue of the Library of Thomas Jefferson* (5 vols.; Washington, D.C., 1952–59), IV, 301–30.

18. Jefferson to Thomson, June 21, 1785, Jefferson to Stockdale, February 1, 1787, Adams to Jefferson, May 22, 1785, in Boyd (ed.), *Papers of Jefferson*, VIII, 245,

XI, 107, VIII, 160; Marquis de Chastellux, *Travels in North America in the Years 1780, 1781, and 1782*, ed. Howard C. Rice, Jr. (2 vols.; Chapel Hill, 1963), II, 606.

19. Quoted in Marie Kimball, *Jefferson: War and Peace, 1776 to 1784* (New York, 1947), 302–303.

20. John Jay to Jefferson, March 15, 22, 1785, Jefferson to Jay, May 11, June 17, 1785, in Boyd (ed.), *Papers of Jefferson*, VIII, 33, 54, 145–46, 226.

21. Adams to William Gordon, April 27, 1785, Adams to Richard Cranch, April 27, 1785, quoted in *ibid.*, VII, 652n.

22. Jefferson to Francis Hopkinson, January 13, 1795, in *ibid.*, 602–603.

23. Ford (ed.), *Works of Jefferson*, I, 98–99; Lawrence S. Kaplan, *Jefferson and France* (New Haven, 1967), 19–20.

24. Boyd (ed.), *Papers of Jefferson*, VII, 263; Dumas Malone, *Jefferson and His Time* (6 vols.; Boston, 1948–81), II, 31.

25. Jefferson to Nathanael Greene, January 12, [1786], Jefferson to Monroe, November 11, 1784, Jefferson to John Page, August 20, 1785, Boyd (ed.), *Papers of Jefferson*, IX, 168, VII, 511–12, VIII, 419.

26. Jefferson to Adams, November 27, 1785, in *ibid.*, IX, 64. See also documents and editorial notes in *ibid.*, X, 560–70.

27. Lafayette to Jefferson, [October 23, 1786], in *ibid.*, 486.

28. Boyd (ed.), *Papers of Jefferson*, X, 565.

29. Jefferson to Jay, March 12, 1786, in *ibid.*, IX, 325–26; Jefferson, Autobiography, in Ford (ed.), *Works of Jefferson*, I, 97.

30. Alfred L. Bush, "The Life Portraits of Thomas Jefferson," in William Howard Adams (ed.), *Jefferson and the Arts: An Extended View* (Washington, D.C., 1976), 21–22; Jefferson, account book, March 22, April 6, 9, 1786, transcript by Bear, in U. Va. library.

31. Notes on a tour of English gardens, in Boyd (ed.), *Papers of Jefferson*, IX, 369–75. See also Edward Dumbauld, "Jefferson and Adams' English Garden Tour," in Adams (ed.), *Jefferson and the Arts*, 137–57.

32. Boyd (ed.), *Papers of Jefferson*, IX, 369–73, 445.

33. Jefferson to Page, May 4, 1786, in *ibid.*, 445–46.

34. Jefferson to Jay, April 23, 1786, Jefferson to William Temple Franklin, May 7, 1786, in *ibid.*, 402, 466–67.

Chapter IX

1. Theodore Sizer (ed.), *The Autobiography of Colonel John Trumbull, Patriot-Artist, 1756–1843* (New Haven, 1953), 92–93.

2. Benjamin Harrison to Jefferson, July 20, 1784, Jefferson to Harrison, January 12, 1785, Jefferson to Washington, December 10, 1784, in Julian P. Boyd (ed.), *The Papers of Thomas Jefferson* (Princeton, 1950–), VII, 378–79, 600, 567.

3. Donald Jackson and Dorothy Twohig (eds.), *The Diaries of George Washington* (6 vols.; Charlottesville, 1976–79), IV, 200–204; Jefferson to William Temple Franklin, May 7, 1786, in Boyd (ed.), *Papers of Jefferson*, IX, 466.

4. The paper is reproduced in Boyd (ed.), *Papers of Jefferson*, X, opposite p. 179.

5. Alfred L. Bush, "Life Portraits of Thomas Jefferson," in William Howard Adams (ed.), *Jefferson and the Arts: An Extended View* (Washington, D.C., 1976), 25; Irma B. Jaffe, *John Trumbull, Patriot-Artist of the American Revolution* (Boston, 1975), 106–107.

6. Sizer (ed.), *Autobiography of Trumbull*, 93, 98–99.

7. Marie Kimball, *Jefferson: The Scene of Europe, 1784–1789* (New York, 1950).

160; Helen Duprey Bullock, *My Head and My Heart: A Little History of Thomas Jefferson and Maria Cosway* (New York, 1945), 13–16.

8. Maria Cosway's relationship with her husband is examined in Fawn M. Brodie, *Thomas Jefferson: An Intimate History* (New York, 1974), 200–203.

9. Sizer (ed.), *Autobiography of Trumbull*, 93, 98.

10. Howard C. Rice, Jr. *Thomas Jefferson's Paris* (Princeton, 1976), 18–21; Jefferson to Maria Cosway, October 12, 1786, in Boyd (ed.), *Papers of Jefferson*, X, 444–45, 446.

11. Sizer (ed.), *Autobiograpy of Trumbull*, 120; Jefferson to Maria Cosway, October 12, 1786, in Boyd (ed.), *Papers of Jefferson*, X, 445–46.

12. Jefferson to William S. Smith, October 22, 1786, in Boyd (ed.), *Papers of Jefferson*, X, 478. The accident occurred on September 18, 1786. *Ibid.*, 432n.

13. Jefferson to Maria Cosway, October 12, 1786, in *ibid.*, 443.

14. Boyd (ed.), *Papers of Jefferson*, X, 450.

15. *Ibid.*, 446–49, 452.

16. *Ibid.*, 453n; Dumas Malone, *Jefferson and His Time* (6 vols.; Boston, 1948–81), II, 77.

17. Jefferson to Maria Cosway, October 12, 1786, Jefferson to Maria Cosway, December 24, 1786, in Boyd (ed.), *Papers of Jefferson*, X, 447, 627.

18. Maria Cosway to Jefferson, [October 30, November 17, November 27, 1786], in *ibid.*, 494–95, 538–39, 552.

19. Jefferson to Maria Cosway, December 24, 1786, Maria Cosway to Jefferson, February 15, 1787, in *ibid.*, X, 627, XI, 150.

20. Maria Cosway to Jefferson, [November 17, 1786], Jefferson to Maria Cosway, July 1, 1787, in *ibid.*, X, 538–39, XI, 519–20.

21. Maria Cosway to Jefferson, July 9, 1787, Trumbull to Jefferson, August 28, 1787, Jefferson to Trumbull, August 30, 1787, in *ibid.*, XI, 568–69, XII, 60, 69.

22. Maria Cosway to Jefferson, [December 1, 1787], Jefferson to Trumbull, November 13, 1787, Jefferson to Maria Cosway, April 24, 1788, in *ibid.*, XII, 387, 358, XIII, 104.

23. Kimball, *Jefferson: Scene of Europe*, 168; Brodie, *Jefferson*, 225.

24. Jefferson to Madison, January 30, 1787, Martha Jefferson to Jefferson, March 8, 1787, in Boyd (ed.), *Papers of Jefferson*, XI, 203.

25. Jefferson's itinerary is in Edward Dumbauld, *Thomas Jefferson, American Tourist* (Norman, 1946), 233–35.

26. Jefferson to William Short, March 15, 1787, Jefferson to Chastellux, April 4, 1787, in Boyd (ed.), *Papers of Jefferson*, XI, 214–15, 261–62.

27. Jefferson to Short, March 15, 1787, in *ibid.*, 214–15; Notes of a Tour, in *ibid.*, 419.

28. Jefferson to Madame de Tessé, March 20, 1787, in *ibid.*, 226.

29. Boyd (ed.), *Papers of Jefferson*, IX, xxvii, 220–21.

30. Jefferson to Short, March 27, and April 17, 1787, Jefferson to Lafayette, April 11, 1787, in *ibid.*, XI, 247, 280–81, 283.

31. Jefferson to Short, April 7, 12, 1787, Jefferson to Jay, May 4, 1787, Jefferson to Maria Cosway, July 1, 1787, in *ibid.*, 280, 287, 338, 520.

32. Hints on European Travel, June 19, 1788, in *ibid.*, XIII, 272; Notes of a Tour, in *ibid.*, XI, 432.

33. Jefferson to Wythe, September 16, 1787, in *ibid.*, XII, 127; Notes of a Tour, in *ibid.*, XI, 435–39.

34. Jefferson to John Jay, May 4, 1787; Jefferson to Edward Rutledge, July 14, 1787, in *ibid.*, XI, 338–39, 587; Notes of a Tour, in *ibid.*, XI, 435–38.

35. Notes of a Tour, in *ibid.*, 437. Jefferson's Italian tour is described in George Green Shackelford, "A Peep into Elysium," in Adams (ed.), *Jefferson and the Arts*, 237–62.

36. Boyd (ed.), *Papers of Jefferson*, XIII, 272.

37. Jefferson to Wythe, September 16, 1787, Jefferson to Maria Cosway, July 1, 1787, in *ibid.*, XII, 127, XI, 519; Notes of a Tour, in *ibid.*, XI, 441–42.

38. Jefferson to William S. Smith, September 13, 1786, in *ibid.*, X, 362.

39. Notes of a Tour, in *ibid.*, XI, 449–54.

40. Jefferson to Short, May 21, 1787, in *ibid.*, 371–72.

41. *Ibid.*, 372.

42. Jefferson to John Banister, Jr., June 19, 1787, in *ibid.*, 477.

Chapter X

1. Abigail Adams to Jefferson, June 26, 1787, in Julian P. Boyd (ed.), *The Papers of Thomas Jefferson* (Princeton, 1950–), XI, 501–502.

2. Jefferson to Francis Eppes, [August 30, 1785], in *ibid.*, VIII, 451.

3. Jefferson to Mary (Polly) Jefferson, September 20, 1785, Mary Jefferson to Jefferson, [*ca.* May 22, 1786], in Edwin M. Betts and James A. Bear, Jr. (eds.), *The Family Letters of Thomas Jefferson* (Columbia, Mo. 1966), 29–30, 31.

4. Jefferson to Francis Eppes, [August 30, 1785], Elizabeth Eppes to Jefferson, [March 31, 1787], in Boyd (ed.), *Papers of Jefferson*, VIII, 451, XI, 260.

5. Elizabeth Eppes to Jefferson, [May 7, 1787], Abigail Adams to Jefferson, June 26, 1787, Jefferson to Francis Eppes, July 2, 1787, Andrew Ramsay to Jefferson, July 6, 1787, in *ibid.*, XI, 356, 501–502, 524, 556; Dumas Malone, *Jefferson and His Time* (6 vols.; Boston, 1948–81), II, 134–35.

6. Abigail Adams to Jefferson, September 10, 1787, Jefferson to Mary Jefferson Bolling, July 23, 1787, Jefferson to Elizabeth Eppes, July 12, 1788, in Boyd (ed.), *Papers of Jefferson*, XII, 112, XI, 612, XIII, 347.

7. Abigail Adams to Jefferson, June 26, 27, 1787, in *ibid.*, XI, 502–503.

8. Fawn M. Brodie, *Thomas Jefferson: An Intimate History* (New York, 1974), 229–30, 234; review of Brodie, *Jefferson*, by Garry Wills in *New York Review of Books*, April 18, 1974, cited in Virginius Dabney, *The Jefferson Scandals: A Rebuttal* (New York, 1981), 127–28; Abigail Adams to Jefferson, July 6, 10, 1787, in Boyd (ed.), *Papers of Jefferson*, XI, 551, 574.

9. For a criticism of Brodie's methods and views of other scholars see Dabney, *The Jefferson Scandals*. Evidence that Jefferson did not father the mulatto children later born to Sally Hemings is presented in Douglass Adair, *Fame and the Founding Fathers*, ed. Trevor Colbourn (New York, 1974), 160–91.

10. Madison to Jefferson, April 23, 1787, Edward Carrington to Jefferson, April 24, 1787, John Jay to Jefferson, April 24, 1787, Jefferson to Carrington, August 4, 1787, in Boyd (ed.), *Papers of Jefferson*, XI, 309–10, 311–12, 313–14, 678.

11. Madison to Edmund Pendleton, February 24, 1787, Madison to Edmund Randolph, February 25, 1787, in William T. Hutchinson, William M. E. Rachal, and Robert A. Rutland (eds.), *The Papers of James Madison* (Chicago and Charlottesville, 1962–), IX, 263, 295, 299.

12. Jefferson to William S. Smith, November 13, 1787, Jefferson to Carrington, August 4, 1787, Jefferson to Monroe, June 17, 1785, in Boyd (ed.), *Papers of Jefferson*, XII, 356, XI, 678, VIII, 231.

13. Jefferson to Washington, August 14, 1787, Madison to Jefferson, September 6, 1787 (received December 13, 1787), Adams to Jefferson, November 10, 1787, in *ibid.*, XII, 36, 102–104, 335.

14. Jefferson to Smith, November 13, 1787, in *ibid.*, 356.

15. Jefferson to Madison, December 20, 1787, in *ibid.*, 439–40.

16. Jefferson to Smith, February 2, 1788, Jefferson to Madison, December 20, 1787, in *ibid.*, 558, 440–41.

17. Jefferson to Smith, February 2, 1788, Madison to Jefferson, July 24, 1778, in *ibid.*, XII, 558, XIII, 412; Malone, *Jefferson*, II, 173–74.

18. Jefferson to Carrington, May 27, 1788, Jefferson to Madison, July 31, 1788, in Boyd (ed.), *Papers of Jefferson*, XIII, 208, 442.

19. Jefferson to Jay, January 9, February 23, June 21, August 6, 1787, Jefferson to Adams, August 30, 1787, in *ibid.*, XI, 31–32, 179–80, 489–90, 697–98, XII, 67–68.

20. For Jefferson's views on human nature see Adrienne Koch, *The Philosophy of Thomas Jefferson* (New York, 1943), 113–23.

21. Jefferson to Madison, June 20, 1787, in Boyd (ed.), *Papers of Jefferson*, XI, 482.

22. Jefferson to Adams, February 6, 1788, Willink and Van Staphorst to Jefferson, January 31, 1788, Jefferson to Jay, March 16, 1788, Adams to Jefferson, February 12, 1788, in *ibid.*, XII, 566, 443–48, 671, 581–82.

23. Jefferson to Madison, June 20, 1787, Jefferson to Adams, March 2, 1788, Jefferson to William Short, March 10, 1788, Jefferson to Jay, March 16, 1788, in *ibid.*, XI, 482, XII, 637–38, 659, 671–72.

24. Edward Dumbauld, *Thomas Jefferson, American Tourist* (Norman, 1946), 114–22, 236–37.

25. Jefferson to Anne Willing Bingham, May 11, 1788, in Boyd (ed.), *Papers of Jefferson*, XIII, 151; Jefferson, Autobiography, in Paul L. Ford (ed.), *The Works of Thomas Jefferson* (Federal Edition; 12 vols.; New York, 1904), I, 127.

26. Jefferson to Jay, May 23, 1788, Jefferson to John B. Cutting, July 24, 1788, Jefferson to Jay, August 3, September 3, 1788, in Boyd (ed.), *Papers of Jefferson*, XIII, 190, 406, 464, 564–65.

27. Jefferson to Jay, November 19, 1788, Jefferson to Madison, November 18, 1788, Jefferson to Washington, December 4, 1788, in *ibid.*, XIV, 212–13, 188, 330.

28. Robert R. Palmer, "The Dubious Democrat: Thomas Jefferson in Bourbon France," *Political Science Quarterly*, LXXII (1957), 396–98; Jefferson to Jay, November 19, 1788, in Boyd (ed.), *Papers of Jefferson*, XIV, 215.

29. See documents in Boyd (ed.), *Papers of Jefferson*, XIV, 66–180.

30. Jefferson to Elizabeth Eppes, December 14, 1788, in *ibid.*, 355.

31. Dugnani to Carroll, July 5, 1787, quoted in Annabelle M. Melville, *John Carroll of Baltimore* (New York, 1955), 102. See also Boyd (ed.), *Papers of Jefferson*, XIV, 356n.

32. Jefferson to Jay, January 11, 1789, Jefferson to Madison, January 12, 1789, in Boyd (ed.), *Papers of Jefferson*, XIV, 429, 437.

33. Robert R. Palmer, *The Age of Democratic Revolution: A Political History of Europe and America, 1760–1800* (2 vols.; Princeton, 1959–64), I, 469–70; Palmer, "The Dubious Democrat," 394–95; Louis Gottschalk and Margaret Maddox, *Lafayette in the French Revolution: Through the October Days* (Chicago, 1969), 14; Jefferson to Jay, March 1, 1789, in Boyd (ed.), *Papers of Jefferson*, XIV, 604.

34. Jefferson to Trumbull, June 18, 1789, Jefferson to Lafayette, May 6, June 3, 1789, Lafayette to Jefferson, June 3, 1789, Jefferson to Rabaut de St. Etienne, June 3, 1789, in Boyd (ed.), *Papers of Jefferson*, XV, 199, 97, 165–66, 166–67; Gottschalk and Maddox, *Lafayette*, 51–52, 55–57.

35. Jefferson to Jay, May 9, 1789, Jefferson to Lafayette, May 6, 1789, in Boyd (ed.), *Papers of Jefferson*, XV, 111, 97.

36. Jefferson to Madison, June 18, 1789, in *ibid.*, 195-96.

37. Jefferson to Jay, June 29, 1789, in *ibid.*, 222-23.

38. Jefferson to Paine, July 11, 1789, in *ibid.*, 267-69.

39. Jefferson to Paine, July 13, 1789, in *ibid.*, 273.

40. Jefferson to Jay, July 19, 1789, Jefferson to Madison, July 22, 1789, in *ibid.*, 287-90, 300; Gottschalk and Maddox, *Lafayette*, 124-29; Beatrix C. Davenport (ed.), *A Diary of the French Revolution by Gouverneur Morris* (2 vols.; Boston, 1939), I, 152-53.

41. Jefferson to Jay, July 19, 1789, Jefferson to Madison, July 22, 1789, Jefferson to Maria Cosway, July 25, 1789, in Boyd (ed.), *Papers of Jefferson*, XV, 290, 299, 301, 305.

42. Lafayette to Jefferson, July 6, 1789, Jefferson to Lafayette, July 6, 1789, Lafayette to Jefferson, [July 9, 1789], in *ibid.*, 249, 250, 255. Lafayette's draft is printed in *ibid.*, 230-33.

43. Gottschalk and Maddox, *Lafayette*, 90-98.

44. Jefferson, Autobiography, in Ford (ed.), *Works of Jefferson*, I, 152; Lafayette to Jefferson, [August 25, 1789], in Boyd (ed.), *Papers of Jefferson*, XV, 354.

45. Jefferson, Autobiography, in Ford (ed.), *Works of Jefferson*, I, 153-55; Boyd (ed.), *Papers of Jefferson*, XV, 355n.

46. Jefferson to Gem, September 9, 1789, in *Papers of Jefferson*, XV, 398. Adrienne Koch speculated that Gem showed the letter to Thomas Paine before the latter wrote his *Rights of Man*. Koch, *Jefferson and Madison: The Great Collaboration* (New York, 1964), 84-88.

47. Jefferson to Madison, September 6, 1789, in Boyd (ed.), *Papers of Jefferson*, XV, 392-97; see also editorial note, in *ibid.*, 384-91.

48. Boyd (ed.), *Papers of Jefferson*, XV, 394-97.

49. Koch, *Jefferson and Madison*, 63, 70-75; Madison to Jefferson, February 4, 1790, in Boyd (ed.), *Papers of Jefferson*, XVI, 147-50.

50. Jefferson to Edward Bancroft, August 5, 1789, Jefferson to Jay, August 27, September 19, 1789, Jefferson to Madison, August 28, 1789, in Boyd (ed.), *Papers of Jefferson*, XV, 333, 356, 366, 457-60.

51. Jefferson to Nathaniel Cutting, September 10, 1789, list of baggage, [*ca.* September 1, 1789], Jefferson to Henry Knox, September 12, 1789, in *ibid.*, 375-77, 412, 422.

52. Jefferson to Trumbull, January 18, February 15, 1789, Trumbull to Jefferson, February 5, 1789, in *ibid.*, XIV, 467-68, 524-25, 561, XV, xxxv.

53. Boyd (ed.), *Papers of Jefferson*, XV, xxxvi-xxxix; Alfred L. Bush, "The Life Portraits of Thomas Jefferson," in William Howard Adams (ed.), *Jefferson and the Arts: An Extended View* (Washington, D.C., 1976), 29-31.

54. Jefferson to Trumbull, September 16, 1789, Trumbull to Jefferson, September 22, 1789, Jefferson to Trumbull, September 24, 1789, in Boyd (ed.), *Papers of Jefferson*, XV, 435, 467-68, 471.

55. Extract from the Diary of Nathaniel Cutting, in *ibid.*, 491-96; Jefferson to Short, October 4, 1789, Jefferson to Maria Cosway, October 14, 1789, in *ibid.*, XV, 506, 521; Jefferson, account book, September 26, 28, October 8, 9, 22, 23, 1789, transcript by James A. Bear, Jr., in University of Virginia library, Charlottesville.

Chapter XI

1. Jefferson to Nathaniel Cutting, November 21, 1789, Jefferson to William Short, November 21, 1789, Jefferson to John Jay, November 23, 1789, Jefferson to

John Trumbull, November 25, 1789, in Julian P. Boyd (ed.), *The Papers of Thomas Jefferson* (Princeton, 1950–), XV, 551–53, 559–60; Sarah N. Randolph, *The Domestic Life of Thomas Jefferson* (1871; rpr. New York, 1958), 151–52.

2. Washington to Jefferson, October 13, 1789, and address of welcome and Jefferson's reply, November 25, 1789, in Boyd (ed.), *Papers of Jefferson*, XV, 519–20, 557–58.

3. Washington to Jefferson, October 13, 1789, Madison to Jefferson, October 8, 1789, in *ibid.*, 519, 509–10.

4. Jefferson to Short, December 14, 1789, in *ibid.*, XVI, 26.

5. Jefferson to Washington, December 15, 1789, in *ibid.*, 34–35.

6. Madison to Washington, January 4, 1790, in William T. Hutchinson, William M. E. Rachal, and Robert A. Rutland (eds.), *The Papers of James Madison* (Chicago and Charlottesville, 1962–), XII, 467; Washington to Jefferson, January 21, 1790, in Boyd (ed.), *Papers of Jefferson*, XVI, 117.

7. Response, February 12, 1790, in Boyd (ed.), *Papers of Jefferson*, XVI, 179. The address, first published in a Richmond newspaper, can be found in the *Gazette of the United States* (New York), March 24, 1790.

8. Jefferson to Washington, February 14, 1790, Diary of Nathaniel Cutting, October 12, 1789, Cutting to Martha Jefferson, March 30, 1790, in Boyd (ed.), *Papers of Jefferson*, XVI, 184, XV, 498, XVI, 207n.

9. William H. Gaines, Jr., *Thomas Mann Randolph: Jefferson's Son-in-Law* (Baton Rouge, 1966), 24n; Boyd (ed.), *Papers of Jefferson*, XIV, 367n–68n.

10. Jefferson to Madame de Corny, April 2, 1790, in Boyd (ed.), *Papers of Jefferson*, XVI, 290.

11. Jefferson to Randolph, February 4, 1790, in *ibid.*, 154.

12. Boyd (ed.), *Papers of Jefferson*, XVI, 189–91; Edwin Morris Betts (ed.), *Thomas Jefferson's Farm Book* (Princeton, 1953), 32.

13. Jefferson to Martha Jefferson Randolph, April 4, 1790, Martha Jefferson Randolph to Jefferson, April 25, 1790, in Boyd (ed.), *Papers of Jefferson*, XVI, 300, 385.

14. Jefferson to Thomas Mann Randolph, Jr., March 28, 1790, Jefferson to Short, April 6, 1790, with enclosure, in *ibid.*, XVI, 278, 279, 321–24.

15. Jefferson to Lafayette, April 2, 1790, in *ibid.*, 293; Leonard D. White, *The Federalists: A Study of Administrative History* (New York, 1948), 107–109.

16. Jefferson to Charles Bellini, June 13, 1790, Jefferson to Hamilton, June 17, 1790, in *Papers of Jefferson*, XVI, 485–86, 512–13.

17. White, *Federalists*, 27. Washington's administrative system is well revealed in Dorothy Twohig (ed.), *The Journal of the Proceedings of the President, 1793–1797* (Charlottesville, 1981), a volume in *The Papers of George Washington*, ed. W. W. Abbot.

18. Jefferson to Peter Carr, June 13, 1790, in Boyd (ed.), *Papers of Jefferson*, XVI, 487.

19. Boyd (ed.), *Papers of Jefferson*, XVI, 602.

20. Final state of the report on weights and measures, [July 4, 1790], in *ibid.*, 653–54.

21. *Ibid.*, 663–64.

22. Transcription from the original manuscript, in *ibid.*, 381n.

23. Jefferson to Short, April 6, 1790, Jefferson to Monroe, June 20, 1790, in *ibid.*, 316, 537.

24. Jefferson's account (in *ibid.*, XVII, 205–207) is undated but was written no earlier than 1791. Boyd suggested that it may have been written in 1792. *Ibid.*, 207n.

25. Jefferson to Monroe, June 20, 1790, in *ibid.*, XVI, 537.

26. Kenneth R. Bowling, "Politics in the First Congress, 1789–1791" (Ph.D. dissertation, University of Wisconsin, 1968), chs. 6–7; Jacob E. Cooke, "The Compromise of 1790," *William and Mary Quarterly*, 3rd Ser., XXVII (1970), 523–45; Bowling, "Dinner at Jefferson's," *William and Mary Quarterly*, 3rd Ser., XXVIII (1971), 629–40. See also Hutchinson, Rachal, and Rutland (eds.), *Papers of Madison*, XIII, 243–46.

27. Jefferson to Washington, September 9, 1792, in Paul L. Ford (ed.), *The Works of Thomas Jefferson* (Federal Edition; 12 vols.; New York, 1904), VII, 137; Jefferson to John Harvie, Jr., July 25, 1790, in Boyd (ed.), *Papers of Jefferson*, XVII, 271.

28. *The Journal of William Maclay, United States Senator from Pennsylvania, 1789–1791*, introduction by Charles A. Beard (1890; rpr. New York, 1965), 296.

29. Boyd (ed.), *Papers of Jefferson*, XVII, 216–31. The diplomatic establishment did not include the consular service, which was also under Jefferson's direction.

30. Morris to Washington, May 29, 1790, in *ibid.*, 64–65.

31. Donald Jackson and Dorothy Twohig (eds.), *The Diaries of George Washington* (6 vols.; Charlottesville, 1976–79), July 8, 1790, VI, 87–89; Harold C. Syrett *et al.* (eds.), *The Papers of Alexander Hamilton* (26 vols.; New York, 1961–79), VI, 484–86.

32. Julian P. Boyd, *Number 7: Alexander Hamilton's Secret Attempts to Control American Foreign Policy* (Princeton, 1964), xiii–xiv, 6–13, 37; Jerald A. Combs, *The Jay Treaty: Political Battleground of the Founding Fathers* (Berkeley, 1970), 51–56.

33. Memorandum, July 12, 1790, enclosed in Jefferson to Washington, July 12, 1790, in Boyd (ed.), *Papers of Jefferson*, XVII, 108–10.

34. Quoted in Boyd, *Number 7*, p. 36.

35. Memorandum, July 12, 1790, enclosed in Jefferson to Washington, July 12, 1790, in Boyd (ed.), *Papers of Jefferson*, XVII, 108–10.

36. Jackson and Twohig (eds.), *Diaries of Washington*, July 14, 1790, VI, 94–95.

37. Syrett *et al.* (eds.), *Papers of Hamilton*, VI, 496n.

38. Report of conversation, [July 15, 1790], in *ibid.*, 497.

39. Jefferson to Morris, August 12, 1790, in Boyd (ed.), *Papers of Jefferson*, XVII, 127–28.

40. Memorandum, August 27, 1790, in *ibid.*, 128–29.

41. Jefferson to Washington, August 28, 1790, in *ibid.*, 129–30.

42. Boyd (ed.), *Papers of Jefferson*, XVII, 134–61; Syrett *et al.* (eds.), *Papers of Hamilton*, VII, 37–57.

43. Jefferson to Carmichael, August 2, 1790, Boyd (ed.), *Papers of Jefferson*, XVII, 111–12.

44. Boyd (ed.), *Papers of Jefferson*, XVII, 277–78, 318–19, 338, 343–87.

45. Edward Dumbauld, *Thomas Jefferson, American Tourist* (Norman, 1946), 156–58; Jefferson to Martha Jefferson Randolph, August 22, 1790, in Boyd (ed.), *Papers of Jefferson*, XVII, 402.

46. Boyd (ed.), *Papers of Jefferson*, XVII, 460–62.

47. Hutchinson, Rachal, and Rutland (eds.), *Papers of Madison*, XIII, 294–96.

48. Virginia appropriated $120,000, and Maryland $72,000. Constance McLaughlin Green, *Washington, Village and Capital, 1800–1878* (Princeton, 1962), 13.

49. Jefferson, account book, September 1–19, 1790, transcript by James A. Bear, Jr., in University of Virginia library, Charlottesville; Irving Brant, *James Madison* (6 vols.; Indianapolis, 1941–61), III, 319–21; Jefferson to Thomas Mann Randolph, Jr., June 20, July 25, October 22, 1790, Jefferson to Thomas Mann Randolph, Sr., July 25, October 22, 1790, Jefferson to Francis Eppes, October 8, 1790, Jefferson to Elizabeth Eppes, October 31, 1790, in Boyd (ed.), *Papers of Jefferson*, XVI, 540, XVII, 274, 581, 622, 623–24, 658; Gaines, *Thomas Mann Randolph*, 31–34.

NOTES TO PAGES 150–64   371

Chapter XII

1. Ralph Ketcham, *James Madison: A Biography* (New York, 1971), 88; Jefferson to Thomas Leiper, August 4, 1790, Jefferson to William Temple Franklin, July 25, 1790, Franklin to Jefferson, August 1, 1790, in Julian P. Boyd (ed.), *The Papers of Thomas Jefferson* (Princeton, 1950–), XVII, 267–68, 293, 309–10.

2. Jefferson, account book, December 11, 19, 1790, January 8, 20, 1791, transcript by James A. Bear, Jr., University of Virginia library, Charlottesville.

3. *Ibid.*, November 30, December 22, 29, 31, 1790; Jefferson to Madison, January 10, 1791, in Boyd (ed.), *Papers of Jefferson*, XVIII, 480.

4. The contents of the crates shipped from France can be found in Boyd (ed.), *Papers of Jefferson*, XVIII, 33–39.

5. Jefferson to Samuel H. Smith, September 21, 1814, in Paul L. Ford (ed.), *The Works of Thomas Jefferson* (Federal Edition; 12 vols.; New York, 1904), XI, 427–28; Jefferson to William Short, March 12, 1790, in Boyd (ed.), *Papers of Jefferson*, XVI, 229–30.

6. Jefferson to Short, January 24, 1791, in *Papers of Jefferson*, XVIII, 600; Jefferson to Martha Jefferson Randolph, May 8, July 24, 1791, in Edwin M. Betts and James A. Bear, Jr. (eds.), *The Family Letters of Thomas Jefferson* (Columbia, Mo., 1966), 81, 88.

7. Jefferson to Short, March 12, 1790, January 24, 1791, Short to Jefferson, June 14, 1790, in Boyd (ed.), *Papers of Jefferson*, XVI, 229, 500–501, XVIII, 600–601.

8. See Dumas Malone, *Jefferson and His Time* (6 vols.; Boston, 1948–81), III, 167.

9. Jefferson to William Temple Franklin, July 16, 25, 1790, Franklin to Jefferson, July 20, 1790, in Boyd (ed.), *Papers of Jefferson*, XVII, 211, 236–37, 267, 378n.

10. Washington to Jefferson, December 11, 1790, Jefferson to Washington, December 15, 1790, in *ibid.*, XVIII, 283–84, 301–303.

11. Boyd (ed.), *Papers of Jefferson*, XIX, 218, 220. On Tench Coxe's contribution to Jefferson's report see Jacob E. Cooke, *Tench Coxe and the Early Republic* (Chapel Hill, 1978), 221–24.

12. William T. Hutchinson, William M. E. Rachal, and Robert A. Rutland (eds.), *The Papers of James Madison* (Chicago and Charlottesville, 1962–), XIII, 259–60, 321n; Jefferson to Short, March 15, 1791, Jefferson to Humphreys, March 15, 1791, Jefferson to Carmichael, March 17, 1791, in Boyd (ed.), *Papers of Jefferson*, XIX, 570–75.

13. Jefferson, Anas, March 11, 1792, in Ford (ed.), *Works of Jefferson*, I, 210–11; Jerald A. Combs, *The Jay Treaty: Political Background of the Founding Fathers* (Berkeley, 1970), 59, 100–104.

14. Donald Jackson and Dorothy Twohig (eds.), *The Diaries of George Washington* (6 vols.; Charlottesville, 1976–79), March 23, 1790, VI, 51; Linda Grant DePauw (ed.), *Documentary History of the First Federal Congress of the United States of America*, III: *House of Representatives Journal* (Baltimore, 1977), 412; Boyd (ed.), *Papers of Jefferson*, XVIII, 403–408, 423–37; *The Journal of William Maclay, United States Senator from Pennsylvania, 1789–1791*, introduction by Charles A. Beard (New York, 1965), 353.

15. Boyd (ed.), *Papers of Jefferson*, XVIII, 410, 413, 444; DePauw (ed.), *Documentary History of the First Federal Congress of the United States of America*, II: *Senate Executive Journal* (Baltimore, 1974), 114–15.

16. Report, January 18, 1791, in Boyd (ed.), *Papers of Jefferson*, XVIII, 570; Jefferson to Washington, September 9, 1792, in Ford (ed.), *Works of Jefferson*, VII, 140.

17. See Noble E. Cunningham, Jr., *The Jeffersonian Republicans: The Formation of Party Organization, 1789–1801* (Chapel Hill, 1957), 8–9.

18. Jefferson, opinion on constitutionality of a national bank, February 15, 1791, in Boyd (ed.), *Papers of Jefferson*, XIX, 275−77.

19. *Ibid.*, 278−80.

20. John J. Reardon, *Edmund Randolph: A Biography* (New York, 1974), 197−98; Washington to Hamilton, February 16, 1791, in Harold C. Syrett *et al.* (eds.), *The Papers of Alexander Hamilton* (26 vols.; New York, 1961−79), VIII, 50.

21. Hamilton, opinion on the constitutionality of a national bank, February 23, 1791, in Syrett *et al.* (eds.), *Papers of Hamilton*, VIII, 97−98, 101−103, 107.

22. Jefferson to Mason, February 4, 1791, in Boyd (ed.), *Papers of Jefferson*, XIX, 242.

23. Text in Boyd (ed.), *Papers of Jefferson*, XX, following p. 384; Jefferson to Madison, May 9, 1791, in *ibid.*, 293.

24. *Ibid.*, 293; see also editorial note in *ibid.*, 268−90. On Adams' "Discourses on Davila," see Peter Shaw, *The Character of John Adams* (Chapel Hill, 1976), 230−37.

25. Jefferson to Adams, July 17, August 30, 1791, in Lester J. Cappon (ed.), *The Adams-Jefferson Letters* (2 vols.; Chapel Hill, 1959), I, 245−46, 250−51.

26. Edward Dumbauld, *Thomas Jefferson, American Tourist* (Norman, 1946), 172−77; Jefferson, account book, May 17−June 19, 1791, transcript by Bear, in U. Va. library; Robert Troup to Hamilton, June 15, 1791, in Syrett *et al.* (eds.), *Papers of Hamilton*, VIII, 478.

27. Jefferson's notes, May 22−June 3, 1791, are in Boyd (ed.), *Papers of Jefferson*, XX, 453−56; Madison's notes, May 31−June 7, 1791, are in Hutchinson, Rachal, and Rutland (eds.), *Papers of Madison*, XIV, 25−29.

28. Jefferson to Martha Jefferson Randolph, May 31, 1791, in Boyd (ed.), *Papers of Jefferson*, XX, 463−64.

29. On political contacts on the journey see editorial note in Boyd (ed.), *Papers of Jefferson*, XX, 434−53.

30. Richard Hofstadter, *The Idea of a Party System: The Rise of Legitimate Opposition in the United States, 1780−1840* (Berkeley, 1969), 24, 27, 29; Jefferson to Freneau, February 28, 1791, in Boyd (ed.), *Papers of Jefferson*, XIX, 351.

31. Cunningham, *Jeffersonian Republicans*, 13−17; Boyd (ed.), *Papers of Jefferson*, XX, 718−36.

32. Jefferson to Madison, July 21, 1791, in James Madison Papers, Library of Congress.

33. Jefferson to Thomas Mann Randolph, Jr., May 15, 1791, in Boyd (ed.), *Papers of Jefferson*, XX, 416; Jefferson to Washington, September 9, 1792, in Ford (ed.), *Works of Jefferson*, VII, 145; Donald H. Stewart, *The Opposition Press of the Federalist Period* (Albany, 1969), 42−43; Lewis Leary, *That Rascal Freneau: A Study in Literary Failure* (New Brunswick, N.J., 1941), 197−246.

34. *Gazette of the United States*, July 25, 1792, in Syrett *et al.* (eds.), *Papers of Hamilton*, XII, 107.

35. "An American," *Gazette of the United States*, August 4, 1792, in *ibid.*, 159.

36. Hamilton's pieces and Freneau's replies are in *ibid.*, 123−25, 157−64, 188−94, 224.

37. *Ibid.*, 125; see also Jacob Axelrad, *Philip Freneau, Champion of Democracy* (Austin, 1967), 236.

38. Jefferson to Washington, September 9, 1792, in Ford (ed.), *Works of Jefferson*, VII, 144−45; Boyd (ed.), *Papers of Jefferson*, XX, 733−53; Hutchinson, Rachal, and Rutland (eds.), *Papers of Madison*, XIV, 110−12.

39. Jefferson, Anas, May 23, 1793, in Ford (ed.), *Works of Jefferson*, I, 274.

40. Cunningham, *Jeffersonian Republicans*, 22, 31, 49, 256–58. See also John F. Hoadley, "The Emergence of Political Parties in Congress, 1789–1803," *American Political Science Review*, LXXIV (1980), 757–79.

41. Jefferson to Martha Jefferson Randolph, March 22, 1792, in Betts and Bear (eds.), *Family Letters*, 96; Hamilton to Edward Carrington, May 26, 1792, in Syrett *et al.* (eds.), *Papers of Hamilton*, XI, 427–44.

42. Washington to Jefferson, April 23, 1792, Washington to Hamilton, August 26, 1792, in John C. Fitzpatrick (ed.), *The Writings of George Washington* (39 vols.; Washington, D.C., 1931–44), XXXII, 128–34.

43. Jefferson to Washington, September 9, 1792, in Ford (ed.), *Works of Jefferson*, VII, 137–38.

44. Syrett *et al.* (eds.), *Papers of Hamilton*, XII, 157, 188, 224; Jefferson to Washington, September 9, 1792, in Ford (ed.), *Works of Jefferson*, VII, 139–46.

45. Hamilton to Washington, September 9, 1792, in Syrett *et al.* (eds.), *Papers of Hamilton*, XII, 347–49.

46. Jefferson, Anas, October 1, 1792, in Ford (ed.), *Works of Jefferson*, I, 235.

47. Syrett *et al.* (eds.), *Papers of Hamilton*, XII, 379–82; Madison to Edmund Randolph, September 13, 1792, in Hutchinson, Rachal, and Rutland (eds.), *Papers of Madison*, XIV, 364–65; Malone, *Jefferson*, II, 469.

48. Syrett *et al.* (eds.), *Papers of Hamilton*, XII, 162–163, 379–85, 393–401, 498–506, 578–87, XIII, 229–31, 348–56.

49. Harry Ammon, *James Monroe: The Quest for National Identity* (New York, 1971), 93–95; Madison to Monroe, September 18, 1792, in Hutchinson, Rachal, and Rutland (eds.), *Papers of Madison*, XIV, 367, 368–70.

50. Hutchinson, Rachal, and Rutland (eds.), *Papers of Madison*, XIV, 299–304, 321–24; Irving Brant, *James Madison* (6 vols.; Indianapolis, 1941–61), III, 356.

51. Madison to Washington, June 20, 1792, in Hutchinson, Rachal, and Rutland (eds.), *Papers of Madison*, XIV, 321; Jefferson to Washington, May 23, 1792, in Ford (ed.), *Works of Jefferson*, VI, 487–95; Hamilton to Washington, July 30, 1792, in Syrett *et al.* (eds.), *Papers of Hamilton*, XII, 137–39.

52. Noble E. Cunningham, Jr., "John Beckley: An Early American Party Manager," *William and Mary Quarterly*, 3rd Ser., XIII (1956), 40–46; Edmund Berkeley and Dorothy Smith Berkeley, *John Beckley: Zealous Partisan in a Nation Divided* (Philadelphia, 1973), 72–73; Rush to Burr, September 24, 1792, in L. H. Butterfield (ed.), *Letters of Benjamin Rush* (2 vols.; Princeton, 1951), I, 623; Cunningham, *Jeffersonian Republicans*, 45–49.

53. Jefferson to Thomas Mann Randolph, Jr., November 16, 1792, Jefferson to Thomas Pinckney, December 3, 1792, in Ford (ed.), *Works of Jefferson*, VII, 179, 191.

Chapter XIII

1. Jefferson to Thomas Pinckney, November 8, 1792, in Paul L. Ford (ed.), *The Works of Thomas Jefferson* (Federal Edition; 12 vols.; New York, 1904), VII, 177.

2. Jefferson, Anas, February 7, 1793, in *ibid.*, I, 240; Jefferson to Martha Jefferson Randolph, January 26, 1793, in Edwin M. Betts and James A. Bear, Jr. (eds.), *The Family Letters of Thomas Jefferson* (Columbia, Mo., 1966), 110.

3. Jefferson, Anas, February 20, 1793, in Ford (ed.), *Works of Jefferson*, I, 255.

4. Jefferson's draft and the resolutions moved by Giles are in Ford (ed.), *Works of Jefferson*, VII, 220–23. See also Dumas Malone, *Jefferson and His Time* (6 vols.; Boston, 1948–81), III, 14–36, and Noble E. Cunningham, Jr., *The Jeffersonian Republicans: The Formation of Party Organization, 1789–1801* (Chapel Hill, 1957), 51–54.

5. Jefferson to George Mason, February 4, 1791, in Julian P. Boyd (ed.), *The Papers of Thomas Jefferson* (Princeton, 1950–), XIX, 241; Jefferson to Short, January 3, 1793, in Ford (ed.), *Works of Jefferson*, VII, 203.

6. Jefferson to Morris, November 7, 1792, in Ford (ed.), *Works of Jefferson*, VII, 175.

7. Jefferson to Morris, December 30, 1792, in *ibid.*, 198. That same day Jefferson wrote similarly to Thomas Pinckney in London. See Andrew A. Lipscomb and Albert E. Bergh (eds.), *The Writings of Thomas Jefferson* (20 vols.; Washington, D.C., 1903), IX, 7–8.

8. Jefferson to Short, January 3, 1793, in Ford (ed.), *Works of Jefferson*, VII, 203–204.

9. Jefferson to Washington, April 7, 1793, in *ibid.*, 275.

10. Jefferson to C. W. F. Dumas, March 24, 1793, in Lipscomb and Bergh (eds.), *Writings of Jefferson*, IX, 56–57; Oliver Wolcott, Sr., to Oliver Wolcott, Jr., March 25, 1793, in George Gibbs (ed.), *Memoirs of the Administrations of Washington and John Adams, Edited from the Papers of Oliver Wolcott, Secretary of the Treasury* (2 vols.; New York, 1846), I, 91; Jefferson to Morris, April 20, 1793, in Ford (ed.), *Works of Jefferson*, VII, 281–82.

11. Washington to Jefferson, Hamilton, Knox, and Randolph, April 18, 1793, in Harold C. Syrett *et al.* (eds.), *The Papers of Alexander Hamilton* (26 vols.; New York, 1961–79), XIV, 326–27; Dorothy Twohig (ed.), *The Journal of the Proceedings of the President, 1793–1797*, a volume in *The Papers of George Washington*, ed. W. W. Abbot (Charlottesville, 1981), April 18, 1793, pp. 108, 113–14; Jefferson, Anas, April 18, 1793, in Ford (ed.), *Works of Jefferson*, I, 267.

12. Jefferson to Madison, June 23, 30, 1793, in Ford (ed.), *Papers of Jefferson*, VII, 407–408, 421. See also Madison to Jefferson, June 10, 13, 1793, in Gaillard Hunt (ed.), *The Writings of James Madison* (9 vols.; New York, 1900–1910), VI, 127n, 130–32.

13. Cabinet meeting, April 19, 1793, in Syrett *et al.* (eds.), *Papers of Hamilton*, XIV, 328.

14. Text of proclamation in Syrett *et al.* (eds.), *Papers of Hamilton*, XIV, 308n.

15. Jefferson, Anas, May 6, 1793, in Ford (ed.), *Works of Jefferson*, I, 267–69.

16. This summary is based on Jefferson's account of the meeting provided to the president, April 28, 1793, in *ibid.*, VII, 284.

17. *Ibid.*, 284–89, 300.

18. Jefferson, Anas, March 30, April 18, 1793, Opinion on French treaties, April 28, 1793, in *ibid.*, I, 263–64, 268–69, VII, 283. On Genet's reception by Washington see John A. Carroll and Mary W. Ashworth, *George Washington: First in Peace* (New York, 1957), 73–75 (this book completes the biography by Douglas Southall Freeman).

19. Jefferson to Madison, April 28, 1793, Jefferson to Monroe, May 5, 1793, Jefferson to George Hammond, May 3, 15, 1793, in Ford (ed.), *Works of Jefferson*, VII, 301–302, 309, 306, 327.

20. Jefferson to Madison, May 19, 1793, Jefferson to Monroe, June 4, 1793, in *ibid.*, 337–38, 361.

21. Jefferson to Morris, August 16, 1793, Jefferson to Ternant, May 15, 1793, in *ibid.*, 481–82, 330–31; Harry Ammon, *The Genet Mission* (New York, 1973), 66; Genet to Jefferson, May 27, 1793, in *American State Papers: Documents, Legislative and Executive of the United States* (38 vols.; Washington, D.C., 1832–61), *Foreign Relations*, I, 149–50.

22. Jefferson, Anas, May 20, 1793, in Ford (ed.), *Works of Jefferson*, I, 271–73.

23. Jefferson, Opinion on French treaties, April 28, 1793, in *ibid.*, VII, 289–90.

24. Jefferson to Genet, June 5, 1793, in *ibid.*, 362–63.

25. Jefferson to Genet, June 17, 1793, Jefferson to Washington, April 28, 1793, in *ibid.*, 397–98, 290; Ammon, *Genet Mission*, 77.

26. Jefferson, Anas, July 5, 1793, in Ford (ed.), *Works of Jefferson*, I, 280–81.

27. Jefferson to Madison, June 23, 1793, *ibid.*, VII, 408; see also Donald Jackson, *Thomas Jefferson and the Stony Mountains: Exploring the West from Monticello* (Urbana, 1981), 74–78; Lawrence S. Kaplan, *Jefferson and France* (New Haven, 1967), 56–57.

28. Jefferson to Morris, June 13, 1793, Jefferson to Thomas Pinckney, June 14, 1793, Jefferson to Madison, June 9, 1793, in Ford (ed.), *Works of Jefferson*, VII, 385, 388, 374.

29. Madison to Jefferson, June 10, 1793, in Hunt (ed.), *Writings of Madison*, VI, 127n; Jefferson to Madison, June 23, 30, 1793, Jefferson to Monroe, May 5, 1793, Jefferson to Madison, May 12, 1793, in Ford (ed.), *Works of Jefferson*, VII, 407–408, 421, 309, 324.

30. Jefferson to Monroe, May 5, June 4, 1793, Jefferson to Madison, June 29, 1793, in Ford (ed.), *Works of Jefferson*, VII, 309, 362, 420; Syrett *et al.* (eds.), *Papers of Hamilton*, XV, 33–43; Broadus Mitchell, *Alexander Hamilton* (2 vols.; New York, 1957–62), II, 232–33.

31. Jefferson to Madison, June 30, 1793, Jefferson to Madison, July 7, 1793, in Ford (ed.), *Works of Jefferson*, VII, 420–22, 436; Madison to Jefferson, July 18, 22, 30, 1793, in Hunt (ed.), *Writings of Madison*, VI, 135, 137–39.

32. Hunt (ed.), *Writings of Madison*, VI, 138–88; Irving Brant, *James Madison* (6 vols.; Indianapolis, 1941–61), III, 377–79.

33. Jefferson to Madison, July 7, 1793, in Ford (ed.), *Works of Jefferson*, VII, 436.

34. Jefferson, Cabinet opinion on "Little Sarah," July 8, 1793, "Reasons for his Dissent," [July 9, 1793], Anas, July 10, 1793, in Ford (ed.), *Works of Jefferson*, VII, 437–43, I, 282–88; Ammon, *Genet Mission*, 80, 86–90.

35. Jefferson, "Reasons for his Dissent, [July 9, 1793]," in Ford (ed.), *Works of Jefferson*, VII, 441–42; Ammon, *Genet Mission*, 89–90; Hamilton, memorandum, July 9, 1793, in Syrett *et al.* (eds.), *Papers of Hamilton*, XV, 76–77.

36. Ammon, *Genet Mission*, 90–92; Jefferson, Anas, July 10, 1793, in Ford (ed.), *Works of Jefferson*, I, 288; Genet to Jefferson, July 9, 1793, in *American State Papers: Foreign Relations*, I, 163.

37. Twohig (ed.), *Journal of the President*, July 11, 1793, p. 191; Washington to Jefferson, July 11, 1793, in John C. Fitzpatrick (ed.), *The Writings of George Washington* (39 vols.; Washington, D.C., 1931–44), XXXIII, 4.

38. Jefferson, Anas, July 13, 1793, in Ford (ed.), *Works of Jefferson*, I, 290; Ammon, *Genet Mission*, 92; Draft, July 18, 1793, in Syrett *et al.* (eds.), *Papers of Hamilton*, XV, 110–16.

39. Ford (ed.), *Works of Jefferson*, VII, 460–62; Syrett *et al.* (eds.), *Papers of Hamilton*, XV, 139–42, 168–69; Carroll and Ashworth, *Washington: First in Peace*, 111.

40. Jefferson, Anas, August 1, 2, 1793, Jefferson to Madison, August 3, 1793, in Ford (ed.), *Works of Jefferson*, I, 305, VII, 464; Twohig (ed.), *Journal of the President*, August 1, 2, 1793, pp. 211–12.

41. Jefferson to Washington, July 31, 1793, in Ford (ed.), *Works of Jefferson*, VII, 462–63; Ammon, *Genet Mission*, 101.

42. Jefferson, Anas, August 6, 1793, Jefferson to Washington, August 11, 1793, in

Ford (ed.), *Works of Jefferson,* I, 310–12, VII, 471. Hamilton did not resign as expected but remained in the cabinet until January 31, 1795.

43. Jefferson to Morris, August 16, 1793, in *ibid.,* 475–507; Syrett *et al.* (eds.), *Papers of Hamilton,* XV, 145, 233, 239–41; Richard R. Beeman, *The Old Dominion and the New Nation, 1788–1801* (Lexington, Ky., 1972), 126–34; Cunningham, *Jeffersonian Republicans,* 58–60.

44. Jefferson to Madison, August 11, 1793, Madison Papers, Library of Congress.

45. Jefferson to Madison, September 1, 1793, Jefferson to Thomas Mann Randolph, Jr., September 2, 1793, in Ford (ed.), *Works of Jefferson,* VIII, 12–13, 17; J. H. Powell, *Bring Out Your Dead: The Great Plague of Yellow Fever in Philadelphia in 1793* (Philadelphia, 1949), 281–82.

46. Jefferson to Martha Jefferson Randolph, September 8, 1793, in Betts and Bear (eds.), *Family Letters,* 124; Twohig (ed.), *Journal of the President,* September 10, 1793, p. 239; Washington to Hamilton, September 6, 1793, in Syrett *et al.* (eds.), *Papers of Hamilton,* XV, 324–25; Jefferson to Washington, September 15, 1793, in Ford (ed.), *Works of Jefferson,* VIII, 45–46.

47. Jefferson, account book, September–October, 1793, transcript by James A. Bear, Jr., in University of Virginia library, Charlottesville; Washington to Hamilton, September 25, 1793, in Syrett *et al.* (eds.), *Papers of Hamilton,* XV, 343; Washington to Jefferson, October 7, 1793, in Fitzpatrick (ed.), *Writings of Washington,* XXXIII, 112; Jefferson to Washington, October 17, 1793, in Ford (ed.), *Works of Jefferson,* VIII, 55.

48. Jefferson to Thomas Mann Randolph, Jr., November 2, 1793, Jefferson to Washington, October 17, 1793, Jefferson to Madison, November 17, 1793, in Ford (ed.), *Works of Jefferson,* 57, 55, 72; John J. Reardon, *Edmund Randolph* (New York, 1974), 241–42.

49. Jefferson, Anas, November 21, 23, 28, 1793, draft of president's message, [November, 1793], Jefferson to Washington, December 2, 1793, in Ford (ed.), *Works of Jefferson,* I, 328–34, VIII, 79–83, 85–88; Twohig (ed.), *Journal of the President,* November 23, 1793, p. 257.

50. Jefferson to Martha Jefferson Randolph, December 1, 1793, in Betts and Bear (eds.), *Family Letters,* 126; Ford (ed.), *Works of Jefferson,* VIII, 98–119; Malone, *Jefferson,* III, 154–55.

51. Ford (ed.), *Works of Jefferson,* VIII, 111, 114, 115; Jacob E. Cooke, *Tench Coxe and the Early Republic* (Chapel Hill, 1978), 252–53; Brant, *Madison,* III, 389.

52. Jefferson to Martha Jefferson Randolph, December 22, 1793, in Betts and Bear (eds.), *Family Letters,* 128; Jefferson to Angelica Church, November 27, 1793, in Ford (ed.), *Works of Jefferson,* VIII, 79.

53. Jefferson to Mary (Maria) Jefferson, December 15, 1793, in Betts and Bear (eds.), *Family Letters,* 127.

Chapter XIV

1. Jefferson to Madison, February 15, 1794, Jefferson to John Adams, April 25, 1794, in Paul L. Ford (ed.), *The Works of Thomas Jefferson* (Federal Edition; 12 vols.; New York, 1904), VIII, 139, 144–45; Jefferson to Philip Mazzei, May 30, 1795, in Edwin Morris Betts (ed.), *Thomas Jefferson's Garden Book, 1764–1824* (Philadelphia, 1944), 236.

2. Jefferson to Monroe, May 26, 1795, in Ford (ed.), *Works of Jefferson,* VIII, 181; Edwin Morris Betts (ed.), *Thomas Jefferson's Farm Book* (Princeton, 1953), 38; Thomas Jefferson, *Notes on the State of Virginia,* ed. William Peden (Chapel Hill, 1954), 152.

3. Betts (ed.), *Jefferson's Farm Book,* 30, 32; Dumas Malone, *Jefferson and His Time* (6

vols.; Boston, 1948–81), III, 119; Thomas Jefferson Memorial Foundation, *Report of the Curator, 1981* (Monticello, [1982]), 25.

4. Washington to Young, June 18–21, 1792, in John C. Fitzpatrick (ed.), *The Writings of George Washington* (39 vols.; Washington, D.C., 1931–44), XXXII, 71; Jefferson, notes, [June 18, 1792], Jefferson to Washington, June 28, 1793, in Ford (ed.), *Works of Jefferson*, VII, 113–21; Malone, *Jefferson*, III, 196; John C. Miller, *The Wolf by the Ears: Thomas Jefferson and Slavery* (New York, 1977), 107; Thomas Jefferson Memorial Foundation, *Report of the Curator, 1981*, pp. 23–25, 28.

5. Jefferson to Jean Nicolas Demeunier, April 29, 1795, in Ford (ed.), *Works of Jefferson*, VIII, 174–75; Jefferson to Adams, May 27, 1795, in Lester J. Cappon (ed.), *The Adams-Jefferson Letters* (2 vols.; Chapel Hill, 1959), I, 258.

6. Jefferson to Archibald Stuart, January 3, 1796, in Ford (ed.), *Works of Jefferson*, VIII, 212–14.

7. Notes of a tour through Holland, April 19, 1788, in Julian P. Boyd (ed.), *The Papers of Thomas Jefferson* (Princeton, 1950–), XIII, 26–27; Jefferson to Jonathan Williams, July 3, 1796, in Ford (ed.), *Works of Jefferson* VIII, 250–51.

8. Betts (ed.), *Jefferson's Farm Book,* "Commentary and Extracts," 50–57, 68–73; Malone, *Jefferson*, III, 216; Jefferson to Washington, June 19, 1796, in Ford (ed.), *Works of Jefferson*, VIII, 248–49.

9. B. L. Rayner, *Sketches of the Life, Writings, and Opinions of Thomas Jefferson* (New York, 1832), 524; Frederick D. Nichols, "Jefferson: The Making of an Architect," in William Howard Adams (ed.), *Jefferson and the Arts: An Extended View* (Washington, D.C., 1976), 163–64; Jefferson to Carlo Bellini, September 30, 1785, Jefferson to Madame de Tessé, March 20, 1787, in Boyd (ed.), *Papers of Jefferson*, VIII, 569, XI, 226; Jefferson to John Brown, April 5, 1797, in Thomas Jefferson Papers, Library of Congress (hereinafter cited LC).

10. Isaac Weld, Jr., *Travels Through the States of North America and the Provinces of Upper and Lower Canada During the Years 1795, 1796, and 1797* (3rd ed.; 2 vols., London, 1800), I, 207; Duc de La Rochefoucauld-Liancourt, *Travels Through the United States of North America, the Country of the Iroquois, and Upper Canada, in the Years 1795, 1796, and 1797* (2 vols.; London, 1799), II, 70; Jefferson to Volney, April 10, 1796, Jefferson Papers, LC.

11. Jefferson to Madison, July 24, 1797, in Ford (ed.), *Works of Jefferson*, VIII, 321; Malone, *Jefferson*, III, 238; Jefferson to Thomas Mann Randolph, Jr., May 3, 1798, in Betts (ed.), *Jefferson's Garden Book*, 259; Jefferson to Mary Jefferson Eppes, March 8, 1799, Edwin M. Betts and James A. Bear, Jr. (eds.), *The Family Letters of Thomas Jefferson* (Columbia, Mo., 1966), 176.

12. Malone, *Jefferson*, III, 240–42. William Howard Adams, *Jefferson's Monticello* (New York, 1983) offers a richly illustrated history of Monticello.

13. Jefferson to Mazzei, May 30, 1795, in Betts (ed.), *Jefferson's Garden Book*, 236.

14. Jefferson to Washington, May 14, 1794, Jefferson to Randolph, September 7, 1794, in Ford (ed.), *Works of Jefferson*, VIII, 150, 152.

15. Jefferson to Coxe, September 10, 1795, in *ibid.*, 190; Noble E. Cunningham, Jr., *The Jeffersonian Republicans: The Formation of Party Organization, 1789–1801* (Chapel Hill, 1957), 86–87; Madison to Jefferson, February 7, 1796, James Madison Papers, LC.

16. Jefferson to Madison, December 28, 1794, Jefferson to Edward Rutledge, November 30, 1795, Jefferson to William B. Giles, December 31, 1795, Jefferson to Monroe, March 2, 1796, Jefferson to Madison, September 21, 1795, Jefferson to Madison, April 27, 1795, in Ford (ed.), *Works of Jefferson*, VIII, 156–58, 200, 201, 221, 192, 169–70.

17. Madison to Monroe, February 26, 1796, in *Letters and Other Writings of James Madison* (Congressional Edition; 4 vols.; Philadelphia, 1865), II, 83. No formal mechanism for nominating presidential candidates existed in 1796, Jefferson's name being brought forward largely by a consensus of Republican members of Congress.

18. Madison to Monroe, September 29, 1796, in Madison Papers, LC; Jefferson to Rutledge, December 27, 1796, in Ford (ed.), *Works of Jefferson*, VIII, 257.

19. John Beckley to William Irvine, September 15, 1796, in William Irvine Papers, Historical Society of Pennsylvania, Philadelphia; Noble E. Cunningham, Jr., "John Beckley: An Early American Party Manager," *William and Mary Quarterly*, 3rd Ser., XIII (1956), 47–50.

20. *State Gazette of North Carolina* (Edenton), September 29, 1796; Circular, September 25, 1796, signed by M. Leib, broadside, Historical Society of Pennsylvania, Philadelphia.

21. Handbill, signed "A Republican," October 3, 1796, broadside, and "Public Notice," [1796], broadside, both in Historical Society of Pennsylvania, Philadelphia.

22. Handbill, signed "A Republican," October 3, 1796, broadside, Historical Society of Pennsylvania, Philadelphia; *President II, Being Observations on the Late Official Address of George Washington* ([Newark, N.J.], 1796), 15; Cunningham, *Jeffersonian Republicans*, 100.

23. Harper, circular letter, January 5, 1797, in Noble E. Cunningham, Jr. (ed.), *Circular Letters of Congressmen to Their Constituents, 1789–1829* (3 vols.; Chapel Hill, 1978), I, 62–63.

24. Adet to Pickering, October 27, November 15, 1796, in *American State Papers: Documents, Legislative and Executive of the United States* (38 vols.; Washington, D.C., 1832–61), *Foreign Relations*, I, 576–77, 582–83; Stephen G. Kurtz, *The Presidency of John Adams: The Collapse of Federalism, 1795–1800* (Philadelphia, 1957), 114, 125–34.

25. Madison to Jefferson, December 5, 1796, in Madison Papers, LC; Oliver Wolcott, Jr., to Oliver Wolcott, Sr., November 19, 1796, in George Gibbs (ed.), *Memoirs of the Administrations of Washington and John Adams, Edited from the Papers of Oliver Wolcott, Secretary of the Treasury* (2 vols.; New York, 1846), I, 397.

26. *Historical Statistics of the United States, Colonial Times to 1970* (Washington, D.C., 1975), 1071; Jefferson to Madison, December 17, 1796, in Ford (ed.), *Works of Jefferson*, VIII, 255.

27. Jefferson to Rutledge, December 27, 1796, in Ford (ed.), *Works of Jefferson*, VIII, 257–58.

28. Madison to Jefferson, December 10, 1796, in Madison Papers, LC; Madison to Jefferson, December 19, 1796, in Gaillard Hunt (ed.), *The Writings of James Madison* (9 vols.; New York, 1900–1910), VI, 296–302; Jefferson to Madison, January 1, 1797, in Ford (ed.), *Works of Jefferson*, VIII, 263.

29. Jefferson to Archibald Stuart, January 4, 1797, in Ford (ed.), *Works of Jefferson*, VIII, 267; Adams to Elbridge Gerry, February 20, 1797, in *Warren-Adams Letters*, Massachusetts Historical Society *Collections*, LXXIII (1925), 331; Benjamin Rush to Jefferson, January 4, 1797, in L. H. Butterfield (ed.), *Letters of Benjamin Rush* (2 vols.; Princeton, 1951), II, 785.

30. Jefferson to Madison, January 22, 1797, Jefferson to Wythe, January 22, 1797, in Ford (ed.), *Works of Jefferson*, VIII, 271, 274.

Chapter XV

1. Jefferson to Madison, January 30, 1797, in Paul L. Ford (ed.), *The Works of Thomas Jefferson* (Federal Edition; 12 vols.; New York, 1904), VIII, 280; Jefferson,

account book, February 20–March 2, 1797, transcript by James A. Bear, Jr., University of Virginia library, Charlottesville; Philadelphia *Minerva*, March 4, 1797.

2. Jefferson, Anas, March 2, 1797, in Ford (ed.), *Works of Jefferson*, I, 334–35.

3. Page Smith, *John Adams* (2 vols.; New York, 1962), II, 917–19; Ralph Adams Brown, *The Presidency of John Adams* (Lawrence, Kan., 1975), 3–4; Jefferson, Anas, March 2, 1797, Jefferson to Elbridge Gerry, May 13, 1797, in Ford (ed.), *Works of Jefferson*, I, 335–36, VIII, 284.

4. Jefferson to Benjamin Rush, January 22, 1797, in Ford (ed.), *Works of Jefferson*, VIII, 278; Dumas Malone, *Jefferson and His Time* (6 vols.; Boston, 1948–81), III, 340–45.

5. Jefferson to Pierre Samuel du Pont de Nemours, March 2, 1809, in Dumas Malone (ed.), *Correspondence Between Thomas Jefferson and Pierre Samuel du Pont de Nemours, 1798–1817* (Boston, 1930), 122.

6. Jefferson to Mazzei, April 24, 1796, in Ford (ed.), *Works of Jefferson*, VIII, 237–40.

7. Jefferson to Madison, August 3, 1797, in *ibid.*, 332–33; Howard R. Marraro, "The Four Versions of Jefferson's Letter to Mazzei," *William and Mary Quarterly*, 2nd Ser., XXII (1942), 23–27.

8. Text from the Philadelphia *Minerva*, May 14, 1797, in Ford (ed.), *Works of Jefferson*, VIII, 238n.

9. Jefferson to Martin Van Buren, June 29, 1824, in *ibid.*, XII, 362, 366.

10. Jefferson to Thomas Bell, May 18, 1797, in Andrew A. Lipscomb and Albert E. Bergh (eds.), *The Writings of Thomas Jefferson* (20 vols.; Washington, D.C., 1903), IX, 387; Jefferson to Peregrine Fitzhugh, June 4, 1797, Jefferson to Madison, August 3, 1797, in Ford (ed.), *Works of Jefferson*, VIII, 302, 332–33; Monroe to Jefferson, July 12, 1797, in Stanislaus M. Hamilton (ed.), *The Writings of James Monroe* (7 vols.; New York, 1898–1903), III, 69–70.

11. Madison to Jefferson, August 5, 1797, in *Letters and Other Writings of James Madison* (Congressional Edition; 4 vols.; Philadelphia, 1865), II, 118; Malone, *Jefferson*, III, 302.

12. Jefferson to Burr, June 17, 1797, Burr to Jefferson, June 21, 1797, in Mary-Jo Kline and Joanne Wood Ryan (eds.), *Political Correspondence and Public Papers of Aaron Burr* (2 vols.; Princeton, 1983), I, 298–300, 301.

13. Gallatin to his wife, June 28, 1797, June 30, 1797, in Henry Adams, *The Life of Albert Gallatin* (New York, 1879), 186–87; Harry Ammon, *James Monroe: The Quest for National Identity* (New York, 1971), 157.

14. Jefferson to Madison, August 3, 1797, in Ford (ed.), *Works of Jefferson*, VIII, 331–34; *Virginia Gazette* (Richmond), May 24, 1797.

15. Noble E. Cunningham, Jr. (ed.), *Circular Letters of Congressmen to Their Constituents, 1789–1829* (3 vols.; Chapel Hill, 1978), I, xxxvii–xxxix, 67–71; Jefferson to Fitzhugh, June 4, 1797, in Ford (ed.), *Works of Jefferson*, VIII, 302.

16. Cunningham (ed.), *Circular Letters of Congressmen to Their Constituents*, I, xxxviii–xxxix; petition, [August, 1797], Jefferson to Madison, August 3, 1797, in Ford (ed.), *Works of Jefferson*, VIII, 322–31, 333–34; Richard R. Beeman, *The Old Dominion and the New Nation, 1788–1801* (Lexington, Ky., 1972), 172.

17. Monroe to Jefferson, September 5, 1797, in Hamilton (ed.), *Writings of Monroe*, III, 85; Jefferson to Monroe, September 7, 1797, in Ford (ed.), *Works of Jefferson*, VIII, 339–40.

18. Jefferson to Monroe, October 25, 1797, in Ford (ed.), *Works of Jefferson*, VIII, 344–46; Jefferson, account book, December 6, 1797, transcript by Bear, in U. Va. library.

19. Jefferson to Madison, January 25, February 22, in Ford (ed.), *Works of Jefferson,* VIII, 358–59, 373; Jackson to John Donelson, January 18, 1798, in Sam B. Smith and Harriet C. Owsley (eds.), *The Papers of Andrew Jackson* (Knoxville, 1980–), I, 167.

20. *Annals of Congress,* 5th Cong., 2nd Sess. (March 5, 1798), 1200–1202; Alexander DeConde, *The Quasi-War: The Politics and Diplomacy of the Undeclared War with France, 1797–1801* (New York, 1966), 66.

21. *Annals of Congress,* 5th Cong., 2nd Sess. (March 19, 1798), 1271–72; DeConde, *Quasi-War,* 68–70.

22. Anthony New, circular letter, March 20, 1798, in Cunningham (ed.), *Circular Letters of Congressmen to Their Constituents,* I, 112; Jefferson to Madison, March 21, 1798, Jefferson to Monroe, Mar. 21, 1798, in Ford (ed.), *Works of Jefferson,* VIII, 386, 389; DeConde, *Quasi-War,* 71–72.

23. Samuel J. Cabell, circular letter, April 6, 1798, Joseph McDowell, circular letter, May 28, 1798, in Cunningham (ed.), *Circular Letters of Congressmen to Their Constituents,* I, 119, 120; Jefferson to Carr, April 12, 1798, in Ford (ed.), *Works of Jefferson,* VIII, 405.

24. *Annals of Congress,* 5th Cong., 1st Sess. (May 16, 1797), 56; Jefferson to Madison, April 6, 1798, in Ford (ed.), *Works of Jefferson,* VIII, 403.

25. Jefferson to Madison, April 6, 1798, in Ford (ed.), *Works of Jefferson,* VIII, 403; Gerard H. Clarfield, *Timothy Pickering and American Diplomacy, 1795–1800* (Columbia, Mo., 1969), 155.

26. Jefferson to Monroe, April 19, 1798, Jefferson to Madison, April 19, 26, 1798, in Ford (ed.), *Works of Jefferson,* VIII, 407–408, 409, 413.

27. *Annals of Congress,* 5th Cong., 2nd Sess., 3722–29; DeConde, *Quasi-War,* 90–91; Richard H. Kohn, *Eagle and Sword: The Federalists and the Creation of the Military Establishment in America, 1783–1802* (New York, 1975), 228–29; John Dawson, circular letter, July 19, 1798, in Cunningham (ed.), *Circular Letters of Congressmen to Their Constituents,* I, 125.

28. Jefferson to Madison, April 26, June 7, 1798, in Ford (ed.), *Works of Jefferson,* VIII, 411–12, 434.

29. Jefferson to Madison, June 21, 1798, in *ibid.,* 439–40; DeConde, *Quasi-War,* 93.

30. Jefferson to John Taylor, June 1, 1798, in Ford (ed.), *Works of Jefferson,* VIII, 432.

31. James Morton Smith, *Freedom's Fetters: The Alien and Sedition Laws and American Civil Liberties* (Ithaca, N.Y., 1956), 35, 50, 61, 438. Smith prints the texts of the acts on pp. 435–42.

32. *Ibid.,* 94–95, 130, 441–42.

33. Jefferson to Stevens Thomson Mason, October 11, 1798, in Ford (ed.), *Works of Jefferson,* VIII, 450.

34. Nicholas to Jefferson, October 4, 1798, Jefferson to Nicholas, October 5, 1798, in Thomas Jefferson Papers, Library of Congress.

35. Jefferson to Madison, October 26, November 17, 1798, in Ford (ed.), *Works of Jefferson,* VIII, 456, 457. On the collaboration of Jefferson and Madison on the Kentucky and Virginia Resolutions see Adrienne Koch and Harry Ammon, "The Virginia and Kentucky Resolutions: An Episode in Jefferson's and Madison's Defense of Civil Liberties," *William and Mary Quarterly,* 3rd Ser., V (1948), 145–76, and Adrienne Koch, *Jefferson and Madison: The Great Collaboration* (New York, 1964), 178–211.

36. Jefferson's "fair copy," in Ford (ed.), *Works of Jefferson,* VIII, 458–61.

37. The resolutions as passed in Kentucky are reproduced along with Jefferson's rough draft and fair copy in *ibid.,* 458–79.

38. *Ibid.*, 458–59, 476–77.

39. Jefferson to Taylor, November 26, 1798, Jefferson to Nicholas, November 29, 1798, in *ibid.*, 458–59, 483; Koch, *Jefferson and Madison*, 190–91.

40. Malone, *Jefferson*, III, 413; Jefferson to Madison, August 23, 1799, in Koch, *Jefferson and Madison*, 197–98; Jefferson to Nicholas, September 5, 1799, in Ford (ed.), *Works of Jefferson*, IX, 79–81.

41. The Kentucky Resolutions are reprinted from the Journal of the House of Representatives of Kentucky, November 14, 1799, in Noble E. Cunningham, Jr. (ed.), *The Early Republic, 1789–1828* (New York, 1968), 145–46.

42. Koch, *Jefferson and Madison*, 206.

Chapter XVI

1. Thomas Jefferson, *A Manual of Parliamentary Practice for the Use of the United States Senate* (Washington, D.C., 1801). Jefferson's *Manual* is still published by Congress today. See *Constitution, Jefferson's Manual, and Rules of the House of Representatives of the United States*, 97th Cong., 2nd Sess., House Document No. 97-271 (Washington, D.C., 1983).

2. Jefferson to Madison, February 5, 1799, Paul L. Ford (ed.), *The Works of Thomas Jefferson* (Federal Edition; 12 vols.; New York, 1904), IX, 34.

3. Jefferson to Monroe, July 15, 1803, Jefferson to Callender, October 5, 1799, in *ibid.*, 388–89, 84–85; John Taylor to Wilson Cary Nicholas, January 31, 1800, in Wilson Cary Nicholas Papers, University of Virginia, Charlottesville; Noble E. Cunningham, Jr., *The Jeffersonian Republicans: The Formation of Party Organization, 1789–1801* (Chapel Hill, 1957), 171.

4. Jefferson to Monroe, February 11, 1799, Jefferson to Philip Norborne Nicholas, April 7, 1800, in Ford (ed.), *Works of Jefferson*, IX, 36, 128; Thomas Cooper, *Political Arithmetic* (N.p., 1798), 3–5.

5. Jefferson to Gerry, January 26, 1799, in Ford (ed.), *Works of Jefferson*, IX, 17–19. See also George A. Billias, *Elbridge Gerry: Founding Father and Republican Statesman* (New York, 1976), 300–301.

6. Cunningham, *Jeffersonian Republicans*, 212–14; Meriwether Jones to Creed Taylor, April 9, 1799, in Creed Taylor Papers, University of Virginia, Charlottesville; *Aurora* (Philadelphia), October 4, 1800.

7. Ames to Oliver Wolcott, June 12, 1800, George Gibbs (ed.), *Memoirs of the Administrations of Washington and John Adams, Edited from the Papers of Oliver Wolcott, Secretary of the Treasury* (2 vols.; New York, 1846), II, 368–70; *A Short Address to the Voters of Delaware*, September 21, 1800, pamphlet in Broadsides Collection, Library of Congress (hereinafter cited LC); *Gazette of the United States* (Philadelphia), September 10, 1800.

8. [William Linn], *Serious Considerations on the Election of a President: Addressed to the Citizens of the United States* (New York, 1800), 4–6, 16–17, 24, 28.

9. [Tunis Wortman], *A Solemn Address, to Christians and Patriots, upon the Approaching Election of a President of the United States: In Answer to a Pamphlet, Entitled, "Serious Considerations"* (New York, 1800), 4; Joseph Bloomfield, *To the People of New Jersey*, September 30, 1800, broadside, Historical Society of Pennsylvania, Philadelphia; William G. McLoughlin (ed.), *Isaac Backus on Church, State, and Calvinism* (Cambridge, Mass., 1968), 16.

10. *An Address to the Citizens of North Carolina on the Subject of the Approaching Elections*, signed "A North Carolina Planter" (N.p., July 1800), 12; Americanus [John Beckley], *Address to the People of the United States; with an Epitome and Vindication of the Public Life and Character of Thomas Jefferson* (Philadelphia, 1800), 32; Joseph Bloom-

field, *To the People of New Jersey,* September 30, 1800, broadside, Historical Society of Pennsylvania; *Virginia Argus* (Richmond), July 11, 1800.

11. William Austin, *An Address, to the Voters for Electors of President and Vice-President of the United States, in the State of Virginia,* Richmond, May 26, 1800, in Broadside Collection, LC.

12. Cunningham, *Jeffersonian Republicans,* 145–46.

13. Thomas B. Adams to John Q. Adams, May 11, 1800, in Adams Family Papers (microfilm edition), Massachusetts Historical Society, Boston.

14. Jefferson to Madison, March 8, 1800, in Ford (ed.), *Works of Jefferson,* IX, 123; Burr to Jefferson, [May 3, 1800], in Mary-Jo Kline and Joanne Wood Ryan (eds.), *Political Correspondence and Public Papers of Aaron Burr* (2 vols.; Princeton, 1983), I, 426; Hamilton to Jay, May 7, 1800, in Harold C. Syrett *et al.* (eds.), *The Papers of Alexander Hamilton* (26 vols.; New York, 1961–79), XXIV, 465.

15. James Nicholson to Albert Gallatin, May 6, 1800, in Henry Adams, *The Life of Albert Gallatin* (New York, 1879), 241.

16. Hamilton to Theodore Sedgwick, May 4, 1800, in Syrett *et al.* (eds.), *Papers of Hamilton,* XXIV, 453.

17. Noble E. Cunningham, Jr., "Election of 1800," in Arthur M. Schlesinger, Jr. (ed.), *History of American Presidential Elections, 1789–1968* (4 vols.; New York, 1971), I, 110–12; Hamilton to Sedgwick, May 10, 1800, in Syrett *et al.* (eds.), *Papers of Hamilton,* XXIV, 475.

18. Jefferson to John Taylor, November 26, 1799, in Massachusetts Historical Society *Collections,* 7th Ser., I (1900), 67–68.

19. Jefferson to Thomas Mann Randolph, Jr., November 30, December 5, 1800, in *ibid.,* 78–79.

20. The election in South Carolina is treated in detail in Cunningham, *Jeffersonian Republicans,* 231–39.

21. Peter Freneau to Seth Paine, December 2, 1800, in Personal Papers, Miscellaneous, LC.

22. *Courier of New Hampshire* (Concord), December 19, 1800; Increase N. Tarbox (ed.), *Diary of Thomas Robbins, D.D., 1796–1854* (2 vols.; Boston, 1886), I, 114, 127–28.

23. Jefferson to Monroe, December 20, 1800, in James Monroe Papers, LC; Douglass Adair (ed.), "James Madison's Autobiography," *William and Mary Quarterly,* 3rd Ser., II (1945), 206; Jefferson, Anas, January 26, 1804, in Ford (ed.), *Works of Jefferson,* I, 378.

24. Burr to John Taylor, October 23, 1800, in Kline and Ryan (eds.), *Papers of Burr,* I, 451; John Hunter to Madison, April 16, 1801, in James Madison Papers, LC; Uriah Tracy to James McHenry, December 30, 1800, in Bernard C. Steiner, *The Life and Correspondence of James McHenry* (Cleveland, 1907), 483–84 (punctuation modernized).

25. Jefferson to Burr, December 15, 1800, Burr to Jefferson, December 23, 1800, in Kline and Ryan (eds.), *Papers of Burr,* I, 469–70, 473–74.

26. Burr to Smith, December 16, 1800, December 29, 1800, in *ibid.,* 471, 479.

27. Kline and Ryan (eds.), *Papers of Burr,* I, 481–85.

28. Hamilton to Oliver Wolcott, Jr., December 16, 1800, in Syrett *et al.* (eds.), *Papers of Hamilton,* XXV, 257.

29. Syrett *et al.* (eds.), *Papers of Hamilton,* 269–324.

30. Hamilton to Bayard, January 16, 1801, in *ibid.,* 319–20.

31. Jefferson to Madison, December 26, 1800, Jefferson to Tench Coxe, December 31, 1800, in Ford (ed.), *Works of Jefferson,* IX, 161–62; Gallatin to his wife, January 22, 1801, in Adams, *Gallatin,* 255–56.

32. *Annals of Congress*, 6th Cong., 2nd Sess. (February 9, 1801), 1009–11; Gallatin to his wife, February 5, 1801, in Adams, *Gallatin*, 260.

33. Jefferson had the votes of New York, New Jersey, Pennsylvania, Virginia, North Carolina, Georgia, Kentucky, and Tennessee; Burr received the votes of New Hampshire, Massachusetts, Rhode Island, Connecticut, Delaware, and South Carolina.

34. Bayard to Richard Bassett, February 12, 1801, in Elizabeth Donnan (ed.), *Papers of James A. Bayard, 1796–1815*, Vol. II of American Historical Association *Annual Report, 1913* (Washington, D.C., 1915), 125; Gallatin to his wife, February 12, 14, 1801, in Adams, *Gallatin*, 260–62.

35. Bayard to Bassett, February 16, February 17, 1801, in Donnan (ed.), *Papers of Bayard*, 126–27; Gallatin to James Nicholson, February 14, 16, 1801, Gallatin to his wife, February 17, 1801, in Adams, *Gallatin*, 261–62.

36. Jefferson to Monroe, February 15, 1801, Jefferson to Madison, February 18, 1801, in Ford (ed.), *Works of Jefferson*, IX, 179, 182; Bayard to Allen McLane, February 17, 1801, in Donnan (ed.), *Papers of Bayard*, 127.

37. Bayard to Bassett, February 16, 1801, in Donnan (ed.), *Papers of Bayard*, 126; John S. Pancake, "Aaron Burr: Would-Be Usurper," *William and Mary Quarterly*, 3rd Ser., VIII (1951), 209.

38. Burr to Gallatin, February 25, 1801, in Kline and Ryan (eds.), *Papers of Burr*, I, 509; Bayard to McLane, February 17, 1801, in Donnan (ed.), *Papers of Bayard*, 128.

39. Deposition of James A. Bayard, April 3, 1806, deposition of Samuel Smith, April 15, 1806, Samuel Smith to Richard H. and James A. Bayard, April 3, 1830, in Matthew L. Davis, *Memoirs of Aaron Burr, with Miscellaneous Selections from His Correspondence* (2 vols.; New York, 1837), II, 107–109, 129–37. On Smith's role see Frank A. Cassell, *Merchant Congressman in the Young Republic: Samuel Smith of Maryland, 1752–1839* (Madison, 1971), 98–102; John S. Pancake, *Samuel Smith and the Politics of Business, 1752–1839* (University, Ala., 1972), 52–58.

40. Jefferson, memorandum on a conversation with Burr, April 15, 1806, in Kline and Ryan (eds.), *Papers of Burr*, II, 963; Jefferson to Monroe, February 15, 1801, in Ford (ed.), *Works of Jefferson*, IX, 179; Robert Williams to his North Carolina constituents, February 26, 1801, in Noble E. Cunningham, Jr. (ed.), *Circular Letters of Congressmen to Their Constituents, 1789–1829* (3 vols.; Chapel Hill, 1978), I, 241; Bayard to McLane, February 17, 1801, in Donnan (ed.), *Papers of Bayard*, 128–29.

41. Jefferson to Spencer Roane, September 6, 1819, in Ford (ed.), *Works of Jefferson*, XII, 136. On the election of 1800 see also Joyce Appleby, *Capitalism and a New Social Order: The Republican Vision of the 1790s* (New York, 1984), 3–4, 79, 103–104.

Chapter XVII

1. *Times* (Alexandria), March 6, 1801; *Examiner* (Richmond), March 13, 1801.

2. Gallatin to his wife, January 15, 1801, in Henry Adams, *The Life of Albert Gallatin* (New York, 1879), 254; Mrs. Smith to Susan B. Smith, March 4, 1801, in Gaillard Hunt (ed.), *The First Forty Years of Washington Society, Portrayed by the Family Letters of Mrs. Samuel Harrison Smith* (New York, 1906), 25.

3. Hunt (ed.), *First Forty Years of Washington Society*, 26.

4. Jefferson to Monroe, [March] 7, 1801, in Paul L. Ford (ed.), *The Works of Thomas Jefferson* (Federal Edition; 12 vols.; New York, 1904), IX, 203.

5. Text of Jefferson's inaugural address, March 4, 1801, transcribed from Jefferson's final manuscript copy, in Thomas Jefferson Papers, Library of Congress (here-

inafter cited LC), in Noble E. Cunningham, Jr. (ed.), *The Early Republic, 1789–1828* (New York, 1968), 70–75.

6. Giles to Jefferson, March 16, 1801, in Jefferson Papers, LC; *American Citizen* (New York), June 5, 1801; *American Mercury* (Hartford), July 30, 1801, reprinted from Philadelphia *Aurora*.

7. Jefferson to Gouverneur Morris, May 18, 1801, in Ford (ed.), *Works of Jefferson*, IX, 251; Noble E. Cunningham, Jr., *The Process of Government Under Jefferson* (Princeton, 1978), 12–14.

8. Jefferson, Anas, March 8, 9, 1801, in Ford (ed.), *Works of Jefferson*, I, 363–65; Dumas Malone, *Jefferson and His Time* (6 vols.; Boston, 1948–81), IV, 35.

9. Jefferson, Anas, May 15, 1801, Jefferson to Wilson Cary Nicholas, June 11, 1801, in Ford (ed.), *Works of Jefferson*, I, 365, IX, 264.

10. Jefferson, Anas, May 15, 1801, in *ibid.*, I, 365–66; Cunningham, *Process of Government Under Jefferson*, 48–50.

11. Jefferson to Nicholas, June 11, 1801, in Ford (ed.), *Works of Jefferson*, IX, 264–65.

12. Cunningham, *Process of Government Under Jefferson*, 64.

13. Jefferson to John Dickinson, June 21, 1801, Jefferson to James Sullivan, March 3, 1808, in Jefferson Papers, LC.

14. Jefferson to Benjamin Rush, March 24, 1801, Jefferson to Giles, March 23, 1801, Jefferson to Monroe, [March] 7, 1801, in Ford (ed.), *Works of Jefferson*, IX, 230–31, 222–23, 204.

15. Pierpont Edwards and others to Levi Lincoln, June 4, 1801, enclosed in Lincoln to Jefferson, June 15, 1801, in Jefferson Papers, LC.

16. Giles to Jefferson, June 1, 1801, in *ibid.*

17. Jefferson to Elias Shipman and others, July 12, 1801, in Ford (ed.), *Works of Jefferson*, IX, 272–73.

18. Harrison Gray Otis to John Rutledge, October 18, 1801, in John Rutledge Papers, University of North Carolina, Chapel Hill; Jefferson to Shipman and others, July 12, 1801, in Ford (ed.), *Works of Jefferson*, IX, 274.

19. Jefferson to Monroe, [March] 7, 1801, Jefferson to Giles, March 23, 1801, in Ford (ed.), *Works of Jefferson*, IX, 204, 222.

20. Jefferson, memorandum, [1803], in Jefferson Papers, LC. A detailed breakdown of this memorandum is in Cunningham, *Process of Government Under Jefferson*, 173–74; see also Carl E. Prince, "The Passing of the Aristocracy: Jefferson's Removal of Federalists, 1804–1805," *Journal of American History*, LVII (1970), 563–75. For an extended treatment of Jefferson's patronage practices see Noble E. Cunningham, Jr., *The Jeffersonian Republicans in Power: Party Operations, 1801–1809* (Chapel Hill, 1963), 12–70.

21. Cunningham, *Process of Government Under Jefferson*, 72–77.

22. Jefferson, draft of first annual message, December 8, 1801, Smith to Jefferson, received November 21, 1801, in Jefferson Papers, LC.

23. Jefferson, marginal note on draft of first annual message, December 8, 1801, in *ibid.*

24. Jefferson to the president of the Senate, December 8, 1801, in Ford (ed.), *Works of Jefferson*, IX, 321; Macon to Jefferson, Apr. 20, 1801, in Jefferson Papers, LC; Michael Leib to Lydia Leib, December 9, 1801, in Leib-Harrison Family Papers, Historical Society of Pennsylvania, Philadelphia.

25. Cunningham, *Process of Government Under Jefferson*, 98. The first session of the Seventh Congress is reviewed in the circular letters of John Clopton, April 3, 1802,

William Dickson, April 5, 1802, and John Stratton, April 22, 1802, in Noble E. Cunningham, Jr. (ed.), *Circular Letters of Congressmen to Their Constituents, 1789–1829* (3 vols.; Chapel Hill, 1978), I, 275–86.

26. *Annals of Congress*, 6th Cong., 2nd Sess., 1534–48; Richard E. Ellis, *The Jeffersonian Crisis: Courts and Politics in the Young Republic* (New York, 1971), 41–50; John Clopton, circular to his constituents, April 3, 1802, in Cunningham (ed.), *Circular Letters of Congressmen to Their Constituents*, I, 276.

27. Jefferson to John Dickinson, December 19, 1801, Andrew A. Lipscomb and Albert E. Bergh (eds.), *The Writings of Thomas Jefferson* (20 vols.; Washington, D.C., 1903), X, 302; Ellis, *Jeffersonian Crisis*, 43–44.

28. Ellis, *Jeffersonian Crisis*, 66.

29. Hillhouse to Simeon Baldwin, February 11, 1802, in Baldwin Family Papers, Yale University Library, New Haven; Henderson to Samuel Johnston, December 16, 1802, in Hayes Collection, transcript, North Carolina Division of Archives and History, Raleigh; Pickering to his wife, January 31, 1806, quoted in Edward H. Phillips, "Timothy Pickering's Portrait of Thomas Jefferson," Essex Institute *Historical Collections*, XCIV (1958), 313; Charles Francis Adams (ed.), *Memoirs of John Quincy Adams, Comprising Portions of His Diary from 1795 to 1848* (12 vols.; Philadelphia, 1874–77), February 7, 1806, I, 403–404.

30. Jefferson to Bidwell, July 5, 1806, in Jefferson Papers, LC; *Annals of Congress*, 9th Cong., 1st Sess., (March 5, 1806), 561.

31. Jefferson to Breckinridge, November 24, 1803, in Ford (ed.), *Works of Jefferson*, X, 52. For examples of legislation drafted by Jefferson see Cunningham, *Process of Government Under Jefferson*, 189–92.

32. Robert M. Johnstone, Jr., in *Jefferson and the Presidency: Leadership in the Young Republic* (Ithaca, N.Y., 1978), 14, argues that Jefferson's presidency fits the bargaining model of presidential leadership employed by modern presidents.

33. Cunningham, *Process of Government Under Jefferson*, 197–209.

34. Jefferson to Thomas Mann Randolph, Jr., November 16, 1801, in Jefferson Papers, LC.

35. Cunningham, *Process of Government Under Jefferson*, 45–47; Jefferson to Gallatin, September 18, 1801, in Henry Adams (ed.), *The Writings of Albert Gallatin* (3 vols.; Philadelphia, 1879), I, 55.

36. Jefferson, circular to the heads of the departments, November 6, 1801, in Jefferson Papers, LC.

37. Jefferson to Lewis, February 23, 1801, in *ibid.;* Cunningham, *Process of Government Under Jefferson*, 5–6, 36–38. See also Silvio Bedini, *Thomas Jefferson and His Copying Machines* (Charlottesville, 1984).

38. Jefferson to Walter Jones, March 5, 1810, Jefferson to Joel Barlow, January 24, 1810, in Ford (ed.), *Works of Jefferson*, XI, 137, 132.

39. Jefferson to Comte Destutt de Tracy, January 26, 1811, in *ibid.*, 185.

40. *Ibid.*

41. Cunningham, *Process of Government Under Jefferson*, 40.

42. Jefferson to David R. Williams, January 31, 1806, in Jefferson Papers, LC; Cunningham, *Process of Government Under Jefferson*, 41–44.

43. Mitchill to his wife, February 10, 1802, November 26, 1804, in Samuel Latham Mitchill Papers, Museum of the City of New York; Everett S. Brown (ed.), *William Plumer's Memorandum of Proceedings in the United States Senate, 1803–1807* (New York, 1923), 212–13. On the mammoth cheese, see Malone, *Jefferson*, IV, 106–108.

44. Jefferson, account book, March 8, 1802, photostatic copy, in LC.

45. Cunningham, *Process of Government Under Jefferson*, 40–41.

46. Jefferson to William Short, October 31, 1819, in Dickinson W. Adams (ed.), *Jefferson's Extracts from the Gospels* (Princeton, 1983), 389, a volume in Series 2 of *The Papers of Thomas Jefferson*.

47. In an excellent introduction to both works published in *ibid.*, Eugene R. Sheridan explains the origins of the works and clarifies the confusion that has surrounded the two compilations.

48. Constance B. Schulz, "'Of Bigotry in Politics and Religion'; Jefferson's Religion, the Federalist Press, and the Syllabus," *Virginia Magazine of History and Biography*, XCI (1983), 73–83.

49. Adams (ed.), *Jefferson's Extracts from the Gospels*, 12–16, 25, 331–34; Schulz, "Jefferson's Religion," 88–89.

50. Jefferson to Adams, October 12, 1813, in Adams (ed.), *Jefferson's Extracts from the Gospels*, 352.

51. Rules of Etiquette, [1803], in Ford (ed.), *Works of Jefferson*, X, 47.

52. On the Merry incident see Henry Adams, *History of the United States of America During the Administration of Thomas Jefferson* (4 vols.; New York, 1889), II, 365–76; Malcolm Lester, *Anthony Merry Redivivus: A Reappraisal of the British Minister to the United States, 1803–6* (Charlottesville, 1978), 29–47.

53. Plumer to Jeremiah Smith, December 9, 1802, in William Plumer Papers, LC; Brown (ed.), *Plumer's Memorandum*, 212–13.

Chapter XVIII

1. King to Madison, March 29, 1801, in *American State Papers: Documents, Legislative and Executive of the United States* (38 vols.; Washington, D.C., 1832–61), *Foreign Relations*, II, 509; Jefferson to Monroe, May 29, 1801, in Paul L. Ford (ed.), *The Works of Thomas Jefferson* (Federal Edition; 12 vols.; New York, 1904), IX, 263. The secret treaty of San Ildefonso was signed October 1, 1800.

2. Madison to Pinckney, June 9, 1801, Madison to Livingston, September 28, 1801, in *American State Papers: Foreign Relations*, II, 510–11; Dumas Malone, *Jefferson and His Time* (6 vols.; Boston, 1948–81), IV, 250.

3. Jefferson to Livingston, April 18, 1802, in Ford (ed.), *Works of Jefferson*, IX, 364–65; Jefferson to Pierre Samuel du Pont de Nemours, April 25, 1802, in Andrew A. Lipscomb and Albert E. Bergh (eds.), *The Writings of Thomas Jefferson* (20 vols.; Washington, D.C., 1903), X, 317.

4. Jefferson to Livingston, April 18, 1802, in Ford (ed.), *Works of Jefferson*, IX, 368; Madison to Charles Pinckney, November 27, 1802, Gaillard Hunt (ed.), *The Writings of James Madison* (9 vols.; New York, 1900–1910), VI, 462; Madison to Livingston, December 16, 1802, quoted in Irving Brant, *James Madison* (6 vols.; Indianapolis, 1941–61), IV, 99.

5. John Stanly to Duncan Cameron, January 20, 1803, in Cameron Family Papers, University of North Carolina, Chapel Hill.

6. Jefferson, second annual message, December 15, 1802, in Ford (ed.), *Works of Jefferson*, IX, 409; Hamilton to Charles C. Pinckney, December 29, 1802, Harold C. Syrett *et al.* (eds.), *The Papers of Alexander Hamilton* (26 vols.; New York, 1961–79), XXVI, 71; *Annals of Congress*, 7th Cong., 2nd Sess. (December 17, 1802), 281; *American State Papers: Foreign Relations*, II, 469–71.

7. Claiborne to Madison, January 3, 1803, in Dunbar Rowland (ed.), *Official Letter Books of W. C. C. Claiborne, 1801–1816* (6 vols.; Jackson, Miss., 1917), I, 253; Mary P. Adams, "Jefferson's Reaction to the Treaty of San Ildefonso," *Journal of Southern His-*

tory, XXI (1955), 173–88; Alexander DeConde, *This Affair of Louisiana* (New York, 1976), 132.

8. *Annals of Congress*, 7th Cong., 2nd Sess. (January 4–11, 1803), 312–14, 326–28, 339–42; *American State Papers: Foreign Relations*, II, 471.

9. Jefferson to Monroe, January 10, 1803, January 13, 1803, in Ford (ed.), *Works of Jefferson*, IX, 416, 418–19; *Journal of the Executive Proceedings of the Senate* (Washington, D.C., 1828), Jauary 12, 1803, I, 436.

10. New York *Evening Post*, February 8, 1803, in Syrett *et al.* (eds.), *Papers of Hamilton*, XXVI, 82–85.

11. Du Pont to Jefferson, April 30, 1802, October 4, 1802, in Dumas Malone (ed.), *Correspondence Between Thomas Jefferson and Pierre Samuel du Pont de Nemours, 1798–1817* (Boston, 1930), 58–60, 68–70; Malone, *Jefferson*, IV, 257.

12. *Annals of Congress*, 7th Cong., 2nd Sess. (January 12, February 26, 1803), 370–74, 602.

13. Madison to Livingston and Monroe, March 2, 1803, in Hunt (ed.), *Writings of Madison*, VII, 19, 24–25. The State Department calculated the exchange rate at $1.10 for every six livres tournois, or a total of $9,166,666.60. *Ibid.*, 19.

14. Livingston to Talleyrand, January 10, 1803, in *American State Papers: Foreign Relations*, II, 531; DeConde, *Louisiana*, 131.

15. Jefferson to Hugh Williamson, April 30, 1803, in Lipscomb and Bergh (eds.), *Writings of Jefferson*, X, 386.

16. Harry Ammon, *James Monroe: The Quest for National Identity* (New York, 1971), 207–208; DeConde, *Louisiana*, 162–64, 172.

17. Monroe to Madison, April 15, 1803, memoranda, April 27–May 3, 1803, in Stanislaus M. Hamilton (ed.), *The Writings of James Monroe* (7 vols.; New York, 1898–1903), IV, 9–19. See also George Dangerfield, *Chancellor Robert R. Livingston of New York, 1746–1813* (New York, 1960), Part 5.

18. *National Intelligencer* (Washington), July 4, 8, 1803; Jefferson to Horatio Gates, July 11, 1803, in Ford (ed.), *Works of Jefferson*, X, 13. See also Jefferson, Anas, May 7, 1803, in Ford (ed.), *Works of Jefferson*, I, 372–73.

19. Jefferson to John Dickinson, August 9, 1803, Jefferson to Wilson Cary Nicholas, September 7, 1803, Jefferson to John Breckinridge, August 12, 1803, in Ford (ed.), *Works of Jefferson*, X, 29, 10–11, 7.

20. Everett S. Brown (ed.), *William Plumer's Memorandum of Proceedings in the United States Senate, 1803–1807* (New York, 1928), 13–14; Noble E. Cunningham, Jr., *The Process of Government Under Jefferson* (Princeton, 1978), 273–75.

21. Jefferson, third annual message, October 17, 1803, in Ford (ed.), *Works of Jefferson*, X, 37.

22. Jefferson, special message to Congress, October 21, 1803, in *ibid.*, 44; DeConde, *Louisiana*, 188.

23. Jefferson, third annual message, October 17, 1803, in Ford (ed.), *Works of Jefferson*, X, 37; Adrienne Koch, *Power, Morals, and the Founding Fathers* (Ithaca, N.Y., 1961), 48; John C. Miller, *The Wolf by the Ears: Thomas Jefferson and Slavery* (New York, 1977), 142–43.

24. Jefferson to Horatio Gates, July 11, 1803, in Ford (ed.), *Works of Jefferson*, X, 14; George Dargo, *Jefferson's Louisiana: Politics and the Clash of Legal Traditions* (Cambridge, Mass., 1975), 107, 169–74.

25. Carlos Martinez de Yrujo to Pedro Cevallos, December 2, 1802, in Donald Jackson (ed.), *Letters of the Lewis and Clark Expedition, with Related Documents, 1783–1854* (2nd ed.; 2 vols.; Urbana, 1978), I, 4–5.

26. Jefferson, message to Congress, January 18, 1803, in *ibid.*, 11–13; *Annals of Congress*, 7th Cong., 2nd Sess., 1565.

27. Jackson (ed.), *Letters of the Lewis and Clark Expedition*, I, 8–9; Jefferson to James Wilkinson, February 23, 1801, Jefferson to Meriwether Lewis, February 23, 1801, in *ibid.*, 1–2; Donald Jackson, *Jefferson and the Stony Mountains: Exploring the West from Monticello* (Urbana, 1981), 117–20.

28. Jefferson's instructions to Lewis are in Jackson, *Jefferson and the Stony Mountains*, 139–44.

29. Gerard H. Clarfield, *Timothy Pickering and the American Republic* (Pittsburgh, 1980), 224–28; Mary-Jo Kline and Joanne Wood Ryan (eds.), *Political Correspondence and Public Papers of Aaron Burr* (2 vols.; Princeton, 1983), II, 862–65; Syrett *et al.* (eds.), *Papers of Hamilton*, XXVI, 310.

30. McKean to Jefferson, February 7, 1803, quoted in Malone, *Jefferson*, IV, 229; Jefferson to McKean, February 19, 1803, in Ford (ed.), *Works of Jefferson*, IX, 451–52.

31. See Leonard W. Levy, *Legacy of Suppression: Freedom of Speech in Early American History* (Cambridge, Mass., 1960), 300–301; Levy, *Jefferson and Civil Liberties: The Darker Side* (Cambridge, Mass., 1963), 58–59; Malone, *Jefferson*, IV, 224–35.

32. Jefferson to Elbridge Gerry, March 3, 1804, in Ford (ed.), *Works of Jefferson*, X, 73; Jacob Crowninshield to Barnabas Bidwell, February 26, 1804, in Henry W. Taft Collection, Massachusetts Historical Society, Boston.

33. Noble E. Cunningham, Jr., *The Jeffersonian Republicans in Power: Party Operations, 1801–1809* (Chapel Hill, 1963), 38–43.

34. Jefferson to Monroe, January 8, 1804, in Ford (ed.), *Works of Jefferson*, X, 61.

35. Mary Jefferson Eppes to Jefferson, February 10, [1804], in Edwin M. Betts and James A. Bear, [Jr.] (eds.), *The Family Letters of Thomas Jefferson* (Columbia, Mo., 1966), 256–57; Noble E. Cunningham, Jr., *The Image of Thomas Jefferson in the Public Eye: Portraits for the People, 1800–1809* (Charlottesville, 1981), 80–84.

36. Jefferson to Nicholson, May 13, 1803, in Lipscomb and Bergh (eds.), *Writings of Jefferson*, X, 390; Richard E. Ellis, *The Jeffersonian Crisis: Courts and Politics in the Young Republic* (New York, 1971), 79–80; Nathaniel Macon to Nicholson, July 26, August 6, 1803, in Joseph H. Nicholson Papers, Library of Congress (hereinafter cited LC); *Annals of Congress*, 8th Cong., 1st Sess. (January 5, 7, 1804), 806, 876; Caesar A. Rodney to George Read, February 7, 1804, in George Read Papers, Historical Society of Pennsylvania, Philadelphia.

37. *Annals of Congress*, 8th Cong., 1st Sess. (March 12, 1804), 1180; Ellis, *Jeffersonian Crisis*, 69–76; Pickering to Theodore Lyman, March 14, 1804, in Timothy Pickering Papers, Massachusetts Historical Society, Boston; Plumer to Isaac Lyman, March 17, 1804, in William Plumer Papers, LC.

38. Charles Francis Adams (ed.), *Memoirs of John Quincy Adams, Comprising Portions of His Diary from 1795 to 1848* (12 vols.; Philadelphia, 1874–77), I, 321. See also Timothy Pickering to James McHenry, December 22, 1804, in Pickering Papers, Massachusetts Historical Society, and William Plumer to Thomas W. Thompson, December 23, 1804, in Plumer Papers, LC.

39. Uriah Tracy, quoted in Ellis, *Jeffersonian Crisis*, 96.

40. Joseph Hiester to John H. Hiester, February 10, 1805, in Joseph Hiester Papers, Gregg Collection, LC; Brown (ed.), *Plumer's Memorandum*, January 2, 1805, pp. 235–36; Ellis, *Jeffersonian Crisis*, 96; William Plumer to Daniel Plumer, February 25, 1805, in Plumer Papers, LC.

41. Jefferson to Joseph H. Nicholson, May 13, 1803, in Lipscomb and Bergh (eds.), *Writings of Jefferson*, X, 390; Ellis, *Jeffersonian Crisis*, 104.

42. Brown (ed.), *Plumer's Memorandum*, 101; Jefferson memorandum, [March, 1805], Jefferson Papers, LC; Adams (ed.), *Memoirs of John Quincy Adams*, I, 362–63; Ellis, *Jeffersonian Crisis*, 101.

Chapter XIX

1. Samuel L. Mitchill to his wife, March 2, 1805, in Samuel Latham Mitchill Papers, Museum of the City of New York; Mary-Jo Kline and Joanne Wood Ryan (eds.), *Political Correspondence and Public Papers of Aaron Burr* (2 vols.; Princeton, 1983), II, 909–17; Augustus John Foster, *Jeffersonian America: Notes on the United States of America, Collected in the Years 1805–6–7 and 11–12*, ed. Richard Beale Davis (San Marino, 1954), 15; Dumas Malone, *Jefferson and His Time* (6 vols.; Boston, 1948–81), V, 3–4.

2. Charles Francis Adams (ed.), *Memoirs of John Quincy Adams, Comprising Portions of His Diary from 1795 to 1848* (12 vols.; Philadelphia, 1874–77), I, 373; Everett S. Brown (ed.), *William Plumer's Memorandum of Proceedings in the United States Senate* (New York, 1928), 315–16.

3. Jefferson, second inaugural address, March 4, 1805, in Paul L. Ford (ed.), *The Works of Thomas Jefferson* (Federal Edition; 12 vols.; New York, 1904), X, 127–31.

4. *Ibid.*, 131–33. On Jefferson and the Indians see Bernard W. Sheehan, *Seeds of Extinction: Jeffersonian Philanthropy and the American Indian* (Chapel Hill, 1973).

5. Jefferson, notes on a draft for second inaugural address, in Ford (ed.), *Works of Jefferson*, X, 127n.

6. *Ibid.*, 135.

7. Foster, *Jeffersonian America*, 15; Address dated March 4, 1805, (capitalization and spelling modernized) in Thomas Jefferson Papers, Library of Congress (hereinafter cited LC); Malone, *Jefferson*, V, 4.

8. Alfred L. Bush, "The Life Portraits of Thomas Jefferson," in William Howard Adams (ed.), *Jefferson and the Arts: An Extended View* (Washington, D.C., 1976), 73–76; Noble E. Cunningham, Jr., *The Image of Thomas Jefferson in the Public Eye: Portraits for the People, 1800–1809* (Charlottesville, 1981), 87–92.

9. Jefferson to John Taylor, January 6, 1805, in Ford (ed.), *Works of Jefferson*, X, 125; *Annals of Congress*, 9th Cong., 1st Sess. (March 13, 1806), 775.

10. Jefferson to Monroe, January 8, 1804, in Ford (ed.), *Works of Jefferson*, X, 63; Harry Ammon, *James Monroe: The Quest for National Identity* (New York, 1971), 233–42; Malone, *Jefferson*, IV, 342–47, V, 45–52.

11. Malone, *Jefferson*, V, 39–41; Jefferson to Madison, August 25, 1805, August 7, 1805, in Ford (ed.), *Writings of Jefferson*, X, 171, 169n.

12. Jefferson to Madison, October 23, 1805, Jefferson, memorandum, [November 14, 1805], in Ford (ed.), *Writings of Jefferson*, 176n, 177n, 180.

13. Jefferson, Anas, November 19, 1805, in *ibid.*, I, 387. See also Henry Adams, *History of the United States of America During the Administration of Thomas Jefferson* (4 vols.; New York, 1889), III, 103–107, and C. Edward Skeen, *John Armstrong, Jr., 1758–1843: A Biography* (Syracuse, New York, 1981), 76–77.

14. Jefferson, fifth annual message, December 3, 1805, in Ford (ed.), *Works of Jefferson*, X, 189–90.

15. Jefferson, confidential message, December 6, 1805, in *ibid.*, 198–205.

16. *Ibid.*, 205; Gallatin to Jefferson, [December 3, 1805], in Henry Adams (ed.), *The Writings of Albert Gallatin* (3 vols.; Philadelphia, 1879), I, 276; John Randolph, "Decius," Richmond *Enquirer*, August 15, 1806; Adams, *History of the U.S. During the*

Administration of Jefferson, III, 133; Norman K. Risjord, *The Old Republicans: Southern Conservatism in the Age of Jefferson* (New York, 1965), 46-47.

17. C. Peter Magrath, *Yazoo: Land and Politics in the New Republic* (Providence, 1966), 5-19, 35-45; Irving Brant, *James Madison* (6 vols.; Indianapolis, 1941-61), IV, 234-40.

18. *Annals of Congress,* 9th Cong., 1st Sess., 88, 1131-32, 1226-27; Randolph, circular letter, April 27, 1806, in Noble E. Cunningham, Jr. (ed.), *Circular Letters of Congressmen to Their Constituents, 1789-1829* (3 vols.; Chapel Hill, 1978), I, 475-76.

19. Jefferson to Thomas Lomax, January 11, 1806, quoted in Malone, *Jefferson,* V, 95.

20. John Quincy Adams to John Adams, February 11, 1806, in Worthington C. Ford (ed.), *Writings of John Quincy Adams* (7 vols.; New York, 1913-17), III, 134; Bradford Perkins, *Prologue to War: England and the United States, 1805-1812* (Berkeley, 1968), 78-81; Jefferson, fifth annual message, December 3, 1805, Jefferson, special message, January 17, 1806, in Ford (ed.), *Works of Jefferson,* X, 187-92, 223-24; *Annals of Congress,* 9th Cong., 1st Sess. (January 17, 1806), 342-43.

21. Brown (ed.), *Plumer's Memorandum,* 388; Ralph Ketcham, *James Madison: A Biography* (New York, 1971), 442-43; Jefferson to Comte de Volney, February 11, 1806, in Ford (ed.), *Works of Jefferson,* X, 227.

22. *Annals of Congress,* 9th Cong., 1st Sess. (December 4, 1805), 262.

23. Randolph to Madison, December 11, 1805, in Original Reports of the Secretary of State, House Records, Record Group 233, National Archives; *Annals of Congress,* 9th Cong., 1st Sess. (January 29, 1806), 409-12.

24. *Annals of Congress,* 9th Cong., 1st Sess., 412-13, 877. After approval by the Senate on April 15, the act was signed by the president on April 18, 1806. *Ibid.,* 240, 1259-62.

25. Adams (ed.), *Memoirs of John Quincy Adams,* I, 415; Jefferson to Paine, March 25, 1806, in Ford (ed.), *Works of Jefferson,* X, 248; *Annals of Congress,* 9th Cong., 1st Sess., 771-72, 851; William Plumer to James Sheafe, March 14, 1806, in William Plumer Papers, LC.

26. Malone, *Jefferson,* V, 113-14.

27. Undated letters received December 1, 5, 1805, in Jefferson Papers, LC.

28. Merry to Lord Harrowby, August 6, 1804, Merry to Harrowby, March 29, 1805, in Kline and Ryan (eds.), *Papers of Burr,* II, 291, 927-29; Adams, *History of the U.S. During the Administration of Jefferson,* III, 233-38.

29. *United States Gazette* (Philadelphia), July 27, 1805; Malone, *Jefferson,* V, 231-32; *Aurora* (Philadelphia), July 30, 1805; Claiborne to Madison, August 6, 1805, in Clarence E. Carter (ed.), *The Territorial Papers of the United States* (26 vols.; Washington, D.C., 1934-62), IX, 489.

30. Daveiss to Jefferson, January 10, 1806, received February 8, 1806, Jefferson Papers, LC, printed in J. H. Daveiss, *A View of the President's Conduct Concerning the Conspiracy of 1806* (Frankfort, Ky., 1807), in Historical and Philosophical Society of Ohio *Quarterly Publications,* XII (1917), 69-71.

31. Gallatin to Jefferson, February 12, 1806, Adams (ed.), *Writings of Gallatin,* I, 290; Jefferson to Daveiss, February 15, 1806, in Ford (ed.), *Works of Jefferson,* X, 231-32; List enclosed in Daveiss to Jefferson, February 10, 1806, in Daveiss, *View of the President's Conduct,* 74-75.

32. Daveiss to Jefferson, July 14, 1806, in Daveiss, *View of the President's Conduct,* 91; Jefferson to Daveiss, September 12, 1806, in Ford (ed.), *Works of Jefferson,* X, 286.

33. Jefferson to Morgan, March 26, 1807, in Andrew A. Lipscomb and Albert E. Bergh (eds.), *The Writings of Thomas Jefferson* (20 vols.; Washington, D.C., 1903), XI, 174. See also Jefferson to Morgan, September 19, 1806, Jefferson to John Nicholson, September 19, 1806, in Ford (ed.) *Works of Jefferson*, X, 291–92; Malone, *Jefferson*, V, 239.

34. Granger to Jefferson, October 16, 1806, in "Burr-Blennerhassett Documents," Historical and Philosophical Society of Ohio *Quarterly Publications*, IX (1914), 10–13; Malone, *Jefferson*, V, 240–41.

35. Jefferson, Anas, October 22, 24, 25, 1806, in Ford (ed.), *Works of Jefferson*, I, 401–403.

36. Thomas P. Abernethy, *The Burr Conspiracy* (New York, 1954), 15.

37. Letter to Wilkinson, [July 22–29, 1806], in Kline and Ryan (eds.), *Papers of Burr*, II, 986–87.

38. Kline and Ryan (eds.), *Papers of Burr*, II, 973–86.

39. Excerpts from Wilkinson to Jefferson, October 21, 1806, and memorandum, dated October 20, 1806, in Abernethy, *Burr Conspiracy*, 150–52.

40. Jefferson, Anas, November 25, 1806, Jefferson, proclamation, November 27, 1806, in Ford (ed.), *Works of Jefferson*, I, 403–404, X, 301–302.

41. Brown (ed.), *Plumer's Memorandum*, 515–16.

42. Jefferson to Caesar A. Rodney, December 5, 1806, Jefferson, sixth annual message, December 2, 1806, in Ford, (ed.) *Works of Jefferson*, X, 322, 311.

43. Jefferson, special message, January 22, 1807, in *ibid.*, 346–56; *Annals of Congress*, 9th Cong., 2nd Sess. (January 22, 1807), 39–43, 1008–12; Malone, *Jefferson*, V, 263–64; Abernethy, *Burr Conspiracy*, 193–94.

44. Abernethy, *Burr Conspiracy*, 113, 117–18, 209, 217–26.

45. *Ibid.*, 230–32; Joseph P. Brady, *The Trial of Aaron Burr* (New York, 1913), 9–11.

46. Jefferson to William B. Giles, April 20, 1807, in Ford (ed.), *Works of Jefferson*, X, 383–84.

47. Abernethy, *Burr Conspiracy*, 234–39.

48. *Ibid.*, 237–38; Malone, *Jefferson*, V, 321; *American State Papers: Documents, Legislative and Executive of the United States* (38 vols.; Washington, D.C., 1832–61), *Miscellaneous*, I, 487.

49. Jefferson to George Hay, June 12, 1807, in Ford (ed.), *Works of Jefferson*, X, 398–99.

50. Jefferson to Hay, June 17, 1807, June 20, 1807, in *ibid.*, 400–401, 404.

51. Randolph to Joseph H. Nicholson, June 25, 1807, quoted in Adams, *History of the U.S. During the Administration of Jefferson*, III, 457–58; Jefferson to Wilkinson, June 21, 1807, in Ford (ed.), *Works of Jefferson*, X, 337n.

52. Abernethy, *Burr Conspiracy*, 240, 244; *American State Papers: Miscellaneous*, I, 488.

53. B. R. Curtis (ed.), *Reports of Decisions in the Supreme Court of the United States* (6th ed.; Boston, 1881), II, 37; Malone, *Jefferson*, V, 336–37; Adams, *History of the U.S. During the Administration of Jefferson*, III, 465–67; David Robertson (ed.), *Reports of the Trials of Colonel Aaron Burr* (2 vols.; Philadelphia, 1808), I, 526, 532.

54. Robertson (ed.), *Reports of the Trials of Burr*, II, 445; Abernethy, *Burr Conspiracy*, 246–48; Hay to Jefferson, September 1, 1807, in Jefferson Papers, LC.

55. Jefferson to du Pont, July 14, 1807, Jefferson to Wilkinson, September 20, 1807, in Ford (ed.), *Works of Jefferson*, X, 461–62, 499–500.

Chapter XX

1. Jefferson, special message, December 3, 1806, in Paul L. Ford (ed.), *The Works of Thomas Jefferson* (Federal Edition; 12 vols.; New York, 1904), X, 320–22; *Annals of Congress*, 9th Cong., 2nd Sess., 16, 1250.

2. Jefferson, Anas, February 2, 1807, in Ford (ed.), *Works of Jefferson*, I, 406–408.

3. Harry Ammon, *James Monroe: The Quest for National Identity* (New York, 1971), 262–64; Erskine to Howick, February 2, 1807, quoted in Dumas Malone, *Jefferson and His Time* (6 vols.; 1948–81), V, 405.

4. Bradford Perkins, *Prologue to War: England and the United States, 1805–1812* (Berkeley, 1968), 141–43; Malone, *Jefferson*, V, 422; Michael Leib to Caesar A. Rodney, July 2, 1807, in Simon Gratz Collection, Historical Society of Pennsylvania, Philadelphia; Beverley Tucker to St. George Tucker, July 11, 1807, in Tucker-Coleman Collection, College of William and Mary, Williamsburg, Va.; C. A. Rodney to Thomas Rodney, July 1, 1807, in H. F. Brown Collection, Historical Society of Delaware, Wilmington.

5. Jefferson to Gallatin, June 25, 1807, text of proclamation, July 2, 1807, in Ford (ed.), *Works of Jefferson*, X, 432, 434–47, 447n.

6. Jefferson to William H. Cabell, June 29, 1807, in *ibid.*, 433.

7. This statement makes it impossible to accept the conclusion in Burton Spivak, *Jefferson's English Crisis: Commerce, Embargo, and the Republican Revolution* (Charlottesville, 1979), 72–73, that Jefferson's preferred policy from the beginning of the crisis was war against England.

8. Jefferson, Anas, July 2, 1807, in Ford (ed.), *Works of Jefferson*, I, 410. Jefferson's proclamation of July 2, 1807, is in *American State Papers: Documents, Legislative and Executive of the United States* (38 vols.; Washington, D.C., 1832–61), *Foreign Relations*, III, 23–24.

9. Robert Smith to Jefferson, July 17, 1807, in Robert and William Smith Papers, Maryland Historical Society, Baltimore; Jefferson, Anas, July 4, 5, 7, 1807, in Ford (ed.), *Works of Jefferson*, I, 411.

10. Jefferson to William Duane, July 20, 1807, in Ford (ed.), *Works of Jefferson*, I, 471.

11. Jefferson to William H. Cabell, July 27, 1807, Jefferson to William Tatham, July 28, 1807, Jefferson to Samuel Smith, July 30, 1807, Jefferson to Cabell, July 31, 1807, in Andrew A. Lipscomb and Albert E. Bergh (eds.), *The Writings of Thomas Jefferson* (20 vols.; Washington, D.C., 1903), XI, 296–99, 301, 303.

12. Madison to Monroe, July 6, 1807, in Gaillard Hunt (ed.), *The Writings of James Madison* (9 vols.; New York, 1900–1910), VII, 455; Canning to Monroe, August 3, 1807, enclosed in Monroe to Madison, August 4, 1807, in *American State Papers: Foreign Relations*, III, 186–88.

13. Madison to Jefferson, September 20, 1807, in Thomas Jefferson Papers, Library of Congress (hereinafter cited LC); Monroe to Madison, August 4, 1807, in *American State Papers: Foreign Relations*, III, 186–87.

14. Jefferson to Madison, August 16, September 1, 1807, Jefferson to Lafayette, July 14, 1807, Jefferson to Thomas Leiper, August 21, 1807, in Ford (ed.), *Works of Jefferson*, X, 476–77, 489, 465, 483–84; Jefferson to James Bowdoin, July 10, 1807, in Lipscomb and Bergh (eds.), *Writings of Jefferson*, XI, 269.

15. Madison to Monroe, October 21, 1807, in Hunt (ed.), *Writings of Madison*, VII, 466–68; Malone, *Jefferson*, V, 455.

16. Humphreys to Jefferson, September 25, 1807, received October 3, 1807, in Jefferson Papers, LC; Malone, *Jefferson*, V, 457.

17. Gallatin to Jefferson, October 21, 1807, in Henry Adams (ed.), *The Writings of Albert Gallatin* (3 vols.; Philadelphia, 1879), I, 358; Smith to Jefferson, received October 19, 1807, in Jefferson Papers, LC.

18. Dearborn to Jefferson, received October 17, 1807, in Jefferson Papers, LC; Gallatin to Jefferson, October 21, 1807, in Adams (ed.), *Writings of Gallatin*, I, 359, 361.

19. Gallatin to his wife, October 30, 1807, in Henry Adams, *The Life of Albert Gallatin* (New York, 1879), 363–64.

20. Jefferson to Paine, October 9, 1807, Jefferson to Robert Williams, November 1, 1807, in Lipscomb and Bergh (eds.), *Writings of Jefferson*, XI, 378–79, 390; see also Jefferson to William H. Cabell, November 1, 1807, in *ibid.*, 389.

21. Jefferson to Thomas Mann Randolph, Jr., November 30, 1807, in Jefferson Papers, LC; *National Intelligencer* (Washington), December 2, 1807; Jefferson, confidential message, December 7, 1807, in Ford (ed.), *Works of Jefferson*, X, 528–29.

22. Canning to Monroe, September 23, 1807, in *American State Papers: Foreign Relations*, III, 199–202; Malone, *Jefferson*, V, 464–65.

23. Jefferson to Randolph, November 30, 1807, in Jefferson Papers, LC; Jefferson, confidential message, December 7, 1807, in Ford (ed.), *Works of Jefferson*, X, 529.

24. Jefferson, special message, December 18, 1807, in Ford (ed.), *Works of Jefferson*, X, 530–31.

25. *American State Papers: Foreign Relations*, III, 25–26; *Aurora* (Philadelphia), December 17, 1807; Jefferson to Madison, July 14, 1824, in Lipscomb and Bergh (eds.), *Writings of Jefferson*, XVI, 69–71; Henry Adams, *History of the United States of America During the Administration of Thomas Jefferson* (4 vols.; New York, 1889), IV, 103; Malone, *Jefferson*, V, 481.

26. Gallatin to Jefferson, December 2, 1807, Jefferson to Gallatin, December 3, 1807, in Adams (ed.), *Writings of Gallatin*, I, 367; Jefferson to John G. Jackson, October 13, 1808, in Jefferson Papers, LC.

27. Gallatin to Jefferson, December 18, 1807, Jefferson to Gallatin, December 18, 1807, in Adams (ed.), *Writings of Gallatin*, I, 368, 369.

28. Jefferson's draft (30603) and Madison's draft (30612) are in the Jefferson Papers, LC. See also Jefferson to Madison, July 14, 1824, in Lipscomb and Bergh (eds.), *Writings of Jefferson*, XVI, 69–70.

29. See Jefferson's discarded draft of message (30603), in Jefferson Papers, LC, printed in Adams, *History of the U.S. During the Administration of Jefferson*, IV, 168–69.

30. Charles Francis Adams (ed.), *Memoirs of John Quincy Adams, Comprising Portions of His Diary from 1795 to 1848* (12 vols.; Philadelphia, 1874–77), I, 491–92; *Annals of Congress*, 10th Cong., 1st Sess. (December 18, 1807), 50–51; Mitchill to his wife, December 23, 1807, in Samuel Latham Mitchill Papers, Museum of the City of New York.

31. *Annals of Congress*, 10th Cong., 1st Sess. (December 21, 1807), 1221–23, 2814–15; Jefferson to Thomas Mann Randolph, Jr., December 22, 1807, in Jefferson Papers, LC.

32. Campbell to his constituents, January 22, 1808, in Noble E. Cunningham, Jr. (ed.), *Circular Letters of Congressmen to Their Constituents, 1789–1829* (3 vols.; Chapel Hill, 1978), II, 525–26.

33. Desha to his constituents, March 29, 1808, in *ibid.*, 540; Timothy Pickering to Timothy Williams, December 31, 1807, in Timothy Pickering Papers (microfilm edition), in Massachusetts Historical Society, Boston.

34. These addresses, dated November, 1806–January, 1808, are in the Jefferson Papers, LC.

35. Vermont, November 5, 1806; Georgia, December 6, 1806; Maryland, January 3, 1807; Michigan Territory, January 31, 1807; Rhode Island, February 27, 1807; New York, March 12–13, 1807; Pennsylvania, April 13, 1807; New Jersey, December 4, 1807; South Carolina, December 10, 1807; North Carolina, December 11–12, 1807; Maryland, January 6–18, 1808. See Jefferson Papers, LC.

36. Leiper to Jefferson, August 28, 1807, in *ibid.*

37. Form letter from Jefferson to legislatures of Vermont, Rhode Island, New York, Pennsylvania, Maryland, Georgia, and New Jersey, December 10, 1807, in *ibid.; Enquirer* (Richmond), December 24, 1807.

38. Samuel L. Mitchill to his wife, November 23, 25, 1807, in Mitchill Papers, Museum of the City of New York.

39. Jefferson to Charles Thomson, January 11, 1808, Jefferson to John Armstrong, May 2, 1808, in Ford (ed.), *Works of Jefferson*, XI, 7, 30.

40. Jefferson to Madison, March 11, 1808, Jefferson to Thomas Leib, June 23, 1808, in *ibid.*, 12–18, 34.

41. Malone, *Jefferson*, V, 591. On the administration of the embargo see Leonard D. White, *The Jeffersonians: A Study in Administrative History, 1801–1829* (New York, 1951), 423–73.

42. Gallatin to Jefferson, July 29, 1808, in Adams (ed.), *Writings of Gallatin*, I, 398–99. On Gallatin and the embargo see Raymond Walters, Jr., *Albert Gallatin: Jeffersonian Financier and Diplomat* (New York, 1957), 200–207.

43. Jefferson to Gallatin, August 11, 1808, in Ford (ed.), *Works of Jefferson*, XI, 41.

44. Jefferson to Dearborn, August 12, 1808, Jefferson to Madison, August 12, 1808, in *ibid.*, 43, 44; Jefferson to Smith, August 12, 1808, in Lipscomb and Bergh (eds.), *Writings of Jefferson*, XII, 124.

45. Letter and list of towns, August 26, 1808, in Jefferson Papers, LC; Jefferson to Smith, September 9, 1808, in Jonathan Bayard Smith Papers, LC.

46. Jefferson to Smith, September 13, 1808, and Jefferson, indexes to letters sent and received in Jefferson Papers, LC.

47. Annual message, November 8, 1808, in Ford (ed.), *Works of Jefferson*, XI, 56–65; Jefferson to Gallatin, October 30, 1808, in Adams (ed.), *Writings of Gallatin*, I, 420.

48. Brant, *Madison*, IV, 466; Noble E. Cunningham, Jr., *The Jeffersonian Republicans in Power: Party Operations, 1801–1809* (Chapel Hill, 1963), 114–23.

49. Jefferson to Levi Lincoln, November 13, 1808, in Ford (ed.), *Works of Jefferson*, XI, 74–75; Macon to Joseph H. Nicholson, December 4, 1808, in Joseph H. Nicholson Papers, LC; Gallatin to Jefferson, November 15, 1808, in Adams (ed.), *Writings of Gallatin*, I, 428.

50. Jefferson to George Logan, December 27, 1808, in Lipscomb and Bergh (eds.), *Writings of Jefferson*, XII, 220; Jefferson to Monroe, January 28, 1809, in Ford (ed.), *Works of Jefferson*, XI, 96.

51. Jefferson to St. George Tucker, December 25, 1808, in Jefferson Papers, LC.

52. John Rhea to his constituents, February 13, 1809, in Cunningham (ed.), *Circular Letters of Congressmen to Their Constituents*, II, 616.

53. Jefferson to Monroe, February 18, 1808, January 28, 1809, in Ford (ed.), *Works of Jefferson*, XI, 11, 96; Jefferson to du Pont, March 2, 1809, in Lipscomb and Bergh (eds.), *Writings of Jefferson*, XII, 259–60.

54. Mrs. Smith to Susan B. Smith, March 1809, in Gaillard Hunt (ed.), *The First Forty Years of Washington Society, Portrayed by the Family Letters of Mrs. Samuel Harrison Smith* (New York, 1906), 59; Noble E. Cunningham, Jr., (ed.), "The Diary of Frances Few, 1808–1809," *Journal of Southern History*, XXIX (1963), 360.

55. Sixth annual message, December 2, 1806, in Ford (ed.), *Works of Jefferson*, X, 317–18.

56. Hunt (ed.), *First Forty Years of Washington Society*, 59; Jefferson to the Citizens of Washington, March 4, 1809, in Lipscomb and Bergh (eds.), *Writings of Jefferson*, XVI, 347.

57. Hunt (ed.), *First Forty Years of Washington Society*, 63; Jefferson to the General Assembly of Virginia, February 16, 1809, in Lipscomb and Bergh (eds.), *Writings of Jefferson*, XVI, 334.

58. Jefferson to du Pont, March 2, 1809, in Lipscomb and Bergh (eds.), *Writings of Jefferson*, XII, 260.

Chapter XXI

1. Martha Jefferson Randolph to Jefferson, February 24, 1809, in Edwin M. Betts and James A. Bear, Jr. (eds.), *The Family Letters of Thomas Jefferson* (Columbia, Mo., 1966), 384; Jefferson to Thomas Mann Randolph, Jr., February 28, 1809, in Thomas Jefferson Papers, Library of Congress (hereinafter cited LC).

2. Jefferson, account book, March 2–11, 1809, transcript by James A. Bear, Jr., in University of Virginia library, Charlottesville; Jefferson to Madison, March 17, 1809, in Andrew A. Lipscomb and Albert E. Bergh (eds.), *The Writings of Thomas Jefferson* (20 vols.; Washington, D.C., 1903), XII, 266.

3. Jefferson to Charles Thomson, December 25, 1808, Jefferson to Madison, March 17, 1809, in Lipscomb and Bergh (eds.), *Writings of Jefferson*, XII, 218, 266; Dumas Malone, *Jefferson and His Time* (6 vols.; Boston, 1948–81), V, 625.

4. Jefferson to Robert R. Livingston, January 3, 1808, Jefferson to Madison, March 17, 1809, in Lipscomb and Bergh (eds.), *Writings of Jefferson*, XI, 411, XII, 266–67; Jefferson to Thomas Jefferson Randolph, February 17, 1809, in Betts and Bear (eds.), *Family Letters*, 382.

5. Jefferson to Comte Diodati, March 28, 1807, in Lipscomb and Bergh (eds.), *Writings of Jefferson*, XI, 182; Jefferson to Martha Jefferson Randolph, February 27, 1809, Martha Jefferson Randolph to Jefferson, March 2, 1809, in Betts and Bear (eds.), *Family Letters*, 386–87.

6. Malone, *Jefferson*, VI, 9; Betts and Bear (eds.), *Family Letters*, 384, n. 2; William H. Gaines, Jr., *Thomas Mann Randolph: Jefferson's Son-in-Law* (Baton Rouge, 1966), 83–91, 115–39.

7. A list of Jefferson's grandchildren can be found in Malone, *Jefferson*, VI, Appendix I.

8. Jefferson to Adams, January 21, 1812, in Lester J. Cappon (ed.), *The Adams-Jefferson Letters* (2 vols.; Chapel Hill, 1959), II, 292; Jefferson to Maria Cosway, December 27, 1820, in Sarah N. Randolph, *The Domestic Life of Thomas Jefferson* (1871; rpr. New York, 1958), 374.

9. Ellen W. Coolidge, *ca.* 1850, in Randolph, *Domestic Life of Jefferson*, 345; Malone, *Jefferson*, VI, 456–58.

10. Virginia J. Trist, May 26, 1839, in Randolph, *Domestic Life of Jefferson*, 346–48; see also recollections of Thomas Jefferson Randolph in Henry S. Randall, *The Life of Thomas Jefferson* (3 vols.; New York, 1858), III, 671–76.

11. Malone, *Jefferson*, VI, 285. Thomas Jefferson Randolph married Jane Hollins Nicholas, daughter of Wilson Cary Nicholas, on March 10, 1815. *Ibid.*, 502.

12. Jefferson to Thaddeus Kosciusko, February 26, 1810, in Lipscomb and Bergh (eds.), *Writings of Jefferson*, XII, 369–70.

13. Malone, *Jefferson*, VI, 15, 290–91.

14. Frederick D. Nichols, "Jefferson: The Making of an Architect," in William

Howard Adams (ed.), *Jefferson and the Arts: An Extended View* (Washington, D.C., 1976), 177; Nichols, *Thomas Jefferson's Architectural Drawings* (3rd ed.; Charlottesville, 1961), 7–8; Adams (ed.), *The Eye of Thomas Jefferson* (Washington, D.C., 1976), 278–79; Malone, *Jefferson*, VI, 390; Paul L. Ford (ed.), *The Works of Thomas Jefferson* (Federal Edition; 12 vols.; New York, 1904), XII, xviii.

15. Jefferson to Thomas Jefferson Randolph, June 20, 1809, Jefferson to Thomas Jefferson Randolph, December 30, 1809, in Betts and Bear (eds.), *Family Letters*, 393, 395.

16. James A. Bear, Jr. (ed.), *Jefferson at Monticello* (Charlottesville, 1967), 51; Edwin Morris Betts (ed.), *Thomas Jefferson's Farm Book* (Princeton, 1953), 201–202.

17. Betts (ed.), *Jefferson's Farm Book*, 426–28, 448–53.

18. *Ibid.*, 342, 343

19. Jefferson to Kosciusko, June 28, 1812, in Ford (ed.), *Works of Jefferson*, XI, 260–61; Jefferson to Richard Fitzhugh, May 27, 1813, Jefferson to William Thornton, June 9, 1814, in Be s (ed.), *Jefferson's Farm Book*, 465, 484, 486.

20. Jefferson to David Humphreys, January 20, 1809, in Lipscomb and Bergh (eds.), *Writings of Jefferson*, XII, 235–36.

21. Jefferson to James Jay, April 7, 1809, in *ibid.*, 271.

22. Jefferson to Kosciusko, June 28, 1812, Jefferson to Philip Mazzei, December 29, 1813, Jefferson to Benjamin Austin, January 9, 1816, in Ford (ed.), *Works of Jefferson*, XI, 261, 366, 502–504.

23. Jefferson to William H. Crawford, June 20, 1816, in *ibid.*, 537–38. See Joyce Appleby, "Commercial Farming and the 'Agrarian Myth' in the Early Republic," *Journal of American History*, LXVIII (1982), 833–49; and Appleby, "What Is Still American in the Political Philosophy of Thomas Jefferson?" *William and Mary Quarterly*, 3rd Ser., XXXIX (1982), 287–309. For a different view see Drew R. McCoy, *The Elusive Republic: Political Economy in Jeffersonian America* (Chapel Hill, 1980), 227–31, 248–54.

24. Abigail Adams to Jefferson, May 20, 1804, October 24, 1804, Jefferson to Abigail Adams, June 13, 1804, in Cappon (ed.), *Adams-Jefferson Letters*, I, 268–71, 280–82.

25. Rush to Adams, October 17, 1809, Rush to Jefferson, January 2, 1811, in L. H. Butterfield (ed.), *Letters of Benjamin Rush* (2 vols.; Princeton, 1951), II, 1021–22, 1075–76; Jefferson to Rush, January 16, 1811, in Ford (ed.), *Works of Jefferson*, XI, 165–73.

26. Jefferson to Rush, December 5, 1811, in *ibid.*, 173n–75n; Rush to Adams, December 16, 1811, in Butterfield (ed.), *Letters of Rush*, II, 1110; Adams to Rush, December 25, 1811, in Charles Francis Adams (ed.), *The Works of John Adams* (10 vols.; Boston, 1856), X, 10–12.

27. Adams to Jefferson, January 1, 1812, in Cappon (ed.), *Adams-Jefferson Letters*, II, 290. In tracing the renewal of correspondence between Jefferson and Adams, I have followed *ibid.*, 283–89.

28. Jefferson to Adams, January 21, 1812, January 23, 1812, in *ibid.*, 290–93.

29. Jefferson to Adams, October 28, 1813, Adams to Jefferson, November 15, 1813, in *ibid.*, 387–92, 397–402.

30. Cappon (ed.), *Adams-Jefferson Letters*, 289. All of the letters are published in *ibid.*

31. Jefferson to Samuel H. Smith, September 21, 1814, in Ford (ed.), *Works of Jefferson*, XI, 427–30.

32. Francis Calley Gray, *Thomas Jefferson in 1814: Being an Account of a Visit to Mon-*

ticello (Boston, 1924), excerpt in Francis C. Rosenberger (ed.), *Jefferson Reader* (New York, 1953), 80; Boston *Gazette,* October 27, 1814, quoted in William D. Johnston, *History of the Library of Congress* (Washington, D.C., 1904), 78, 84–89; *Annals of Congress,* 13th Cong., 3rd Sess. (January 26, 1815), 1105–1106.

33. Jefferson to Samuel H. Smith, May 8, 1815, in Thomas Jefferson Papers, LC.

34. Jefferson to Adams, June 19, 1815, in Cappon (ed.), *Adams-Jefferson Letters,* II, 443; Jefferson, account book, May 10, 1815, transcript by Bear, in U. Va. library; William Peden, "Some Notes Concerning Thomas Jefferson's Libraries," *William and Mary Quarterly,* 3rd Ser., I (1944), 268.

35. Jefferson to Madison, May 25, June 6, 1812, Jefferson to Adams, June 11, 1812, in Ford (ed.), *Works of Jefferson,* XI, 247, 249, 255. On Jefferson's support of the war see Jefferson to Thaddeus Kosciusko, June 28, 1812, in *ibid.,* 258–60.

36. Jefferson to John W. Eppes, June 24, 1813, in *ibid.,* 297.

37. Jefferson to Eppes, June 24, September 11, November 6, 1813, in *ibid.,* 297–306, 306n–22n; Malone, *Jefferson,* VI, 135–46.

38. Monroe to Jefferson, October 1, 1813, in Stanislaus M. Hamilton (ed.), *The Writings of James Monroe* (7 vols.; New York, 1898–1903), V, 273–74; Jefferson to Madison, October 15, 1814, in Ford (ed.), *Works of Jefferson,* XI, 432–36; Jefferson to Joseph C. Cabell, January 17, 1814, in Lipscomb and Bergh (eds.), *Writings of Jefferson,* XIV, 68.

39. Malone, *Jefferson,* VI, 145; Irving Brant, *James Madison* (6 vols.; Indianapolis, 1941–61), VI, 400–403; Bray Hammond, *Banks and Politics in America from the Revolution to the Civil War* (Princeton, 1957), 238–40.

40. Jefferson to Roane, September 6, 1819, in Ford (ed.), *Works of Jefferson,* XII, 135–40.

41. Jefferson to John Holmes, April 22, 1820, in *ibid.,* 158–60.

42. Jefferson to William B. Giles, December 26, 1825, in *ibid.,* 424.

Chapter XXII

1. Jefferson to John Tyler, May 26, 1810, in Paul L. Ford (ed.), *The Works of Thomas Jefferson* (Federal Edition; 12 vols.; New York, 1904), XI, 143n.

2. Jefferson to Priestley, January 18, 1800, in Andrew A. Lipscomb and Albert E. Bergh (eds.), *The Writings of Thomas Jefferson* (20 vols.; Washington, D.C., 1903), X, 140–42.

3. Jefferson to Tazewell, January 5, 1805, in [Merrill D. Peterson (ed.)], *Thomas Jefferson: Writings,* The Library of America (New York, 1984), 1149–52; Nora L. Peterson, *Littleton Waller Tazewell* (Charlottesville, 1983), 37–39; Jefferson to Hugh L. White and others, trustees for the lottery of East Tennessee College, May 6, 1810, in Lipscomb and Bergh (eds.), *Writings of Jefferson,* XII, 387.

4. Dumas Malone, *Jefferson and His Time* (6 vols.; Boston, 1848–81), VI, 234, 241–42; Jefferson to Peter Carr, September 7, 1814, in Lipscomb and Bergh (eds.), *Writings of Jefferson,* XIX, 211–20.

5. Malone, *Jefferson,* VI, 244–45, 250, 255–57; Minutes of Board of Visitors, May 5, 1817, in Lipscomb and Bergh (eds.), *Writings of Jefferson,* XIX, 361–65.

6. Latrobe to Jefferson, June 17, 1817, in Fiske Kimball, *Thomas Jefferson, Architect* (Boston, 1916), 188; Malone, *Jefferson,* VI, 257–58; Frederick D. Nichols, *Thomas Jefferson's Architectural Drawings* (3rd ed.; Charlottesville, 1961), 8; William Howard Adams (ed.), *The Eye of Thomas Jefferson* (Washington, D.C., 1976), 131.

7. Latrobe to Jefferson, July 24, 1817, Jefferson to Latrobe, August 3, 1817, in Kimball, *Jefferson, Architect,* 189–91, and fig. 213; Malone, *Jefferson,* VI, 259, 261;

Roy J. Honeywell, *The Educational Work of Thomas Jefferson* (Cambridge, Mass., 1931), 80.

8. Jefferson to Cocke, July 19, 1817, in Thomas Jefferson Papers, Library of Congress (hereinafter cited LC).

9. Jefferson to Correa de Serra, November 25, 1817, in Lipscomb and Bergh (eds.), *Writings of Jefferson*, XV, 156; Malone, *Jefferson* VI, 265–68. The bill is printed in Honeywell, *Educational Work of Jefferson*, 233–43.

10. Jefferson to Ticknor, November 25, 1817, in Ford (ed.), *Works of Jefferson*, XII, 77–78; Malone, *Jefferson*, VI, 269–74.

11. Malone, *Jefferson*, VI, 269–74, 275–78; Honeywell, *Educational Work of Jefferson*, 248–49, 260.

12. Report of the commissioners on the site of the university, August 4, 1818, in Honeywell, *Educational Work of Jefferson*, 248–60.

13. Jefferson to Tazewell, January 5, 1805, in [Peterson (ed.)], *Jefferson: Writings*, 1149, 1152; Jefferson to William Short, June 22, 1819, in Lipscomb and Bergh (eds.), *Writings of Jefferson*, XVIII, 304–305.

14. Jefferson to Wilson C. Nicholas, April 2, 1816, in Lipscomb and Bergh (eds.), *Writings of Jefferson*, XIV, 453.

15. Jefferson to William Thornton, May 9, 1817, reproduced in *ibid.*, XVII, following p. 396.

16. William C. Rives to Jefferson, January 20, 1819, in Jefferson Papers, LC; Malone, *Jefferson*, VI, 280–82.

17. Nicholas to Jefferson, January 25, 1819, Jefferson to Nicholas, January 28, 1819, in Jefferson Papers, LC.

18. Minutes of Board of Visitors, March 29, 1819, Jefferson to Robert Taylor, May 16, 1820, in Lipscomb and Bergh (eds.), *Writings of Jefferson*, XIX, 373–79, XV, 254–56; Malone, *Jefferson*, VI, 368–69, 376–80. See also Dumas Malone, *The Public Life of Thomas Cooper, 1783–1839* (New Haven, 1926), 234–46.

19. Jefferson to Joseph C. Cabell, February 19, 1819, quoted in Malone, *Jefferson*, VI, 366. See also Jefferson to James Breckenridge, April 9, 1822, in Lipscomb and Bergh (eds.), *Writings of Jefferson*, XV, 363.

20. Malone, *Jefferson*, VI, 374–75; Jefferson to Cabell, January 31, 1821, in Lipscomb and Bergh (eds.), *Writings of Jefferson*, XV, 310.

21. Jefferson's estimates of expenditures and needs, enclosed in Jefferson to Cabell, November 28, 1820, in Honeywell, *Educational Work of Jefferson*, 83–84; Malone, *Jefferson*, VI, 382–84.

22. Jefferson to Cabell, November 28, 1820, in Ford (ed.), *Works of Jefferson*, XII, 169–70; Malone, *Jefferson*, VI, 385; Honeywell, *Educational Work of Jefferson*, 84; Jefferson to James Breckenridge, February 15, 1821, Jefferson to Cabell, January 31, 1821, in Lipscomb and Bergh (eds.), *Writings of Jefferson*, XV, 315, 311.

23. Jefferson to Cabell, December 28, 1822, in Jefferson Papers, LC.

24. William B. O'Neal, *Jefferson's Buildings at the University of Virginia: The Rotunda* (Charlottesville, 1960), 2–3, 24–28; Malone, *Jefferson*, VI, 394–95.

25. Jefferson to Gilmer, December 3, 1823, in Richard Beale Davis (ed.), *Correspondence of Thomas Jefferson and Francis Walker Gilmer, 1814–1826* (Columbia, S.C., 1946), 81–82; Malone, *Jefferson*, VI, 397–98.

26. Gilmer to Jefferson, November 12, 1824, in Davis (ed.), *Jefferson-Gilmer Correspondence*, 113; Malone, *Jefferson*, VI, 400–402, 409–10; Robert C. McLean, *George Tucker, Moral Philosopher and Man of Letters* (Chapel Hill, 1961), 25–28.

27. Minutes of Board of Visitors, October 4 and 5, 1824, March 4, 1825, in Lipscomb and Bergh (eds.), *Writings of Jefferson*, XIX, 439−52, 455−56, 460−61.

28. Jefferson to Madison, February 1, 1825, Jefferson to Joseph C. Cabell, February 3, 1825, in Jefferson Papers, LC; Jefferson to William Roscoe, December 27, 1820, in Lipscomb and Bergh (eds.), *Writings of Jefferson*, XV, 303. For a fuller treatment of the incident see Arthur Bestor, "Thomas Jefferson and the Freedom of Books," in *Three Presidents and Their Books* (Urbana, 1955), 24−44; see also Leonard W. Levy, *Jefferson and Civil Liberties: The Darker Side* (Cambridge, Mass., 1963), 151−57.

29. Jefferson, Thoughts on Lotteries, February 1826, in Ford (ed.), *Works of Jefferson*, XII, 448.

30. Jefferson to Lafayette, September 3, 1824, in Gilbert Chinard (ed.), *The Letters of Lafayette and Jefferson* (Baltimore, 1929), 420−21; Richmond *Enquirer*, November 16, 1824; Edgar E. Brandon (ed.), *Lafayette, Guest of the Nation* (3 vols.; Oxford, Ohio, 1950−57), III, 126−31; Malone, *Jefferson*, VI, 402−408.

31. Richmond *Enquirer*, November 16, 1824.

32. Ticknor to William H. Prescott, December 16, 1824, in [George S. Hillard (ed.)], *Life, Letters, and Journals of George Ticknor* (2 vols.; Boston, 1876), I, 348; Cocke to Cabell, February 6, 1826, quoted in Malone, *Jefferson*, VI, 482.

33. Jefferson to Augustus B. Woodward, April 3, 1825, in Ford (ed.), *Works of Jefferson*, XII, 408.

34. Jefferson, account book, April 29, 1815, July 28, 1818, transcript by James A. Bear, Jr., in University of Virginia library, Charlottesville; Jefferson to Alexander K. Dallas, April 18, 1815, in Ford (ed.), *Works of Jefferson*, XI, 469−70; Malone, *Jefferson*, VI, 301, 302, 304.

35. Jefferson to Adams, November 7, 1819, in Lester J. Cappon (ed.), *The Adams-Jefferson Letters* (2 vols.; Chapel Hill, 1959), II, 547; Malone, *Jefferson*, VI, 303, 304, 309, 310; Jefferson to Madison, February 17, 1826, in Ford (ed.), *Works of Jefferson*, XII, 457.

36. William H. Gaines, Jr., *Thomas Mann Randolph: Jefferson's Son-in-Law* (Baton Rouge, 1966), 161−62; Malone, *Jefferson*, VI, 472−73.

37. Jefferson to Cabell, February 7, 1826, in Ford (ed.), *Works of Jefferson*, XII, 451; Francis Eppes to Jefferson, February 23, 1826, in Edwin M. Betts and James A. Bear, Jr. (eds.), *The Family Letters of Thomas Jefferson* (Columbia, Mo., 1966), 470−71.

38. Plans called for selling 11,480 lottery tickets at ten dollars each. Jefferson's debts on July 4, 1826, were calculated at $107,273.63. Malone, *Jefferson*, VI, 477, 479, 488, 511.

39. Jefferson's will, March 16, 1826, and codicil, March 17, 1826, in Ford (ed.), *Works of Jefferson*, XII, 478−83; Malone, *Jefferson*, VI, 488; Jefferson to Wright, August 7, 1825, in Lipscomb and Bergh (eds.), *Writings of Jefferson*, XVI, 119−20.

40. Edward Coles to Jefferson, July 31, 1814, Massachusetts Historical Society *Collections*, 7th Ser., I (1900), 200−202; David Brion Davis, *The Problem of Slavery in the Age of Revolution, 1770−1823* (Ithaca, N.Y., 1975), 180−81.

41. Jefferson to Coles, August 25, 1814, in Ford (ed.), *Works of Jefferson*, XI, 416−20.

42. *Ibid.*, XII, 481.

43. Jefferson to Madison, February 17, 1826, in *ibid.*, 458−59.

44. Malone, *Jefferson*, VI, 493−94; Jefferson to Roger Weightman, June 24, 1826, in Ford (ed.), *Works of Jefferson*, XII, 476−77.

45. Sarah N. Randolph, *The Domestic Life of Thomas Jefferson* (1871; rpr. New York,

1958), 428–29; Malone, *Jefferson*, VI, 496–97; Samuel X. Radbill (ed.), "The Auto-biographical Ana of Robley Dunglison, M.D.," American Philosophical Society *Transactions*, n.s., LIII, Part 8 (1963), 32–33.

46. Page Smith, *John Adams* (2 vols.; New York, 1962), II, 1136–37; Charles Francis Adams (ed.), *Memoirs of John Quincy Adams, Comprising Portions of His Diary from 1795 to 1848* (12 vols.; Philadelphia, 1874–77), VII, 122, 125.

47. Jefferson Papers, LC.

Bibliographical Note

"The letters of a person, especially of one whose business has been chiefly transacted by letters, form the only full and genuine journal of his life," Jefferson wrote late in life. Viewing the letters of a person as embracing all correspondence sent and received, Jefferson systematically and diligently retained copies of his papers throughout his life. As a result, Jefferson's papers form one of the largest and most valuable collections of manuscripts relating to his time. Indeed, one earlier biographer of Jefferson, Gilbert Chinard, called the record left by Jefferson "the richest treasure house of historical information ever left by a single man." The major collection of Jefferson manuscripts is in the Library of Congress and has been reproduced on microfilm in the presidential papers series. Other important collections of Jefferson manuscripts are at the Massachusetts Historical Society, the University of Virginia, and the Missouri Historical Society. The Library of Congress houses major collections of the papers of James Madison and James Monroe, two of Jefferson's closest political associates; these also are available in microfilm editions. Among other major collections of Jefferson's close associates, the Papers of Albert Gallatin at the New-York Historical Society are indispensable. A microfilm edition of the Gallatin Papers, edited by Carl E. Prince, is invaluable. The extensive collection of Adams Family Papers at the Massachusetts Historical Society is also available on microfilm.

Printed editions of Jefferson's papers are widely available. The definitive edition is Julian P. Boyd *et al.*, eds., *The Papers of Thomas Jefferson* (Princeton, 1950–), a continuing project in which Jefferson's correspondence to August, 1791, has been published in the first 20 volumes; Series 2 of *The Papers of Thomas Jefferson* includes Dickinson W. Adams, ed., *Jefferson's Extracts from the Gospels* (Princeton, 1983). The best earlier edition of Jefferson's writings, containing only his own letters and papers, is Paul L. Ford, ed., *The Works of Thomas Jefferson* (Federal Edition; 12 vols.; New York, 1904). Major supplements include Edwin M. Betts and James A. Bear Jr., eds., *The Family Letters of Thomas Jefferson* (Columbia, Mo., 1966); Lester Cappon, ed., *The Adams-Jefferson Letters* (2 vols.; Chapel Hill, 1959); Edwin Morris Betts, ed., *Thomas Jefferson's Garden Book, 1766–1824* (Philadelphia, 1944) and *Thomas Jefferson's Farm Book* (Princeton, 1953). Still useful is Andrew A. Lipscomb and Albert E. Bergh, eds., *The Writings of Thomas Jefferson* (20 vols.; Washington, D.C., 1903). The best one-volume edition of selections from Jefferson's letters and other writings is [Merrill D. Peterson, ed.], *Thomas Jefferson: Writings*, The Library of America (New York, 1984). The best scholarly edition of Jefferson's only book is William Peden, ed., *Notes on the State of Virginia* (Chapel Hill, 1954).

In any study of Jefferson's life the papers of his contemporaries are essential. Among the most important published collections are Harold C. Syrett *et al.*, eds., *The Papers of Alexander Hamilton* (26 vols.; New York, 1961–79); William T. Hutchinson, William M. E. Rachal, Robert A. Rutland *et al.*, eds., *The Papers of James Madison* (Chicago and Charlottesville, 1962–); Gaillard Hunt, ed., *The Writings of James Madison* (9 vols.; New York, 1900–1910); W. W. Abbot, Dorothy Twohig *et al.*, eds., *The Papers of George Washington* (Charlottesville, 1981–); John C. Fitzpatrick, ed., *The Writings of George Washington* (39 vols.; Washington, D.C., 1939–44); Mary-Jo Kline and Joanne Wood Ryan, eds., *Political Correspondence and Public Papers of Aaron Burr* (2 vols.; Princeton, 1983); Stanislaus M. Hamilton, ed., *The Writings of James Monroe* (7 vols.; New York, 1898–1903); Henry Adams, ed., *The Writings of Albert Gallatin* (3 vols.; Philadelphia, 1879); and Robert A. Rutland, ed., *The Papers of George Mason* (3 vols.; Chapel Hill, 1970). Important diaries and journals include L. H. Butterfield, ed., *Diary and Autobiography of John Adams* (4 vols.; Cambridge, Mass., 1961); Charles Francis Adams, ed., *Memoirs of John Quincy Adams, Comprising Portions of His Diary from 1795 to 1848* (12 vols.; Philadelphia, 1874–77); Donald Jackson and Dorothy Twohig, eds., *The Diaries of George Washington* (6 vols.; Charlottesville, 1976–79); and Everett S. Brown, ed., *William Plumer's Memorandum of Proceedings in the United States Senate, 1803–1807* (New York, 1923).

The most extensive and definitive biography of Jefferson is Dumas Malone, *Jefferson and His Time* (6 vols.; Boston, 1948–81); Merrill D. Peterson, *Thomas Jefferson and the New Nation: A Biography* (New York, 1970) is also a major study. Still useful for Jefferson's youth and early career are the volumes by Marie Kimball: *Jefferson: The Road to Glory, 1743 to 1776* (New York, 1943); *Jefferson: War and Peace, 1776 to 1784* (New York, 1947); and *Jefferson: The Scene of Europe, 1784 to 1789* (New York, 1950). Fawn M. Brodie's *Thomas Jefferson: An Intimate History* (New York, 1974) has been seriously challenged by scholars; see Virginius Dabney, *The Jefferson Scandals: A Rebuttal* (New York, 1981). Merrill D. Peterson, *The Jefferson Image in the American Mind* (New York, 1960) skillfully traces Jefferson's image and influence through history after his death. Portraits and other images of Jefferson are examined in Alfred L. Bush, *The Life Portraits of Thomas Jefferson* (Charlottesville, 1962) and Noble E. Cunningham, Jr., *The Image of Thomas Jefferson in the Public Eye: Portraits for the People, 1800–1809* (Charlottesville, 1981).

Jefferson's many-faceted life has been explored in a number of specialized studies. Works relating to Jefferson and the arts include William Howard Adams, ed., *Jefferson and the Arts: An Extended View* (Washington, D.C., 1976) and *The Eye of Thomas Jefferson* (Washington, D.C., 1976); Eleanor D. Berman, *Thomas Jefferson Among the Arts* (New York, 1947); Fiske Kimball, *Thomas Jefferson, Architect* (Boston, 1916); Frederick D. Nichols, *Thomas Jefferson's Architectural Drawings* (3rd ed.; Charlottesville, 1961); William B. O'Neal, *Jefferson's Fine Arts Library* (Charlottesville, 1976); and Howard C. Rice, Jr., *Thomas Jefferson's Paris* (Princeton, 1976). On Jefferson's library, the definitive work is E. Millicent Sowerby, ed., *Catalogue of the Library of Thomas Jefferson* (5 vols.; Washington, D. C., 1952–59). Works exploring other of Jefferson's interests include Helen Cripe, *Thomas Jefferson and Music* (Charlottesville, 1974); Edward Dumbauld, *Thomas Jefferson, American Tourist* (Norman, 1946) and *Thomas Jefferson and the Law* (Norman, 1978); and Roy J. Honeywell, *The Educational Work of Thomas Jefferson* (Cambridge, Mass., 1931).

Considerable scholarly study has been given to Jefferson's thought. Valuable studies include Adrienne Koch, *The Philosophy of Thomas Jefferson* (New York, 1943) and *Jefferson and Madison: The Great Collaboration* (New York, 1964); and Joyce Appleby, "What Is Still American in the Political Philosophy of Thomas Jefferson," *William and Mary Quarterly,* 3rd Ser., XXXIX (1982), 287–309. Garry Wills focused on ideas in *Inventing America: Jefferson's Declaration of Independence* (New York, 1978). Daniel J. Boorstin explores the mind-set of Jefferson's world in *The Lost World of Thomas Jefferson* (1948; rpr. Chicago, 1981). Among important works that have focused on the ideology of republicanism are Lance Banning, *The Jeffersonian Persuasion: Evolution of Party Ideology* (Ithaca, N.Y., 1978);

Richard Buel, Jr., *Securing the Revolution: Ideology in American Politics, 1789–1815* (Ithaca, N.Y., 1972); Joyce Appleby, *Capitalism and a New Social Order: The Republican Vision of the 1790s* (New York, 1984); and Drew R. McCoy, *The Elusive Republic: Political Economy in Jeffersonian America* (Chapel Hill, 1980). For the scholarly debate over the terms in which Jeffersonian ideology may best be understood, see Lance Banning, "Jeffersonian Ideology Revisited: Liberal and Classical Ideas in the New American Republic," *William and Mary Quarterly*, 3rd Ser., XLIII (1986), 3–19, and Joyce Appleby, "Republicanism in Old and New Contexts," *William and Mary Quarterly*, 3rd Ser., XLIII (1986), 20–34.

Jefferson as a party leader can be viewed in Noble E. Cunningham, Jr., *The Jeffersonian Republicans: The Formation of Party Organization, 1789–1801* (Chapel Hill, 1957) and *The Jeffersonian Republicans in Power: Party Operations, 1801–1809* (Chapel Hill, 1963); see also Dumas Malone, *Thomas Jefferson as Political Leader* (Berkeley, 1963), and Joseph Charles, *The Origins of the American Party System: Three Essays* (Williamsburg, 1956). Party opposition to Jefferson has been examined in David Hackett Fischer, *The Revolution of American Conservatism: The Federalist Party in the Era of Jeffersonian Democracy* (New York, 1965). Jefferson as president has been studied in Noble E. Cunningham, Jr., *The Process of Government Under Jefferson* (Princeton, 1978) and Robert M. Johnstone, Jr., *Jefferson and the Presidency: Leadership in the Young Republic* (Ithaca, N.Y., 1978); see also Ralph Ketcham, *Presidents Above Party: The American Presidency, 1789–1829* (Chapel Hill, 1984). On the judiciary during Jefferson's presidency see Richard E. Ellis, *The Jeffersonian Crisis: Courts and Politics in the Young Republic* (New York, 1971). Henry Adams' classic *History of the United States of America During the Administration of Thomas Jefferson* (4 vols.; New York, 1889), while still valuable, has been much revised by subsequent scholarship.

Among important biographies of Jefferson's contemporaries are the following: Irving Brant, *James Madison* (6 vols.; Indianapolis, 1941–61); Ralph Ketcham, *James Madison: A Biography* (New York, 1971); Harry Ammon, *James Monroe: The Quest for National Identity* (New York, 1971); Broadus Mitchell, *Alexander Hamilton* (2 vols.; New York, 1957–62); Jacob Ernest Cooke, *Alexander Hamilton* (New York, 1982); Raymond Walters, Jr., *Albert Gallatin: Jeffersonian Financier and Diplomat* (New York, 1957); Page Smith, *John Adams* (2 vols.; New York, 1962); William H. Gaines, Jr., *Thomas Mann Randolph: Jefferson's Son-in-Law* (Baton Rouge, 1966); Jacob E. Cooke, *Tench Coxe and the Early Republic* (Chapel Hill, 1978); Douglas Southhall Freeman, *George Washington: A Biography* (7 vols.; New York, 1948–57); John R. Alden, *George Washington: A Biography* (Baton Rouge, 1984); Lowell H. Harrison, *John Breckinridge: Jeffersonian Republican* (Louisville, 1969); Gerard H. Clarfield, *Timothy Pickering and the American Republic* (Pittsburgh, 1980); George A. Billias, *Elbridge Gerry: Founding Father and Republican Statesman* (New York, 1976); C. Edward Skeen, *John Armstrong, Jr.: A Biography* (Syracuse, 1981); John J. Reardon, *Edmund Randolph: A Biography* (New York, 1974); and George Dangerfield, *Chancellor Robert R. Livingston of New York* (New York, 1960).

Important studies relating to Jefferson and foreign affairs include Harry Ammon, *The Genet Mission* (New York, 1973); Lawrence S. Kaplan, *Jefferson and France: An Essay on Politics and Political Ideas* (New Haven, 1967); Jerald A. Combs, *The Jay Treaty: Political Battleground of the Founding Fathers* (Berkeley, 1970); Alexander DeConde, *This Affair of Louisiana* (New York, 1976); Bradford Perkins, *Prologue to War: England and the United States, 1805–1812* (Berkeley, 1968); and Burton Spivak, *Jefferson's English Crisis: Commerce, Embargo, and the Republican Revolution* (Charlottesville, 1979).

Other relevant specialized studies include Bernard W. Sheehan, *Seeds of Extinction: Jeffersonian Philanthropy and the American Indian* (Chapel Hill, 1973); James Morton Smith, *Freedom's Fetters: The Alien and Sedition Laws and American Civil Liberties* (Ithaca, N.Y., 1956); Leonard W. Levy, *Jefferson and Civil Liberties: The Darker Side* (Cambridge, Mass., 1963); John C. Miller, *The Wolf by the Ears: Thomas Jefferson and Slavery* (New York, 1977); Robert McColley, *Slavery and Jeffersonian Virginia* (Urbana, 1964); George Dargo, *Jefferson's Louisiana: Politics and the Clash of Legal Traditions* (Cambridge, Mass., 1975); Donald Jackson, *Thomas Jefferson and the Stony Mountains: Exploring the West from Monticello* (Urbana, 1981); Daniel P. Jordan, *Political Leadership in Jefferson's Virginia* (Charlottesville, 1983); John C. Greene, *American Science in the Age of Jefferson* (Ames, 1984); and Richard Beale Davis, *Intellectual Life in Jefferson's Virginia, 1790–1830* (Chapel Hill, 1964).

Comprehensive bibliographies of writings about Jefferson are Eugene L. Huddleston, *Thomas Jefferson: A Reference Guide* (Boston, 1982) and Frank Shuffelton, *Thomas Jefferson: A Comprehensive Annotated Bibliography of Writings About Him, 1826–1980* (New York, 1983).

Index

Morris, Robert (American financier), 160

Morris, Robert (English architect), 19

Napoleon I, 263–65, 279, 284, 295, 300, 311
National Gazette, 169–71, 173
Nelson, Thomas, 39, 42, 64, 71, 72
Newton, Isaac, 6, 129, 138
Nicholas, George, 73
Nicholas, Robert Carter, 25, 34
Nicholas, Wilson Cary, 217, 338, 340, 346
Nicholson, Joseph H., 235, 272, 274
North, Frederick, Lord, 23, 34, 37, 38–39
Northwest Ordinance, 85, 86
Notes on the State of Virginia: TJ's writing of, 76–79; publication of, 94–96; John Adams on, 96; Chastellux on, 96; quoted in 1800 campaign, 225

Otis, James, 48

Page, John, 6–7, 17, 42, 64
Paine, Thomas, 42, 125, 167, 284
Palladio, Andrea, 19, 20, 197
Peale, Rembrandt, 278
Pendleton, Edmund, 10, 36, 44, 46, 53, 57–58
Petit, Adrien, 160
Phillips, William, 70–71
Pickering, John, 273
Pickering, Timothy, 212, 214, 250, 269, 273
Pinckney, Charles, 229–30, 259, 260
Pinckney, Charles Cotesworth, 207, 212, 229, 231, 271, 317
Pinckney, Thomas, 197, 204, 228
Pinkney, William, 295, 296, 316
Pitt, William, 141
Plumer, William, 255, 258, 274, 275–76, 289
Poplar Forest, 73, 325–26, 346
Preston, James P., 339
Priestley, Joseph, 207, 256

Rabaut de St. Etienne, Jean Paul, 123
Ramsay, Andrew, 114, 115
Randolph, Edmund: on TJ, 19, 32; attorney general, 137; on national

bank, 164, 166; drafts neutrality proclamation, 181; and Genet, 182, 189; secretary of state, 199; at Burr trial, 290; mentioned, 12, 13, 74, 175
Randolph, Ellen, 324
Randolph, Isham, 2
Randolph, John, 39–40
Randolph, John (of Roanoke): as House leader, 250, 274, 284; and election of 1808, pp. 278, 314; opposes TJ, 281–82
Randolph, Peyton, 10, 15, 24, 26–27, 32–34, 36, 39, 40
Randolph, Thomas Jefferson, 319, 324, 325
Randolph, Thomas Mann, Jr., 134–35, 148–49, 282, 310, 323–24, 346
Randolph, Thomas Mann, Sr., 3, 135, 148–49
Randolph, Virginia, 324
Randolph, William, 2, 3, 135
Raymond, Robert, 8
Republican party: beginnings of, 171–74; in election of 1792, pp. 176–77; and Genet, 190–91; in election of 1796, pp. 200–203; TJ's leadership of, 209–11, 221–23, 245, 249–51; in election of 1800, pp. 221, 226–28
Rhea, John, 318
Ritchie, Thomas, 314
Rittenhouse, David, 78, 83, 207
Roane, Spencer, 334, 339
Rodney, Caesar A., 290, 292, 297
Rose, George, 312
Rush, Benjamin, 177, 329–30
Rushworth, John, 25
Rutledge, Edward, 110

Saint-Mémin, Charles-Balthazar-Julien Fevret de, 271–72
Salkeld, William, 8
Shadwell, 1, 2, 9, 16–18, 196
Shays's Rebellion, 116
Sherman, Roger, 46
Short, William: private secretary to TJ, 87, 91, 109, 112; diplomatic service of, 161; mentioned, 135, 179
Sidney, Algernon, 30, 344
Skelton, Bathhurst, 21
Skelton, Martha Wayles, 20–21